For
Jay Adams
*an outstanding teacher
of preachers*

and

Tom Stewart
*a discerning listener
to sermons*

TONGUES AFLAME

LEARNING TO PREACH FROM THE APOSTLES

ROGER WAGNER

MENTOR

© Roger Wagner
ISBN 1- 85792- 965- 9

Published in 2004
in the
Mentor Imprint
by
Christian Focus Publications
Geanies House, Fearn, Tain, Ross-shire,
IV20 1TW, Great Britain

www.christianfocus.com

Edited by Malcolm Maclean
Cover design by Alister MacInnes

Printed and bound by
Bell & Bain, Glasgow

Contents

Introduction

Some of you have heard the words of the old spiritual, 'Balm in Gilead'.

> You may not preach like Peter,
> You may not pray like Paul,
> But you can tell the love of Jesus,
> Who died to save us all.

Is this the way you view your present preaching ministry? As a minister of the gospel you are to 'tell the love of Jesus' – to bring to lost sinners the message of forgiveness for sins and reconciliation with God through the shed blood of Jesus Christ. But you freely admit that you cannot 'preach like Peter,' or 'pray like Paul' (and perhaps you don't see yourself preaching like Paul either).

When you left seminary and entered your first pastorate you hoped to set the church and the world aflame with your sound biblical exposition, your penetrating theological insights, your persuasive applications, and your homiletical eloquence. But after a few years those dreams disappeared.

But should they?

Why not preach like Peter and Paul?

Why not preach *better* than these great giants of the pulpit?

'Ah,' you say, 'what vanity!'

I am not talking about vanity. I am talking about powerful preaching in your ministry. If it were merely a matter of aspiring to their position as masters of the presentation of the 'good news,' there would be no reason for a book such as this. But I am assuming here (and will throughout this book) that you, as an evangelical pastor, have a deep desire to be as effective in your ministry as possible, and especially so in the pulpit.

I assume that (if you are like me) you are *unsatisfied* with the present state of your preaching. With Paul you rejoice in the glorious wonders of the message to be preached, but with him you also know that the treasure is deposited in 'pots of clay' (2 Cor. 4:7). You know the message deserves more than you give it, and you want to give it more. But how?

Perhaps that is why you have allowed yourself to become disappointed, and have drawn, at least implicitly, the conclusion of the old song that you may *never* preach like Peter. You'd like to, but things are too locked in now, and you are far from having achieved that goal. You have become resigned to the status quo.

Well, don't!!

These are great days for preaching, and you must make the most of them! While some in our day are speaking of the *death* of preaching in the face of our modern communications explosion, God is still determined by the 'foolishness of preaching to save them that believe' (1 Cor. 1:21, AV). More and more evangelicals are relying on 'gimmicky' tools and techniques – on overhead projectors (splashing power point sermon outlines and cartoon illustrations on the wall) and other 'communications technology', on sermon-replacing 'dramas' and hip, upbeat musical performances to help get them through the Sunday morning hour. Meanwhile, if the truth were known, many of God's people – and even some non-Christians – are still looking for the man who is convicted by the truth of God and fired by the Holy Spirit who will take his place in the pulpit and *preach* to them.

Church members by and large are not sick of preaching, they are sick of *not hearing* preaching. Some of our congregations have not heard a decent sermon in years!

Lectures? Yes.

Bible studies with good content? Sometimes.

Moving personal testimonies? Yes.

But powerful preaching of solid sermons week after week? All too seldom.

The purpose of this book is to help you realize that it doesn't have to be that way. You don't have to surrender to the status quo. You can grow. Your preaching can change for the better. This book is an effort to show you one of the sources to which you can look to find help in growing and changing in your preaching.

You may not preach like Peter or Paul, but you can do the next best thing. *You can learn about preaching from them*. You can become an imitator of their preaching

Imagine if one day, in that pile of mailings and flyers that comes to the church every day, there was a brochure announcing a preaching seminar in your town, and as you looked to see who the key speakers would be, you found (to your utter amazement) that they were Peter and Paul, with Stephen thrown in for good measure! Would you attend? How much time and money would you be willing to devote to participating in such a seminar.

Well, you don't have to do that. You already have access to a seminar by these great apostolic preachers in the Book of Acts.

As a Bible-believing minister you are already accustomed to using the Scriptures for the *content* of your messages. Now I am calling you to examine the way the sermons in Acts can also give you insights into how to shape the *form* of your messages, and to let the apostolic preachers become your examples of how to *deliver* sermons that will be *powerful* and *effective*.

I do not know how you would evaluate your personal strengths and weaknesses as a preacher, but since there is seldom anything 'new under the sun', you probably share problems with other preachers.

- The press of pastoral duties takes away time needed to develop your messages fully so sometimes you feel unprepared to preach effectively.

- The dulling sense of routine that can become part of the weekly ministry of the Word can rob you of the sense of majesty and glory you once had when faced with the prospect of declaring the 'whole counsel of God'.

- You are intimidated by the responses you get (or fear you may get) from your congregation if you preach in certain ways or on certain topics, so you blunt the cutting edge of your preaching out of fear of men.

- Your own walk with the Lord has its periods of dryness, and you know well what that does to your preaching.

Entries on this list of common preaching ailments could be multiplied, and our individual problems would all find a place on the list.

If you now face, or have at one time faced, these or other problems in your preaching ministry, then this book is for you. A careful study of the preaching in Acts will greatly help you identify some of your problems, and give you clear directions for implementing useful correction.

It is my prayer that as we work through this study together you will be challenged and encouraged to 'preach like Peter' and the other apostolic witnesses in the Book of Acts, and that in so doing you will recapture the exhilaration of the preaching ministry once again. If you are a student or new preacher, perhaps these studies will help you get started in the right direction. Your people in turn will know the deep satisfaction of being fed week by week with the good food of the Word by a shepherd who speaks as an 'oracle of God' (1 Pet. 4:11).

I worked on this book for a long time before I settled upon the present title. All the working titles were so boring, while I found the subject matter so challenging and exciting. I like this title: *Tongues Aflame.* Not only does it carry the allusion to the Pentecostal tongues of the apostles as they were set afire by the Spirit of God in the first century, but it suggests that today's preacher must, and can, also possess a tongue (and heart) set aflame by that same Spirit of gospel grace and hope. And the title captures the *connection* between the apostolic preachers of those early days and preachers like you and me in the twenty-first century, which I want you to understand is at the heart of my concern in this book.

We all realize that we share the message with the apostles – the 'good news' of the death, resurrection, and transforming power of Jesus Christ. My prayer is that this book will help you share in their preaching methods and abilities as well.

This book was a long time in the making. Many have helped along the way. I'm thankful to the faculty and staff of Westminster Theological Seminary in California. This book is the fruit of my participation in the seminary's Doctor of Ministry degree program in preaching. Special thanks to my advisors Jay Adams and Joseph Pipa. I would also like to thank my wife, Sherry, and my family, as well as the elders and congregation of Bayview Orthodox Presbyterian Church, Chula Vista, California, who all kept prodding me (gently but persistently) to complete this project. Finally, thanks to Alan Wares and Mike Pasarilla who helped me whip the manuscript into shape at various stages.

This book is dedicated to two men who are bound together in my heart around the preaching of the Word of God. Jay Adams is well known to many for his seminal thinking and writing on the subject of biblical counseling. He is also an outstanding preacher, and perhaps more importantly, an able teacher and trainer of young preachers. He was my first instructor in preaching at Westminster Seminary in

Philadelphia in 1970. It was he who, during the evaluation conference following my first 'practice sermon', first suggested (strongly) that I should consider becoming a pastor (I had had no such intention in entering seminary). He has had a profound effect on me as a Christian and as a pastor-preacher (as the text before you will demonstrate clearly). And it was at his urging, years later, that I entered the D.Min program in preaching at Westminster Seminary in California, out of which the present study grew. Thank you, Dr. Adams, and praise be to God, for all you have done for me.

The late Tom Stewart was a member of my first congregation in Sonora, California. He was the kind of sermon listener for which every preacher longs: eager, discerning, verbally responsive, a 'doer of the word' and not merely a hearer. Tom and his wife Grace were a great encouragement to me over the ten years I labored in Sonora. When I told Tom about the prospect of entering the D.Min program under Dr. Adams, he urged me to do so, and generously provided the financial support for the first phase of my studies. After I moved on to my present pastoral charge in Southern California, I did not see much of Tom and Grace, but on those few occasions we did visit one another, the conversation soon turned to preaching. Tom went home to be with our Lord a few years ago, but I was so grateful to God that before he died he had the opportunity to read the manuscript of this study. The last time we spoke, he had phoned me to say he had finished reading the manuscript, and had found it a great blessing to his heart. Thank the Lord, whose glorious gospel we proclaim, for modern day 'Bereans' like Tom.

Roger Wagner
September 2004
Chula Vista, California

Part 1

Characteristics of the
Preaching in Acts

1

Apostolic Examples for Preachers Today

It is rather remarkable to realize that neither the preaching of Jesus himself, nor the sermons of the apostolic preachers in the Book of Acts have been extensively considered or analyzed as models for developing methods and practices for preachers in our day. Several authors on the history of preaching pass over the sermons in Acts with little or no commentary. Broadus' comment is typical:

> I have time for but a few words as to the preaching of the Apostles. I regret this, because we may find in their discourses a greater number of practical lessons as to preaching, than in other parts of Scripture. But it is also easier to find those lessons here than elsewhere, and one who is interested in the matter will have comparatively little need of help.[1]

Accordingly, Broadus moves on to study the post-canonical development of Christian preaching, leaving us to discover the lessons of apostolic preaching on our own.

To be sure, these sermons have been discussed in detail with regard to their historical and theological interest. They have been used to construct a theology of the New Testament – in some cases multiple 'theologies' of the New Testament. Paul and Peter, or Paul and Jesus, have been made 'team captains', and New Testament theologians have 'chosen up sides' – some have said, 'I am of Peter,' others, 'I am of Paul,' and still others, 'I am of Christ.'

Yet students and teachers of the 'art of preaching' have been largely absent from this discussion. Little attempt has been made to discover what made the apostles such great preachers, and what gave their preaching such a profound effect on the first-century Roman world.

In this book we are going to make a small effort to reverse that trend of neglect by looking carefully at the sermons in Acts *as students of preaching*. While there is a great deal of valuable and helpful information about the sermons in the various historical and theological studies that have been written (which we in our turn will draw from),

it still remains for specific conclusions to be drawn and applications
made for preachers and preaching.

That is what we are going to attempt. We will distill from an
examination of these sermons some directives and guidelines that, it
is hoped, will make our preaching better today. As we look at the
apostolic preaching, it will be possible for us to reflect on some of the
strengths and weaknesses of contemporary preaching from the
perspective of these biblical models, so that we can learn how to
improve the effectiveness of our own efforts.

The first part of our study will be synthetic – drawing together
several features that we find characteristic of all the sermons in Acts.
Then, in the second section of our study, we will look in depth at the
sermons individually in order to learn what makes them so effective
in their peculiar setting. In all this our goal will be to become
accomplished imitators of apostolic preaching.

Perhaps you find a question forming in your minds at this point. As
a committed evangelical you have no question regarding the abiding
validity of the historical and theological content of the Acts sermons.
But we have been talking about their form and presentation. You may
be thinking, 'Why study these ancient sermons as a pattern for
preaching in the early twenty-first century?' Times have really
changed, and in many ways people and society have changed too.
Are these old messages still relevant?

I think so. Let me give you a few reasons for studying these sermons
as models for our preaching today. Some arise from Luke's purpose
in including these sermons in the Acts narrative in the first place.
Others are bound up with the nature of preaching, and its unique
function in God's redemptive purposes for mankind.

The Sermons and Luke's Purpose in Acts
As you are no doubt aware, Acts is really the second of two volumes
by Luke in which he chronicles the historical progress of the foundation
of the Christian church. Volume one, the Gospel of Luke, tells us of
the ministry of Jesus in word and deed, culminating in his resurrection
and ascension. Luke tells us of his purpose in writing his second volume,
the Book of Acts, in the very beginning of that book: 'In my former
book, Theophilus, I wrote about all that Jesus began to do and to
teach until the day he was taken up to heaven, after giving instructions
through the Holy Spirit to the apostles he had chosen' (1:1-2).

Thus Luke implies that his narrative in Acts will be a continuation of his account of what Jesus 'did and taught' – this time through the apostolic witnesses. Luke is about to unfold more details concerning the ministry of Christ – but now it is the Holy Spirit working through the apostles that will become the focus of his attention. The Holy Spirit, sent by the Father (John 15:26) and the Son (Acts 2:33; cf. John 16:25), will come in the name of Jesus, and on his behalf continue his post-resurrection ministry of glory (cf. 2 Cor. 3). Specifically, Jesus will accomplish this through the 'witness' of the apostles, borne in the power of the Spirit to the nations in ever-widening circles of expansion.

Consider Luke's introduction to his Gospel (which may indeed be an introduction intended for the whole two-volume work). He wrote:

> Many have undertaken to draw up an account of the things that have been fulfilled among us, just as they were handed down to us by those who were from the first eyewitnesses and servants of the word. Therefore, since I myself have carefully investigated everything from the beginning, it seemed good also to me to write an orderly account for you, most excellent Theophilus, so that you may know the certainty of the things you have been taught (Luke 1:1-4).

Luke is self-conscious in stating his purpose. He knows that his writing will be foundational for Theophilus, and for others who, like him, have come to put their faith in the Lord Jesus Christ. These new converts need to come to an exact understanding about what they have been taught and believe. Luke's intention in writing is to meet that need. His method will be to bring together the reports of earlier eyewitnesses, having personally investigated, compared, and collated them. He will then set them down in a unified narrative.

Luke's thematic emphasis on the role of the Holy Spirit in the spread of the gospel to the world is seen in his version of the 'Great Commission' in Luke 24:46-49:

> He told them, 'This is what is written: The Christ will suffer and rise from the dead on the third day, and repentance and forgiveness of sins will be preached in his name to all nations, beginning at Jerusalem. You are witnesses of these things. I am going to send you what my Father has promised; but stay in the city until you have been clothed with power from on high.'

Acts is the story of the spread of the Church *through preaching* –
the 'preaching of repentance and forgiveness of sins'. This preaching
constitutes the mission of the apostles, and it is to be done in the
power of the Holy Spirit. With this commission the stage is set for the
narrative of the Book of Acts.

Herman Ridderbos has commented that the purpose of Luke in
Acts is to describe 'the continuing work here on earth performed by
the ascended Christ through the service of His apostles'.[2] He goes
on to say, 'it is [Luke's] purpose to depict the confirmation of the
Gospel in the deeds and in the preaching of the apostles. Therefore
the content of the preaching and the manner in which it was done
were no less important than its geographical extension.'[3]

The sermons of the apostles, of which there are so many fine
examples in Acts (they make up one-fifth of the book), are not,
therefore, incidental additions to the account, chosen arbitrarily for
the purposes of narrative 'color'. These sermons are cited to
emphasize the central role preaching played in the witness of the
apostles to Christ.[4] According to Luke, the salvation of God which
has appeared in Christ must be proclaimed to the ends of the earth in
order to accomplish the redemptive purposes that began their realization
in the earthly ministry, death, and resurrection of Jesus Christ. For
this reason the speeches in Acts have a critical role to play in the
fulfillment of Luke's stated purpose. He intends to accomplish that
purpose both through the details of the historical narrative and through
the citation of the speeches.[5]

With regard to Luke's selection of sermonic materials for inclusion
in the Acts narrative, it has been noted that the speeches are 'typical,
carefully selected examples or illustrations of the witness to Christ in
its progress from Jerusalem to the end of the earth.'[6] Luke chooses
carefully to indicate what kind of message Jesus was preaching by
his Spirit through the apostles under different circumstances to various
sorts of people. As students of preaching we note that these sermons
are instructive not only for *what* is said, but for *how* that content is
arranged, and the method by which it is presented. A careful
examination of these sermons, therefore, is vital for the training of
today's preachers in the 'art' of biblical preaching.

The Reliability of Luke's Record

Questions have been raised concerning the reliability of Luke as a
reporter of the apostolic speeches. The sermons in Acts which we

propose to study would be of little value to us as models of apostolic message and method if they were not, in fact, accurate examples of the preaching of Peter and Paul, but rather literary creations of Luke himself. We must look at this question briefly in laying the foundation of our study.

Some scholars, notably Martin Dibelius, have argued that Luke took the liberty of creating the speeches he attributes to the apostles in the Book of Acts. Like the Greek historian Thucydides, Dibelius argues, Luke 'created' speeches and put them in the mouths of his principal characters. These speeches, again on the classical analogy, allegedly represent the historian's own interpretation of events in the narrative, formulated into speeches which are then attributed (by way of literary convention) to the participants for the dramatic purpose of enriching the historical narrative.[7] Thus according to this line of argument the sermons tell us more about Luke – about his theological point of view and style – than about Peter or Paul and their ministry as preachers.

In a 1943 booklet entitled *The Speeches in the Acts of the Apostles*, F. F. Bruce raised several trenchant criticisms of Dibelius' understanding of Luke's work.[8] More recently, Ward Gasque has defended Luke's method of recording the apostolic speeches against critics like Dibelius.[9] Gasque first criticizes Dibelius' reading of Thucydides' famous quotation concerning his method of recording speeches. According to Gasque,

> The celebrated passage from Thucydides, if taken at its face value, contradicts the thesis of Dibelius.... Although Dibelius admits that the interpretation of this passage is open to debate, he interprets it as an attempted justification by Thucydides of the practice of composing speeches with little or no regard for what actually may have been said. In point of fact, the natural interpretation of the passage would have Thucydides making the exact opposite claim, *viz.* that he did *not* invent speeches! 'For some of the speeches,' he says, 'I was present and heard what was actually spoken. For others I am dependent on the report of other people who heard them. It has been, of course, difficult to recall verbatim what was said on each occasion; therefore, I have made the speeches say what I thought was appropriate to the occasion, keeping as closely as possible to the general idea of what was actually spoken.' Some scholars, it is true, have questioned whether Thucydides really lived up to the high standard which he claims. Others, however, have given a good case for the view that he did. At any rate, it is clear that the

invention of speeches was not an acceptable historiographical method insofar as Thucydides was concerned – at least, in principle.[10]

Gasque gives other reasons for believing the speeches in Acts were not the creations of Luke: their brevity and placement,[11] their linguistic and theological diversity,[12] and the sometimes awkwardness of their style.[13] Gasque concludes:

> [The speeches] are intended to be regarded as the author's synopses of actual addresses, although, admittedly, the author would probably consider them to be models of good preaching even in his own day ... enough has been said to give some indication of the reason many New Testament critics take a very different view of the speeches in Acts from that advocated by Dibelius. The student of Acts must make up his own mind on the subject by making a careful study of the speeches for himself and then examining the arguments of Dibelius and those who follow him on one hand and their critics on the other.[14]

Others who share our particular interest in the study of preaching methods have come forward to debate the propriety of the claim that Luke is an inventor, rather than an accurate recorder, of sermons. In an appendix to his book, *Audience Adaptation in the Preaching of Paul*, Jay E. Adams addresses this question in some detail.[15] He argues for the historical reliability of Luke's record of the apostolic sermons. Based on the strong evidence for Lukan authorship of the book and an early date for composition (AD 61–63), Adams concludes that Luke was not composing a narrative of events that took place several hundred years before he lived, as Thucydides sometimes did. Instead, Luke was a contemporary of Peter and Paul. The general accuracy of Luke's historiography has been so thoroughly vindicated by even theologically unsympathetic scholarship as to put it beyond question.[16] He was personally involved and immediately concerned with many of the events included in the Acts narrative. He had no need to attempt to 'reconstruct' events (or statements) from the distant past. Luke was recording events in contemporary history, and he was recording them with remarkable accuracy.

Luke was a frequent companion of Paul,[17] and as such had repeated exposure to his apostolic preaching and teaching. He did not have to depend on one or two examples of sermons he personally heard, much less rely wholly on his imagination. Since he was present much of the time when Paul was ministering and preaching, his accounts of the sermons are often firsthand. Adams argues that it is even plausible to think that transcriptions and summaries of the sermons of Paul, prepared by Luke, may have been reviewed, corrected, and approved by Paul prior to their inclusion in the narrative.[18] The sermons, though not recorded in accordance with the modern custom of verbatim quotation, are nevertheless accurately reported, and they are typical examples of things that Luke heard said again and again over a period of some twelve years during which he was a participant in the ministry of the apostles.[19]

It must also be remembered that Luke is a theologian/historian. As such he is aware of the great significance of the events he is recording in the unfolding of redemptive history. Unlike many historians, he does not need the benefit of the perspective afforded by historical 'hindsight' in order to determine the relative significance of the events he is recording. He was aware of the estimation of the risen Lord that the apostolic 'witness' would be of earth-changing historical importance. This was bound to affect the manner in which he gathered and presented the factual information contained in his narrative, and it certainly controlled his assessment of the significance of the occasions and contents of the apostolic sermons.

Momentous events tend to call forth extraordinary effort and care on the part of those who have the responsibility to record and report those events. Often historians must rely on sketchy or biased reports from a geographical or historical distance. This limits their ability to report with accuracy and completeness, no matter what their intention. Luke, however, had no such problem. He was the reporter 'on the scene', and he knew he had the story of the ages to tell.

Beyond this, it is important to remember that Luke himself was an instrument of revelation, as much so as Peter and Paul. They were to bear 'witness,' and so was Luke. They had received the eschatological gift of the Holy Spirit for that purpose, and so had he. Their sermons were 'God-breathed', and so were Luke's records of those messages. What results is historiography of the highest order – at once humanly careful and accurate (Luke 1:1-4) and divinely inspired (2 Tim. 3:16).

The parallels between the speeches in Acts and the language, content, and style of the epistles of Paul and Peter also confirm the accuracy of Luke's record.[20] Donald Guthrie also points up the striking similarities between James' speeches in Acts 15 and the epistle that bears his name.[21] The Acts speeches retain their personal distinctiveness. They do not reflect the uniformity of a process by which apostolic teaching was gathered, digested, and regurgitated by Luke. The sermons are 'Petrine' and 'Pauline', not 'Lukan'.

Having said all this, it is nevertheless important to recognize that the sermons are not precise or complete transcriptions as one might be accustomed to finding today in an issue of *Vital Speeches*. Luke's brevity (the longest of the speeches only takes a few minutes to read) is accounted for by the fact that he is summarizing. It would be unwise, however, to conclude from this that Luke is therefore inaccurate in his reporting. On the contrary, Luke's habit is to give the actual words of men where they are relevant to the narrative. Adams points out that an example of Luke's accuracy can be found in the speech in Acts 22:1-21, which he argues was probably delivered in Aramaic and translated into Greek. This sermon as translated contains no characteristic Pauline words or expressions, though the ideas are typically Paul's. This may well be because Luke translated the sermon into his own Greek words, and thus the translation has a Lukan style rather than the style characteristic of the sermons that Luke records which were originally delivered by Paul in Greek.[22]

How could Luke have made such accurate summary transcripts? Shorthand! It should be remembered that a rather sophisticated method of shorthand was in use during the first century. It was developed for the very purpose of taking down speeches by Cicero. In later times it was used in the church, and by physicians.[23] Luke, a physician, may well have had a mastery of this skill which would have facilitated his ability to record the sermons while they were being delivered, and later to draw characteristic excerpts from those transcripts when including sermonic material in his narrative. In this light the process of editorial selection would not necessarily entail any diminution of the accuracy of the reports.

Christ Preaching Through the Apostles

A second reason that we ought to give our attention to the sermons in Acts as models for preaching today is that the preaching of the apostles in Acts is nothing less than the preaching of the risen Christ himself. We have already noticed that preaching was not incidental to the apostles' fulfillment of their mission. As with Jesus before them, the 'witness' the disciples were sent out to bear was to be conveyed through preaching. The 'witness' spoken of in Acts 1:8 was to be a witness-in-proclamation.

The Greek term *kērussō*, used so prominently in describing preaching in the New Testament, means 'to herald forth'.[24] The practice of the 'herald' (*kērux*) was well known in the ancient world. In the Greek city-states it was the task of the herald to call forth the citizens of the town to meet together in order to address themselves to the affairs of the city. This model helps us understand the function of preaching in God's redemptive economy. The preacher is sent forth as a *kērux* to proclaim the mighty redemptive acts of God (Acts 2:11), and by means of that witness-bearing, he calls out and calls together the church, which is the 'assembly' of the saints.[25] These 'saints' are those who put their trust in the finished work of Christ, whose saving work is the subject of the apostolic kerygma, and they thereby become 'citizens' of the kingdom of God (cf. Phil. 3:20).

Preaching, therefore, is central to the ministry of the apostles, because it is the direct extension of the preaching ministry of Jesus Christ. Jesus began his ministry by 'doing and teaching', and his appointed ambassadors are to continue that ministry by acting and teaching as his agents in the post-resurrection extension of his ministry.

In Mark 3:14f, the gathering of the twelve who are to become the 'apostles' is described in this way: 'He appointed twelve – designating them apostles – that they might be with him and that he might send them out to preach and to have authority to drive out demons.'

The disciples were gathered together by Jesus so that he might personally prepare them. Jesus' purpose in training and discipling these men is to equip them for the time when he would send them out (*apostellō*) to preach and teach. 'Being with him' is the phrase that Mark uses to indicate this personal, direct relationship the apostle-designates had to the Master. Having thus prepared them, he sent them out to test their gifts in ministry. In Luke 9:2, we read that Jesus 'sent them out to preach the kingdom of God and to heal the sick'. The account in Acts 4:13 of the response of the Sanhedrin to the preaching of Peter tells us, 'When they saw the courage of Peter and John and realized that they were unschooled and ordinary men, they were astonished and they took note that these men had been with Jesus.'

The convicting quality of Peter's preaching was the result of his having 'been with Jesus'. But this remark is more than a simple observation that Peter was a follower of Jesus. Rather, Luke is drawing our attention in this setting to the fact (related in the Gospels) that these simple men – fishermen, tax collectors, etc. – had been trained by Jesus himself, and the evidence of that training was not lost on the Jewish leaders. They made the connection. Though these men lacked formal theological or homiletical education, because of their personal training under Jesus, they were bold and powerful preachers.[26]

The nature of the apostolic commission, and its attendant authority, depends upon the *identification* of the one sent with the One sending. The Greek verb *apostellō* describes this unique sort of 'sending'. In Matthew 10 (as well as the parallel passage in Luke 9), we have the record of Jesus' sending the Twelve on a mission of preaching and miracle-working during the time when Jesus was still engaged in public ministry. It is a sort of training mission for the 'Great Commission' which will come later following Jesus' resurrection. 'He called his twelve disciples to him and gave them authority to drive out evil spirits and to heal every disease and sickness.... These twelve Jesus sent out' (Matt. 10:1, 5).

In his commission to the Twelve on this occasion, Jesus explains to them that the closest kind of identification exists between their *mission* and his. With regard to the nature of their mission he says, 'Do not go among the Gentiles or enter any town of the Samaritans. Go rather to the lost sheep of Israel' (v. 6). The scope of their mission at this stage was identical to that of Jesus' own personal mission (cf. Matt. 15:24). In verse 18, Jesus says, 'On my account (*eneken emou*) you will be brought before governors and kings as witnesses to them and to the Gentiles,' and in verse 22 he tells them, 'All men will hate you because of me (lit., "on account of my name").' This emphasis on the ministry of the apostles in the place of Christ is carried through by Luke in the Book of Acts by his repeated emphasis on the fact that the apostolic work is done 'in Jesus' name' (cf. 2:38; 3:6, 16; 4:10, 12, 17, 18, 30; 5:40-41; 8:12; etc.).

Not only is the mission of the apostles (and its scope) identical with that of Jesus, but they are also commanded to preach the very same *message* that Jesus preached – namely, 'the kingdom of heaven is near' (v. 7; cf. Mark 1:15; Luke 9:2). Finally, they share his *authority*, because they are identified with him in their preaching and healing, and in the response of men to them: 'He who listens to you listens to me; he who rejects you rejects me; but he who rejects me rejects him who sent me' (Luke 10:16).

The 'Great Commission' as given in Matthew 28:18ff. is predicated on the total authority of Jesus Christ, who has now been 'declared to be the Son of God with power through the resurrection from the dead' (cf. Rom. 1:4), and by this authority the apostles are sent out to 'disciple' (i.e., baptize and teach) all the nations in Jesus' name. Historically, the scope of the post-resurrection mission has now extended from 'the lost sheep of Israel' to 'all the nations'.

To attend them in this mission, Jesus promises his personal presence: he will be with them to the 'end of the age' (Matt. 28:20). According to Luke in his narrative of the progressive accomplishment of the apostolic mission, Jesus is present in and with the apostles by the Holy Spirit with whom Jesus baptizes them (indeed the whole Church) on the day of Pentecost, and in whose power and authority he sends them forth (Acts 1:8; cf. Luke 24:44-49; Acts 2:32; 26:16-18).

Thus an 'apostle' of Jesus Christ in the strict, technical sense refers to one commissioned and sent by Christ the Lord to carry his message for him, one who bears his full authority as the One sending, and one who in effect is identified with the ministry of Christ himself.

This explains why the teaching of the apostles became theologically and ethically foundational to the early Church (Acts 2:42; Eph. 2:20; Gal. 1:6ff), and to believers ever since. Paul has no qualms about identifying himself as a 'foundation layer', and therefore as one having a ministry distinct from other preachers who will come after him, and who will build upon that one unique foundation which he, as an apostle, can lay (1 Cor. 3:10f). He can readily identify his apostolic instructions to the churches as the 'Lord's command' (1 Cor. 14:37-38).

Since a wedge cannot be driven between the ministry and message of Jesus, on the one hand, and the ministry and message of the apostles, on the other, Luke can describe the ministry of the latter as a *continuation* of that which Jesus 'began to do and to teach' when he was on the earth (Acts 1:1). In a sense, then, the sermons in Acts are the messages of the risen Lord: both because he personally taught the apostolic preachers what and how to preach, and because, by his Spirit, he was preaching through them.[27]

The apostolic preaching we find in Acts, therefore, is not only theologically and ethically foundational to the new covenant – it is *homiletically* foundational as well. These sermons have a unique character. It is distinctive from other collections of great Christian sermons, such as those of Chrysostom, Whitefield, or Spurgeon. These apostolic sermons are 'God-breathed' and thus can serve as valuable models of the art of preaching in both their *content* (which is often acknowledged) and in their *form* and *presentation* (which is often overlooked). We can certainly learn much from the example of Whitefield and Spurgeon, but the preacher of today will do well to look carefully at the patterns here in these apostolic sermons for insights that will help make his preaching more effective.

The Holy Spirit and the Preaching of the Apostles

One final reason should be considered for studying the sermons in Acts as patterns for our preaching today. Apostolic preaching is the result of a *special ministry of the Holy Spirit in the apostles*. A unique and powerful ministry of the Spirit was given to them which reflects the place of this preaching in the history of redemption.

This kind of preaching was not possible in the Old Testament era. It was not possible for any of the prophets, including John the Baptist. Indeed, it was not possible at any time before the ascension of Jesus. Such proclamation of the gospel only became possible when the Holy Spirit was poured out upon men by means of the 'baptism with the Spirit' promised by both John the Baptist and Jesus (cf. Matt. 3:11; Acts 1:4). That 'baptism' was wholly conditioned by the dawning of the new era occasioned by the historic accomplishment of Jesus' atoning work through his death and resurrection (cf. Acts 2:31-33). Apostolic preaching presupposes and announces the *glorification* of the Lord Jesus Christ (cf. Acts 2:36). Thus the apostles were told to wait in Jerusalem until they were 'clothed with power from on high' (Luke 24:49; Acts 1:8). We will have more to say later about the central importance of this historical dimension in apostolic preaching, but for now we want to emphasize the unique role of the Holy Spirit in preparing the preaching of the apostles in Acts.

During the time of Jesus' earthly ministry with his disciples, he had promised them special 'help' from the Holy Spirit for their future witness bearing: 'But when they arrest you, do not worry about what to say or how to say it. At that time you will be given what to say, for it will not be you speaking, but the Spirit of your Father speaking through you' (Matt. 10:19-20).

You can see here a striking distinction between your situation as a preacher and that of the apostles. You share their preaching task, but the Lord Jesus made a unique provision for their preaching that he has not made for yours, at least not in the same way.

You prepare your sermons very carefully, and rightly so. But what do you suppose would happen if you made no preparations at all for your Sunday message? Quite likely the results would be disastrous, at least in most cases. I have heard of sermons where the preacher tried to claim the Lord's special 'leading' (as a substitute for adequate study and preparation). Perhaps you have too. The results are usually very shabby, and it is a shameful scandal to blame the Spirit of the Lord for the awful results.

With that in mind, can you imagine actually being told by Jesus not to prepare at all? Yet, according to Matthew in the passage cited above, that is exactly what Jesus told the apostles. He promised them that both the content ('what') and the form ('how') of their speeches would be 'given' them or 'taught' to them by the Spirit apart from any specific study and preparation. The Spirit would be speaking through them[28] as they made their defenses.

The same point is made by Jesus in Mark 13:11: 'Whenever you are arrested and brought to trial, do not worry beforehand about what to say. Just say whatever is given you at the time, for it is not you speaking, but the Holy Spirit.' Similarly, Luke records our Lord's words in his Gospel as follows: 'When you are brought before synagogues, rulers and authorities, do not worry about how you will defend yourselves or what you will say, for the Holy Spirit will teach you at that time what you should say' (12:11, 12). 'But make up your mind not to worry beforehand how you will defend yourselves. For I will give you words and wisdom that none of your adversaries will be able to resist or contradict' (21:14-15).

When called upon by the authorities to answer for their ministry, the apostles were not to prepare defenses beforehand (by extensive rehearsal, etc.), nor were they to be worried. Jesus would give or teach them the words they would need for their defense (Luke 21:14), and he promised to do that by the Holy Spirit (cf. similar language in the other passages cited). So powerful and convincing will be these words of wisdom (carrying the sense of skill in form and presentation as well as truthfulness, cf. Exod. 31:3), that none of their enemies would be able to answer or contradict their words.

Acts contains several accounts of the apostles giving defenses of their gospel in various settings, and it is clear, especially from the formal defenses before the Sanhedrin and the Roman magistrates, that the promise of Christ for special assistance was fulfilled.

We have already noted the response of the Jewish council to the preaching of Peter (Acts 4:13) – they were astonished at the authority of his defense. This is also the case with Stephen in Acts 6:10, where Luke reports that 'they could not stand up against his wisdom or the Spirit by whom he spoke'. The echo of the language of Luke 21:15 is unmistakable. John Calvin's comment on Acts 6:10 is interesting:

> Stephen's adversaries ... were not able to withstand the wisdom with which the Spirit of God supplied him ... the reason why the enemies of the Gospel were broken was that they were fighting with the Spirit of God, who was speaking through the mouth of Stephen.
>
> As far as we are concerned, since Christ has promised the same Spirit to all His servants ... let us ask for a mouth and wisdom from Him, and we shall be sufficiently equipped for speaking, so that neither the shrewdness nor the garrulity of our enemies may ever put us to shame....[29]

In emphasizing this point, I do not want to overstate the case and give you a false impression. It is not that the apostles made no preparation for their preaching ministry. We have already seen that they were intensively trained for their task by Jesus during his public ministry. In addition, as Jews they were well schooled in the Old Testament Scriptures, and we are told in Luke 24:44-45 that Jesus explained the Scriptures to the newly-opened minds of the disciples in light of his recent resurrection. It is likely that the forty-day period between the resurrection and ascension of Christ was taken up with further preparation of the apostles for their coming ministry. In the case of Paul, the time that he spent alone in the desert was probably a time of training in preparation for his ministry of the gospel. Further, he had as part of his religious background the finest rabbinic education available at the time (cf. Acts 22:3). The request that he makes that 'the books and parchments' be brought to him (2 Tim. 4:13) implies that he continued during his ministry to study the Scriptures under the illumination of the Spirit.

So this special involvement of the Holy Spirit in 'giving' messages to the apostles is not so much his creating sermons in the minds of the apostles *ex nihilo,* as it is his *bringing to expression the thoughts shaped by Jesus* through personal instruction in the Scriptures as well as their own study of the Word. Further, that expression will be given in the appropriate form suiting the occasion.

This function of the Spirit can be seen clearly in the comments

Jesus made in his last addresses to his disciples before his suffering and death, as recorded by John in his Gospel. Jesus taught the disciples about the ministry they were to have when he would leave them. In that connection Jesus promises to send the Holy Spirit who will be present with them as another Helper (John 14:16). He goes on to say, 'But the Counselor, the Holy Spirit, whom the Father will send in my name, will teach you all things and will remind you of everything I have said to you' (14:26). Jesus adds, 'But when he, the Spirit of truth, comes, he will guide you into all truth ... and he will tell you what is yet to come' (16:13).

In these statements, Jesus couples the idea that the Holy Spirit will be the source both of *perfect recall* of things said in the past (as he 'reminds' them of what Jesus had already taught them), and of *new revelations* regarding things in the near and distant future. In these ways the Holy Spirit will 'lead the way' for the disciples into the whole truth. The disciples will be equipped like good scribes of the kingdom to bring out of their treasure stores both old and new (Matt. 13:52) under the guidance of the Holy Spirit.

Taken together, these statements by our Lord indicate the unique character of the apostolic preaching. The Holy Spirit will enable the apostles to say the right thing with the right words in the right way at the right time.

> We have not received the spirit of the world but the Spirit who is from God, that we may understand what God has freely given us. This is what we speak, not in words taught us by human wisdom but in words taught by the Spirit, expressing spiritual truths in spiritual words (1 Cor. 2:12, 13).

Thus content, style, form, and occasion all come within the scope of our Savior's concern for, and the Spirit's ministry in, preparing the apostles for their preaching task. The sermons in Acts therefore are vital for study by today's preachers, because they represent how God himself delivered his gospel in the situations recorded in Acts.

In considering the character of the Acts sermons themselves as they reflect this unique character as Christ-prepared and Spirit-delivered, the comments of J. M. Stifler, in his book *An Introduction to the Study of the Acts of the Apostles*, are instructive. Stifler speaks of the 'Spirit-inspired' oratory of the formerly weak and vacillating Peter on the day of Pentecost:

Christian eloquence is not a gift of nature, but of grace. Piety is necessary to the best oratory.

But when Peter's address on this morning is studied, we have still more convincing proof of the Spirit's presence. In its adroitness, in the arrangement of the arguments, in its analysis, in its steering clear of Jewish prejudices, in its appeal and effect, it is without a peer among the products of uninspired men. As an example of persuasive argument it has no rival. The more it is studied the more its beauty and power are disclosed, and yet it is the work of a Galilean fisherman, without culture or training, and his maiden effort....

Who taught the unschooled Peter this perfection in argumentation? It implies a metaphysician's knowledge of the hearer's reason and feeling. He knows just how the auditor must be addressed to be won. Beethoven could not play on the pianoforte with more masterfulness than Peter shows in touching the many keys of the human heart.

Pages might be written on the grandeur of this address, which, it must not be forgotten, was extemporaneous. But this is sufficient to show that he who wrote it was either under supernatural influence, or was a supernatural person. To deny the inspiration of the address is to cast us on the other horn of the dilemma, that Peter was more than mortal man.... The structure of the speech transcends human power. It must have come from God's Spirit.[30]

Can you still remember your first sermon? I can. It was an exposition of James 5:7-9. At the time I thought it was a pretty decent sermon, but when looking back at it I came to see its many deficiencies. Though I believe the Spirit was present and blessed in my effort, it would nevertheless admit of later improvement. The Spirit was at work in Peter and the other preachers in Acts in an additional, unique way. The skill of Peter's first sermon is such that it shows clearly the superintending involvement of the Holy Spirit in fulfilling the promise of Christ by giving his words and wisdom to Peter. Peter would not look back upon it in later years and say, 'I could have done better.'

The Sermons and You

We have said so much about the unique characteristics of these sermons, and the special promises of the influence of the Holy Spirit to the preachers, that you may be asking, 'What then is the point of my trying to imitate these messages when I am *not* one of the apostles, and have *not* been given these same promises of help?' Has Christ simply left us to our own feeble devices? Should we abandon preaching in despair and replace it with drama or musical showmanship as some have? No, not at all!

Remember Calvin's comment quoted earlier?

> And forasmuch as Christ hath promised the same Spirit to all his servants, let us only defend the truth faithfully, and let us crave a mouth and wisdom of him, and we shall be sufficiently furnished to speak.

While it is true that we do not help ourselves by trying to erase the 'gulf' that exists between the authority and ministry of the apostles, and our post-apostolic ministry of the Word, nevertheless, it is not right to ignore the fact that we stand *with the apostles* in very significant ways. We will have more to say about this at a later point in our discussion (cf. ch. 9), but for now let us remember that as in theology and ethics, so in preaching, we participate in *apostolic authority and power* by following *apostolic precept and example* as they are set forth in the pages of Scripture. Our way of access to preaching in a manner similar to the apostles is through the Bible. We know that good preaching is full of biblical content. Our preaching methodology should be equally formed by the Bible. God, who gives us the 'new wine' of the gospel, will also furnish the sermonic 'wine skins' in which to contain and dispense that sweet, life-transforming message.

We ought to study and imitate these sermons precisely because we do *not* share the special commission or authority of the apostles. We will preach well as we follow their example, and build upon their foundation. That foundation is the Word, and, specifically, the sermons we propose to examine in the Book of Acts.

It is worthwhile to note in closing this chapter that these sermons are not only characterized by the remarkable influence of the Spirit of God mentioned above, they also evidence the rich human diversity of the apostolic preachers themselves. The sovereignty of God's operations in guiding these preachers does not violate the personal individuality of the preachers themselves. The diversity of personality, background, training, vocabulary, and style shine through in the messages in Acts.

God plays a number of different instruments, and the individual personality and background of the preacher is as much a part of powerful preaching as is the divine influence. Charles Spurgeon encouraged his students, 'Be yourselves, plus Christ.' It should be an encouragement to you that God will use your personal distinctiveness to his glory in the molding of effective preachers. We are not all the same, and we do not all have to be a George Whitefield or a Billy Graham in order to preach with power and effect. You do not need to become a slavish imitator of the preachers you admire. On the contrary, such imitation can be devastating to the preacher trying to be 'another Spurgeon'. You can never be anyone but yourself. And God will use you as he did Peter or Stephen to speak forth the great news of the mighty acts of God in Christ.

For men like us, who are not inspired preachers of the Word of God, these sermons become especially important as examples. They show us how the Holy Spirit preaches. If you want a preacher to imitate, who better than the Spirit of Christ at work in the apostolic witnesses? Just because you must prepare your sermons, study and carefully arrange your material, consider your audience and situation, you need these sermons as examples of proper content, form, audience adaptation, situational flexibility, and manner of presentation. Your 'preparation' as a preacher must include the study and mastery of these apostolic sermons as guides for the proper presentation of the Word of God today.

May God give you a deeper appreciation for what he was doing through the apostolic preachers in Acts, and may he bless you as you discipline yourself to achieve all that God has promised to you as you follow their lead.

2

Surveying the Sermons

I hope your enthusiasm for studying the sermons in Acts was not dampened by the somewhat technical discussions in the previous chapter. If it has, don't worry, we're about to dive in. But first let's ask a few orientation questions: Exactly what kind of study are we talking about? How many sermons are there? What kinds of sermons are they? How do they fit into the Acts narrative? A few minutes' consideration of these questions will set before us the scope of our study. It will also serve to introduce us to the speakers and occasions for the speeches as well.

We have already noted that fully one-fifth of the Book of Acts is taken up with the sermons Luke records. This means we have a great deal of material to draw from in our study, though there are also some significant limitations.

Consider first the way these messages are distributed throughout Luke's narrative. If we use Acts 1:8 and 9:15 as starting points, we can catch a glimpse of the structural outline for the whole book. Many have noted the schematic significance for Luke's narrative of the geographical expansion of the gospel mentioned in Acts 1:8: 'you will be my witnesses in Jerusalem, and in all Judea and Samaria, and to the ends of the earth.' With this outline in view, we can recognize that in chapters 2–7 Luke tells us of the progress of events 'in Jerusalem'. In this section the principal speeches are those of Peter: to the pilgrims assembled on the Day of Pentecost (2:14-40), to the crowd that gathered after the healing of the blind man (3:12-26), and to the Sanhedrin after his arrest with John (4:8-12). This section concludes with the sermon by Stephen, preached in his own defense before the Jewish leaders (7:2-53).

The persecution that arose in connection with the martyrdom of Stephen forced the beginning of the geographical extension of the apostolic witness (8:1). Chapters 8–11 record the spread of the gospel 'in all Judea and Samaria'. Peter's sermon to the household of Cornelius (10:34-43) is the significant speech which Luke includes in this section.

The introduction of the person of Saul with the story of his conversion in chapter 9 sets the stage for the narrative of the spread of the gospel 'to the ends of the earth' which begins in chapter 13. This section comprises the remainder of the book and centers around the missionary journeys of Paul. This larger section can be further subdivided in the terms outlined in the Lord's commissioning word to Paul through the prophet Ananias in Acts 9:15: 'This man is my chosen instrument to carry my name before the Gentiles and kings and before the children of Israel.'

The events of Paul's missionary career (chs. 13–20) describe how he carried Jesus' name to the Gentiles. Paul's evangelistic sermons to Gentile audiences in Pisidian Antioch and Athens are strategically placed in this section (13:16-41; 17:22-31) as well as his 'farewell' message to the elders of the Gentile church in Ephesus during his return trip to Jerusalem (20:18-35).

Paul's arrest in Jerusalem (21:27-36) precipitates the events that bring him 'before kings' for the defense of the name of Jesus (chs. 24–26). In this section we find the formal 'defenses' before Felix, the Roman governor (24:10-21), and Herod Agrippa, the Roman vassal king (26:2-23). Finally, Paul is called upon to bear the name of Christ to his brothers in the flesh, the sons of Israel. While there were Jews present and involved throughout Paul's missionary enterprise, Luke focuses our attention on Paul's speech to the angry crowd in Jerusalem (22:1-21), the abortive defense before the Sanhedrin (23:1-10), and the deliverances to the Jews in Rome with which Luke closes the book (28:23-29).

Scanning the sermons and their distribution through the book as we have done, we note not only their strategic placement in the narrative, but we are also struck with the wide variety of occasion, audience, and response evident in the sermons Luke includes.

Audiences include Jews and proselytes in Jerusalem, the hardened leaders of the Sanhedrin, the inquiring proselytes and 'God-fearers' in Cornelius' household, common 'man-in-the-street' Gentiles as well as Gentile intellectuals and leaders, leaders in the churches converted from both Judaism and Gentile paganism, Roman imperial magistrates, and Jews of the Diaspora.

There are a variety of occasions as well. Some sermons are prompted by miraculous displays at public celebrations (Pentecost), others by quiet, out of the way miracles (healing the crippled beggar).

Sometimes it is a routine synagogue service that gives rise to a sermon (Pisidian Antioch), sometimes a life and death confrontation with a murderous crowd (at the Temple in Jerusalem). While in every one of these varied circumstances the apostolic witness maintains a consistent message (*kerygma*), yet the preachers are well aware of, and often capitalize upon, the special occasions for preaching in which they find themselves.

The responses to the sermons are as varied as the audiences and occasions. Sometimes the preaching brings comfort and encouragement to the distressed (the Ephesian elders), at other times it creates a furor and division (as Paul did before the Sanhedrin), at still other times the response may be a chilly dismissal (as at the Areopagus). Sometimes the hearers rejoice in the message (the 3,000 at Pentecost), on other occasions they murder the preacher (as the Jewish leaders did Stephen).

Despite the great abundance and variety of sermonic material in Acts, we must acknowledge that there are also some significant *limitations* inherent in our study. One, which is more apparent than real, is the fact that we are studying the work of essentially only two preachers in Acts – Peter and Paul.[1] I say this is only apparent, because it seems very likely that Luke focuses our attention on these two men and their ministries, not only because of the central importance of their ministries to the advancement of the gospel kingdom in redemptive history, but also because they can be taken as typical. This includes the way in which they conducted their missions – specifically, the way they approached preaching.

I think we can take it for granted that wherever the other apostles went, the message they preached, and the manner in which they preached it, was essentially the same as what we see in Peter and Paul. No doubt they encountered different people in different cultures and preached under different circumstances. Perhaps they were called upon to exercise adaptability to a greater or lesser degree, but we have sufficient variety in Acts to give us a good indication of how they would have approached the challenges of their ministries. Acts can give us enough direction to enable us to become flexible enough to adapt ourselves to the situations in which we find ourselves preaching.

The most glaring limitation arising from our study is the absence in Acts of even a single example of what we would consider 'regular Sunday preaching' in the worship assemblies of the church. The closest we come to such preaching in a stable, friendly environment is Paul's address to the Ephesian elders in Acts 20.[2] But this message is unusual as well, occasioned as it was by Paul's dramatic leave-taking, and his profound conviction that he would never see these beloved brethren again.

Most of the messages in Acts are missionary sermons of one sort or another, or else defenses of the faith before inquiring or hostile audiences. While many of the methods and practices of such evangelistic or apologetical preaching are readily adaptable to weekly preaching in the church, there are some differences, and we will have to take these differences into account as we go along. Most of the apostolic preachers did not enjoy the benefit we have of the weekly continuity afforded by the abiding relationship which exists between most of us as pastors and one local congregation. When they did enjoy a longer pastoral tenure, as Paul did for a time in Ephesus, Luke has not left us an example of the sort of preaching that was carried on in that setting.

We must, therefore, take this cautionary word to heart – in studying these messages with a view to imitating them as examples of sound preaching practices, our imitation cannot be slavish or wooden. There is a need to learn the lessons of the apostolic preachers, and then apply them carefully and sensitively *to our particular situations.* If you are a missionary or evangelist, you may find more of immediate and direct relevance to your situation than the man who does the bulk of his preaching during the weekly public worship of the local church. You need to be influenced deeply by the apostolic examples, and not settle for just a superficial conformity to their practices. You still want to be yourself at the end of this study, but you also want Peter, Stephen, and Paul to have become part of you.

I believe that if you who are pastor-preachers come to understand these sermons properly, it will likely change your concept of what is, or should be, going on in the weekly assemblies of your churches. If you evangelize, defend the faith, confront your people with the challenges of the Christian life, carefully handle their reactions to what you say, and even at times preach to provoke a response, you will revitalize even the most drab and routine of your worship services.[3]

Thus if there is a gap between what you do week by week and what the preachers in Acts are doing, do not assume that they have nothing to say to you or show you. Follow their lead, and you will find the Spirit of God breathing fresh life and power not only into your sermons, but into the circumstances in which those sermons are preached.

3

The Preaching in Acts is
Bold Preaching

In the next few chapters we will consider some of the most striking characteristics of the sermons in Acts taken together, then we will turn (in Part 2) to a more detailed examination of the individual sermons.

The heart of the 'good news' carried to the world by the apostolic preachers in the first several decades of the Christian era was the staggering announcement that God had glorified his Son, Jesus of Nazareth, through his resurrection and ascension to God's right hand (Rom. 1:3-4; 1 Tim. 3:16). In the name of this triumphant King of kings and Lord of lords repentance and the forgiveness of sins was to be preached to all nations (Luke 24:47). That was the apostolic *message*.

The hallmark of the apostolic *method* of preaching was *boldness*. Again and again as we read Luke's account we are arrested by the power and boldness that characterized the way in which the gospel was proclaimed by those early preachers.

The message preached and the method of delivery go hand in hand. Form and content are mutually appropriate to one another – 'spiritual truths in spiritual words' (1 Cor. 2:13).

This characteristic boldness is all the more striking when we compare it with the preaching of our day, which is so often lacking in this biblical boldness. We may not like to admit it, but it is nevertheless a fact that many of today's preachers may be loud and bombastic at times, may even become tactless and offensive at times, but for all that, they lack the boldness that is so obviously evident in the apostolic preaching of Acts.

If you were to ask the members of your congregation to describe your preaching in one word, what do you think they would say? How many would use the term 'bold'? Have you ever asked your congregation such a question? If you did, was 'bold' one of the top three adjectives they used to describe your preaching? One of the top ten? Would anyone characterize your preaching as bold? How would you evaluate your own preaching? Is boldness a trait that you think is important, and that you would like to cultivate in your proclamation of the gospel?

Perhaps as you reflect on these questions you would have to admit that you have not cultivated boldness in your preaching. Perhaps you have not even missed it. Perhaps your congregation would not really appreciate preaching that was biblically bold if you did preach that way. As we will see a little later, apostolic boldness is something people are not likely to understand until they actually hear it, and then they are not exactly sure that it is what they wanted after all!

In our day many churchgoers favor a kind of preaching that is at once 'laid-back' and 'upbeat'. Preachers who want to attract big crowds need to be able to ooze a 'be-(happy) attitude'. Their sermons – or should we call them simply 'messages' or 'informal monologues' – must be strong on 'affirmation'. They would likely find preaching that is bold in the biblical sense to be oppressive, meddling, confrontational, and not a little disconcerting. They may be glad that they do not have to face it.

While it may not be difficult to find churchgoing people who are pleased with 'preaching' that lacks biblical boldness, it is not at all possible, as a preacher, *to please God* without it.

If biblical boldness is not characteristic of your preaching, there is something seriously wrong, for true preaching is – above all else – bold. In this chapter and the next we will try to come to a clear understanding of what *true* boldness is – and what it is *not* – and how it comes to expression in the sermons recorded in Acts. By so doing I hope you will learn to be bold in your own preaching. It is very important that, as we study and reflect on the Scriptures regarding this point, we sincerely ask God to give us, first, the desire of heart to become bold preachers of his truth, and then the grace and discipline to practice such boldness in our proclamation of the Word.

We must begin by asking what this boldness is. The Greek word *parrēsia* – translated 'boldness' (often 'confidence' in the NIV) – is scattered throughout Luke's narrative as he describes the preaching of those early days.[1] Peter said to the crowd at Pentecost, 'Brothers, I can tell you confidently (*parrēsias*) that the patriarch David died. But ... he spoke of the resurrection of the Christ' (Acts 2:29, 31). Again in 4:13 (AV) we read, 'Now when [the Sanhedrin] saw the boldness (*parrēsian*) of Peter and John ... they marvelled.' The boldness and confidence of these simple and (as they thought) untrained men was enough to penetrate even the jaded ears of the Jewish council (they had heard it someplace before!).

Immediately after his conversion, Paul's preaching ministry in Damascus became more and more powerful, and is described by Barnabas as fearless. Later the brethren in Jerusalem are treated to a sample of that same sort of preaching and debating (vv. 28 f.).

> Yet Saul grew more and more powerful and baffled the Jews living in Damascus by proving that Jesus is the Christ.... Barnabas ... told [the apostles] how Saul on his journey had seen the Lord and that the Lord had spoken to him, and how in Damascus he had preached fearlessly in the name of Jesus. So Saul stayed with them and moved about freely in Jerusalem, speaking boldly in the name of the Lord (Acts 9:22, 27-28).

Much later in his ministry, the closing words of Acts summarily describe Paul's activities: 'Boldly and without hindrance he preached the kingdom of God and taught about the Lord Jesus Christ' (28:31).

As far as the preaching of the apostles in Acts is concerned, the first and last word is boldness. So what is this boldness? If the apostles had it, what did they have?

Essentially, whether the Greek term is translated 'boldness' or 'confidence' (or 'plainness' or 'sincerity'), at the heart of the idea is *freedom to make the truth of God known without fear of opposition or consequences*. It is critical that you understand this point clearly, for only so will you be able to distinguish true (i.e., biblical) boldness from its counterfeits.

Paul includes in his letters to the Ephesians and the Colossians personal prayer requests for his ministry. These requests shed particular light on the question before us.

> Pray also for me, that whenever I open my mouth, words may be given me so that I will fearlessly make known the mystery of the gospel, for which I am an ambassador in chains. Pray that I may declare it fearlessly, as I should (Eph. 6:19 f.).

> And pray for us, too, that God may open a door for our message, so that we may proclaim the mystery of Christ, for which I am in chains. Pray that I may proclaim it clearly, as I should (Col. 4:3 f.).

In the Colossians passage Paul asks the church to pray that he will preach the 'mystery of Christ' (i.e., the gospel, cf. Eph. 3:2-6) 'as he should'.[2] In Ephesians the request takes the form of asking that 'words may be given me so that I will fearlessly[3] make known the mystery'. In the parallel passage he asks that he 'may proclaim [the gospel message] clearly [*phanerōsō*].' In collating these two texts, we find that in Paul's mind 'boldness' equals 'clarity'. The apostle believes that boldness in preaching is at heart a question of getting the message of Christ out clearly, despite the fearful threat of unpleasant consequences. In short, as I said before, boldness in the preacher is the willingness and ability *to be clear in the face of fear.*

This means that true boldness is not a *personality trait*. Some people imagine that boldness is to have a strong, outgoing personality. Boldness and brashness are taken as virtually synonymous. This is not so. Men with this sort of personality will not necessarily have the boldness that describes the apostles in Acts. As a matter of fact, such an overpowering personality may well get in the way of the growth of genuine boldness, just because it can be such a ready substitute for it.

Peter certainly had such a strong, overbearing personality. He was always the man on the spot with the decisive mouth. Remember the boldness of his promise to the Lord of constant faithfulness – even to the death? 'Lord, I am ready to go with you to prison and to death' (Luke 22:33). Sounds impressive. But bold? Not long afterwards, when faced with the accusing questions of a young maiden, Peter first cracked, and finally crumbled. Why? He was afraid. Afraid that if he openly confessed his association with Jesus he would join him in his condemnation at the hands of the Jews. Peter had the brash personality, but did it make him bold? Not at all. He was not bold in the biblical sense, because he lacked real freedom in the face of his fears. Under the pressure of the girl's question, he caved in completely.

But by the time we meet Peter in the Book of Acts, he has become a broken, humbled man – confronted with his sinful cowardice and restored by the grace of Christ. Only then can Peter demonstrate the rocklike boldness of which his name speaks.

I myself have the same kind of loud, brash, outgoing personality as Peter. My voice can make sleeping babies jump two houses away. I am happy enough to make the grand gesture, the brave declaration in a friendly environment. But also like Peter I have succumbed to fear more often than I would care to admit. Perhaps you have too. If we are going to discover what real boldness is, we cannot rely on our natural personality. True boldness does not arise from the flesh.

There is another danger in confusing boldness with a strong personality. Preachers that are thus confused may draw the conclusion that they could never be bold in their preaching or witnessing, just because they do not have the personality for it. 'It's just not my style,' they think. But remember, biblical boldness is not a matter of personal style; it is the result, not of native ability, but of grace.

It may come as a surprise to you that it is often the people that do not have the personality for it – the quiet, retiring, self-effacing people – who evidence the greatest boldness in ministry. I remember sitting in a chapel service at a Christian college one day in the late 1960s when the speaker (usually a rather brash and overbearing sort), who had been harried by a hostile and outspoken student body for a few days, 'faced the lions' for the last time. With a voice at once quiet, calm, and strong – never rising above a conversational level – he told the students what they needed to hear, but so far had been unwilling to hear. The impact of his sermon was overpowering. He was bold, even when (uncharacteristically) withdrawn in manner, because he told the truth to his audience in clear and unequivocal terms, even though (humanly speaking) there was a high probability that his message would be rejected.

On another occasion, a seminary professor found himself feeling rather out of place speaking about Jesus Christ to a room full of semi-freaked-out 'hippies' in the back of a restaurant. He was the last person on earth you would have chosen – if you were choosing on the basis of 'natural' considerations like background, personality, style of delivery, etc. – yet he spoke with such simplicity, such clarity, such sincere love, that many of these outcast young people came up at the end of his presentation to inquire further concerning 'the Way'.

Paul directs us to the heart of the matter when he indicates the true source of boldness. He says, 'Therefore, since we have such a hope, we are very bold' (2 Cor. 3:12). Boldness comes from hope. And that hope arises from the glorious revelation of God's saving grace in the work of Jesus Christ. It is a hope manifested in history by the coming of the new covenant. It is a hope that reaches its fullness through the Holy Spirit and his ministry of glory (3:4-11, 18). By reason of this hope, ministers of the new covenant 'do not lose heart' (4:1), but know that 'our light and momentary troubles are achieving for us an eternal glory that far outweighs them all' (v. 17).

> We are hard pressed on every side, but not crushed; perplexed, but not in despair; persecuted, but not abandoned; struck down, but not destroyed. We always carry around in our body the death of Jesus, so that the life of Jesus may also be revealed in our body. For we who are alive are always being given over to death for Jesus' sake, so that his life may be revealed in our mortal body. So then, death is at work in us, but life is at work in you (4:8-12).

With such a confident perspective on the things which threaten the preacher of the gospel, one can be fearless and therefore *bold.*

We have already stated that the gospel – by the very nature of the message – demands the sincere openness of bold proclamation. There is something totally incongruous about gospel preaching that is not bold. It is a contradiction in terms. Your personality and your natural abilities are part of the 'vessel of clay' in which the glorious gospel treasure is deposited. But it is the presence of the message itself – as you embrace it by faith and proclaim it with love – that transfigures your weak and common vessel with its glory, 'to show that this all-surpassing power is from God and not from us' (4:7).

This necessity for clarity in the proclamation of the gospel is also altogether appropriate in light of the character of the message itself. Paul explains in 2 Corinthians 4:1-6:

> Therefore, since through God's mercy we have this ministry, we do not lose heart. Rather, we have renounced secret and shameful ways; we do not use deception, nor do we distort the word of God. On the contrary, by setting forth the truth plainly we commend ourselves to every man's conscience in the sight of God.... For we do not preach ourselves, but Jesus Christ as Lord, and ourselves as your servants for Jesus' sake. For God, who said, 'Let light shine out of darkness,' made his light shine in our hearts to give us the light of the knowledge of the glory of God in the face of Jesus Christ.

Again Paul ties his comments about the manner in which the gospel should be preached to the nature of the message itself: 'since we have this ministry...' The proclamation of the gospel is an extension of the revelation of the light of God's glory in the coming of Christ into the world – i.e., the incarnation, death, and resurrection of the God-Man. As the light had shone clearly heretofore in the person and work of Christ, so now it must shine clearly through the faithful proclamation of the gospel by men to men. Thus Paul (and every faithful preacher) must 'renounce secret and shameful ways' which includes, in particular, distorting the message or using deception. On the contrary, gospel preaching must 'set forth the truth plainly' (i.e., clearly, boldly). Only so will the preacher's message commend itself 'to every man's conscience in the sight of God'.

In Paul's day, as in ours, there were many temptations to be influenced by the fear of people to tone down the message of the gospel. He faced pressures, just as you do, to avoid 'stepping on people's toes' – to steer clear of their prejudices, to jettison unpopular doctrines, or to soft-peddle painful exhortations. All this amounts to sacrificing the clarity and power of the gospel message under the wicked influence of fear.

Paul could declare that he was not ashamed of the gospel of Christ (Rom. 1:16), but it was a matter of daily concern – concern expressed, as we have seen, in his prayer requests to the Ephesians and Colossians – that he be given grace and strength from God to make good on his pledge to boldly proclaim the mystery of Christ, as he should. Far from relying on his natural ability or personality, Paul knew, and we need to learn, that the only way to resist the many temptations to fear that press in on the preacher is to pray (and get our churches to pray) that we, like him, will preach boldly in the face of whatever threat.

So you can see that when it comes right down to it, boldness is a matter of speaking the truth, clearly and to the point, regardless of circumstances or consequences. The preacher who stands before his people and roundly denounces the sins of others, and yet fails to confront his hearers with their own greed, lust, hard-heartedness, and pride, is not bold, no matter how loudly he may thunder.

It is relatively easy for a preacher to let fly the salvos of Scripture against the communists, the Roman Catholics, the homosexuals, the drunks, or the secular humanists – most of whom are probably absent from his Sunday services. But how many will clearly and boldly address in relevant and challenging ways the evils of broken relationships between members of the church, poisonous envy among church leaders, generally tolerated compromises with worldliness among the affluent sheep who believe they have earned it, or the chronic laziness of the poor man who likes to think of himself as a victim? The pastor who withholds from his people anything that is profitable from the Word of God, because he is uncertain that his congregation will willingly receive it, is not a faithful shepherd (cf. Acts 20:20). Jesus warned pastors of the danger of being, or becoming, a hireling who flees in the face of danger, abandoning the sheep (John 10:12-13).

A quiet man who, from his pulpit week by week, and face to face with his people individually, speaks humbly from the heart of God to the hearts of his people is the one who knows the power of apostolic boldness. He is the one who is constrained to preach fearlessly by the conviction that God in his Word has a message for his people.

Don't get me wrong. There are times for vocal thunder from the pulpit (perhaps more often that we are inclined to use it nowadays), but often, as in days of old, it is in the 'still small voice' of truth clearly proclaimed that God's message resonates deeply within the conscience of people, and brings the conviction that bears fruit in transformed lives and new holiness.

> Since, then, we know what it is to fear the Lord, we try to persuade men. What we are is *plain to God*, and I hope it is also *plain to your conscience*. We are not trying to commend ourselves to you again, but are giving you an opportunity to take pride in us, so that you can answer those who take pride in what is seen rather than what is in the heart.... For Christ's love compels us, because we are convinced that one died for all, and therefore all died. And he died for all, that those who live should no longer live for themselves but for him who died for them and was raised again (2 Cor. 5:11-12, 14-15, emphasis added).

Note well the connection between the 'plainness' (the same term which is used in Colossians 4:4) of the message and the clarity of its presentation. In the next chapter we will explore further the connection between integrity and boldness – plainness before God and plainness in the consciences of men. But for now I hope you can plainly see that for the faithful, effective preacher of the gospel it is necessary that he put a very high premium on the quality of clarity and truthfulness in his preaching. The pulpit is no place for fudging or faking it. And if necessary, like Paul, he must be willing to risk being considered an enemy by his congregation for the sake of telling them the truth (Gal. 4:16). For it is the truth from God which alone will set them free (John 8:32).

Jay Adams has commented on the importance of clarity in preaching:

> Paul's one goal was to avoid anything that might obscure God's truth and to do everything that he could to present it as clearly as possible....

Clarity is the one prerequisite pertaining to form that is essential to preaching to the heart. How sad it is that preachers do not work more on this matter of clarity. How important it must be if the apostle Paul himself was concerned enough about it to ask for prayer.[4]

Adams raises another important feature of this concern for boldness/clarity which we should consider before closing this chapter. Not all lack of clarity is the result of fear. Some may be the result of fuzzy thinking, a lack of training, or insufficient care and self-discipline in the matter of making our preaching clear. I would challenge you to consider your own customary ways of expressing yourself – in casual conversation and in formal presentations. Do you (can you) identify the heart of the matter about which you are speaking? Do you bring all the divergent elements of what you are thinking or saying into a clear, organized pattern around that central idea or purpose? Are you easily sidetracked in conversation? Do you often move in a 'stream-of-consciousness' fashion from one idea to another in your thinking or speaking?

It is no insult to those who do not to admit that others have special gifts in this area. They can lock on to a concept – in casual conversation or in a prepared sermon – and bring every thought that is relevant to bear on expressing the idea. They can resist the temptation to follow every bypath that will prove (for the purposes at hand) irrelevant. They can generate a persuasive, logical, and coherent argument to bring the auditor from point A to point C by clearly expressed steps.

Even if you don't have special native abilities for clear verbal expression, these skills can be learned. University level speech and debate classes are designed to train students in these skills. Mortimer Adler's little book, *How to Speak, How to Listen,*[5] is a valuable guide to the improvement of these important communication skills. Jay Adams' *Pulpit Speech*[6] is another very helpful tool which has benefited many seminary students and preachers in becoming clearer in their presentations of the message of the Bible.

Mentioning these helps does, however, point up a more general problem we face as preachers today. Our culture does not put a high priority on clear thinking and speaking. Truth (and with it clarity and accuracy) has been displaced by sincerity. And one does not have to know what one is thinking, or what one is talking about, in order to be sincere. Unhappily, the church is not significantly different from the world on this score. A random perusal of the articles in Christian magazines, a few minutes listening to Christian television talk shows, or a glance at the most popular titles in evangelical bookstores, will confirm the fact that the church doesn't know how to think and speak very clearly either. I myself would happily trade fifteen seminars on 'The Organization of Small Groups in the Local Church' for one class for pastors devoted to 'Understanding and Developing the Skill of Theological Argument'. And I do not say that to be snobbish, but because our need for such understanding and skill today – when we face clever and deceitful enemies from inside and outside the church – is so urgent.

One serious consequence of this cultural devaluation of clarity is the fact that our educational institutions no longer require students to learn clarity of thought and speech. Logic, for example, is no longer one of the basic skills required of the educated man. College philosophy majors may still have to sit through a class, but the general run of students need not study or master logical thinking. Public speaking used to be required of college students as part of the general graduation requirements, but that is no longer the case in many universities.

For these reasons and others, you may find yourself handicapped with respect to being able to preach clearly and cogently, due to a lack of training or self-discipline. You may have some problems with theological sloppiness. You may have tried to cover up weaknesses in your argumentation by dogmatism, or by relying on the fact that you will not face a challenge from your people, because they love and respect you. You may find the structural demands of preparing a sermon outline to be sheer devilment. Whatever your problem, you are going to have to deal with it if you prize apostolic boldness, for clarity is its essential ingredient.

You may have to begin by getting some books together that will help you learn to think, speak, argue, and persuade in a clear way. You may have to find a friend or colleague in the ministry whom you prize for these very abilities, and become his disciple. Let him show you how he thinks through problems, how he reads the Bible, how he prepares sermon outlines, etc. You may not be blessed with a naturally analytical mind. Your personality may be quite disinclined to that kind of thinking and speaking. But you can, and must, make some effort in this direction if you want to be all you should be as a preacher. It is not accidental that part of God's sovereign pre-conversion preparation of the Apostle Paul was the rigorous rabbinic training he had at the feet of Gamaliel.

Now I know what you're thinking: 'What about Peter? I'll follow Peter the simple fisherman.' Let me challenge you to examine Peter's sermons as we look at them in the second part of this book, and on your own. Read over his letters and see if he is not every bit as clear, logical, and persuasive as Paul. He sat at the feet of a greater One than Gamaliel.

4

Preaching Before the Face of God

We have been looking at the nature of biblical boldness as a characteristic of the preaching in Acts. This boldness is a fearless commitment to speak the truth honestly and clearly, regardless of possible consequences.

In considering the source of such boldness, we have argued that it is not a trait of personality, or a rhetorical technique. It is bound up with the very character of the message proclaimed. There is more, however, that needs to be explained in order to show how a preacher can become bold in that biblical way. Let us think again of the apostles. What turned a band of frightened and discouraged men into preachers who turned the world upside down in a few short years?

The answer to that question lies in the intimate personal relationship these men had with the risen Christ.

'Ministers of the New Covenant'
We know from the Gospel accounts that it was the news that Christ had risen from the dead that turned the apostles' lives around and gave them their ministries. More than that, it was the exposure they had to Jesus' post-resurrection ministry of the Word, in which he opened up the Scriptures to them in the light of the new era that had broken through in his resurrection. They came to understand that indeed 'the time had fully come' (i.e., God's plan of salvation had come to fulfillment in history, cf. Gal. 4:4; Mark 1:15), and that the new day had dawned. What is more, they had been called and trained to go forth and announce these great things to the whole world!

We have already discussed their commission, and the way in which Jesus identified their future ministry with his own. Jesus promised to be with them 'until the end of the age' as they went about their task of discipling the nations (Matt. 28:20). When the promised Holy Spirit was poured out on the Day of Pentecost (Acts 1:4-5; 2:1 ff.), Jesus came upon them and upon the whole church in the power and glory of the new resurrection age.

This ministry of the 'new covenant' impressed the Apostle Paul, who, though a latecomer, was nevertheless an eyewitness of the glory revealed in the resurrection of Christ (1 Cor. 15:8). For Paul and the other apostles, boldness arises out of a keen sense of living and ministering in the presence of the Lord of glory. They are sent forth as messengers before his face. With the old veil taken away in Christ, the new covenant preacher beholds the glory of Christ (2 Cor. 3:18), and proclaims that glory to the nations with powerful boldness.

For the preacher today, then, boldness comes (in part) from knowing who you are and where you stand in the historic unfolding of God's program of redemption. It is true that there is a gulf between ourselves and the apostles with regard to the receiving of direct revelation from the Spirit. Ours is not the apostolic task of foundation laying for the church (1 Cor. 3:12 ff). We build upon the foundation that the apostles laid down. They gave the new covenant Scriptures. Our task is to proclaim and apply those apostolic Scriptures today.

Nevertheless, in another sense, we stand in the same historic position as Paul and the other New Testament preachers, because we too are 'ministers of the new covenant' (2 Cor. 3:6). As theirs was a ministry of glory, so is ours. As they were to bear witness to the reality and the significance of the resurrection, so are we. As they had full right to expect the attendant power and blessing of the Holy Spirit upon their witness, so may we. As we stand between the resurrection of Christ and his second coming, we stand with them. Our mission is the same as theirs, and our hope is the same as theirs. Should not our boldness in preaching, then, be like theirs?

Yet there is a problem at just this point. As preachers you are students of the Bible, and presumably are aware of these things already. Perhaps as you began reading the last paragraph you thought, 'Oh, I'm fully aware of my role as a minister,' and skimmed over it. If so, I hope you will go back and read it again, because even though theologically you may know the significance of these truths, nevertheless ministering as you do two thousand years after the time when these earth-upending events – the death and glorious resurrection of the Lord Jesus Christ – took place, they may have ceased to influence your life practically as they should. These inaugural events of the 'new covenant' era may not have a compelling effect upon how you live your life and conduct your ministry.

In the middle of trying to plan a Tuesday morning Bible study for the ladies' group, settle the claim on your auto insurance, make a call at the hospital in the afternoon, arbitrate a disagreement between two of the deacons, and get your boys signed up for baseball, who has time to remember that he is a 'minister of the new covenant'? Who appreciates as he should the freshness and newness this ministry has in virtue of its being filled with the power and the glory of the triumphant Christ, who changed everything when he came forth alive from that Judean tomb?

If you lose sight of these things in the week by week crush of mundane (and not so mundane) activities, how will they ever consume you when you enter the pulpit on Sunday? The answer is simple – they won't.

You, like thousands of your colleagues in the ministry, will enter the pulpit again next Sunday conscious primarily of the routineness of what is done each week. That monotony will only be broken by the occasional crisis or the occasional happy surprise. Basically things will go as planned in a predictable way. In that condition of 'business as usual', you will never preach with the boldness of the apostolic preachers.

Now you might say, 'But everything the apostolic preachers did was so heroic, so historic, so momentous.... If I were invited to preach on the Day of Pentecost, I'd rise to the occasion. If I could stand before the Areopagus, then I'd preach like Paul.' And so you would. But that is never going to happen to you. And it is fine that it will not, for in the final analysis it does not really matter.

Do you imagine that the apostles themselves were untroubled by the thousands of tedious little details of daily responsibility you have to face? Of course they weren't. When Paul mentions 'the daily pressure of my concern for all the churches' (2 Cor. 11:28), it has a familiar ring to it. He, like you, had to consider all the unromantic decisions that go into a missionary or pastoral ministry. Paul may have been more efficient than you at getting others to help see the jobs get done, but the concerns were there. Just like you he would be tempted each day to be overwhelmed by those details. In addition there were fears that you and I know nothing, or very little, about (e.g., the matters mentioned in verses 23-26).

So what really made the apostles different?

It was simply this: they had a vivid sense of ministering before the face of God, and it is just this sense which you and I too often lack in our ministry in general, and in our preaching in particular. In their preaching they were gripped by the reality of knowing that they were standing before the Lord of glory – Jesus Christ now freshly risen in power from the dead – announcing to men the majesty of his Name and the wonder of his works. They realized that history had reached its center in Jesus Christ, who had come 'to make all things new'. They understood that the ages had now come to their fullness – that a new page had turned, and that they stood on the threshold of a new era in which the exalted Lord would accomplish his redemptive harvest of the nations in accordance with the Father's word (Ps. 110:1; cf. Matt. 24:31-34). The conviction that they were called by Christ to enter into that great harvest work through their proclamation of the gospel made them preach with boldness.

Listen to the ringing words of the Apostle Paul as he glories in the ministry of this new covenant:

> But thanks be to God, who always leads us in triumphal procession in Christ and through us spreads everywhere the fragrance of the knowledge of him. For we are to God the aroma of Christ among those who are being saved and those who are perishing. To the one we are the smell of death; to the other, the fragrance of life. And who is equal to such a task? Unlike so many, we do not peddle the word of God for profit. On the contrary, in Christ we speak before God with sincerity, like men sent from God (2 Cor. 2:14-17).

Preacher, if you would daily place yourself in that scene, you too would preach with that kind of sincerity and power. That is the work God has called you to, and it is a ministry of glory!

You might want to argue that it was easier for Paul or Peter to be impressed with these realities, since they had seen the risen Lord with their own eyes. That might be true, though I doubt it. But even if it were, it only means that you will have to work harder at cultivating that same sense of living in the presence of God, and preaching before the Lord of glory. Remember, Jesus has a special blessing for you who, though you have not seen him in the flesh, yet believe (John 20:29). For a preacher like yourself, that blessing no doubt includes the realization of the full impact of the resurrection glory in your ministry of preaching as well as in your whole life.

Sincerity and Holiness in the Presence of God

The mention of 'sincerity' (*eilikrineias*) by Paul in the passage just cited from 2 Corinthians 2 brings to our attention another dimension of this matter of preaching in the presence of God. What we have been talking about so far has to do with orienting ourselves properly to our place in the unfolding history of redemption. This is vital, as I hope you now see. Only with this perspective can you minister before God as a bold herald of the new covenant.

But there is another equally important aspect to consider, and that is chiefly ethical in its significance. I am speaking of the fact that boldness before men presupposes a *sincerity of heart* which comes from an open relationship with God.

Sincerity, as Paul speaks of it here and elsewhere, refers to inward honesty of conscience before God that comes through the cleansing of the heart and purity in living. He said to the troubled church at Corinth, beset with many ethical problems:

> Get rid of the old yeast that you may be a new batch without yeast – as you really are. For Christ, our Passover lamb, has been sacrificed. Therefore let us keep the Festival, not with the old yeast, the yeast of malice and wickedness, but with bread without yeast, the bread of sincerity and truth (1 Cor. 5:7-8).

In this context Paul is talking about the purification of the congregational body through proper application of church discipline. Through such wholesome discipline the yeast of wickedness will be removed so that the body can fellowship with Christ in sincerity and truth.

In a parallel way the principle can be applied to the individual life. Individually, each of you is called upon by Christ to put away the evil yeast from your heart and life so that you may enjoy personal fellowship with God in sincerity and truth (cf. Phil. 1:10; 2 Pet. 3:1). The sincerity of an open intimacy with God distinguishes the new way of life of the people of God (individually and corporately) from their old ways (the 'old yeast').

As a minister of the gospel, Paul cherishes this sincerity before God very highly, for himself and for those who labor with him. In 2 Corinthians, where he is concerned (among other things) with attacks on his personal integrity and honesty, Paul refers to this sincerity at significant places. 'Now this is our boast: Our conscience testifies that we have conducted ourselves in the world, and especially in our relations with you, in holiness and sincerity that are from God' (1:12).

We have already noticed in our earlier consideration of this letter that this sincerity has an important role to play in bold ministry in the presence of God (2:17). Sincerity involves renouncing 'secret and shameful ways' – deception and distorting or adulterating the message preached – and instead 'setting forth the truth plainly ... commend[ing] ourselves to every man's conscience in the sight of God' (4:2). Boldness – speaking the truth clearly before men – has its roots in honesty and sincerity before God.

The Apostle John adds his testimony in speaking of the necessity of boldness before God – a confidence that arises from the conscientious practice of righteousness (1 John 2:28 f.), from genuine, active love for the brethren (3:21), and from being like Christ in this world (3:17).

Notice the consistent ethical emphasis in what John is saying – conformity to Jesus in the world involves the consistent practice of righteousness, including an active love for the brethren (as opposed to mere words of love). Without a serious concern for your personal holiness, you cannot know boldness before God, and without that boldness before God you will not speak with boldness before men.

The Epistle to the Hebrews speaks in the same vein, using the same term for 'confidence' before God (*parrēsia*) that Luke used in Acts to describe the 'boldness' towards men that was characteristic of the apostolic preaching :

> Let us then approach the throne of grace with confidence [*parrēsias*], so that we may receive mercy and find grace to help us in our time of need (4:16).

> Therefore, brothers, since we have confidence [*parrēsian*] to enter the Most Holy Place by the blood of Jesus, by a new and living way opened for us through the curtain, that is, his body, and since we have a great priest over the house of God, let us draw near to God with a sincere heart in full assurance of faith, having our hearts sprinkled to cleanse us from a guilty conscience and having our bodies washed with pure water (10:19-22).

Note well the connection here between boldness before God, and the gracious cleansing of the conscience through the blood of Christ on the one hand, and a true heart and a confident faith on the other.

There is nothing here of a proud, self-sufficient boldness before God that boasts in personal moral or spiritual merit. On the contrary, this boldness is marked by its brokenness and humble reliance upon the saving grace of God alone. But neither is there in this boldness a lack of aggressive concern with personal holiness, integrity, and righteousness before God. Reliance upon grace does not lead to moral laxness, but drives one deliberately on toward the goal of holiness, for 'without holiness no one will see the Lord' (Heb. 12:14).

Guilt-Induced Powerlessness in Preaching

It may appear that we have moved far afield from our study in Acts, but in reality we have not. I make no apology for taking the time to develop fully this connection between boldness before God and boldness toward men, for it is absolutely essential to our effective imitation of the apostolic model.

Most of us would agree that the church today is suffering from a lack of truly bold preaching. As a preacher you are responsible to do your part to recapture the precious prize. You need to know where boldness in your preaching will come from. It is urgent that you and I realize that if we are careless about our personal integrity and holiness before God, if we are lax about making use of the cleansing blood of Jesus for our guilty conscience when we fall into sin, then we will never preach with biblical boldness, no matter how hard you may seek it by other means. To pray for boldness is, in effect, to pray for holiness, and preachers may find their prayers for boldness unanswered, because they do not want to face the commitment to holiness that God demands in order to gain pulpit power.[1]

Consider the way in which a guilty conscience can rob you of boldness in making the truth clear to men. Guilt is always morally debilitating, because it inhibits the freedom to act, or even think, in categories of righteousness. Many is the time that a jury of guilt-ridden sinners have found themselves unable to pass judgment on even the clearest cases of criminal activity, because they know in their hearts that they have done similar things, or worse. How can they condemn another when they stand under the same condemnation of conscience? Lawyers have learned to make good use of guilt-manipulation. The same sort of thing happens daily in our private lives.

It is no different for the preacher who finds himself unwilling to deal seriously with sin in his life. Let us say that he has a bad temper, and regularly ventilates his anger at members of his family. He knows what the Bible says about it, but is unwilling to repent. Perhaps he has tried to excuse himself by attributing the problem to a strong personality, by shifting the blame to others, or by pitying himself in his difficult circumstances. But it is no use, his conscience will not stay quiet. Such a man is going to find it impossible to preach freely on a passage like Ephesians 4:26-27 or verses 31-32, or the many other passages in the Bible that confront him with his sin. He will attempt to ignore them altogether, or touch them lightly, and then only by surrendering to hypocrisy and its conscience-searing effects. Nor will he have much to say about the Christ-reflecting love that a husband should show his wife (Eph. 5:25 ff.) if he regularly uses his wife for a verbal punching bag.

In addition to this kind of guilt-induced selectivity, there is the further serious problem of becoming unwilling to press the claims of Christ for repentance and right thinking and right living in any area. If one is consumed by guilt over unconfessed sin, and harbors unresolved problems in the personal life, one will always let up too soon in pleading with men to repent, lest one hear the voice of conscience saying, 'You are the man!'

In his classic American novel, *The Scarlet Letter*, Nathaniel Hawthorne gives us an agonizing glimpse into the heart of the guilt-ridden Puritan preacher, Arthur Dimmesdale, in a chapter aptly titled, 'The Interior of A Heart.' The preacher has become involved in an adulterous relationship with a member of his community, Hester Prynne. While her sin is exposed through the revelation of her pregnancy, for which she is ostracized and required to wear the scarlet letter 'A' upon her breast for the remainder of her life, his sin remains hidden and gnaws at his conscience while he continues his ministry. Hawthorne describes him:

> He longed to speak out, from his own pulpit, at the full height of his voice, and tell the people what he was. 'I, whom you behold in these black garments of the priesthood, – I, who ascend the sacred desk, and turn my pale face heavenward, taking upon myself to hold communion, in your behalf, with the Most High Omniscience, – I, in whose daily life you discern the sanctity of Enoch, – I, whose footsteps, as you suppose, leave a gleam along my earthly track, whereby the pilgrims that shall come after me may be guided to the regions of the blest, – I, who have laid the hand of baptism upon your children, – I, who have breathed the

parting prayer over your dying friends, to whom the Amen sounded faintly from a world which they had quitted, – I, your pastor, whom you so reverence and trust, am utterly a pollution and a lie!'

This desperate preacher even tried to confess his sin indirectly, but to no avail. His people only admired his supposed piety the more, adding to his guilty misery. The author continues:

The minister well knew – subtle, but remorseful hypocrite that he was! – the light in which his vague confession would be viewed. He had striven to put a cheat upon himself by making the avowal of a guilty conscience, but had gained only one other sin, and a self-acknowledged shame, without the momentary relief of being self-deceived. He had spoken the very truth, and transformed it into the veriest falsehood. And yet, by the constitution of his nature, he loved the truth, and loathed the lie, as few men ever did. Therefore, above all things else, he loathed his miserable self![2]

Such is the agony of the heart – especially the minister's heart – caught in the grip of guilt while trying to maintain his ministry! Can there be real power and boldness for such a preacher? Hawthorne vividly portrayed the Puritan vision of sin and guilt, but had lost sight by this time of the Puritan vision of sovereign, saving grace through the cleansing blood of Jesus Christ. For that reason his ministers must wear their 'black veils' over their faces. But you and I can come with unveiled face, and behold as in a mirror the glory of the Lord. We can be transformed into his image from glory to glory, through the powerful inward work of cleansing and renewal wrought within the heart by the Holy Spirit (2 Cor. 3:18).

Bold preaching is pointed, deeply challenging, and specific. As such it requires a preacher that is himself acquainted every day with the specific convictions of the Word of God as the Spirit uses it to bring him around to repentance in his own life. As we confess our sins daily, and experience the faithfulness and justice of God in forgiving our sins for Jesus' sake, and cleansing us from all unrighteousness (1 John 1:9), we will thereby be equipped to preach that grace to our people with clarity and power.

Facing Opposition Fearlessly

It is important to remember that bold preaching will surely bring opposition from some. You must be prepared for opposition, even persecution. It is part of the cost that must be counted as you seek to become a better preacher. But you are not to be afraid, for the Lord himself declares:

> Hear me, you who know what is right, you people who have my law in your hearts: Do not fear the reproach of men or be terrified by their insults. For the moth will eat them up like a garment; the worm will devour them like wool. But my righteousness will last forever, my salvation through all generations (Isa. 51:7-8).

> Brother will betray brother to death, and a father his child; children will rebel against their parents and have them put to death. All men will hate you because of me, but he who stands firm to the end will be saved. When you are persecuted in one place, flee to another.... So do not be afraid of them. There is nothing concealed that will not be disclosed, or hidden that will not be made known. What I tell you in the dark, speak in the daylight; what is whispered in your ear, proclaim from the roofs. Do not be afraid of those who kill the body but cannot kill the soul. Rather, be afraid of the One who can destroy both soul and body in hell (Matt. 10:21-28).

Thus we can say with the Psalmist (boldly echoed by the writer of Hebrews): 'The LORD is with me; I will not be afraid. What can man do to me?' (Ps. 118:6; cf. Heb. 13:6).

Opposition to bold preaching may take the form of personal criticism or attacks against your ministry. 'You've stopped preaching and started meddling,' the old saying goes. You must be prepared to face the criticisms which bold, confrontational preaching will elicit from the unrepentant – including those in your own congregation. Imagine, if you were the angry man I mentioned above, how vulnerable you would be to attack by someone who took offense at your preaching (on any subject), and how powerless you would be to respond to such attacks. You could well be silenced, and your ministry rendered impotent, because you did not maintain a clear conscience before God.

How absolutely essential it is, therefore, that when you come under this kind of attack you have the ethical and spiritual confidence that comes from a conscience cleansed by the blood of Christ from acts that lead to death, so that you may serve the living God with boldness (Heb. 9:14).

Paul's experience with the members of the Corinthian church included that kind of hostility and accusation on the part of some. He was attacked personally and his ministry was also maligned. Much of his second letter to the Corinthians is devoted to a defense of his ministry and message, and it is in that book especially (as we have seen) that he speaks of the importance of this matter of 'sincerity' before God. The basis for his bold defense was the assurance of a clear conscience before God. 'We are not like Moses, who would put a veil over his face' (2 Cor. 3:13). Nearness to God, ministering openly before the face of Christ, made Paul bold, even in the presence of the stiff opposition of his detractors.

> Therefore, since through God's mercy we have this ministry, we do not lose heart. Rather, we have renounced secret and shameful ways; we do not use deception, nor do we distort the word of God. On the contrary, by setting forth the truth plainly we commend ourselves to every man's conscience in the sight of God. And even if our gospel is veiled, it is veiled to those who are perishing. The god of this age has blinded the minds of unbelievers, so that they cannot see the light of the gospel of the glory of Christ, who is the image of God. For we do not preach ourselves, but Jesus Christ as Lord, and ourselves as your servants for Jesus' sake. For God, who said, 'Let light shine out of darkness,' made his light shine in our hearts to give us the light of the knowledge of the glory of God in the face of Christ. But we have this treasure in jars of clay to show that this all-surpassing power is from God and not from us (2 Cor. 4:1-7).

Our desire in seeking to preach boldly should be that 'by setting forth the truth plainly we commend ourselves to every man's conscience in the sight of God'. The second-generation pastor Timothy was exhorted to minister in 'love, which comes from a pure heart and a good conscience and a sincere faith' (1 Tim. 1:5). You and I are called to the same goal. Any preacher today who would know apostolic boldness in his preaching ministry will do well to remember Paul's instruction, which is also confirmed by Peter who commands, 'keep a clear conscience, so that those who speak maliciously against your good behavior in Christ may be ashamed of their slander' (1 Pet. 3:16).

Fearing Men or Fearing God? – a Biblical Example

Let me close this chapter about boldness with a brief example from the Old Testament of the relationship between the fear of men and the fear of God.[3] Genesis 27 describes for us the way in which the scheming Jacob deceitfully secured the birthright of Esau. As a result he fled the land and sojourned for a while with Laban. When it was time for Jacob to return, he was understandably fearful of Esau's wrath (Gen. 32:11). He made arrangements to appease his brother by sending gifts, women, and children before him in the caravan (vv. 13-21), but he was still fearful and uncertain about how Esau would receive him. Jacob had a serious problem with the fear of man.

That night, by the river Jabbok, Jacob was confronted by the 'angel of the Lord' in a life and death struggle. Jacob was willing to presume upon the promise of God, and to seek divine assistance on that basis, but he failed to understand that a relationship with God involved humility and repentance, and a commitment to love God deeply and continue faithful to him. Apart from these things, God is a fearful and dangerous adversary. As Jacob struggled with the angel that night, and prevailed (vv. 22-32), he came to realize that it was not Esau he must fear, but God. Having been thus humbled, and brought to a place of both brokenness and bold confidence before God, Jacob was now ready to face his brother Esau without fear (33:1-4).

Though it is not likely that you will face a confrontation with God as outwardly dramatic as Jacob's, you must be committed to wrestle with God daily in maintaining an open, confident freedom before him – a confidence rooted in the power of the cleansing blood of Jesus, and issuing in a serious pursuit of holiness. Then you will know the boldness of the apostles in the face of even the most hostile of men. It is not your personality that will give you boldness, it is your nearness to God.

5

Preaching in the Fullness of the Spirit

The connection between boldness before God and boldness before people leads us to consider the relationship between the apostolic preaching in the Book of Acts and the post-resurrection ministry of the Holy Spirit. We have already observed that, according to the Lord's command, the apostolic mission must await the 'baptism' (i.e., the outpouring) of the Holy Spirit to be accomplished on the day of Pentecost (Luke 24:49; Acts 1:4-5). When the Spirit is given at Pentecost, Peter interprets the miraculous outpouring in light of the prophecy of Joel 2:28-32 (cf. Acts 2:16-21), explaining that the Spirit has now been given as an indication of the glorious exaltation of the Messiah, Jesus Christ, who had so recently been crucified in weakness and shame (Acts 2:33-36). Peter's explanatory message was the first instance of the fulfillment of Jesus' commission to the apostolic preachers that 'repentance and forgiveness of sins ... be preached to all nations' (Luke 24:47). Peter accordingly responds to the desperate inquiry of his hearers by calling them to 'repent and be baptized ... in the name of the Lord Jesus Christ for the forgiveness of your sins' (Acts 2:38).

Because the Spirit had now been given, the apostolic message could be proclaimed, and its immediate effect was the saving of some three thousand souls that day (2:41). The intimate connection between the Holy Spirit as the personal representative of the risen Christ and the boldness and effectiveness of the apostolic preaching is clear. The witness of the apostles is what it is because of the witness of the Holy Spirit.

> When the Counselor comes, whom I will send to you from the Father, the Spirit of truth, who goes out from the Father, he will testify about me. And you also must testify for you have been with me from the beginning (John 15:26-27).

> And it is the Spirit who testifies, because the Spirit is the truth. For there are three that testify: the Spirit, the water and the blood; and the three are in agreement (1 John 5:6b-7).

The testimony to be borne to the truth by the Spirit and by the apostles is the same witness, and for that reason it is convincing (cf. John 16:7-11). The preaching in Acts shows the characteristic boldness of such conviction. There is no 'It seems to me,' or 'Let me suggest to you', in the preaching of the apostles. It is preaching with certainty and conviction, because it is preaching the truth, and it is preaching in the Spirit. The words with which Luke describes the preaching of Stephen make this point clear: 'they could not stand up against his wisdom or the Spirit by whom he spoke' (Acts 6:10; cf. Luke 21:14-15).

Luke uses the phrase 'filled with the Spirit' frequently in Acts to describe the manner of the Spirit's involvement in the ministry of the apostles (and others). The effect of the coming of the Spirit at Pentecost was to 'fill' those in the upper room, and they began to speak, 'declaring the mighty acts of God' in various foreign languages (Acts 2:4, 8-11). Peter preached as the spokesman for the apostles as 'filled with the Holy Spirit' (that is expressly stated in 4:8 of his sermon before the Sanhedrin, and is no doubt implicit in 2:14 as he addressed the crowd in Jerusalem at the feast).

Being 'full of the Holy Spirit' was characteristic of the leaders and preachers in those early days. Stephen (6:5; 7:55), Barnabas (11:24), and Paul (9:17; 13:9) are all described in this way. When it was determined to augment the leadership of the church for diaconal ministries, the characteristic 'filling' was sought in the candidates (6:3). All this language looks back to Luke's description of the signal involvement of the Holy Spirit in the witness borne to Jesus Christ in his advent (cf. Luke 1:15, 41, 67), and his characterization of the inauguration of Jesus' own ministry (4:1).

Unfortunately, the significance of this 'filling' by the Holy Spirit has been missed to a large degree as a result of the attempts to connect this filling with some sort of personal 'second blessing' upon individual believers derived from the 'baptism of the Holy Spirit' as understood according to a 'pentecostal' or 'charismatic' paradigm. Without entering the debate on those questions,[1] let me emphasize the importance of this 'filling' for Luke, and therefore for us. For the apostolic preachers, who were called by Jesus Christ to be messengers before his face, and bear a unique witness to his redemptive glory before the nations, this filling of the Holy Spirit represents the fulfillment of Jesus' promise that he would be with them always, even to the very end of history. When he had told them in the upper room that he must go away, he promised to come back to them personally: 'I will not leave you as orphans, I will come to you' (John 14:18). In the context that promise comes right on the heels of the promise to send the Holy Spirit in his place (v. 16). Luke is highlighting both the *existential* (personal, experiential) 'filling' and the *redemptive-historical* significance of the role of the One with whom the apostles (and others) are filled – the Holy Spirit as the Spirit of Christ (cf. 1 Cor. 15:45).

Now as to the existential significance of the 'filling' Adams has written:

> What does it mean to be filled with the Spirit? In that phrase, the idea of domination is uppermost. When the Bible speaks of being filled with amazement, with fear, with jealousy, or with joy, similarly, the idea of domination is in view. A person who is filled with fear is dominated by fear; everything he does or says in that condition is colored by fear.... The same is true of one who is 'filled' with jealousy, joy, or amazement.[2]

In Ephesians 5:18, Paul contrasts living under the control of wine with living under the control of the Holy Spirit. The former is to be 'filled' with wine, the latter, to be 'filled with the Holy Spirit'. Adams continues:

> ... when a person is filled with the Spirit, every aspect of his life is under the Spirit's influence; there are no areas that are untouched by Him. That does not mean the person filled with the Holy Spirit is perfect, but it does mean that the Spirit is at work in the totality of his life.[3]

The way Luke speaks of the filling of the Holy Spirit in those early chapters of Acts suggests that the filling was not a one-time occurrence in the life of an individual. Rather the picture is of repeated 'fillings', or better, of an ongoing filling as with an overwhelming flood, as the witness of the apostles is carried on the crest of the fullness of the Spirit's presence in the coming of the new covenant age. As the 'last days' of redemptive fulfillment and gospel prosperity have broken in to the present order of things in the coming of Christ, that event is witnessed to by the powerful fullness of the presence of the Spirit in the human witnesses, the preachers.

Another very important feature of this filling of the Holy Spirit must be examined. The Holy Spirit came upon the apostolic preachers and the early saints *when they prayed*. The disciples had been told to wait in Jerusalem for the coming of the promised Spirit (Luke 24:49). The 'waiting' of the apostles was not, however, idly killing time. Rather it was the *expectant* waiting of constant and united *prayer* – 'they went upstairs to the room where they were staying.... They all joined together constantly in prayer' (Acts 1:13-14). It was as they remained there, giving themselves to prayer, that the Spirit was soon given (2:1ff.), and as a result of Peter's first sermon, the many who were converted immediately 'devoted themselves ... to prayer' (2:42).

Prayer is that which unites the historical and existential aspects of the 'filling of the Spirit' in the lives and ministries of God's people, and especially the preachers. Calvin has called prayer 'the chief exercise of faith',[4] and so it is. The apostolic faith is expressed in their witness to the great events of Calvary and the resurrection and exaltation of Christ. This faith involves, as we have seen, the historical understanding that now the 'fullness of times have come' (Gal. 4:1 ff.), that the old has 'passed away', and that the 'new has come' (2 Cor. 5:17). The hallmark of the newness of the new covenant age is the presence of the Holy Spirit in his fullness (cf. 3:6, 11, 17). Preaching and calling people to peace with God through the death and resurrection of the Lord Jesus Christ is the apostolic activity of this new age. Paul calls it 'the ministry of reconciliation' (5:18 ff.). With this conviction of faith, the apostles carry out their ministry with boldness – 'since we have such a hope, we are very bold' (3:12).

It is prayer, as the chief expression of this historical faith, that brings the apostolic preachers into experiential contact with the powerful fullness of the Holy Spirit in their preaching and other ministries. Though the new era is one of the presence of the Spirit, he does not work *ex opere operato* (i.e., mechanically, automatically) in the human witnesses. He comes to them in response to their prayers, and fills them with confident boldness, and makes their preaching effective.

This can be seen in the incidents recorded by Luke in Acts 4:23-31. Let us read that dramatic account in full.

> On their release, Peter and John went back to their own people and reported all that the chief priests and elders had said to them. When they heard this, they raised their voices together in prayer to God. 'Sovereign Lord,' they said, 'you made the heaven and the earth and the sea, and everything in them. You spoke by the Holy Spirit through the mouth of

your servant, our father David: 'Why do the nations rage and the peoples plot in vain? The kings of the earth take their stand and the rulers gather together against the Lord and against his Anointed One.' Indeed Herod and Pontius Pilate met together with the Gentiles and the people of Israel in this city to conspire against your holy servant Jesus, whom you anointed. They did what your power and will had decided beforehand should happen. Now, Lord, consider their threats and enable your servants to speak your word with great boldness. Stretch out your hand to heal and perform miraculous signs and wonders through the name of your holy servant Jesus.' After they prayed, the place where they were meeting was shaken. And they were all filled with the Holy Spirit and spoke the word of God boldly.

How powerfully Luke brings together the elements we have been discussing. The disciples respond to the report by Peter and John with united, corporate, audible prayer ('they raised their voices together in prayer'). In this prayer their faith comes to clear expression. They recognize the historic significance of the events that took place in Jerusalem under Pilate, and they interpret those events in light of the messianic Psalm 2, which speaks of the triumphant exaltation of the Lord's Anointed, and the inauguration of his reign over the nations. They know precisely where they stand and what is going on in the official hostility of the authorities to their preaching. This confidence in the triumph of the resurrected Christ leads them to ask the Sovereign Lord for boldness in the face of the threats of the enemies. And God answers by 'filling' them with the Spirit, who is present as the Spirit of Christ, and as a result they 'proclaim the word of God boldly'.

Boldness in the preaching of the Word, therefore, is an index of the Spirit's presence in the ministry of the preacher. This may seem a lot of ink spilt on the obvious, but let me ask you, 'Are you satisfied with your life of prayer – in its own right, and as a support of your preaching ministry?' I think we might be astounded at how many preachers struggle with prayerlessness as a chronic spiritual problem. They do alright at 'official' prayer – prayer meetings, leading the congregation in prayer, saying blessings over meals, etc. But beyond that they are strangers much of the time to the practice of prayer. It is so much easier to study than to pray. It is often more attractive to be a 'people person' than a man of prayer. In a pastor's demanding and busy schedule, how often is it the ministry of vital prayer that suffers? Though there are many 'how-to-pray' books that have been written and read, I often wonder if the amount of good praying in the church has increased, for the truth is, it is easier to read about how to pray than it is to pray.

In the face of the increasing pressures arising from the ministry demands of the growing church in Jerusalem, the apostles are zealous to protect the time needed to 'devote themselves to prayer and to the ministry of the Word' (Acts 6:4). Note well the order of their concerns: they wanted ample time for prayer, and also for study, sermon preparation, etc. Judging by your practice of prayer, would you say it is equally obvious that you understand that boldness comes only from the fullness of the Spirit whose presence is sought in prayer? I confess that this is a lesson which I could never learn too well, and I would be a fool to take these truths for granted.

Some of you reading this chapter may be men of constant faithfulness in prayer. You may also be bold and powerful preachers. Praise the Lord! Keep it up. But some of you might be forced to admit that, while you are mighty in the closet, you are still all too fearful and weak in the pulpit. You still have difficulty preaching the Word with challenging clarity. For all your praying you are still afraid of men. For you, reading a chapter like this may be a discouragement. You may say, 'I have prayed, but the boldness does not come. It is not working for me.'

I would like you to go back over this chapter again. There may be a problem with your praying. You see, I have tried to stress that prayer is not just a commodity that you need 'enough of' in order to become a bold preacher. Please remember that, above everything else, prayer is communion with the living God in the full awareness of who he is and who you are. Prayer of this sort presupposes the humble repentance and faith, the concern for personal holiness, about which we spoke in the previous chapter. In prayer we do not do something for God, we make contact with him in personal fellowship, and in that setting we are cleansed and renewed experientially as the Spirit of Christ fills our hearts and lives. Many good Protestants have fallen into the habit of making prayer a sort of 'rosary', a litany of requests that have very little to do with actually drawing near to God. That kind of praying will not bring the Spirit's fullness or the boldness that results.

The apostles prayed as they drew themselves together into the presence of God. They sought the fullness of the Spirit, because they longed for the promised presence of Christ with them. The boldness came as a result.

In closing let me touch briefly on one other reason that boldness may not presently come as a result of your praying. It may be that you, unlike the apostles, do not understand as you should the connection I have been stressing between your existential experience of the fullness of the Spirit, and your place in the history of God's redemptive activities. Prayer is an act of faith, and thus *what* you believe specifically about the working of God in your ministry is very important to the effectiveness of your prayer. Vague and fuzzy convictions will lead you to miss the mark in your praying. You may, for example, have a problem with your eschatology (the doctrine of 'last things,' including your understanding of the character of the present interadvent period of history) that makes it difficult (or impossible) for you to appreciate the glorious nature of the present ministry of the risen Christ through his Spirit. You may be confidently looking forward to the time of Christ's power, while at the same time being quite sure that your present ministry will not (or cannot) partake of that power.

It is impossible for you to pray as the apostles did if you do not share their conviction concerning the significance of the death and resurrection of Christ, not only for your personal life, but for the present period in the history of God's unfolding plan for mankind.

Boldness will come to you when you commune with God in the confident assurance that God, in Christ, has taken his almighty power and begun to reign (Rev. 11:15, 17). In the face of that conviction, what can the enemies of your preaching do? Of such fearless certainty, in the apostles and in you, is bold preaching born.

6

What Does Bold Preaching Sound Like?

Having considered at length the boldness that was characteristic of the preaching of the apostles in the Book of Acts, let us now take a look at how this boldness showed itself in the sermons. I would like to stress two things in this connection. The boldness of the apostolic preaching can be seen first in its *directness*, and second in its being challenging or *confrontational*. These two features are closely related, and both leap off the page as you read the sermons in Acts.

The Sermons Speak Directly to You

The characteristic directness of the apostolic preaching is seen in the fact that it is so often couched in the *second person*. The apostolic sermons address the hearers directly. And because they are recorded by Luke in direct address they also confront the readers as 'YOU'. Evangelist C. John Miller made the following observations about his study of these sermons:

> I discovered that ... the apostolic heralds in Acts preached to me in the second person. Sometimes they used 'we' as one sinner speaking to another, but at the point of confrontation they took aim at particular men and said 'you.' This startled me. My preaching had often been earnest, but it had been third person or first person exclusively – never a direct exhortation to come to Christ. But once I made the matter one of special prayer, almost immediately two people responded to the exhortation and showed evidence of new life. I had the same experience meeting people on a one-to-one basis. I began to ask, 'Do you know personally about the love of God? Do you love Jesus because he died at Calvary for the sins of men?'[1]

Two things are significant about Miller's experience. It was rooted in coming to an awareness of the apostolic practice, and when he adopted the practice, it began to show immediate effects. Is Miller's observation about the apostolic practice correct? Let's look briefly at a few of the sermons.

Peter addresses the crowd at Pentecost directly: 'Fellow Jews and all of you who live in Jerusalem, let me explain this to you; listen carefully to what I say' (Acts 2:14). After citing Joel (with its own second person form), Peter goes on to say, 'Men of Israel, listen to this: Jesus of Nazareth was a man accredited by God to you by miracles, wonders and signs, which God did among you through him, as you yourselves know' (v. 22).

Later the indictment regarding the murder of Jesus Christ is addressed to the crowd in the second person 'you': 'You, with the help of wicked men, put him to death by nailing him to the cross' (v. 23). Throughout the sermon the second person is used consistently (cf. vv. 29, 33, 36). When at last the invitation is given in verse 38, it too is addressed directly to the hearers: 'Repent and be baptized every one of you ... for the forgiveness of your sins.'

Stephen adopts the same posture, speaking directly to the Sanhedrin. Though most of his sermon is a rehearsal of crucial events in the history of Israel, when it comes time to draw his conclusions, he forthrightly uses the second person: 'You stiff-necked people, with uncircumcised hearts and ears! You are just like your fathers: You always resist the Holy Spirit' (7:51).

The examples of the preaching of Paul and Barnabas show the same characteristic use of the second person. At Lystra, when they addressed the crowd that wanted to sacrifice to them as gods, they said, 'Men, why are you doing this? We too are only men, human like you. We are bringing you good news...' (14:14 ff.).

Because of the form in which these sermons were delivered and recorded, they (and the others in Acts) demand that *you* the reader respond as one directly and personally confronted by the apostolic preacher. There is no third person indirection here. Though the 'we' or 'they' is sometimes used (as Miller pointed out), these men customarily speak from God *directly to you*.

Is that the way you preach? No doubt when you give an invitation to people to come to Christ in faith, you speak in the second person. But what about the rest of the time? Are your messages sprinkled liberally with 'we' or the tactfully indirect 'they?' Do you ever directly accuse, or directly encourage your congregation? Bold preaching is direct, and often the clearest indication that preaching lacks biblical boldness is the fact that it comes in language designed to maintain a distance – language that is comfortably abstract.

There are a number of reasons why preachers fail to use the second person consistently. First of all, there is a genuine feeling of awkwardness about speaking to others with such directness. For all its talk about honesty, our culture has refined the art of indirection and euphemism in an attempt not to have to say directly what we really mean. Even in personal conversation there is something disconcerting about someone who looks you right in the eye, and tells you candidly what he thinks about something, and all the more so since it is so rare.

This feeling of strangeness is heightened in the pulpit. You may be willing to speak a word of approval or encouragement to the congregation in the second person. But it is far less comfortable to take the 'you' upon your lips when it comes to correcting them for false doctrine, or rebuking the people for moral error. In these latter cases it is much easier to slip into saying, 'some men believe,' or 'the problem with the Corinthian church,' or 'Ahab's sin.' You hope from that indirect way of speaking to get the point across without the congregation feeling you are getting after them. You hope that the more spiritually sensitive people (those guilty of the particular sin you have in mind) will take the generic indictment and make the necessary applications. You may even try to assure this by concluding your message with a phrase like, 'May the Lord apply these words to your hearts today.'

That kind of preaching may be more comfortable for all concerned, but it doesn't sound much like Peter or Paul.

Many of us were trained for several years in seminary before embarking on our preaching careers. In such an academic environment dispassionate analytical expression is prized as a virtue and may well have its place in such a setting. The lectures you listened to, and the papers you wrote, may well have served to teach you some bad habits of expression that have been carried over into your pulpit ministry. Those habits simply amplify the ease with which you can slip into abstract and impersonal expressions when you experience the awkwardness of personally facing your people from the pulpit. When things get tense, you put a little verbal distance between yourself and the congregation. The real problem, however, is that in doing so you also put distance between them and God.

Your ability to freely express yourself with the directness of the second person, as the apostles did, depends upon your awareness of your role in relation to God and the congregation. You are God's herald, proclaiming his name to the congregation for their salvation and edification. You speak for him to them. As such you must address the people as he would, personally and directly.

Many preachers are tempted to identify themselves with the congregation in preaching, rather than with God. This may be the most significant reason for their feeling ill at ease in speaking to their congregation in the second person. Such preachers do not want their people to get the impression that the preacher is holier than them — for preachers know they are not. Conscious as they are of their sin, it is natural for them to identify themselves with their people as being in need of the grace of God, ready and willing to hear what God has to say from his Word. The genuine piety behind such an attitude is indeed commendable. Nevertheless, this point of view can come to expression in the wrong way, and create problems for the preacher.

If a man, even for the most noble of motives, identifies himself primarily with the congregation in preaching, rather than with God, the best he will be able to do is speak as one sinner to other sinners about God. He will not be able to speak from God to them. He will not function as God's mouthpiece, bringing God's life-giving message to the people – correcting, rebuking, and encouraging them in God's Name (i.e., on his behalf).

Don't get the wrong impression from what I am saying. I am not suggesting that the preacher speaks for God because he deserves to. It is not by the merit of his personal piety or godliness that he stands at the pulpit. Rather it is because he has been called of God to do so. It is his commission that entitles him to speak for God, not his personal worthiness. But that commission is not a call to stand before the congregation as a priest, representing them before God. It is rather to stand before the congregation on God's behalf – a herald commissioned to deliver God's message to the people.

Is this not how it has always been? With the exception of Jesus Christ, all of God's prophets have been sinners, and many of them truly remarkable sinners. Yet they have been called to speak for God. Moses – despite his failures and weaknesses, despite his repeated excuses when faced with the task – was appointed God's spokesman to Pharaoh. But Moses said, 'O Lord, please send someone else to do it.'

> Then the LORD's anger burned against Moses and he said, 'What about your brother, Aaron the Levite? I know he can speak well. He is already on his way to meet you, and his heart will be glad when he sees you. You shall speak to him and put words in his mouth; I will help both of you speak and will teach you what to do. He will speak to the people for you,

and it will be as if he were your mouth and as if you were God to him. But take this staff in your hand so you can perform miraculous signs with it' (Exod. 4:13-17).

The prophetic formula, 'Thus says the Lord,' was not something the prophets were entitled to speak because they earned it, but because God spoke through them.

Consider these bold apostolic preachers who speak so eloquently and directly to the people, who make the pointed second-person accusations and give the comforting personal invitations to come to Christ. Do you imagine that Peter was ever for a moment unconscious of his failure in denying the Lord three times? Not at all: he remembered his failure vividly. And what was the testimony of Paul?

I was once a blasphemer and a persecutor and a violent man, ... Here is a trustworthy saying that deserves full acceptance: Christ Jesus came into the world to save sinners – of whom I am the worst. But for that very reason I was shown mercy so that in me, the worst of sinners, Christ Jesus might display his unlimited patience as an example for those who would believe on him and receive eternal life (1 Tim. 1:13-16).

As you can see, Paul had no illusions about his worthiness. He carried the daily reminder in his heart of hearts of personal wickedness and rebellion. But it is for that very reason – that the grace of Christ, which is the central message of the gospel to sinners, might be exemplified in its working – that God chose one such as Paul to be his herald of that grace. And it is for that same reason that God chose you and me to be his preachers – to show forth the wonder of his grace through such unworthy instruments.

These men did not speak for God because they knew they were spiritually above the congregation. They did not express themselves as they did because they no longer had need of grace. It was not their arrogance and self-sufficiency that spoke, but rather their deep humility and reliance upon the grace of God at work in and through them. Paul reminds us that God has chosen weak and unworthy vessels in which to carry the treasure of the gospel: 'But we have this treasure in jars of clay to show that this all-surpassing power is from God and not from us' (2 Cor. 4:7).

No preacher dare forget this for a moment. The apostles knew they were sinners, but they also knew that they had been called by God to speak to men on his behalf. That is what made them preach the way they did, and use the forms of address they chose. For this reason they did not, by and large, speak out of a sense of identity with the hearers, rather they spoke as 'oracles' sent from God.

In discussing this matter with another pastor, he expressed a genuine fear that if he preached directly to his people, in the second person, they would get the impression that he did consider himself spiritually or morally superior to them. Is there a way around this problem? I suggest a couple of ways.

The first is to make very sure that part of your preparation of every sermon includes preaching the message to yourself. I do not mean preaching it in order to hear how it sounds, or to time its length. I mean that you need to make yourself hear every sermon as a sinner in need of what that message has to say. This may seem obvious, but it is critically important. You not only must prepare the sermon, you must *let the sermon prepare you.* By faith you must appropriate everything you are going to say to your congregation, since the message is from God. In this way the message will be taken up by you, and you will become the instrument of the message – of the Lord whose message you speak.

If you are thus prepared by the message, your congregation will know it. Even if you speak directly to them, as standing with God (as you should), they will know that you too have been touched and changed by the message you bring. There will be no sense in which they imagine you climbing a spiritual ladder to exalt yourself above them. They will know that the man who, at that moment in the pulpit, speaks for God is the same man who has been himself confronted by the Lord, and has come away broken, humbled, and changed. Your whole life will become an example to the flock of how sinners are to receive and respond to the Word of God.

That leads to the other matter I want to mention in this connection. Remember that for most of you who are reading this – being pastors with a fixed charge in a local congregation – your preaching ministry does not exist in a vacuum. Your preaching task functions in the context of your whole life before the people of God. The man they see and hear in the pulpit is the same man that they know in many other ways. They know you in your family. They know what you say to them, and how you say it, in personal conversation. They have received your ministry when they were ill or otherwise troubled. In short, they know you as a whole man with a complete ministry. If you live a life of humble piety and willing service in all your ways, as God would have you do, your people will know that the man speaking to them so personally and directly from the pulpit on Sunday is their pastor, and what they know of your whole life in relationship to God will affect their response to your pulpit ministry. You will be able to say with Paul,

> You know how I lived the whole time I was with you, from the first day I came into the province of Asia. I served the Lord with great humility and with tears, although I was severely tested by the plots of the Jews. You know that I have not hesitated to preach anything that would be helpful to you but have taught you publicly and from house to house (Acts 20:18-20).

Or,

> ... we were gentle among you, like a mother caring for her little children. We loved you so much that we were delighted to share with you not only the gospel of God but our lives as well, because you had become so dear to us.... For you know that we dealt with each of you as a father deals with his own children, encouraging, comforting and urging you to live lives worthy of God, who calls you into his kingdom and glory (1 Thess. 2:7-8, 11-12).

Don't be afraid to speak to your people directly from God, as the apostles did. That is a manifestation of what bold preaching should be: directly personal and sincere. Notice that Paul, far from lording it over his people from the pulpit, wept with them, for though he spoke from God, he was one of them – a sinner, saved by grace. If you begin to preach this way, your congregations will notice the difference, and while sometimes they may feel the pinch (sometimes they should), on the whole they will rejoice in the change. Many times I have had members of my own congregation come to me at the door after the sermon and say, 'Thank you, pastor, you were really speaking to me today.' And I was – because God was.

The Sermons Challenge You

The other phenomenon we discover in the sermons in Acts that is evidence of their boldness is the fact that they are *challenging* and *confrontational*. The apostles are preaching for effect, and they receive strong reactions to their sermons – both positive and negative. One of the most distressing things about contemporary preaching is that it seems to have so little effect of any kind. People sit week after week under the preaching of the Word and are largely unchallenged, unchanged, unedified.

There is a reason for this: the modern church has become so fearful of 'turning off' anyone to the gospel that it is unwilling to sound forth clearly and with certainty the trumpet call of the gospel. It is paradoxical in a sense. Evangelicals (at least) claim to understand that the gospel to which they are committed includes the 'scandal of the cross' which is a 'stumbling block' to men (1 Cor. 1:18-25). Yet when it comes to the matter of presenting that gospel, even evangelicals are tempted to lighten up the message in the hope of winning more to Christ.[2]

The paradox comes in trying to tell men and women that they are hell-bound sinners without letting them know that God is offended by their sin. Listening to sermons today that try to get off the horns of this dilemma is at once comical and tragic. Some pastors try to 'solve' the problem by being real hard on the mutually acknowledged 'bad guys' (i.e., the notorious sinners who do not come to church) and real easy on the presumed 'good guys' (i.e., the members of the church that are listening to the sermon and supporting the pastor). In its worst form this kind of preaching degenerates into a kind of 'Home on the Range' sermon, 'where never is heard a discouraging word, and the skies are not cloudy all day.'

By contrast, the preachers in Acts do not seem at all concerned to adapt their message to the prejudices of their unbelieving audiences. This is not because they are unaware that the gospel may drive some men away, but just because they realize that possibility so acutely. As Paul says elsewhere, 'For we are to God the aroma of Christ among those who are being saved and those who are perishing. To the one we are the smell of death; to the other, the fragrance of life' (2 Cor. 2:15 f.). And again, 'And even if our gospel is veiled, it is veiled to those who are perishing. The god of this age has blinded the minds of unbelievers, so that they cannot see the light of the gospel of the glory of Christ, who is the image of God' (4:3-4). Better than many evangelicals today, the apostles realized that 'God has mercy on whom he wants to have mercy, and he hardens whom he wants to harden' (Rom. 9:18). It is a humbling realization – 'Who is equal to such a task?' (2 Cor. 2:16). Yet such an understanding of the sovereignty of God in conversion also sets them free to proclaim the gospel unafraid of the possible consequences. Paul, and the others, also know that the gospel alone is 'the power of God for the salvation of everyone who believes' (Rom. 1:16). Therefore they preach with the boldness and power we have already observed, understanding that their proclamation will have its divinely designed effects – either converting or hardening the heart of the hearers. The manner in which they confront their hearers with the enormity of their sins, and the even greater wonder of the grace of God – grace that has now been fully revealed in the atonement of Christ and his powerful resurrection from the dead – staggers even those of us who have grown accustomed to reading these sermons.

Would you begin one of your sermons by contradicting the settled opinions of your hearers? Peter does.

He begins his first sermon on the day of Pentecost by saying, 'These men are not drunk as you suppose. It's only nine in the morning!' (Acts 2:15). He goes on a little later to challenge them for attempting to escape the inevitable conclusion to be drawn from things that they themselves knew about Jesus from their own firsthand experience. Peter declares, 'Jesus of Nazareth was a man accredited by God to you by miracles, ... as you yourselves know' (v. 22). Remember also that this was a crowd that not many weeks before had consented to Jesus' death, crying for his blood, because they refused to believe the import of Jesus' miracles. Peter says they ought to have known better. He seems to be poking his stick in the lion's eye! Finally he goes over the edge, and bluntly accuses them of murdering the Lord's Christ. He says (can you believe it?), 'This man ... you ... put to death by nailing him to the cross' (v. 23, NIV). Then he delivers the *coup de grâce* (or signs his own death warrant) in verse 36: 'Therefore let all Israel be assured of this: God has made this Jesus, whom you crucified, both Lord and Christ.'

Peter brings everything he has said to focus in this personal challenge, and he boldly shapes the challenge in the most direct and confrontational terms he can find.

Can you imagine yourself as a solitary unarmed individual confronting a rowdy gang of street thugs with the murder of your brother, of which they are guilty. If you can see yourself confronting the gang and threatening to expose their crime to the authorities, then perhaps you can catch the feeling of that moment for Peter. Remember, not many weeks before he had been scared to death because a servant girl might tattle on him to the Jewish authorities! Truly, to speak to the assembly in Jerusalem at the feast of Pentecost, as he did, with this sort of direct, personal confrontation, took the sort of boldness that comes from God alone.

That is the way all of the preachers in Acts deliver the message of the gospel, because they are the heralds of God. 'Because God has said, "Never will I leave you; never will I forsake you." So we say with confidence, "The Lord is my helper; I will not be afraid. What can man do to me?"' (Heb. 13:5-6).

Soon afterwards, still in Jerusalem, Peter faces the multitude again, they having witnessed the healing of the crippled man 'in the Name of Jesus Christ of Nazareth' (Acts 3:6). In preaching to the Jews on that occasion, Peter makes the same kind of direct accusations against them. They themselves are guilty of conspiracy and murder, says Peter: 'You handed [Jesus] over to be killed, and you disowned him before Pilate, though he had decided to let him go. You disowned the Holy and Righteous One and asked that a murderer be released to you. You killed the author of life' (3:13-15).

In this situation Peter was truly 'out of the frying pan and into the fire', but he did not moderate his directness or the confrontational elements in his sermon at all. He not only accused the Jews of 'disowning' the Messiah, he actually repeated the accusation a second time, driving the point home forcefully! He was preaching to get through to men, and he did. Many were converted as a result of this sort of preaching, and the church grew to about 5,000 men (cf. 4:4).

We find the same directness in Stephen, though with a very different effect. Like Peter, Stephen brings his challenge to the Sanhedrin in pointed and personal terms:

> You stiff-necked people, with uncircumcised hearts and ears! You are just like your fathers: You always resist the Holy Spirit! Was there ever a prophet your fathers did not persecute? They even killed those who predicted the coming of the Righteous One. And now you have betrayed and murdered him – you who have received the law that was put into effect through angels but have not obeyed it (7:51-53).

There are further examples of this sort of direct challenge in the other sermons, but I think you can see the point clearly. The preaching of the apostles recorded in Acts is consistently confrontational and challenging. The apostles never approach their hearers on a take-it-or-leave-it basis. They want a response. They know the message of the gospel is designed by God to elicit a response. This is why the sermons in Acts so often include, or are followed immediately by discussion, debate, reasoned argument, etc. The apostles are busy teaching sound doctrine, persuading their audience, and refuting any and every attempt to contradict the truth and import of their messages (cf. Titus 1:9). This kind of preaching gets more than a comment like 'Nice sermon, pastor,' at the door as the people leave. Men and women are deeply affected by this preaching, and they respond – strongly, inevitably.

What about these varied responses? On the basis of what Paul says in 1 Corinthians 1:18 ff. and 2 Corinthians 2:12 ff., we can expect two general kinds of response: humble repentance and faith from some, and rebellious and hard-hearted hostility from others. We have examples of both kinds of responses to sermons in Acts.

In Acts 2:37 we have an example of the first kind of response: 'When the people heard this, they were cut to the heart and said to Peter and the other apostles, "Brothers, what shall we do?"' In the case of those assembled in Jerusalem on the day of Pentecost, Peter's hard-hitting and penetrating indictment of their sin and his pointed call to repentance moved thousands in the crowd to turn from their sins and entrust themselves to this Messiah whom, until that moment, they had not recognized.

The opposite response is recorded by Luke in reference to Stephen's sermon before the council: 'When they heard this, they were furious and gnashed their teeth at him ... they covered their ears and, yelling at the top of their voices, they all rushed at him, dragged him out of the city and began to stone him' (7:54 ff.).

The leaders of the Sanhedrin, who had themselves been guilty of delivering Jesus to the Romans for execution, were provoked by Stephen's clear accusations, but rather than turning in sorrow and true repentance, they inflicted upon Stephen what they had so recently visited upon his Lord.

One response is that of desperate seeking for salvation in light of deep conviction, the other is that of murderous rage resulting from the offense of the message. Both sermons were equally true – equally pointed and direct. What made the difference? Luke's language indicates that the difference was in the hearts of the hearers.

Clearly, the different responses to heavenly influences are due not to any difference in preaching ... but to differences in the hearts of the ones who hear it. In one case the Word is mixed with faith, while in the other it is not (cf. Heb. 4:2). So, the reason why the response to Peter's sermon was faith and the response to Stephen's was fury is that God's rain fell on two distinct types of ground.[3]

The Bible teaches that no natural person can or will receive the things spoken of God (1 Cor. 2:14; cf. Rom. 8:7). They make no sense to him, and he is disposed by nature to reject them. In his natural condition he has a heart of stone (Ezek. 36:26). He is in need of God's all-powerful converting grace if he is to respond to the gospel in repentance and faith. Theologians have classically understood this in terms of the relationship between 'regeneration' and 'effectual calling.' The former refers to the sovereign re-creative act of the Holy Spirit quickening and renewing the 'inner man', the 'heart'.[4] Jesus, in his conversation with Nicodemus, described this divine activity as the 'new birth' (John 3:3 ff.; cf. Ezek 36:26 ff.). Apart from this secret operation of the divine Spirit, a man cannot 'see' (understand, appreciate, respond favorably to) the Kingdom of God.

'Effectual calling' describes the irresistable summons of the Father in drawing the sinner to God.[5] The outward preaching of the Word (the gospel call) penetrates to the inner life of the individual through the power of God. While the outward call comes to all people equally, the call is rendered effectual only to the hearts of those who are inwardly renewed by the sovereign power of God's Spirit.

Putting this in terms of the preaching of Peter and Stephen, they both issue the outward call with equal power, boldness, and conviction to both groups. The crowd at Pentecost and the members of the Sanhedrin alike hear the gospel – the indictment, the promise of salvation in Christ, and the call to repentance and faith – but only the former respond favorably to the invitation, for they alone have received new hearts from God through regeneration. The latter, being left in their native hardness of heart, respond to the same message, preached in the same way, by giving full vent to their murderous rage in the martyrdom of Stephen.

Luke's language intimates the difference between the two groups on the level of their hearts' response to the Word of God.[6] The term Luke uses in Acts 2:37, *katanussō*, means 'to prick, puncture, or sting'. It has the sense of a sharp dart making a strong, even violent, impact upon the inner life of the hearer. For such people Peter's words 'are like goads ... like firmly embedded nails, ... given by one

Shepherd' (Eccles. 12:11). They reach the hearts of the people, and they are wounded with deep conviction. This leads them to cry out, 'What must we do?' Later, when Peter answers their question, they respond by repenting and receiving baptism at the hands of the apostles.

The word Luke chooses in Acts 7:54, rendered (somewhat vaguely) 'they were furious' in the NIV, is *diapriō*, meaning 'to saw asunder,' or 'cut through to.' This term suggests the remaining hardness of the natural, unchanged hearts of the members of the Sanhedrin. Again, Stephen gets through to his hearers, but here they are unconvicted, unconverted. Their hearts are left only 'torn', and for this reason they do not seek grace and forgiveness. They rather drag Stephen out to his death.

The preaching of the Word of God always has a powerful effect. As the Lord promised through the prophet Isaiah, 'My word that goes out from my mouth; it will not return to me empty, but will accomplish what I desire and achieve the purpose for which I send it' (Isa. 55:11).

Please note carefully, the response to the Word of God is not a matter of human calculation. It is a matter of the purpose of God. In the context of sending out his disciples to preach, Jesus said that he came to bring not peace, but a 'sword' of division to bear upon the hearts of people (Matt. 10:34-39). The message you are called to preach as a minister of the Word will never return empty to the Lord who sends it out. It is either an 'aroma of life' or the 'smell of death' to those who hear it, depending upon the condition of their hearts. Realizing these things, the apostles humbly, but confidently and clearly, preach to the heart for effect – and they always get one or the other of these responses.

Let me ask you: When was the last time people took up stones to kill you at the conclusion of your sermon? When was the last time they broke down in true humility under your preaching of the Word, and pled with God for mercy? Ever? Can you honestly say that you preach for that kind of effect? Is that part of your goal in preaching? You may even issue an 'altar call' at the end of every sermon as a matter of course. But do you sincerely expect that people will respond immediately and decisively to the proclamation of the Word? Perhaps this sort of response has been so rare in your experience that you no longer really expect such things to happen.

Some of you might object to this emphasis on preaching that seeks results, and remind us of the abuses – the many forms of empty emotional manipulation – made in the name of getting people to respond to a sermon. We acknowledge that this occurs. The use of such manipulative techniques is current in the evangelical church today. There are preachers who make a last-ditch effort to make something out of a sermon which was generally disorganized, vague, and lacking biblical content. Such a pastor may recognize (too late) that he isn't getting anywhere, so he moves into his 'two-minute offense', trying to hit pay dirt quickly. There may be a change in his tone of voice, he may appeal to emotion, he may linger over the personal appeal of the altar call for too many verses of 'Just As I Am'. All this by way of trying desperately to get people who have not been moved by the content and presentation of the message itself to respond by slipping up their hand or coming forward to the prayer room. Such manipulation is so gross and vain that we rightly recoil from it.

This is definitely not what we find in the direct, confrontational message we have heard from the apostles, and in our desire to avoid abuses, let's not close ourselves off from what God would have us do in imitation of them. Surely the Word of God encourages an emotional, as well as an intellectual and moral response to the message of the gospel, but in the case of the sermons in Acts, it is emotion that arises from *heart felt conviction*, not superficial psychological manipulation. This latter kind of emotionalism is unattended by the necessary deep changes in thinking and doing that characterize true repentance, and in the long run may serve to *harden the heart* rather than render a person more willing to hear and heed the demands of the Word of God. Some who are satisfied to shed a tear each week over a sermon may think they have done their duty, but, in fact, they never face the deeper demands of God for truthfulness and holiness in life. At the same time, others who do hear and heed the message properly, but make little or no display of emotion, may be discouraged by thinking that their experiences are somehow inauthentic.

It is precisely because you want to, and must, preach effectively for genuine repentance and faith, that you must resist every temptation to give in to this sort of manipulation. Don't trade the results brought forth by the direct, confrontational preaching (in the style of the apostles) for the 'pottage' of an emotional appeal which, when tacked on to the end of even the poorest of sermons, may promise to bring someone forward.

There is, however, a ditch on the other side of this right path as well. Those who reject such emotional manipulation may be inclined to say, 'It's the Holy Spirit's job to convict and convert the heart. (That much is true.) Therefore I must not do anything that would intrude upon this work of the Holy Spirit.' Preaching for the kind of responses we have been examining, therefore, makes them very nervous. But is their conclusion true?

Such preachers may build magnificent sermons, but they hold the gospel at a distance from the sinner. They are hesitant to challenge, to invite, to persuade, or to plead with tears, for fear of somehow compromising the sovereign work of the Holy Spirit. Some, of a particular Calvinistic stripe, may even resist actually calling hearers to repentance, claiming that we cannot command them to do what they are naturally unable to do. The natural person cannot respond to the gospel in his own strength, so there is no point in calling him to turn from his sin to Christ. They claim, as a matter of fact, that such a gospel invitation implies natural human ability, and is therefore theologically suspect.

One of my preaching professors described such preachers as those who build sermons like exquisitely beautiful Byzantine mosaics, which they shellac a few times, and then hold them up before their listeners to admire. But they seldom really bring the message near to the hearts of sinful, needy people. 'God is able,' they say, 'to convert sinners under any circumstances.' Again, this is true enough, but that truth can never be allowed to tempt preachers to fail to do their job. The Holy Spirit will bring conviction and change to the hearts of hearers through preaching that is clear, personal, challenging, and directed to their hearts. You see, it is in commanding them to do what they cannot do by themselves – to repent and believe the gospel – that we magnify the sovereignty of God in conversion.[7] Dead people hear and respond to the gospel, for God, who raises the dead, calls them by our preaching, and makes them to respond to our invitations.

You are always prophesying to the 'dry bones' (Ezek. 37). Preach clearly, boldly, directly to those bones, and they will live! And if you preach that way, you need never fear that you will be getting in the way of the Spirit, or that you will be usurping his divine prerogatives. You will be doing your part just because you truly believe that he is doing his part – in you and through you.

Paul was the greatest 'Calvinist' of all time, teaching as he did the sovereignty of God in salvation. Yet it is this same Paul who confronts, argues, persuades, and even begs with tears in his preaching. All this in the conviction that through his message God will sovereignly convert sinners to Christ.

If you wish to imitate the apostolic example of boldness in preaching, you will have to examine your sermons for these two marks of directness: first, the use of the second person, and second, challenging confrontation. These are the marks of biblical, apostolic boldness. If they are not present in your sermons, you are not as bold as you may think. Changing your preaching style in this way will not be easy. At first it may seem very awkward and forced. But work at it anyway. You will be pleased with the difference it makes. But please remember again, it is much more than a *technique* that you need to master. In changing your style of presentation, reflect again on what we have said about preaching before the face of God and in the fullness of the Spirit, and then you will be increasingly empowered and emboldened to speak directly to your hearers in that light, and it will be much more natural, and effective.

7

Adapting to the Audience Without Compromise

In the ninth chapter of 1 Corinthians, Paul makes the following well-known comments about his ministry:

> Though I am free and belong to no man, I make myself a slave to everyone, to win as many as possible. To the Jews I became like a Jew, to win the Jews. To those under the law I became like one under the law (though I myself am not under the law), so as to win those under the law. To those not having the law I became like one not having the law (though I am not free from God's law but am under Christ's law), so as to win those not having the law. To the weak I became weak, to win the weak. I have become all things to all men so that by all possible means I might save some. I do all this for the sake of the gospel, that I may share in its blessings (vv. 19-23).

This straightforward language has occasioned a good deal of debate over the apostle's missionary methods. Clearly, Paul was willing and able to adapt himself to his audience in order to win as many as possible. Equally clearly, he was not willing to adapt his message – 'I resolved to know nothing while I was with you except Jesus Christ and him crucified' (1 Cor. 2:2) – even when under pressure to conform that message to the prejudices of Jews or Gentiles (cf. 1:22 ff.).

Adaptation without compromise thus becomes the duty of the apostolic preacher, and the 'trick' to learn in order to preach effectively. What may legitimately affect your approach to different kinds of audiences, and what must remain constant and sure?

As we noted in our brief overview of the sermons in chapter 2, the apostles addressed a wide variety of audiences in a wide variety of situations. In his book, *Studies in Preaching II: Audience Adaptation in the Sermons and Speeches of Paul*, Jay Adams began a systematic investigation of Paul's actual practice of flexibility vis-à-vis his audiences. In that study, Adams set out to determine if Paul practiced the kind of audience adaptation he preached in 1 Corinthians 9:19 ff., and, if so, how effective it proved to be, based on the evidence Luke gives in his narrative. He then went on to distill some basic principles from the Pauline practice for application to contemporary preaching practice. It is a very helpful study.[1]

Adams sets forth a 'Check List for Audience Analysis' and a 'Check List for Modes of Adaptation' based on studies of public speaking and audience adaptation in general, and with special reference to discussions of these questions by theological writers. In the former he lists matters like the size of the audience, the occasion for gathering, the cultural backgrounds, homogeneity, interests, hopes, fears, and needs of the hearers, and the attitudes toward the speaker and his subject. In the latter list Adams includes the central idea set forth in the speech, the mode of approach, the choice of language, persuasive appeal, appeals to authority, etc.[2] He then discusses each of the eight sermons or speeches (defenses) of Paul recorded in Acts in light of these two checklists, and offers his conclusions.

I will not attempt to reproduce Adams's findings here, though we will try to consider some of his insights when we look at the individual sermons in the second part of this study. I would, however, like to draw some of Adams's conclusions to your attention at this point. First, Adams highlights the general characteristics of the men of the first-century Roman world to which Paul's messages were originally delivered, comparing the similarities to our own day.

> New Testament days were much like ours. That too was a time of breakdown of old institutions. Faith in polytheism largely was dead (except in remote areas like Lystra). Poets openly jeered at the gods. The *Pax Romana* was disturbed by internal strife and 'wars and rumors of wars.' It was a period of moral degradation. To a society tired of the past and apprehensive about the future Paul carried the 'good news,' a message of *hope.* Upon the wreckage of the past it spread like a blanket, bringing a purpose to live that many had doubted could be found. The unequaled response of that generation of yearning souls is now a page of history. Today's children of Paul are challenged by a generation even more deeply plunged into despair; a generation probably more hungry than any previous to it; and ... a generation that could respond with equal enthusiasm to a proclamation of the gospel rightly adapted to its needs.[3]

One does not need to know much about contemporary Western culture to realize that Adams is right. Institutions are breaking down. The family is under attack from an escalating rate of divorce, the promotion of 'alternative' sexual lifestyles (homosexuality, lesbianism, transvestitism, etc.) through the media and in the sex-education classes of the public schools, and from the genocide of abortion, which encourages parents to wantonly and selfishly destroy their own children. Governmental institutions are shaken by political scandal, power-struggles between the branches of government, and a general civil impotence in the face of pressing domestic and foreign problems. Gang wars and random violence rage in many urban neighborhoods.

Our cultural religion is dead. Historically, Christianity, not pagan polytheism, provided the fundamental structures which shaped the life and thought of the Western world. But with the growing humanism of our cultural consensus, the ties between the culture and Christianity are disintegrating. While general illiteracy is a growing problem, biblical illiteracy is already commonplace, even among 'educated' people. The film maker, the media guru, and the rock singer (our modern 'poets') openly jeer at Christianity, and its institutions – the Church and the clergy. Newspapers and magazines are becoming both more frequent and more bold in their denunciations of the Church and the Christian ministry. Culturally, we are living in a 'post-Christian age.'

The moral degradation is reflected in the quality of our 'artistic' productions (including pornography of every kind), the lust and licentiousness reflected in the appeals of our advertizers, the greed and corruption that afflict businesses and labor organizations, and the general loss of integrity on the part of so many citizens which causes the passage of more and more laws 'to keep people honest.' And behind it all is the ominous emergence of a new occultism – ranging from the increasingly popular 'New Age philosophy' to outright, vicious Satanism.[4]

In the midst of all these cultural changes, many people are unhappy, without hope, and hungry for something – they know not what – that will truly satisfy. Adams is right – the times are ripe for a fresh resurgence of clear, powerful gospel proclamation in the mold of the apostles' preaching in Acts. That is the reason for a book like this.

Today's preachers need to be able to meet this challenge by understanding where their audiences are (intellectually, morally, even physically). Adams says:

> Paul *knew* his people. In Antioch and before the Sanhedrin, he was conscious of the factions. He knew Felix well enough to trust to simple exposition. He had taken Agrippa's measure, and made the supreme bid for his soul. He trapped the Athenians at their own game, and commanded their respect. Conservatives today too frequently are found fighting

yesterday's battles; building straw men, and employing outmoded modes of adaptation. They often preach to faces, not to well-known and thoroughly understood persons. Paul's preaching loudly proclaims to us that there is a need for better analysis.[5]

How well do you know your audience? For those of you who, like me, have a pastoral charge in a local congregation, there is little need for significant adaptation on an ongoing basis. We may have visitors each week, but they are not usually radically different from the folks that are already part of the congregation – they speak the same language, are from the same general economic and social stratum, and are attracted because they think the people in the church will be more or less like them. We are in a situation much like Paul was when he entered the synagogues of the Jews. There he was very much 'at home', though he did have a bomb to set off in their midst when they heard what message he was preaching.

If, on the other hand, you are called as a missionary or evangelist, you will face the need to adapt much more often, and perhaps, much more radically. You may find yourself feeling like Peter in the Gentile household of Cornelius, or Paul before the Athenian intellectuals. But whether or not you must adapt greatly to your audience, you do need to know and understand them. So I ask again, 'How well do you know your audience?'

Are you similar to your congregation in terms of regional culture, educational background, economic factors, etc., or quite different? What efforts do you make to know and understand your people? You would do well to learn as much as you can about the backgrounds of individuals and families in your congregation, and perhaps you have. This can be done well during times of informal socializing in your home, or during visits you make among the congregation. May I say, some ministers enjoy talking more than they like to listen. We need to cultivate the skill of listening actively and carefully to what our people have to say. You must learn to ask questions effectively so as to draw your people out in conversation in the most natural way. In addition to this you must be observant, watching how your sheep behave with different people and in different situations. Having a (more-or-less) fixed congregation is a real blessing from God, if you are careful to take advantage of it. Make your congregation your 'second book' – as you study your Bible, study your people as well, and God will richly repay your efforts.

Pastors in larger churches, which have a staff of pastoral workers, face a special potential danger in this regard. Specialization tends to distance the preacher (the 'senior pastor') from the work of pastoral counseling and family visitation. The preacher may have less and less in-depth contact with the members of his congregation, and a distance will surely grow between them which will make it more difficult for him to 'connect' with them from the pulpit, and for them to sustain the kind of personal rapport with him which will make them good hearers. Care should be taken to assure that preaching, counseling, and visitation are always closely interconnected in the ministry of any pastor who would be the most effective preacher he can become.

What kinds of things do you need to know about your people? There are many things I could suggest. You should graciously find out about how they came to know the Lord, what experiences and events have profoundly shaped their lives (before and after their conversion), how they best learn and grow (by their reading, through personal advice, by trial-and-error efforts, by the example of others, etc.). Do they have any obvious prejudices that will get in the way of their Christian discipleship? You should also get a clear idea about the level of their Bible understanding. How sophisticated and self-disciplined are they in listening to sermons, personal Bible study, prayer, etc.? All of these things, and more, will help you more effectively adapt in order to communicate the message of the Word to them.

Flexibility is a reflection of our willingness to *know* our audience well and bring our messages *to them*. Most pastors have preached the same sermon (with little modification) to different audiences on different occasions and have seen differing responses. Generic, cooky-cutter sermon outlines are inadequate to the task of real communication from the pulpit.

> Paul's method of beginning with people where they are depends largely upon *knowing* where they are, but it also demands patience, in bringing them to the Christian position. Conservative Christians (unlike Paul) often have assumed too much knowledge and acceptance of Christian presuppositions on the part of audiences. From Paul, they must learn how to approach modern man, who knows and accepts little more of the Scriptures than the Lycaonians. Knowing man's contemporary disillusionment, the modern preacher may begin with sin and despair (most contemporaries even approach these concepts under the labels of psychological or scientific jargon). To induce sick men (who know they

are sick) to see the doctor should not be quite so difficult as in the earlier part of this century when they thought (wrongly) that they were healthy. Obscurantists stand off and demand that people accept Christianity in terms of its own theological jargon. They grapple with psychological terminology rather than recognizing its insufficiency but at the same time they learn how to penetrate its most significant meanings. Such preachers never would have been able to use the Athenian altar as Paul did. They never could have brought themselves to say 'The Deity you worship but do not know I can make known to you.' If they tried, they would compromise.[6]

To be an effective preacher you need to know where you want to take your people – the goal of all your biblical instruction. And you need to know where to find your people. Then the requirement is to find those paths that will best bring them from the start to the finish of their journey under your care. That is where the flexibility comes in.

I love the language of Christian theology. Much of it is clear and precise, and most helpful in understanding and expressing our faith, to God and to people. I am personally sorry that terms like propitiation, expiation, forensic, etc. have passed from the vocabulary of most modern Christians. Yet I also realize that men and women in general, and converted men and women in particular, do not come equipped with a built-in mental glossary of theological terms. If we carelessly use the terms without proper, patient explanation and review, we *are* guilty of sloganizing. We are 'obscurantists' who, as Adams said, 'stand off and demand that people accept Christianity in terms of its own theological jargon.' More than that, we are guilty of inconsiderateness and a breach of brotherly love.

One last point to glean from Adams' conclusions at this point, concerns the preacher's knowledge and understanding of the literature and learning of our age:

Paul's knowledge and use of Greek poetry exhibits a principle that cannot be stressed too strongly. Christian preachers must study the literature and learning of the 'other side,' not only to stay abreast of changing currents of thought in their audiences, but also to enable them to communicate with contemporary society in terms of the literature that they are reading and the concepts they understand. The conservative preacher who is unfamiliar with existential writing, for example, does not comprehend the drift of the times. He must know enough about various areas of life to be 'at home' with people.[7]

It still amazes me to find that people are genuinely surprised to find that I, their pastor, have read a book that they enjoyed, or saw the same movie as they, or like the same kind of music. Many modern Christians think ministers come from, and live in, 'Never-Never-Land.' They live with the suspicion that our lives are so different from theirs, and that our interests are so foreign to theirs, that they will never really be able to live the Christian life as we do, and that we do not truly understand where their deepest interests and concerns lie.

I have been blessed, in the providence of God, with having held down a wide variety of jobs — carpentry, electronic assembly, hospital work, construction labor, etc. – during the summers and vacations during my high school and college years. I say blessed, because having those kinds of work experiences in common with members of my churches over the years has meant a great deal in helping me both to build rapport with them (especially other men, who often think ministers don't know anything about working for a living), and communicate the biblical message clearly and practically to them. I am also interested in many things (I think *too* many things) and tend to read widely. But that too has been a blessing in helping me understand the broader culture in which we are trying to minister today. The richer you are as a person – in terms of your reading, listening, and experience – the more imaginative and versatile you will be in finding those paths along which to lead your people from where you find them to where they need to be at last.

Though Adams' conclusions arise from a study of the Apostle Paul, I think we would find much of what he says borne out in the preaching of Peter and Stephen as well, as we shall try to notice later in considering their individual sermons. All of the apostolic preachers shared in an alertness and sensitivity to the make-up of their audiences, and a willingness to approach them thoughtfully.

Most of us were told in seminary to pay attention to the make-up of our audiences, but I'm afraid this point does not get enough practical attention in the development of preachers. Student preachers begin their sermon preparation with a careful study of their text – as they should. They then proceed to a consideration of the theological and ethical implications of the text in view of the whole message of Scripture. They seek to discover the centrality of Christ to the message of the passage they are preaching – since he is the center of the message of the whole Bible. But when, on the basis of all this study and preparation, they have developed an outline, they do not yet have a sermon outline. They need next to 'study' their audience with equal care, bringing to mind those factors that will affect their listeners' ability really to *hear* the message from the Word of God. What is the purpose of this sermon in view of the teaching of the passage and the true needs of the audience? Does the congregation know what its true needs are in this area of concern? Where is the point of contact for this sermon? What do they already know that will help them grasp the message? What do they need to have explained? What vocabulary and form of argument is best suited to their ability to understand? Many other similar questions must be asked and answered in the process of sermon preparation.[8] Then the preacher has the other 'leg' of his sermon, without which his message will not stand up.

In closing this chapter, I want to touch on one more point – one having more to do with the compromise side of our subject than with the adaptation side. There is a great deal said these days about the need for 'homogeneity' between the preacher and his audience. Many assume that people are most responsive to those who are most like them, and familiar (either personally or culturally) to them. An analysis of the audiences in Acts discloses that sometimes the preachers are right at home with their hearers: Peter with an audience of fellow Jews in Jerusalem, Paul with the Jews of the Diaspora in Asia Minor. Other times they find themselves in very foreign audience environments: Peter to the Gentiles of Cornelius' household, Paul before the Greek intellectuals and philosophers in Athens, and *anybody* before the Sanhedrin!

What ought we to make of the principle of 'homogeneity' in light of the data from Acts? Our response should be balanced. On the one hand it is true that the apostolic preachers shared some significant things in common with their different audiences. Most notably their language. It has been often remarked that the spread of the use of *koine* Greek in the first-century Roman world was part of God's providential preparation for the spread of the gospel message through the preaching of the apostles. At least as far as the Acts narrative is concerned, neither Peter nor Paul experienced the kind of situation that is commonly faced, for example, by a modern-day Wycliffe translator upon first arriving on the field. Wherever they went they could readily find a Greek-speaking audience, be they Jewish or Gentile. The language barrier was thus not a significant problem.

It seems obvious that on a basic level there must be some common cultural bridges between speaker and audience. As we have already noted, Paul spoke of his willingness to 'become all things to all men' in his efforts to win men to the gospel (1 Cor. 9:19-22). This is certainly a call to adaptability. We will have occasion to observe this flexibility in action in the sermons of Paul in Acts as he confronts different audiences on different occasions (e.g., his apologetic method with Jews differs from his approach to an audience made up of Gentiles). We can say, then, that it is important for a preacher to be able to adapt to various audiences and situations in his proclamation of the Word of God.

In my judgment this kind of adaptation falls far short of what has come to be called 'contextualization'. The call to 'contextualize the gospel' often leads to the pressing of culturally legitimate principles of adaptation to extremes, leading to a distortion of the message itself. It is sometimes alleged that only a certain kind of man is able to preach effectively to certain kinds of people (in various cultures or subcultures). It is even asserted by some that adjustments must be made in the content and presentation of the gospel message in order to overcome the cultural prejudices of some groups (e.g., a 'liberation theology,' a 'black theology,' a 'feminist gospel'). The evidence we have from the preaching in Acts does not confirm the necessity of such 'contextualization'. While there are some efforts at adaptation, there are also significant differences between the preachers and their audience at times (e.g., it took a divine revelation to prompt Peter to 'adapt' by taking the gospel to Cornelius and his family). Paul, for his part, makes 'contact' with the Greek philosophers without accommodating his message to the thought system of classical philosophy and pagan religion.[9]

There are favorable and unfavorable responses to the preaching in Acts, but it is the *message* rather than the *man* that elicits the response. The hostile reactions of people, when they come, are not the reaction of merely cultural prejudices (though that may enter the picture at times) or a superficial lack of affinity with the messenger. Rather it is an expression of the basic antipathy and hostility of the 'natural man' to the things of the Spirit of God – including the message preached, and the means of its propagation. 'The man without the Spirit does not accept the things that come from the Spirit of God, for they are foolishness to him, and he cannot understand them, because they are spiritually discerned' (1 Cor. 2:14).

As regards the messengers, it is true that God uses certain men for certain jobs, but any preacher who preaches God's Word faithfully and powerfully, and is sensitive to differences of audience and situation, should be able to freely preach that life-saving gospel anywhere, even in the most alien and hostile of environments (with the use of a translator if need be!), and be assured that God will use him to communicate to men, and that they will respond to the message from God (cf. Acts 28:28).

8

Preaching the Mighty Acts of God

All the sermons in Acts have one essential point – Jesus Christ is risen from the dead. The apostles, as eyewitnesses of the resurrection of Christ (Acts 1:22), were called to bear witness before the nations to this great event in redemptive history (Luke 24:48; Acts 1:8). Thus everything they preach, explicitly or implicitly, has reference to this historic center – the redemption accomplished by Jesus Christ, the Son of God, in his death and resurrection. Paul summarizes the gospel he and the other apostles preached, and which the people who heard them had believed:

> Now, brothers, I want to remind you of the gospel I preached to you, which you received and on which you have taken your stand. By this gospel you are saved, if you hold firmly to the word I preached to you. Otherwise you have believed in vain. For what I received I passed on to you as of first importance: that Christ died for our sins according to the Scriptures, that he was buried, that he was raised on the third day according to the Scriptures.... Whether, then, it was I or they, this is what we preach, and this is what you believed (1 Cor. 15:1-11).

It is especially noteworthy, particularly in light of present day preaching emphases, that Paul does not say that he and the other apostles preached faith, or the new birth, or justification, or obedience, or spiritual wholeness. As critical as all these elements are, they are responses to, and results from, the preaching of the gospel. The 'good news' itself is the proclamation of a historic message – the death and resurrection of Jesus Christ in the light of the explanations thereof given in the teachings of the Scriptures. This gospel, which God 'promised beforehand through his prophets in the Holy Scriptures', was a message concerning his own Son, 'who as to his human nature was a descendant of David, and who through the Spirit of holiness was declared with power to be the Son of God by his resurrection from the dead' (Rom 1:2-4).

Apostolic Preaching is the Preaching of History

Even when the preaching and teaching concerns other elements in the life of faith, these things cannot be far separated from the historical events that stand at the heart of the apostolic message. C. H. Dodd has described the apostolic *kerygma* in this way:

> In its most summary form the kerygma consists of the announcement of certain historical events in a setting which displays the significance of those events. The events in question are those of the appearance of Jesus in history – His ministry, sufferings and death and His subsequent manifestation of Himself to His followers as risen from the dead and invested with the glory of another world – and the emergence of the Church as a society distinguished by the power and activity of the Holy Spirit, and looking forward to the return of its Lord as Judge and Savior of the world.[1]

When the Spirit came upon the disciples at Pentecost, and they began to speak in different languages, the content of their miraculous speech was to declare 'the mighty acts of God' (Acts 2:11). As Peter rises to preach in explanation of the phenomena of the multiple languages being spoken, his message develops around the dual theme of the death and resurrection of Christ (2:23 f.), together with the sequel, Jesus' exaltation to the right hand of God in power and glory (vv. 33 ff.).

Peter's sermon near the Temple again focuses on the announcement of the death and resurrection of Jesus (3:13 ff.). Peter again expresses the purpose of the apostolic preaching: 'We are witnesses of [the resurrection]' (v. 15). In explaining the healing of the crippled beggar to the Sanhedrin, Peter again calls attention to the significance of the death and resurrection of Christ: 'It is by the name of Jesus Christ of Nazareth, whom you crucified but whom God raised from the dead, that this man stands before you healed' (4:10). When forbidden to preach further by the Council, the apostles again affirm that they must obey God in the discharge of their commission as witnesses – with the Holy Spirit – of the central redemptive acts of God in Christ (5:29-32). When Peter is sent to the Gentiles of Cornelius' household to preach, the death and resurrection of Christ remains the heart of his proclamation. Peter declares: 'We are witnesses of everything he [Christ] did in the country of the Jews and in Jerusalem. They killed him by hanging him on a tree, but God raised him from the dead on the third day and caused him to be seen' (10:39-40).

Paul addresses the congregation of the Jewish synagogue at Pisidian Antioch with a sermon that focuses on an explanation of the death of Christ and his resurrection (13:26-31), reminding them that this word of testimony comes to them from eyewitnesses. At Athens it is Paul's preaching 'about Jesus and the resurrection' (17:18) that attracts the attention of the Areopagus, and in his speech before these Greek intellectuals, Paul again announces the reality and significance of Jesus' resurrection: 'For he has set a day when he will judge the world with justice by the man he has appointed. He has given proof of this to all men by raising him from the dead' (v. 31). When the Apostle Paul faces a divided and hostile Sanhedrin, he brings down the house by proclaiming, 'I stand on trial because of my hope in the resurrection of the dead' (23:6). The news of the historic resurrection of Christ also figures prominently in Paul's defense before Festus (26:24).

The constant theme of the apostolic sermons is that Jesus of Nazareth, a contemporary historical figure well known to many who heard the apostolic preaching, is none other than the Lord's Christ. He was rejected, suffered, and put to death by the hands of wicked men. Yet God was in Christ reconciling the world unto himself. Jesus has risen from the dead, and that fact, understood in light of its scriptural significance, forces people to face the crisis of decision and respond to the offer of salvation and forgiveness made in Jesus' Name (cf. 17:30).

This apostolic emphasis on the *historical core of the gospel* is very important for today's preachers. While fundamentalists and evangelicals have distinguished themselves by affirming again and again the historical and factual accuracy of the Bible, and the reliability of the historical accounts contained in Scripture, that emphasis has not kept evangelical preaching from drifting into a kind of *unhistorical moralism*. I recently had occasion to listen to several sermons from the Gospel of John by a prominent evangelical preacher. In sermon after sermon the heart of the message revolved around a moralistic application of the text. Never was the historicity of the passage denied, but neither was it clearly emphasized or explained. Rather the text was characteristically used as an *example* of faith, or obedience, or love, or compassion, etc. The congregation was urged again and again to respond by imitating the spiritual or moral qualities practically illustrated in the biblical story which was the basis of the message.

I do not mean to say that there are not moral principles embodied in the human action described in the historical narratives of the Bible.

Nor am I suggesting that those principles ought not to be identified and applied by preachers.[2] But I am saying that these narratives are not given to us primarily as examples of how or how not to live today. They are given to tell us *what God has done in our world* of space and time to solve the deadly, damning problem we face with sin, and the impending judgment our sin deserves and will surely receive if something does not change radically. This change has been accomplished by God through the redemptive work of his Son, Jesus Christ.

An example may help you understand the distinction I am making between moralism and a proper concern with the ethical applications of biblical history. If your house is on fire, and you are in danger of being trapped on the second floor and burned to death, and if I come to warn you of the danger by crying, 'Your house is on fire! Get out quickly! The ladder is leaning against the second story bedroom window!', you would be foolish to respond by saying, 'What a wonderful example of neighborly concern. Thank you. I resolve in future to work harder at showing that kind of compassion to my neighbor,' and then go back to bed. In light of your present circumstances, such a response would be ridiculous – and deadly!

The historic reality of the fire puts you in immediate and mortal danger, and the only appropriate way to make use of my warning is to get out the window and down the ladder as fast as possible. In the morning, at your leisure, and in the security of new circumstances, you may reflect profitably on my neighborly concern, and draw a lesson or two about your future behavior from my example.

To put this matter back into a first century setting, then, the apostles came (after centuries of prophetic activity and written Scripture) to announce that God had acted in a conspicuous redemptive fashion in history. Through the giving of his Son, the sacrificial death of that Son on the cross in space and time, and the resurrection of the Son to new life and power to save, God has acted to provide a way of escape for people from the real, historic threat of judgment. When the apostles announce the death and resurrection of Christ, therefore, they do not expect their listeners to draw simple moral insights about Jesus' trust in his heavenly Father, or his love for others, or his personal commitment to righteous living. Rather, they plead with their hearers to cast themselves upon Jesus as their only hope to escape the wrath to come (Acts 2:40; cf. Matt. 3:7 ff.), and they expect a response.

According to the apostles, the events surrounding the coming of Jesus Christ have precipitated a *crisis in human history* that puts all people everywhere under *obligation* to repent and believe the gospel (Acts 17:30; cf. 3:23). This is a historic obligation forced by the mighty acts of God. 'As God's fellow workers we urge you not to receive God's grace in vain. For he says, "In the time of my favor I heard you, and in the day of salvation I helped you." I tell you, now is the time of God's favor, now is the day of salvation' (2 Cor. 6:1-2).

These historic concerns are at the forefront of the apostolic preaching in Acts, and they are equally critical in importance to faithful and effective preaching on our part today.

There is a vital need for us to recapture this historical emphasis. The influences of existentialism and psychology, with their emphasis on personal experience without significant relationship to the external world of objective reality, have created an atmosphere of dangerous *subjectivism*, even within the church. Faith, hope, and love have come to be understood as self-defining and self-perpetuating. No longer is faith understood in relation to the *object* of faith, Jesus Christ.

The empty subjectivism of much of what passes for faith is evident in statements (heard even from the pulpits of evangelical churches) like: 'The doctrinal disagreements that divide us are not important so long as we all share the same faith together.' We are told it does not matter *what* we believe as long as we *believe*. That's nothing more than 'faith in faith'. This kind of name-it-and-claim-it 'faith' bears no resemblance (beyond the name) to biblical faith. It has much more in common with Maria's attempt (in the movie *The Sound of Music*) to lift her spirits by singing, 'I have confidence in confidence alone, besides which you see, I have confidence in me.'

Similarly, hope has become dissociated from the historic goals of God's redemptive plans to which hope properly attaches itself. I have heard ministers, who deny the historicity of the personal return of Christ and even the gospel itself, who nevertheless want to speak of the Christian's 'hope'. What can such hope possibly be under those circumstances? Surely nothing more than a vague 'openness to the future'. Certainly not the hope about which the New Testament speaks.

Love is also commended to men as a way of life without reference to its definition, or to the holy standard of God's law, which is the substance of true love (Rom. 13:8-10). This law of love was historically revealed through Moses and the prophets, and confirmed in these last times by none other than Jesus himself (cf. Matt. 5:17-20). Yet without that law love is no more than an undefined emotion. Sometimes, in the name of love, churchmen and Christians even set aside God's expressed commands, pitting 'love' against 'law'. Christian ethics needs an historical context.

You see the point, I trust. It is vitally important that the *subjective* realities of the Christian life always be kept in the closest contact with the *objective* realities of what God has done for us in his Son. It is the job of preachers and preaching to make that connection clear. Every time you and I preach it must be our concern to 'proclaim the mighty acts of God', and to call men to repentance and faith *in light of those historic acts*. If we do not, the dangerous drift into subjectivism which the contemporary church is experiencing will continue, and grow worse, until genuine Christian faith all but disappears, replaced by illusionary 'word magic' – using the familiar old terms without their biblical meaning and historical mooring. Too much of the church has already lost sight of this important matter, and may not even know it is missing.[3]

I have a simple test for you to apply to your own preaching to test yourself on this question. Review one of your recent sermons, and ask yourself, 'Would it make any difference to what I said in this sermon, or how I said it, if the biblical account was not true?' You may find that sometimes (I hope not often) you will have to admit, 'No, not really.'

If your main emphasis in preaching is to use the narrative texts as lessons in faith, love, etc., you will find that the possibility that the stories did not really happen would not significantly change your presentation. If, for example, you preached on the miracle of the feeding of the five thousand in such a way as to make the primary point, or application, a lesson in sharing, then the story will do just as well if the account was no more than a fable. Remember Aesop's *Fables* work very well as moral tales, even though everyone knows they are made up. Similarly, when you are preaching about faith, or Christian relationships, or behavior, etc. if there is not a direct connection – in your mind at least, if not explicitly in your sermon – between what the people of God are to believe, think, or do, and what God has done in raising Jesus Christ up from the dead, then you will get along fine even if he did not.

The apostolic preachers had a very different view, however. Paul argues that if Jesus did not come back from the dead, there is nothing left of our faith – nothing left to preach. 'If there is no resurrection of the dead, then not even Christ has been raised. And if Christ has not been raised, our preaching is useless and so is your faith' (1 Cor. 15:13-14, cf. vv. 13-19). 'If the dead are not raised, "Let us eat and drink, for tomorrow we die" ' (v. 32b). If Jesus is not raised there is nothing! No moral precepts, no new relationships, no transformed attitudes, no *nothing*. We are *not* encouraged to 'rescue morality' by teaching men to do the best they can, to love one another even, if the 'good news' is but an ancient fabrication.

But judging from a lot of preaching that people hear today, I think they might well conclude that Paul is overstating the case. While they rejoice in the reality of the resurrection, and are glad that it is true, and cannot conceive of its not being true, they nevertheless do not have any clear or keen sense of why everything depends on it. They might be inclined to think that, if it turned out that Jesus did not rise from the dead, while a very important doctrine would be missing, life and faith would still go on, albeit in a modified form.

'Exhibit A' for my contention is the continued existence in the Western world today of the liberal, modernist churches who deny the historical resurrection of Jesus Christ. They continue to hold their worship services, preach their sermons, and talk a great deal in an approving way of 'faith,' 'hope,' and 'love'. They collect their offerings, and erect their buildings. But they do not realize the problem. That is the bitter irony of 'modernism' (and 'neo-orthodoxy') – if God is dead, if Jesus is not risen, then Nietzsche was right. Everything is permissible.

If the resurrection were proved to be false (though it could never be), Paul would have quit and gone home. Many preachers today would simply change the message, and carry on.

We evangelicals are facing a most serious problem. By embracing a dangerous subjectivism, many of our churches have started down the same road as the modernists at the beginning of the twentieth century. Soon we will lose sight of the integral relationship between faith and history – between the historic accomplishment of redemption in the work of Christ and the whole structure of the Christian faith and life. Church historians have pointed out that the first stage in the decline into unbelief on the part of a church is this very slide into a faith centered in subjectivism. If we preachers are going to guard the flocks which the Holy Spirit has entrusted to us, we need to apply the brakes as soon as possible, and effect a reversal.

Since as evangelicals we do still appreciate and confess the central importance of God's redemptive works in history, let us see to it that we preach that way every time we preach. You must preach every aspect of the Scripture from the standpoint of the resurrection, as Paul and the other apostles did. Paul declared: 'For I resolved to know nothing while I was with you except Jesus Christ and him crucified' (1 Cor. 2:2). Your congregations need to realize afresh that Christianity is, before anything else, an historical faith. Because God accomplished certain things by acting in our world, in our history, everything is different for people. As you preach to the lost, and to your congregation of God's people, you must call upon them to respond in light of these historic realities, if they are to escape the wrath to come in the end.

Your people need to understand again that the whole edifice which is Christianity collapses if Jesus did not come back from the dead. They will only understand it if you preach that way.

9

Standing With the Apostles –
in the Twenty-first Century

Before I leave the consideration of these general characteristics of apostolic preaching and turn to look at the sermons in Acts individually, I would bring one more consideration to your attention. It is closely related to what we have already been looking at in the last chapter. It is the need for the contemporary preacher of the gospel to bridge a tremendous gap, for himself and his listeners, between the first and twenty-first centuries, and between Palestine and wherever you do your preaching. In short, you as a preacher must work hard to close the distance between the world of the New Testament preachers and yourself, between the churches of AD 50–70 and your congregation of the 2000s.

Other able writers have discussed this question from the standpoint of cultural differences, and the need for adaptation without compromising the truth of the Word.[1] I want to focus our attention on the need for you to create immediacy through your preaching, so that your hearers will be confronted with the sense of urgency brought about by the impact upon them of the historic events we discussed in the last chapter.

We all face the problem of fading memory. No matter how significant the event, or how personally important it was to you, time has a way of erasing both the vividness of the recollection and the urgency of responding to the event. No doubt there are things that have happened to you that were so overwhelming at the time that you were certain you would never forget that day, and that you would never be the same again as a result of what happened. But as the years went by, your memory faded, your emotions evoked by the event weakened, and your resolve to act differently in the light of that event disappeared.

The man who comes upon the scene of an auto accident and discovers the dead body of the driver, thrown through the windshield because he did not have his seatbelt on, will (no doubt) be affected deeply by that experience. He will relive all the chilling emotions – sickening excitement as the adrenalin surged through his bloodstream, terrible fear, and later, oppressive sadness and disappointment that nothing more could have been done. Then after the experience and the memories have sunk deeply into his consciousness, he may make an absolute commitment never to get in a car again without fastening his seatbelt. But time will pass, he will not come upon a similar accident, or even see one at a distance. The recollections will gradually become less vivid. Other day by day concerns will squeeze the urgency of the need for caution from his mind. And at last his resolution to change will dissolve into the old habits again.

God has made us the kind of creatures that are profoundly affected by events. But events affect us only as long as we continue under their influence – what I have called this 'sense of urgency'. And that depends to a very large degree on *memory*.

It is the blessing and curse of memory that both the tragedies and bitter disappointments, as well as the vivid joys and blessings, fade with time. The same is the case with the religious memory of individual Christians and of the church as a whole. God realizes this, and has taken steps to deal with the problem.

In the old covenant era Jehovah laid a great deal of stress on the importance of *remembering*.

> Ask now about the former days, long before your time, from the day God created man on the earth; ask from one end of the heavens to the other. Has anything so great as this ever happened, or has anything like it ever been heard of? Has any other people heard the voice of God speaking out of fire, as you have, and lived? Has any god ever tried to take for himself one nation out of another nation, by testings, by miraculous signs and wonders, by war, by a mighty hand and an outstretched arm, or by great and awesome deeds, like all the things the Lord your God did for you in Egypt before your very eyes? You were shown these things so that you might know that the Lord is God; besides him there is no other.... Acknowledge and take to heart this day that the Lord is God in heaven above and on the earth below. There is no other. Keep his decrees and commands, which I am giving you today, so that it may go well with you and your children after you and that you may live long in the land the Lord your God gives you for all time (Deut. 4:32-35, 39-40).

Note the vital connection between remembering and covenant faithfulness – the faith and obedience of God's people to his law of life. Moses calls Israel to remember what God had done in Egypt – a period forty years earlier, when the adults to whom he is speaking were no more than children, and the young people before him had not even been born. He calls them to compare that with the memories of events that took place 'long before their time', which they had heard of only through the effort of one generation to pass on to the next the memory of the mighty acts of God. Only as they remember what God had done in the *past* – things done 'so that you might know that the LORD is God; besides him there is not other' – would they put their trust in him *today*, and pledge themselves to loyalty and obedience to the covenant in the *future*. Moses the preacher is the one called by God to bridge the gap between past and present for the people. His sermons (which form the bulk of the Book of Deuteronomy) have as their purpose to stir the people's corporate memory, so that they will continue to live in light of the urgency created by a knowledge of what God has done for them in history. If their memory fails, so will their faithfulness.

Further, God prescribed that a part of the regular observance of Passover would be a question: 'What does this ceremony mean to you?' (Exod. 12:26). The use of the question would be the occasion for an exercise in remembering – deliberately calling to mind the struggle between Moses and Pharaoh, the plagues, the death of Egypt's firstborn, and the deliverance from bondage. Without it the people were sure to forget these things, and as a consequence would stop living in the light of those events.

In the same way God commanded Moses to write a 'Song of Witness' (Deut. 32) for the people to memorize and rehearse frequently, so that they would not forget what God had done, what he promised to them, and what he had threatened. Many of the psalms function to remind the people of their history so that they will not drift from the faith (e.g., Ps. 78; 103; etc.).

As you can see from these few examples, God is very concerned to keep the memory of his people vividly alive to the things that he has done for them. As we observed in the last chapter, without the history of these redemptive events clearly in mind our faith is rootless and fruitless – dead.

The reason that God's special redemptive revelation was committed to writing was so that an accurate historical record of the history of redemption would be preserved in a durable form. Without the Scriptures, there would be no living faith. For this reason the Scriptures are foundational to the faith and life of the church (cf. Eph. 2:20; etc.). They constitute the infallible, life-transforming historical memory of the people of God.

As we observed in the previous chapter, this concern for a living historical memory is no less central to the New Testament and the purpose of apostolic preaching. The apostolic preachers proclaim 'the mighty acts of God' in history as foundational for the faith of the church in the living Christ.

There is more. Not only has God left us with this unsurpassably excellent record in Scripture, he has commanded post-apostolic preachers to continue the proclamation of that Word (2 Tim. 4:2). You see, there is still a danger that the church's memory will fade. That is where you come in as a preacher. You are not apostles. You do not supplement (or supplant) God's revelation in Scripture (1 Cor. 3:10-15), but you are commanded to proclaim it afresh in your generation.

As a minister of the Word, you have committed your life to a work that has at its heart the proclamation of events, and God's scriptural explanation of their significance, to the people of God. To do justice to your task, you must consistently preach with the kind of vividness and urgency that will close the gap between your twenty-first century congregation and the witness of the first-century apostles. Like Moses, you must preach events that happened years, even generations before, as if they had happened only yesterday. Quite a commission is it not?

When you were in seminary you ate, drank, and slept biblical studies. Systematic theology, Semitic languages and culture, Greek and Roman history were your daily bread. Perhaps many of you were, for a time, more at home in that world than you were in your own (just ask your wife to remind you if you have forgotten!). You steeped yourself in that world and those events to such an extent that they presented themselves to your heart and mind with great clarity and vividness.

I remember dozing off one time while reading the early chapters of Acts, and actually dreaming that I was walking in Jerusalem with Peter and John! I overheard, as an immediate spectator, the quiet interchange between Peter and the crippled beggar near the Temple, 'Silver and gold have I none: but such as I have give I thee: In the name of Jesus Christ of Nazareth rise up and walk.' (Peter spoke the King's English in my dream!) It was all so real that it took me the rest of the day to shake off the impression it made on me.

Soon you graduated, and stepped into your first pulpit only to face a serious problem. You tried out all that good seminary stuff (the very air you breathed) on your congregation, and ... nothing. The subtle significance of a Greek verb form did not stir their blood. A piece of interesting archaeological information about ancient fishing practices did not do much for them. And (worst of all!) they cared little for the theological debates that kept you and your classmates up all night.

For them your ancient world was just that – ancient, and all too remote. They had a difficult time understanding what you were so steamed up about, though at first they were too polite to tell you. Later you heard rumors that some were 'not getting anything out of your preaching'. For your congregation, the truly vivid concerns revolve around their job, their family, their bills, and the threat of terrorism. They began to ask you to be more 'practical' in your preaching. By this they probably meant, 'Just tell us what to do and spare us all the ancient history and systematic theology.'

If this describes something of your experience, you faced a crisis of sorts in your ministry. I don't know how you solved the problem. I think if you were unwise, you probably simply gave in, and began to preach 'practical' sermons about daily life in the twenty-first century. If you did, then by now the first century – with the grisly event that took place on a splintery cross of wood on a hot, sweaty morning, or the secret mysteries of life and power that unfolded in the cool morning mists of the garden – may have become as remote to you as they were (and are) to your people. Your faith, and your preaching, may have become abstracted from the very historical events to which you are called by God to testify. By now you are perhaps more influenced by contemporary answers to today's issues than by the solutions God provided when he brought forth his Son from the grave in resurrection power.

Indeed you do preach 'practically' now. You talk a lot about what God's people need to do. But tell me this. Are you frustrated because you see so little change in them? You know, and they know, that though you tell them week after week what God expects from them, they are not consistently doing it. Perhaps in moments of soul searching and prayer you have even begun to fear that you are leading your people into a 'form of godliness' which is long on practicality but void of power. Has your own life become that as well?

Where did you go wrong? How can you get back on track? How can you lead your people back into a fruitful faith and godliness?

Consider this. Your problem is that your preaching did not effectively bridge the distance between your people and Christ's work. Instead you hurdled it and ended up on this side. You may have become (no matter how unwittingly) a pulpit proclaimer of practical ethics or a sermonic psychologist. But you are no longer – in any vital way – a 'witness of the resurrection'. You have lost touch with the apostles. There is now a gap between your work and theirs.

When, as a preacher, you face the wide chasm that yawns before you between your congregation and the Bible's life and history, the wisest course is to recognize this reality as a fact of life, and deal with it. It is not a new problem, and it is not a problem that God has failed to notice. Indeed he has already solved it for us. He invented your job for just this reason! God has ordained your task as a preacher and witness to overcome this problematic historical distance. As he sent the apostles to preach peace to those who were near, and to those who were far off (cf. Eph. 2:17), so he has called you to preach that same message – to give that same testimony – to those who are far off, and to those who are farther off.

You must determine to work with all your might to bring your people near, so that the earth-changing impact of Jesus' work will strike them with the same urgency as those who were there. You must work at your sermons so that in them, and through you, God is announcing his mighty acts directly to your people across the ages and the miles.

Your preaching must force your congregation to realize that they – no less than their first century brothers and sisters who first listened to the apostolic message – can become partakers of that new world called the Kingdom of God. They too are called to repent and believe in light of the urgency created by the announcement of the resurrection.

Only in this way can your preaching become truly *practical*. Only so can you avoid becoming either a purveyor of a detached and lifeless theology, or a psychologizer about faith and love in the categories familiar to modern people. Only so can you keep from the temptation to flights of biblical-theological fancy, or the temptation to turn the Christian faith into simply one more vain morality or self-help technique. Your preaching must remain at bottom the proclamation of the cross and the resurrection, and an explanation of the significant impact of these world-changing events upon the lives of your people facing the demands of Christian living today.

In a sense you have to do the same thing the apostles themselves had to do as they carried the Word away from Jerusalem geographically, and (with the passing of the years) historically. They had to proclaim the good news of God's work in Christ in such a way that their hearers were confronted directly with the urgency of responding, even when those events had happened years before and far away. The distance for us may be greater, but our task is not essentially different from that which the apostles, or the post-apostolic preachers like Timothy and Titus, had to face.

As we shall see in our next chapter, Peter had no real difficulty in his Pentecost sermon announcing the good news with this sense of freshness and urgency. He preached right after these things happened, and right where they happened. In the same way, John the Baptist had the benefit of the immediacy of the historic moment when he announced the imminent coming of the King and his Kingdom – 'Repent, for the Kingdom of heaven is at hand' (Matt. 3:1 ff.). Jesus is waiting in the wings, and indeed he arrives on the scene even as John proclaims his coming.

You do not have the advantage of these historical circumstances, of course. Does that mean you cannot bear witness to these events in the same way? Not at all. But you must craft and direct your sermons to accomplish this goal. What you preach and how you preach it are the means God has given you to trigger this crisis of confrontation. You have to preach so as to bring the work of Christ – first in its historical, but also in its forensic and existential reality – before your people vividly, and with a sense of immediacy. That of course presupposes that you have this sense yourself, and that you continually cultivate it.

It is a great tragedy to hear a pastor standing in the pulpit, handling the very Word of God, droning on like the murmuring of innumerable bees in some dusty empty cloister. How can we legitimately expect our people to listen with eagerness to our messages if, in our demeanor and delivery, we convey the impression that proclaiming these great and holy mysteries of redemption is all very routine? Even preachers who are known for a little 'fire' in the pulpit are more often stirred to zeal by the sins they are denouncing than by the events to which they are (supposedly) bearing witness.

Isn't it interesting that many Christians take expensive and potentially dangerous trips to the 'Holy Land' in order to make their faith more *real* and alive? To visit the historic sites – even the bogus and crassly commercialized ones – brings to them a vivid sense of the *reality* of the gospel. They know Jesus is no myth – he really came to our world, he lived and died and rose again in our history. The old stories are not fables – they are as true and relevant as last week's newspaper headlines. Truly, they are far more important. And yet for so many contemporary Christians there is a vague sense of unreality about the whole thing. Why?

I think it is wonderful that believing people can make those trips, and that they get that sense from their visit to Israel and the Middle East. But it is very sad if they cannot get that sense of reality and immediacy unless they can make such a trip. They should not have to. Christians today should be brought to that same realization week after week as they sit under the preaching of a pastor who is a witness to them of the death and resurrection of Jesus. A man who in the twenty-first century preaches with the apostles.

Without a sense of the urgency of the moment, people are less inclined to repent, to entrust themselves to Christ, and to devote themselves to a new way of life and to a new community of relationships. That is just the way they are, and always have been. It is a truism that people are often much more responsive to the gospel during situations of crisis. Preaching at a funeral, if you will boldly seize the occasion, can be a wonderful opportunity to confront people when they are especially open, because they are thinking of life and death, and may by God's grace be softened by the loss of a loved one.

Several years ago a gunman entered a nearby McDonalds and killed several people. A couple of days later I scrapped my regular Sunday sermon, and preached instead on Luke 13:1-5. I called the sermon, 'The Reason Why.' Because of the situation God had graciously prepared the congregation, which was especially responsive. They were deeply challenged by the preaching. We reflected together on the tragedy of such an event. We considered the brevity of life, and the uncertain, yet inevitable, time of our death. Young and old alike lost their lives in that tragedy, and the congregation took seriously the Lord's call, when I was able to declare to them in Jesus' Name, 'Repent or you will perish in the same way.' How urgent was the call! How precious was the good news that Jesus receives and saves sinners. We are all often at our most open, most honest when we face a crisis, and we know it.

The point that I want to leave you with is that the preacher who would preach like the apostles does not have to lead his people on a tour to the Holy Land – as nice as that might be. Nor does he have to depend on a circumstantial crisis in the lives of his people – with the knowledge that we, any one of us, could die at any moment – in order to convey a sense of urgency to his people. Rather, it is his preaching of the Word itself that ought to create the immediacy out of which a sense of urgency arises. The message of the apostles was that God himself precipitated the historic crisis for the whole world, and for each and every person, by bringing Jesus back from the dead. God creates the urgency for this whole age by sending out his preachers with this message that will turn the world, and the life of every person, upside down: 'Therefore let all Israel be assured of this: God has made this Jesus, whom you crucified, both Lord and Christ' (Acts 2:36). 'In the past God overlooked such ignorance, but now he commands all people everywhere to repent. For he has set a day when he will judge the world with justice by the man he has appointed. He has given proof of this to all men by raising him from the dead' (17:30-31).

> Since, then, we know what it is to fear the Lord, we try to persuade men.... For Christ's love compels us, because we are convinced that one died for all, and therefore all died. And he died for all, that those who live should no longer live for themselves, but for him who died for them, and was raised again ... the old has gone, the new has come! All this is from God, who reconciled us to himself through Christ and gave us the ministry of reconciliation.... We are therefore Christ's ambassadors, as though God were making his appeal through us. We implore you on Christ's behalf: Be reconciled to God.... As God's fellow workers we urge you not to receive God's grace in vain.... I tell you, now is the time of God's favor, now is the day of salvation (2 Cor. 5:11–6:2).

Each of these declarations by Peter and by Paul rings with urgency – the urgency occasioned by the death and resurrection of Jesus Christ. These events have ushered in a 'new creation'. By them God has inaugurated the time of his favor – the 'day of salvation'. We still live in that day of grace and patience, and that same message – proclaimed in that same way, with that same sense of urgency and immediacy – is what God expects you to preach from your pulpit *every week*.

How can you do it? I have already mentioned that you must begin with yourself. If you do not have, or have lost, a sense of the historic reality and significance of these events, you need to recapture and cultivate one. For example there are pastors that have read practically every book written on church growth methods, or building proper relationships in the family, and yet have never read, for example, Alfred Edersheim's *Life and Times of Jesus the Messiah*.[2] They pore over journals devoted to psychology and Christianity, but know next to nothing about the significance of the history of redemption for the shape and content of Paul's thought. They cultivate all that makes them 'right at home' here in the world today. They are well abreast of contemporary problems. But they neglect those readings, those studies, those meditations that would help bring them back into vital contact with the world and events about which they are supposed to be bearing witness. Small wonder that their preaching does not help the people of God bridge the gap.

I have strongly emphasized this point. I do not think I have overstated its importance. I realize that the contemporary 'whipping-boy' for many who find fault with the church today is the dry, irrelevant, scholastic pastor. He is the one who is supposedly killing our churches. And perhaps he is. But I myself have not met very many of that kind of pastor. I have met men who are dry and dead in their preaching, but it was not usually because they were too much in touch with the world of the New Testament. On the contrary, they were often trying so hard to be 'relevant' and 'practical' that they had very little to say. They had become lecturers in the techniques and technology of faith. They were no longer, in any meaningful sense, 'witnesses of the resurrection' and 'ministers of the new covenant'.

Please do not mistake what I am saying as an appeal for some kind of elitist, esoteric, or impractical ministry of preaching. But if we can only have practical, relevant preaching at the expense of testifying to and proclaiming the powerful impact of the death and resurrection of Christ upon the lives of people today, then it is too high a price to pay. Such preaching will make us no different from the Pharisees. We may compass heaven and earth for one disciple, but we will make him twice over a child of hell.

Preaching that is distanced from the historic center and life-transforming power of the gospel quickly becomes simply another 'yoke' of moralism that neither our fathers, nor their fathers before them, were able to bear. I am convinced that this failure in much preaching today is responsible for much of the powerless formalism apparent in contemporary Christian 'piety' – where people know *what* to do, and sometimes even *how* to do it. But they cannot remember *why* they should, and thus they lack the power to change.

If you have read this chapter carefully and thoughtfully, I hope you will understand that here we are touching one of the major keys to revitalizing the preaching ministry of the church in our day. If you catch the vision for what I am saying, I think you will be pleased and excited by what this will mean for your own ministry of the Word in preaching. You must allow yourself the freedom in the pulpit to be gripped and taken up by the immediacy and urgency of the message you proclaim. This will come to expression in different ways in different messages but, in general, you will allow yourself to express more of the wonder and enthusiasm for what you are saying, much like a child might do in describing things or events that have absolutely captivated him. As I mentioned earlier, too many pastors come across in the pulpit as so jaded in their sensibilities that they can describe the heaven-rending, earth-shaking wonders of the Scriptures in the dullest and drabbest of monotones. I realize this is often not what they really think and feel, but they are so bound by routine that they can hardly break free.

I might also mention in passing that this goes for the way in which you read the Scriptures themselves aloud to your people during worship. The art of reading dramatically from the Scripture should be developed by anyone, but especially a pastor, for he is called upon week by week to read aloud from the Bible before the congregation. It is the best-written book of all time, and it deserves to be read much better than it often is. If you read it properly, you will immediately have your congregation taken up in what you will be expounding, and will be well on your way to success in achieving what we have been considering in this chapter.

Jay Adams has stressed the need to use strong, vivid, concrete, and varied language in preaching, and that recommendation is very much to the point here.[3] A good storyteller or reporter can give you the thrilling sense of 'being there' through the use of expressive language, and by marshalling details for description and the setting of tone. These skills are very useful in learning how to 'close the gap' for your people, and confronting them with the immediacy of the mighty saving acts of God. In the same way, what we have already said about preaching directly to your congregation in the second person is helpful in this connection as well.

God has done a mighty work of salvation in our world and in our history. The apostles proclaimed it at first in Acts, and you are called to stand with them in preaching it in the same way today. It is your great privilege to preach so as to help your people live today in the grip of those wonderful realities of yesterday, so that they too know what it means to enter into the new creation through faith in Jesus Christ.

Part 2

A Closer Look at the Sermons

10

Peter at Pentecost:
A New Kind of Preaching

Peter's sermon to the Jewish multitude during the Pentecost festival in Jerusalem is both chronologically and thematically primary in Luke's account of the apostolic preaching of those early years. Chronologically, it stands in the first position because the sermon itself was occasioned by the very giving of the Holy Spirit for which Jesus, in his parting words to the disciples at his ascension, commanded the apostles to wait in Jerusalem (Acts 1:4-8). Their mission as witnesses was not to begin until the Spirit was given in that historic 'baptism' prophesied by John the Baptist (v. 5). When the Spirit came upon them in power, then they would begin the spread of their witness to the ends of the earth (v. 8). Thus Peter's sermon, occasioned by and explaining the miraculous 'outpouring' of the Holy Spirit on the Church, is the first message conveying the unique apostolic witness to the resurrection of Christ.

Peter's Pentecost sermon is also thematically primary, because it defines the witness of the apostles in the clearest and most comprehensive way. All the subsequent sermons in Acts are thus bound up in Peter's first sermon. Though they differ in several ways, they all (implicitly or explicitly) express the same witness – centered in the resurrection of Christ and its significance in the redemptive plan of God – that Peter so eloquently and fully expounds in this inaugural sermon. Whether it is Peter, or Stephen, or Paul, all the preaching set before us in Acts is *resurrection preaching*, and should be understood against the benchmark of Peter's message on the Day of Pentecost.

Peter the Apostolic Spokesman
Luke tells us in Acts 2:14, 'Then Peter stood up with the Eleven, raised his voice and addressed the crowd.' Why Peter?

Anyone familiar with the Gospel accounts is already aware of the central importance of Peter. For better or worse, Peter is more often than not at center stage in Jesus' dealings with his disciples. Among the original disciples, whom we find waiting in Jerusalem at the opening of the Book of Acts, Peter is the spokesman. Even when Peter and John are together (Acts 3–4), it is Peter who preaches. Later we hear from Stephen (ch. 7), a deacon, and (briefly) from James (ch. 15), the leader of the Jerusalem church, but neither of these men play the strategic role Peter does.

The centrality of Peter, as leader of the other Jerusalem disciples and counterpart of Paul, 'the apostle to the Gentiles,' is to be understood in terms of Peter's role as *apostolic representative*. He does not speak in distinction from the other apostles, but on their behalf. So in recording his sermons, Luke is giving us a clear picture of what *all* the apostles, at various times and in various ways, would preach.

Behind this special emphasis on Peter and his preaching is the event recorded for us in Matthew 16:13-19:

> When Jesus came to the region of Caesarea Philippi, he asked his disciples, 'Who do people say the Son of Man is?' They replied, 'Some say John the Baptist; others say Elijah; and still others, Jeremiah or one of the prophets.' 'But what about you?' he asked. 'Who do you say I am?' Simon Peter answered, 'You are the Christ, the Son of the living God.' Jesus replied, 'Blessed are you, Simon son of Jonah, for this was not revealed to you by man, but by my Father in heaven. And I tell you that you are Peter, and on this rock I will build my church, and the gates of Hades will not overcome it. I will give you the keys of the kingdom of heaven; whatever you bind on earth will be bound in heaven, and whatever you loose on earth will be loosed in heaven.'

This passage has been much debated, especially in connection with the claims of the Church of Rome to establish its view of the primacy of Peter (and the Pope) upon the basis of this text, and it would take us beyond our present purposes to enter into that debate. Suffice it to say that Peter's confession is given in answer to Jesus' question to the apostles collectively: 'Who do you [plural] say that I am?' Thus Peter is answering *for* the Twelve, not in distinction from them. His confession – that Jesus is the Christ, the Son of the living God – is the confession of *all* the apostles. Therefore, when Jesus commends Peter and his confession, he is commending him as a *representative* of the Twelve. In that capacity he gives Peter the 'keys' of authority within the kingdom of heaven. This is further borne out in Matthew 18:18 and John 20:23, where the same authority of the 'keys' is given more explicitly to all the disciples in general. The 'primacy of Peter' is therefore, the primacy of the *apostolate* (cf. 1 Cor. 12:28). It is the primacy of the apostolic confession and their witness to Christ as the Son of God, and all that that confession entails for men and their personal relationships to Christ.

Coming back then to Peter's central role in the Book of Acts, we can say that, just as Peter's 'confession' expressed the confession of the apostolic band as a whole, so also his 'witness' in preaching conveys the substance of their witness to Christ wherever they carried it in the world. In that unique capacity, Peter stands to address the crowd in Jerusalem on the Day of Pentecost.

An Arresting Miracle

What occasioned the sermon? We have already noted Jesus' prediction (and John the Baptist's before him) of the coming gift of the Holy Spirit, soon to be received by the apostles in accordance with the Father's promise (Acts 1:4-5). That prophecy was fulfilled at Pentecost by an open display of miraculous 'signs and wonders' that arrested the attention of the crowd, and provided the direct impetus for Peter's sermon. According to Acts 2:1-4, 'all of the believers' (which included at least the apostles, and quite likely the 120 disciples mentioned in 1:15) were 'together in one place'. Suddenly a violent wind tore through the place where they were thus gathered, and dividing tongues of fire descended from heaven 'resting on each of them'. At the same time the believers were 'filled with the Holy Spirit, and began to speak in other tongues, as the Spirit enabled them' (v. 4).

It is quite probable that this group of believers was in the Temple precincts somewhere, as it was their custom to gather there regularly (cf. Luke 24:53). In that case the filling of 'the house' with audible winds and visible flames of fire, would have been a filling of the Temple itself (cf. Isa. 6:4). Quite a dramatic and unsettling experience for those multitudes who packed the Temple for worship on such an important religious festival day! No wonder the crowd took notice, and in their bewilderment gathered around this small band of believers (v. 6). There they heard even more amazing things – each *in his own language* heard these people 'declaring the wonders of God' to them (vv. 7, 11). Because of this miraculous display of the power of God in bestowing his Spirit upon his people, this vast multitude of visitors in Jerusalem was ready to listen.

Who made up this ready audience? Luke takes care here, as elsewhere in Acts, to tell us who was present. We find in verses 9-11 that the congregation was made up of Jews and converts to Judaism who were visiting Jerusalem from all over the Roman world. Thirteen different groups are mentioned by Luke. These people were in Jerusalem for the feast of Pentecost. This may indicate a certain level of devotion to the Law of Moses, which required Jewish males to appear in the Temple for the three major annual feasts (cf. Deut. 16:16). In view of the distance traveled by some of these visitors, it is quite possible that they had also been in Jerusalem for the Passover, seven weeks before, and had continued in town awaiting the Pentecost celebration. If so, they were in town at the time of Jesus' crucifixion. As we will see below, this becomes relevant to Peter's sermon in a specific way.

Luke does not tell us how much time elapsed during which the disciples in general were declaring the 'mighty acts of God' (NIV, 'wonders of God'), and the crowd was taking in the messages in their own languages. We do know that it formed the immediate background of Peter's sermon, and served as good preparation for it.

An Authoritative Address

'Then Peter stood up with the Eleven, raised his voice and addressed the crowd: "Fellow Jews and all of you who live in Jerusalem"' (v. 14). Notice the formality of Peter's introduction to his sermon. He and the other apostles (note Peter's place as representative spokesman for all the apostles) stood up in some prominent place so as to attract the attention of the large crowd that had gathered. He then raised his voice in order to be heard over the din of the crowd, and spoke out in a clear, loud fashion. The Greek word used here by Luke to describe Peter's 'speaking out' is a most interesting term (*apophtheggomai*) used only rarely in the New Testament (cf. v. 4). It means 'to speak out clearly and loudly,'[1] and carries the connotation (from classical Greek, where it is used to describe the utterance of 'oracles' and 'seers' under divine influence) of speaking with supernatural inspiration and authority. In the Septuagint translation of the Old Testament it is often used to describe prophesying (cf. Deut. 32:2; 1 Chron. 25:1; Ezek. 13:9; Zech. 10:2). Thus Luke uses a term loaded with suggestions of divine influence and revelation in describing both the declarations in other languages by the disciples generally (v. 4) and Peter's sermon itself, which is designed to give an explanation to the crowd of what they have been seeing and hearing.

Fearful No More

As we noted earlier in our study, apostolic preaching is noted for its boldness.[2] Certainly the example of Peter here on the Day of Pentecost is one of the most dramatic illustrations of the transformation which took place in the lives and perspectives of the apostles as a result of the resurrection and ascension of the Lord.

A scant two months earlier Peter had stood shivering in the early morning darkness in the high priest's courtyard not far from where he stood now to deliver his sermon. A servant girl approached him and said, 'You also were with Jesus of Galilee' (Matt. 26:69). Peter denied it. 'I don't know what you're talking about,' he said. Again he was identified as one who had been with Jesus of Nazareth; again by a girl. He denied a second time, with an oath. Then his accent gave him away. They knew he had been with Jesus. But a third time he swore his denial. Immediately a rooster crowed and Peter remembered both the words of Jesus – 'Before the rooster crows, you will disown me three times' – and his own – 'Even if all fall away on account of you, I never will.... Even if I have to die with you, I will never disown you' (Matt. 26:33, 35). And he went outside and wept bitterly.

On that day fear overcame Peter. He was not willing to lose his life for Jesus' sake (Matt. 10:39; 16:25). He denied the truth he had been called to bear witness to, because he was afraid of the consequences. But Christ had forgiven him and restored him to his apostolic calling (John 21:4-19). Now he faces a situation in many ways even more threatening than on the day he denied the Lord. But Peter is a new man. Now he will lift up his voice as an oracle of the risen Christ. Jesus himself, through the agency of the Holy Spirit, will speak out of the mouth of Peter to the crowd that crucified him. The man who was formerly self-sufficient, and therefore vacillating, has become 'the Rock,' because he no longer trusts in himself, but in the Christ whom he has been called to proclaim. As a sinner who has come to see the fearful depths of his sin, and has yet found pardon, and who lives by faith in the Savior, Jesus Christ, he now addresses his fellow Jews, calling them from their sins to salvation through the blood of the One whom they crucified.

The Structure of the Sermon

Let us now return to Peter's sermon, and take an overview of the whole so as to discover how it is structured, and how it achieves its purpose. As we scan the verses beginning with verse 14, we note several things as to the form of the sermon. First, as we mentioned, Peter's address to the crowd is quite formal, 'Fellow Jews and all of you who live in Jerusalem,...' (v. 14). This opening conforms to the kind of model introduction we might find in a source like Lysias.[3] Paul used a similarly formal opening in his address to the Areopagus (cf. 17:22). This is a very important occasion and calls forth an address appropriate to the circumstances. Peter addresses the crowd with respect, for he expects them to respond to his words with the same respect, and more.

Secondly, Peter calls upon them to give careful attention to what he is about to say. The word used in verse 14, translated 'listen carefully,'[4] occurs only here in the New Testament, and literally means to 'get this in your ears.' Often God addresses men with the command, 'Hear!' (e.g., Deut. 6:4; etc.). When God speaks – directly or through his appointed messengers – it will not do for hearers to give casual or indifferent attention to what he has to say. Their lives depend upon their hearing.

Thirdly, Peter begins by offering the audience an explanation, 'Let me explain this to you ...' (v. 14). The crowd had been 'utterly amazed' by the miraculous signs and wonders they had seen (v. 7), and were 'amazed and perplexed' by the declarations they had heard in their own languages concerning the wonders of God's dealings with men (vv. 11 f.). They had even asked, 'What does this mean?' (v. 12). From a formal standpoint that question shapes the first portion of Peter's sermon, which is an elaborate answer to it. It stands parallel to a second question from the crowd – 'Brothers, what should we do?' (v. 37) – which Peter answers in the second part of his sermon. The message as a whole then is an extended answer to the two questions put by the crowd in response to the amazing events they had witnessed with their own eyes.

Fourthly, Peter challenges the audience to listen to his explanation of the events they have witnessed by, at the very outset, rejecting out of hand the proposed explanation from some vocal members of the assembly. Some had cried out sarcastically, 'They have had too much wine' (v. 13). Peter replies, 'These men are not drunk, as you suppose.

It's only nine in the morning!' Peter openly contradicts the opinion of some in his audience. 'You've got it all wrong,' he says, 'and obviously so. Let me tell you what is really going on here.' This may not be the best way to win friends and influence people, but it is a good way to insure the attention of the audience, at least for a time. Your explanation has to be good, however. And Peter's is very good.

The Purpose of Peter's Sermon

It's time for us to try to grasp the *overall purpose* of Peter's sermon. I would summarize the purpose of the sermon as follows: *Peter's purpose is to persuade the Jewish crowd that the man, Jesus of Nazareth, is the divine Messiah promised in the Scriptures, and so to convince them that his coming heralds an imminent judgment upon them, requiring that they repent and believe on him.*

Central to Peter's effective realization of this purpose is his explanation of the significance of the miraculous 'signs and wonders' already seen and heard (but so far misunderstood) by the crowd. The primary text for the sermon is Joel 2:28-32, which Peter quotes at the outset of the message, because this passage gives the proper, scriptural explanation of the significance of what the people have just seen and heard.

By convincing the crowd of the fact that the miracles of that day are the exact fulfillment of the prophecy of Joel, Peter leaves himself in a position to move backward to sketch the connection between Pentecost and the death, resurrection, and ascension of Jesus. By so doing he will fulfill the first part of his purpose, viz. to persuade the crowd that the man Jesus of Nazareth is the divine Messiah promised in the Scriptures. Then, because the second part of his purpose is bound up implicitly in the meaning and purpose of Joel's prophecy, Peter can go on to the second part of his purpose, viz. to convince them that Jesus' coming heralds an imminent judgment upon them, so that they will be led to repent and believe in him. This Peter accomplishes very quickly by declaring that God has made Jesus both Lord and Christ by raising him from the dead (v. 36). This announcement in turn precipitates the crisis of realization that forces from the crowd the urgent question, 'What shall we do?' Peter closes his sermon with an invitation and a promise which answers that desperate question, and brings over 3,000 to faith in Jesus on that very day!

Judgment is Coming!

Let's go through the sermon now, in light of this overview, and pick up some of the details. Peter introduces, in verse 16, the passage that will be the heart of his explanation of the Pentecostal miracles: 'This is what was spoken by the prophet Joel....' Peter argues that what the crowd has observed – the rushing wind and spreading airborne flames – was described and explained by Joel in his ancient prophecy. In so doing, Peter announces the historic fulfillment of Joel's prediction.

In using Joel, Peter is adopting the purpose of Joel's prophecy as his own. Thus the urgency created by Joel's announcement is intensified in Peter's declaration that the ancient prophecy has at last found its fulfillment in the events of the Day of Pentecost. In the context of the book of Joel, this prophecy is an announcement of the coming of 'the great and dreadful day of the Lord' (Joel 2:31b). This day will be one of earth-shattering, cataclysmic judgment. Joel uses apocalyptic language in verses 30-31: 'I will show wonders in the heavens and on the earth, blood and fire and billows of smoke. The sun will be turned to darkness and the moon to blood.' To a Jewish audience, with a background in the Old Testament Scriptures and the intertestamental apocalyptic literature, this would be familiar terminology. It is used here and elsewhere in Scripture to describe the shaking and rending of the present world order in judgment.[5]

This well-known formula of judgment is used (with variations) to describe the overthrow of that which seemingly cannot be shaken in preparation for the emergence of a new post-judgment order. Thus it is used in the case of the destruction of Babylon (Isa. 13:10), Edom (Isa. 34:3-4), and Jerusalem (Jer. 4:23-26). If you look at each of these passages, and others,[6] you will find the language of shaking, the total destruction of crops, trees, animals, commerce, etc., and heavenly portents (a 'darkened' sun, 'bloody' moon, 'falling stars,' etc.) in various combinations. In these passages the vivid and terrifying figures of speech give expression to God's overwhelming judgment upon sinful man. The Lord shakes and purges his creation, sweeping away his enemies, to make room again for his people.

It is such a time of judgment – 'the great and dreadful day of the Lord' – which Joel announced in the passage cited by Peter. Joel's purpose was to warn God's people of the harbingers of that coming judgment, including the outpouring of the Spirit (which is of special concern to Peter), with its accompanying 'signs and wonders', so that the people will heed the prophet's call to repentance – 'and everyone who calls on the name of the LORD will be saved' (Joel 2:32a) – and return to the Lord for salvation.

When Peter calls this ancient prophecy of judgment to the minds of his hearers – minds already amazed and perplexed by the miraculous signs and wonders they have see and heard – they have no trouble getting Peter's point when he says 'this is THAT.' They sense and understand that Peter is announcing an impending cataclysmic judgment. In using the more specific phrase 'last days' (in place of Joel's 'afterwards') to introduce his citation, they understand that Peter is announcing an eschatological judgment. The phrase 'last days,' as used in the Scriptures, refers to the last days of the old covenant economy, or conversely, the time of the beginning of the messianic age of restoration and salvation (cf. Heb. 1:1).[7]

I realize that I have made a lot of assumptions about the interpretation of prophecy in what I have said in the previous paragraphs. I also understand that there is a great deal of heated controversy over these very questions. And I also recognize, as I hope you do, that an extended discussion of the eschatological questions involved in this sermon would take us away from our stated purpose of dealing with Peter's preaching methods. I have only raised these issues in order to help you understand why, in my view, Peter's announcement of the fulfillment of Joel's prophecy precipitated such an *immediate crisis* in the thinking of the multitude, and drove them with such *urgency* to ask Peter for help.

I know that a large segment of evangelical preachers assume that the language of Joel quoted in Acts 2:19-20 must refer to the 'Second Coming' of Christ at the end of history. They would also identify the phrase 'day of the Lord' as a technical term for the Second Coming, as many respected commentators do. Finally, most of them would probably not apply the terminology of 'the last days' to the period leading up to the destruction of Jerusalem and the nation of Israel by the Romans in AD 70. I cannot enter into the debate on that question, but shall simply reply briefly that the apocalyptic judgment formula of Joel 2:30-31 is frequently used in a figurative sense in the Old Testament (check the citations listed above), and is, I believe, used in that way by Peter in Acts 2:19-20. The 'day of the Lord,' as mentioned in the Scriptures, cannot, in my judgment, be simply identified with the Second Coming, but refers more broadly to an eschatological complex of events that includes the destruction of Jerusalem in AD 70, intervening historic judgments, and the final consummate judgment at the end of human history. The 'last days' must be understood in terms of biblical history and the redemptive plan of God, not our modern evangelical sense of chronology (i.e., every generation tends to think it is the 'last'). If so understood, I believe it points to the end of the old covenant economy and its passing away, as mentioned above. Finally, and most importantly for the purposes of my exposition here, I must say that if Joel was not looking to events preceding the destruction of Jerusalem in AD 70, and Peter did not know it, then Peter was mistaken, or deliberately ambiguous, when he applied Joel's words to the events of the Day of Pentecost, and allowed his hearers to conclude that judgment was upon them, and encouraged them to believe that they needed to repent immediately, or else risk the impending historical judgment.

I ask you now to hold these questions in abeyance, and bear with me a little longer as I finish my comments on Peter's method of communicating urgency to his audience. To recap: Peter addresses his audience, already deeply anxious over the signs and wonders they have seen, by telling them that Joel was speaking of these events when he announced the coming of an outpouring of the Spirit of God upon all kinds of people – young and old, men and women (Acts 2:17) – immediately preceding a coming day of the Lord's judgment.

Jesus of Nazareth is the Messiah

Having established this point, Peter begins to develop the portion of his argument designed to convince his hearers that Jesus of Nazareth is the Messiah promised in the Scriptures. Again Peter addresses the crowd formally, 'Men of Israel, listen to this...' (v. 22). He abruptly introduces Jesus as 'a man' well known to them (v. 22b),[8] and draws their attention to the 'miracles, wonders, and signs which God did' in order to 'accredit' Jesus as (at least) a prophet. Here Peter is treading fairly safe ground. From the early days of Jesus' public ministry it was freely admitted by many, including Nicodemus the Pharisee, that Jesus 'was a teacher who has come from God' (John 3:2). As a nation taught by long tradition to acknowledge the authority of the prophetic office and its attesting 'signs', the Jews would generally admit that Jesus shared that prophetic authority attested by such miraculous signs. Nicodemus acknowledged, 'No one could perform the miraculous signs you are doing if God were not with him.' Thus when Peter calls upon his hearers to acknowledge the public authority of Jesus,[9] because they themselves can bear witness to the God-given signs that accompanied Jesus' public ministry, he is standing on solid argumentative ground. So far so good.

Then comes 'the first blast of the trumpet' against Israel's heinous sin: 'This man was turned over [to you] by God's set purpose and foreknowledge; and you, with the help of wicked men, put him to death by nailing him to the cross' (v. 23). Peter accuses his audience of murdering God's prophet! Like their fathers before them who rejected the prophets (cf. Matt. 23:29-39; etc.), this generation of Jews, represented by the crowd standing before Peter, had rejected Jesus. Though they knew full well that this man was a messenger of God, they murdered him by crucifixion. Peter's accusation is penetrating: Though the actual deed was done by the 'lawless' Romans, it was the Jews, God's own people, who through their leaders put Pilate up to the bloody deed!

This is a bold and startling confrontation. Why did it not inflame the crowd on the spot (as later happened to Stephen when he made a similar blunt accusation against the Sanhedrin)? We have already considered the difference in the heart disposition of the two groups.[10] Is there a more proximate explanation in light of Peter's presentation of his argument? I think so. Two things should be kept in mind.

The first is the fact that the audience is already 'on the ropes', in a sense, because of the effect upon them of the miraculous display they had witnessed, intensified by Peter's forceful claim that judgment was at hand. They are a frightened group, and fright often takes the fight out of people (at least temporarily).

Secondly, Peter brings his charge against their sinful complicity in the death of Jesus in two strategic steps. At first he accuses them of murdering a man whom they themselves acknowledged to be a prophet. This point is hardly debatable. They might, upon further reflection, have found ways to escape the force of the accusation – excusing themselves, or shifting the blame to others (which Peter anticipates in verse 23). But they could not deny that they had been witnesses of the attesting signs, had drawn the conclusion that Jesus was a prophet, and yet they had consented to his death.

They Killed the Lord's Anointed

Before they have an opportunity to organize their defense, Peter moves on to the second stage of his indictment. By drawing their attention to the historical reality and redemptive significance of Jesus' resurrection, Peter demonstrates that, in fact, these Jews are guilty of nothing less than murdering the Lord's 'Anointed' (v. 36). By proceeding in this fashion, Peter is able to keep his audience with him right up to the end, even though he has some strongly confrontational, potentially inflammatory things to say to them along the way.

Peter's accusation against the Jews emphasizes both God's sovereignty and man's responsibility. Perhaps no single text in all of Scripture brings these two supposedly disparate theological elements together so naturally as this one: 'This man was handed over to you by God's set purpose and foreknowledge; and you, with the help of wicked men, put him to death by nailing him to the cross (v. 23).

Theologians often force God's people to choose one side or the other – emphasizing the sovereignty of God to the exclusion of human responsibility, or (perhaps more often) laying such stress on human 'free will' as to nullify the power of God. Peter says 'both ... and.' He has already stated that the events of that very day are the result of divine sovereignty acting in the fulfillment of ancient promises. No less so is the 'delivering up' of the Messiah to death an act of the divine will in wisdom and mercy (cf. 4:28; John 3:16; Isa. 53:10). The death and resurrection of Christ, as much as the outpouring of the Holy Spirit, are fulfillments of the Scriptures by the power of God. This is a central element of the case Peter is building. Thus in speaking of the crucifixion, Peter boldly states, 'this man was handed over ... by God's set purpose.'

Peter does not think it necessary (as some evangelical pastors might) to 'protect' God from any involvement in this hideous event, as if his holy reputation could thereby be sullied. For Peter, as for Paul and the other apostles, God is he 'who works out everything in conformity with the purpose of his will' (Eph. 1:11), without whose will 'not even a sparrow can fall to the ground' (Matt. 10:29). How much less could the Lord of glory be handed over to death apart from his predetermined purpose. Nevertheless, God cannot sin (1 John 1:5), neither is he the author of sin in humans (James 1:13). Peter is not willing to preserve the holiness of the divine character at the expense of making a clear declaration of the sovereign will of God at work in the death of Christ. Preachers today should take this leaf from Peter's book.

On the other hand, Peter also knows that God's sovereignty in no way nullifies, or even compromises, human responsibility. It rather establishes it. The crucifixion of Jesus was a criminal wickedness, and Peter pronounces the Jews guilty for it. They 'disowned him before Pilate' (to borrow Peter's later phrase from 3:13b), and thus conspired in Jesus' death. The force of Peter's indictment is rooted in the clarity and truthfulness of his public declaration that the Jews had acted culpably. They are fully responsible for their choices and actions, and any attempt to escape responsibility through an appeal to the sovereignty of God is the most vain and blasphemous kind of blame-shifting. Peter will have none of it.

It is worth noting also the blanket form of this indictment. It may be that some who were present in the crowd to which Peter was speaking were personally present in the mob that cried out for Jesus' blood only a few short weeks before. Others no doubt were newly arrived in the city. But the crowd was primarily Jewish, and thus Peter addresses them in terms of their covenantal and national solidarity. In this sermon God is still dealing with the covenant people of Israel, and this crowd stands as a representative of the whole nation. As such Peter indicts them, and later calls them to repentance. The fact that some of the people present may not have been personally involved in the events surrounding Jesus' crucifixion does not really make any difference. As Jews they stand condemned, and as Jews they need to repent.

Jesus is Alive!

Then Peter makes a most startling announcement, 'But God raised him from the dead' (v. 24). Jesus is ALIVE! This is the first statement in the sermon concerning the resurrection, and coming as it does on the heels of this strong accusation of the Jews' willful attempt to get rid of Jesus the prophet once and for all – it packs quite a punch!

No doubt many of the Jews in Jerusalem had heard rumors of Jesus' resurrection. But what is unique about Peter's announcement is the fact that it comes on the authority of eyewitness testimony (v.32b), and it is confirmed by the Scriptures (vv. 25-28, 34-35). This is the heart of the apostolic witness.

Peter confirms the holiness of Jesus by pointing out not only that God raised him from the dead, but further that 'it was impossible for death to keep its hold on him' (v. 24). Death, as the 'wages of sin', cannot keep hold on the 'Holy One of God' – the name by which Jesus will be identified in the quotation from David which Peter introduces next. Those who saw Jesus die a criminal's death on the cross may still be harboring the opinion that he somehow deserved that death. They might not understand yet that he died as *sin-bearer* – the innocent in the place of the guilty (Isa. 53:6, 12; 2 Cor. 5:21). Peter wants to straighten out that mistaken impression right away. He is demonstrating that Jesus is the uniquely 'Holy One,' the Lord's Messiah. He is declaring the resurrection of Jesus as his vindication by God (cf. 1 Tim. 3:16), and even Peter's passing turns of phrase, and his choice of vocabulary, are designed to accomplish that purpose.

Peter again turns to the Scriptures for confirmation and explanation, and again (as with the prophecy of Joel) we see him making use of the passages cited in a manner consistent with their original purpose. He first calls forth the testimony of David in Psalm 16:8-11. David was a prophet as well as a king (Acts 2:30), and in both those capacities he spoke in Psalm 16. As the Lord's anointed king, David was confident of God's daily presence with him. Indeed that constituted the foundation of his reign and his promised dynasty (v. 25; cf. 2 Sam. 7:25-29). As a prophet David knew that God would fulfill his promises to him of an eternal kingdom by raising his descendant, the Messiah, from the dead: 'You will not abandon me to the grave, nor will you let your Holy One see decay. You have made known to me the paths of life; you will fill me with joy in your presence' (vv. 27-28).

Peter argues that David could not have been speaking about himself personally when he spoke of this deliverance from death, for David knew he would die, and so he did. His tomb, said Peter, was there in Jerusalem for all to see that day (v. 29). Since David was a prophet, 'seeing what was ahead,' it was his purpose, in writing these verses, to speak of another – his descendant, 'the Christ' (Heb., 'Messiah') – whom God did not abandon to the grave, nor allow to decay (v. 31).

This is a richly nuanced argument, and much could be said in its exposition, but we are interested to note how Peter ties these things together. Just as Joel was looking forward to the miraculous events of the Day of Pentecost, so David was looking forward to the day of Jesus' resurrection. Both these words from the prophets confirm and explain the events which they anticipate. The crowd itself had been witness to the events of that day – they could testify for themselves.

The apostles (represented by Peter) had seen the resurrected Christ, and they bear witness to that fact through Peter's words (v. 32b).

The Exalted Christ Gives the Spirit to the Church

Peter takes his argument one step further in order to cement the testimony of the apostles and the testimony of the crowd together. That will close the 'circle of proof', and provide the foundation for his second powerful indictment of their sin. If convincing under the heart-opening power of the Holy Spirit it will drive this crowd to repentance and faith at the feet of the One whom they have pierced. In verses 33-35, Peter connects Pentecost with the resurrection through the exaltation of Christ and, by means of another confirming word from Scripture (Ps. 110:1), closes the net around this school of human fish which he means to catch for the Lord (cf. Luke 5:10). The steps in the argument are simple and clear,

> Exalted to the right hand of God, he has received from the Father the promised Holy Spirit and has poured out what you now see and hear. For David did not ascend to heaven, and yet he said, 'The Lord said to my Lord: "Sit at my right hand until I make your enemies a footstool for your feet."'

The same Lord who had promised to Joel that there would be an outpouring of the Holy Spirit upon all kinds of people in the last days (v. 17), promised David's 'Son' and 'Lord' (cf. Matt. 22:41-46) – the divine-human Messiah – to make him the agent of that outpouring, and to make the Spirit the agent of Messiah's reign. Therefore Jesus, in ascending to the place of honor and dominion beside his heavenly Father, received the Spirit as promised, and poured him forth upon humans (v. 33). By so saying, Peter demonstrates to the crowd that the events to which they themselves can bear witness ('what they now see and hear') is both a *proof* of the enthronement of the exalted Messiah in glory, and the *initial manifestation* of his reign upon the earth. Such a reign, once begun, will not cease until Jesus the Messiah, in the power of his Father, has made his enemies a footstool for his feet (v. 35; cf. 1 Cor. 15:24; Eph. 1:20 ff.).

That Jesus truly is the Christ is thus confirmed in Peter's sermon by the coalescence of three strands of witness – the testimony of the Scriptures, the testimony of the apostolic eyewitnesses, and the testimony of the crowd itself! By this masterfully persuasive argument,

Peter has charmed the fish into stillness as he cast his net about them, and with these words – 'Therefore let all Israel be assured of this: God has made this Jesus, whom you crucified, both Lord and Christ' (v. 36) – he draws it shut.

They are more than prophet-killers, they now see themselves as they are in truth – murderers of their Messiah! The amazement and perplexity caused by the day's events, which became fear of judgment under the influence of Joel's prophecy, have now become abject terror as they realize both what they have done, and the fact that the Lord whom they have offended is alive in glory and 'at the door' in judgment!

Can you see the way in which Peter has so wonderfully accomplished his purpose in this sermon? The crowd standing before Peter *knows* that Jesus is the Messiah promised by the Scriptures, and they are *convinced* that his coming has brought with it the prospect of immediate judgment at his hands. Is it any wonder that they were pierced through to the hearts, and their only response was to cry out, 'Brothers, what shall we do?'

There is Hope for Those Who Repent

Peter has more to say. It is truly 'good news'. 'Repent and be baptized, every one of you, in the name of Jesus Christ for the forgiveness of your sins. And you will receive the gift of the Holy Spirit. The promise is for you and your children and for all who are far off – for all whom the Lord our God will call' (vv. 38-39). The burden of this invitation, and the 'many other words' which followed (v. 40) was that these people would 'save themselves' from this corrupt generation, and from the judgment that would soon fall upon it. According to the words of Jesus himself:

> And so upon you will come all the righteous blood that has been shed on earth, from the blood of righteous Abel to the blood of Zechariah son of Berekiah, whom you murdered between the temple and the altar. I tell you the truth, all this will come upon this generation (Matt. 23:35-36; cf. Luke 23:28-31).

Jesus Christ, the King whom they have rejected, now extends through Peter an invitation and a welcome to the very people who had cried out for his blood. Repentance is absolutely necessary if they are to escape the coming judgment. There must be a turning away from proud self-sufficiency and rebellion against God, even on the part of his own covenant people. But repentance is also *possible*, for God himself is extending this gospel call – a summons to the Jews and their children, and even to those who are far off. The death of their Messiah, which they had meant for evil, God meant for good, for through his death, a fountain of cleansing and forgiveness was opened for sinners.[11] 'God was reconciling the world to himself in Christ, not counting men's sins against them' (2 Cor. 5:19). To Peter and the other apostles, God had committed the message and ministry of reconciliation.

Christ had given Peter and the Twelve the commission to preach repentance and the forgiveness of sins in his Name to the nations, beginning in Jerusalem (Luke 24:47), and in exact fulfillment of that commission Peter now welcomes these first converts to Christ. The promise of the Holy Spirit, who came that day with such unsettling displays of power and glory, is promised to them (v. 38) as the 'down-payment' of the inheritance which is theirs in union and communion with Christ (cf. Eph. 1:14).

A Great Catch of (Human) Fish

As Jesus had indicated by the miraculous catch of fish he granted Peter on the Sea of Galilee just before calling him to fish for men (Luke 5:1-11), and as he had confirmed again after his resurrection by a similar catch when he restored the apostle who had denied him three times (John 21:4-19), so now Jesus blesses Peter's first sermon with a net-tearing catch – 'Those who accepted his message were baptized, and about three thousand were added to their number that day' (v. 41).

These converts continued to imbibe the apostles' teaching daily in the Temple courts (v. 46) as they grew in grace and in the knowledge of Christ (2 Pet. 3:18). They were bound together in a new fellowship, devoting themselves to one another, even to the sharing of their goods to alleviate the needs of the poor brethren (vv. 44-45). 'They broke bread in their homes and ate together with glad and sincere hearts, praising God and enjoying the favor of all the people' (vv. 46-47). And the Lord continually blessed the apostolic preaching with fruitful results as new converts were added daily to the number of those who believed that Jesus of Nazareth was the Christ (v. 48). Thus the church of the new covenant was established and began to grow.

Some Lessons for Your Preaching

I trust that our analysis of this sermon has already suggested many ways in which you can personally refine your preaching practices. To take the time and space to draw out the details of such applications would be prohibitive, and perhaps unnecessary. Yet I do want to conclude this chapter with a few summary observations.

First of all, notice that most of the sermons in Acts are 'occasional' – they are instigated by a particular situation or event (like the miraculous outpouring of the Holy Spirit in Acts 2 or the healing of the crippled beggar in Acts 3). But the essence of preaching is the exposition and application of the Word of God, therefore, though Peter began his sermon with reference to the events that were taking place on the Day of Pentecost, and with the initial reactions of the crowd to them, he quickly moved their attention to the Scriptures. He set before his hearers the teachings of Scripture as they explained what was going on in the presence of the crowd, and called them to action (repentance and faith) in light of what the Word of God threatened. He was not content to simply discuss 'current events'. He was to proclaim the resurrection of Christ in its scriptural framework of meaning.

Your regular preaching is less event oriented. You preach because it is Sunday morning and that is the time to preach. Your people come to worship with the expectation that they will hear and benefit from a sermon. It is not always easy for you to move your congregation into a challenging study and application of a biblical text. Too many preachers, in the introduction to their messages, lead their people *away* from the text of Scripture into the realms of world affairs, pop-psychology, sociological trends, political theory, etc., and some never bring the congregation *back* to the Word! You must resist the temptation to believe that the Bible is not interesting or relevant enough to inform and challenge your people. Don't go off in search of novelties that will tickle their ears (2 Tim. 4:3). Rather, week by week dig deeply into the mine of Scripture, and from its treasures correct, rebuke and encourage your people with great patience and careful instruction (2 Tim. 4:2).

Secondly, Peter uses all of the passages in his sermon in a way consistent with the purposes for which they were given. He is never guilty of using a passage out of context, or as a pretext for getting to the point he wants to make. Too often pastors are not so conscientious.

They may read from the Bible to introduce their sermon (some don't even do that) and then launch off into a discourse which has little or nothing to do with the passage read – it certainly could not be called an *exposition* of a portion of the Word of God. Even if all that is said is theologically orthodox, the pastor is still not preaching *biblically*.[12]

Much has been written about the blessings – indeed the necessity – of 'expository' preaching.[13] I will not reproduce those discussions here, except to note two important benefits of such an approach to preaching. First, it keeps the preacher honest. He must wrestle each week with the meaning of the text of Scripture. He cannot simply rely upon his memory (or review) of the creed, or of the loci of systematic theology from his seminary days. He must grapple with the words and sentences given by the Holy Spirit for the building up of the Church. He must teach his people through his sermons how they must (and can) read, interpret, and apply the message of particular portions of God's Word for themselves.

In addition, consistent biblical exposition requires the pastor to bring a 'balanced diet' of spiritual food to his congregation. Every preacher has his favorite topics for preaching. Sometimes we have a rather limited view of what our congregations need to hear. Consequently, the scope of our preaching can become dangerously narrow. For example, some evangelical churches are heavily committed to evangelistic preaching (in the narrow sense[14]) on Sunday mornings or to the subject of Bible prophecy on Sunday evening. Consistent preaching through books (or large sections) of the Bible will help correct this imbalance. When bound to the exposition of the text of Scripture, the pastor must preach on easy doctrines and difficult ones, familiar as well as unfamiliar subjects, commonly held and more controversial teachings. He cannot 'play it safe' and stick to the well-worn paths of his own favorite subjects. As a preacher works through the books of the Bible, he must take what comes and give it all to his people. Thus they will be well fed with a broad range of biblical instruction.[15]

I do not believe this means that every sermon must be 'textual' rather than 'topical' in form (as some champions of expository preaching claim). Certainly most of the sermons we are studying in Acts are 'topical' (occasional). But what Peter and the other apostolic preachers show us by their preaching is that, even when you are preaching 'topically,' you have an obligation to use the biblical passages you select for the sermon in a manner consistent with the purpose for which they were given by the Holy Spirit. We may not simply go off in search of 'proof texts' to support the thesis of our sermon. This requirement makes 'topical' preaching (when done properly) even more difficult in some ways than 'textual' preaching, contrary to what we might think.

Jay Adams has written:

> Preachers today have no authority for preaching their own notions and opinions; they must 'preach the Word' – the apostolic Word recorded in the Scriptures. Whenever preachers depart from the purpose and the intent of a biblical portion, to that extent they lose their authority to preach.[16]

He goes on to discuss in depth a purpose-oriented approach to preaching that is very helpful in our day. 'It is only when a preacher knows he is saying what the Holy Spirit said, for the purpose of the Holy Spirit in saying it, that he speaks with power and with authority.'[17]

A third observation based on Peter's preaching at Pentecost: though the circumstances of Peter's Pentecost sermon are in many ways most unusual, the audience itself was similar to our congregations in weekly assembly in at least one respect. They did not begin listening to the sermon with a particular sense of 'need'. To be sure, the miraculous outpouring of the Spirit stirred them up with questions right away, but they did not approach Peter with a preconceived notion of what they needed or wanted from his sermon.

Our congregations often come to church with a general desire to hear the Word, but often without any particular idea of what they want to get out of the sermon. We may think at times that this problem makes our preaching task more difficult. We might imagine it easier to be preaching to people who are 'hurting' – people who know that they are needy, people who have already been 'softened-up' by circumstances, or otherwise prepared for the gospel – than to those who seem content and satisfied. God will always be providentially preparing some people *for* sermons, but more often he will prepare them *by* sermons.

We preachers need to realize – and be encouraged by the realization – that the preaching of the Word itself *creates* the need which it is designed to *meet*. As a matter of fact, only the Word of God adequately defines a man's problem, and only as it convicts him of his desperate condition before God will that man see the biblical 'good news' as the true solution to his problem.

Much contemporary preaching goes awry because the preacher allows people to make their own diagnoses of their problems, and then he tries to find a way to offer the gospel so that it will appear to be the solution to the person's perceived problem. This is what is wrong with much of the preaching that tries to meet people's needs. Before long such preaching deteriorates into the 'name-it-and-claim-it-faith' heresy.

Christ is the Great Physician of souls and, as such, only he is competent to judge each person's problem, to define it for him forcefully and clearly through the preaching of the Word, and then to offer the only solution for it. The Holy Spirit must convict people of sin, righteousness, and judgment (John 16:8) through our sermons, just as he did through Peter's, before they will turn from their sins and make an authentic commitment to Christ. The sooner we preachers who are so often tyrannized by the demand that we be 'practical' and 'relevant' or enslaved to the requirement that we 'meet people's needs' learn this, the happier and more effective we will be as ministers of Christ.

Whatever the crowd on the Day of Pentecost thought it needed, it was *not* the forgiveness of sins through the blood of Christ. Before they would ever accept Peter's message, he had to teach them, and convict them, that they had no need like their need for forgiveness, and that Jesus alone is the one who can give it.

Fourthly, notice how often Peter used an appeal to the audience itself to confirm what he was saying. They themselves knew of the attesting signs of Jesus' authority (v. 22). They knew of David's tomb (v. 29). They themselves could attest to the miraculous signs of the Spirit's outpouring (v. 33). Over and over Peter calls upon his audience for assent to what he is saying. This is an effective persuasive tool, and you would do well to learn to incorporate it in your preaching practice where appropriate. You can appeal to things which are (more or less) common knowledge – shared personal experiences, particular events in congregational life, etc. – to capture (and recapture) your audience's attention (they tend to 'perk up' when they hear a reference to something they recognize), to lay a foundation stone in a line of argument you are developing, or to evoke a particular response to the teaching of God's Word.

Recently when preaching about the danger of a merely superficial conformity to God's will in obedience, rather than an obedience driven by the gratitude and love of an eager heart, I said to the congregation, 'You parents know what I'm talking about, don't you? You can tell the difference in your children between grudging obedience and cheerful service, can't you?' I went on briefly to sketch the 'looks', the body language, etc. that we have all witnessed in our children as they have responded to our commands. There were nods of recognition all over the congregation. I had engaged them afresh through an appeal to our common knowledge and experience. Then I was able to ask the pertinent question: 'What does our heavenly Father see in you when you respond to his commands – a willing heart or mere outward conformity?'

Another time, in addressing a more skeptical crowd on a point of biblical ethics, I used as part of my argument an appeal to their own common sense of justice and fair play, and challenged them to give an account for such a sense if (as many of them believed) there was no God – or if there were, that he has no authoritative place in ethical decision-making. Their own commonly held ethical presuppositions were turned against them in much the same way Peter turned the common Jewish respect for the prophets, and for the attestive value of their miracles, against them in proving that Jesus of Nazareth was both a prophet of God and the Messiah.

Fifthly, when Peter made his charges against the Jewish crowd regarding the murder of Jesus, he made a 'blanket' accusation against all the people equally. We observed that that was because of the fact that Peter was addressing the Jews in terms of their covenantal and national solidarity. There are times in our preaching when we too can address our congregations as a whole with calls to repent for specific sins. Some pastors are hesitant to do this. They are fearful that those in the congregation to whom the generalization may not apply will be offended at a 'false accusation' by the preacher. One must be cautious with all sorts of generalizations, but in view of the biblical truth that 'no temptation has seized you except what is common to man' (1 Cor. 10:13), it is appropriate to offer general exhortations, rebukes, and encouragements to our congregations. You will find that, under the convicting power of the Holy Spirit, some who might not think they fit the generalization in fact do, and others will remember times when they have fit the profile and will be warned against future times when they may again.

At the same time you need to have the understanding of your people and sensitivity to distinguish between the sin problems of individuals, and make applications which are more specific within the congregation. The Apostle John does this when he identifies certain groups within the congregation to whom he has particular things to say:

> I write to you, fathers, because you have known him who is from the beginning. I write to you, young men, because you have overcome the evil one. I write to you, dear children, because you have known the Father. I write to you, fathers, because you have known him who is from the beginning. I write to you, young men, because you are strong, and the word of God lives in you, and you have overcome the evil one.... Dear children, this is the last hour; and as you have heard that the antichrist is coming, even now many antichrists have come. This is how we know it is the last hour (1 John 2:13-14, 18).

This is a very important principle because it is so tempting, especially when confronting sin, to simply leave our exhortations vague and general. There is a real need for particularity, but that very particularity requires that we aim the arrows carefully.

Sixthly, we had a great deal to say in chapter 6 about the central role of the heart, and the inward renewal of the heart by the Holy Spirit, with respect to people's reception of preaching. The 'natural man' will not, and cannot, receive biblical preaching, for it is foolishness to him (1 Cor. 2:14). Only after inward transformation by the Holy Spirit, which is called the 'new birth' (John 3:3), is a person capable of hearing and receiving the Word that is preached. Understanding these things is vitally important for the preacher.

Here I would like to balance that emphasis with an equally important one. Please remember, and take special note of the fact that, even though Peter knew these things as well as any preacher, he did not let that cause him to become sloppy as a preacher. He did not 'let go and let God' in his preaching. Trust in the sovereign converting power of God the Holy Spirit did not make him slack as a preacher. He was not willing to say just anything that came to mind knowing that God would have to bless it for it to do any good anyway. On the contrary, he was careful in his choice of the Scripture used in the sermon. He was brilliantly insightful in his formulation of the argument he wanted to follow in bringing the audience to the realization of their sin, and of the mercy of Christ. The craft of his sermon was in no way diminished by his consciousness that it is the Spirit who gives life. Let your confidence in the power of the Holy Spirit make you *even more careful* in the way in which you craft your sermons, rather than less so. Only with this kind of care will you discharge your duty to proclaim the truth of God clearly and persuasively. In this way you, like Peter, can do justice to both the sovereign working of God and your human responsibility as a good steward of God's mercy.

Finally, Luke's reference to Peter 'raising his voice' as he delivered his sermon brings to light another practical matter which may seem so obvious that it can be safely overlooked. I'm thinking of the problem so many preachers seem to have of failing to take pains to make themselves heard. The day of Demosthenes standing by the seashore, mouth full of pebbles, training himself to be heard above the crashing of the waves is apparently long gone. The style of preaching favored by many today seems to be little more than conversational. Perhaps this reflects our overdependence upon electronic amplification systems. Or perhaps this preference is an attempt to deliberately move away from a one-sided, authoritative-sounding proclamation in favor of a more 'low key' and 'accessible' style of delivery on the part of the preacher. Some pastors may be reacting to the stereotypical 'hell-fire-and-brimstone' style that is associated with a 'Bible-belt' pulpit thumper.

Whatever the reasons, adopting this style of delivery can create a problem. In a public setting, in a room of any size, and especially if unaided by electronic amplification, it can make your speaking very difficult, if not impossible, to hear. Mixed with a lack of clear diction, and a tendency to drop the volume at the end of a sentence (which many men have), it can make hearing and making sense of your sermon virtually impossible. This is not an uncommon problem among preachers. In one of my pastoral charges, the commonest criticism of visiting ministers, who preached while I was away on vacation, was that they could not be readily heard and audibly understood.

If your sermon cannot be heard it cannot be believed.[18] It is of no value to prepare a message carefully and prayerfully from the Word of God which will edify the people of God, only to fail to deliver it to them vocally in such a way that they can profit from it. A housewife who slaves over a hot oven all day long preparing dinner, but spills the whole delightful dish on the carpet en route to the dining room, is in much the same frustrating position. It may have been the most wonderful meal imaginable, but it will not do anyone much good. In the actual delivery of the sermon many pastors are concentrating so much on their outline, and their ideas about how to express themselves, that they give little or no thought to what the people in the pews are hearing – or not hearing. For that reason you must work at the skill of making yourself heard to such an extent that you can be confident that you are coming through loud and clear even when you are not consciously thinking about your delivery at all. Some kind of elocution lessons (formal or self-taught) would be a great help to many preachers.[19]

Lest you get the wrong idea, let me say that I am not saying you should all learn how to 'shout up a good camp meeting', or adopt a kind of phony, thundering pulpit style that is not you. It is actually more subtle than that. You want to be 'natural' in the pulpit (most of the time), and yet enable everyone in the audience to hear you. Public preaching is not the same as conversation, and a 'natural pulpit style' is not simply a conversational style writ large. There must be a measure of formality in it. Sentences must flow easily without all the 'uhs' and 'ya knows' that salt so much conversation these days. There must be a studied – even, at times, dramatic – use of changes in volume and silent pauses. There must be the ability to build to climaxes in the content of your sermon by the use of vocal means (similar to the uses of the sustained crescendo and decrescendo in musical composition).

None of these things come naturally to most of us. They need to be considered and worked on until they become natural to us and sound natural to our audiences. In a way it is like turning up the volume on your stereo set. Without losing the variety of tone and volume, and without distorting even its subtle nuances, you yet are able to raise the decibel level across the whole range of sounds. You get the 'natural sound' just a little bit louder.

I was made aware of this problem unintentionally years ago when early in my ministry I was called upon to tape a weekly radio program sponsored by the church I was serving. As I mentioned in an earlier chapter, speaking loudly has never been a problem for me. But in listening to the tapes of the broadcasts I found that, though I thought I was speaking very naturally, my recorded voice sounded very flat, dull, unexpressive – monotonous. I thought, 'I pity the poor person who has to listen to *that* voice for an hour!' What could be done?

I tried exaggerating my vocal inflection (not volume, for taping is much closer to conversation than public preaching) to the point that listening to myself speak into the microphone sounded embarrassingly *unnatural*. To my surprise, however, on playback my voice sounded just right (except for the fact that we never think we sound like ourselves on tape) – very natural and much more interesting to listen to. I found that discipline very helpful in improving my delivery during public preaching as well. Of course in that setting the volume had to be increased as well, but the exaggerated inflections, extended pauses,[20] etc., served well to more clearly punctuate my messages audibly, and made them much more interesting to listen to from the back row of the sanctuary.

A discipline of that sort may prove helpful to you if you find yourself weak in this area of vocal sound, diction, and inflection. Good preachers are even better when they can be easily heard and clearly understood by their audiences, even at a distance. I once came across an interesting passage in Benjamin Franklin's *Autobiography*, which I leave with you to ponder. Franklin describes a visit to Philadelphia by the great open-air evangelist, George Whitefield, and a sermon that Franklin went to hear.

> He had a loud and clear voice and articulated his words and sentences so perfectly that he might be heard and understood at a great distance, especially as his auditories, however numerous, observ'd the most exact silence. He preach'd one evening from the top of the Court-house steps, which are in the middle of Market-street and on the west side of Second-street which crosses at right angles. Both streets were filled with his hearers to a considerable distance. Being among the hindmost in Market-street, I had the curiosity to learn how far he could be heard, by retiring backwards down the street towards the river; and I found his voice distinct till I came near Front-street when some noise in that street obscur'd it. Imagining then a semi-circle, of which my distance should be the radius and that it were fill'd with auditors, to each of whom I allowed two square feet, I computed that he might well be heard by more than thirty thousand. This reconcil'd me to the newspaper accounts of his having preach'd to twenty-five thousand people in the fields and to the ancient histories of generals haranguing whole armies, of which I had some times doubted.
>
> By hearing him often, I came to distinguish easily between sermons newly compos'd, and those which he had often preach'd in the course of his travels. His delivery of the latter was so improv'd by frequent

repetitions that every accent, every emphasis, every modulation of voice, was so perfectly well turn'd and well plac'd that without being interested in the subject one could not help being pleas'd with the discourse; a pleasure of much the same kind with that receiv'd from an excellent piece of musick. This is an advantage itinerant preachers have over those who are stationary as the latter cannot well improve their delivery of a sermon by so many rehearsals.[21]

So much the worse for Franklin, who apparently did not have much interest in Whitefield's subject, else he would have been converted. But it is a good reminder for us who are preachers of what can be done with some disciplined effort. And while Franklin may be correct in his closing remark about our not being able to polish the delivery of a given sermon if we are preaching in the same place week after week, I believe we can nevertheless refine our skills to a much higher degree if we will take the trouble to do so.

11

Peter's Further Messages to the Jews: 'We Cannot But Speak the Things We Have Seen and Heard'

> Everyone was filled with awe, and many wonders and miraculous signs were done by the apostles.... Every day they continued to meet together in the temple courts ... enjoying the favor of all the people. And the Lord added to their number daily those who were being saved (Acts 2:43-47).

Thus Luke summarizes the response of the people of Jerusalem to Peter's first sermon on the Day of Pentecost, and to the preaching and teaching that followed. The Jews were awed – both by the message of the apostles, and by the signs and wonders that accompanied their ministry. They respected the testimony of the public life of the new converts and the mutual love and care evidenced by the new community of believers in Jesus the Messiah. Every day, other Jews were being added to the multitude of those who, through repentance and faith in the name of Jesus Christ, had found forgiveness for their sins and new life in the power of the Holy Spirit. The spread of the gospel was off to a magnificent start!

Soon, however, storm clouds began to gather in Jerusalem. The Jewish leaders, who had dogged the steps of Jesus throughout his public ministry, seeking some occasion to destroy him, now turned their attention to his 'witnesses' who were spreading the good news throughout Jerusalem (cf. 5:28). First, Peter and John were arrested (Acts 4:1-3), and later all the apostles were taken into custody (5:17-18). On two separate occasions the Sanhedrin 'commanded them not to speak or teach at all in the name of Jesus' (4:18; cf. 5:40).

The events recorded by Luke in Acts 3–5 begin his account of the growing opposition by the Jews – first in Jerusalem and later throughout the Roman world – to the preaching of the gospel by Jesus' appointed messengers. This is one of Luke's major themes in Acts, and culminates years later in the dramatic confrontation between Paul and the Sanhedrin, when the apostle declared: 'I stand on trial because of my hope in the resurrection of the dead!' (23:6) and with those words reduced the Sanhedrin to confusion.[1] What provoked this seething hatred and abiding persecution? A gracious miracle of healing by the 'Beautiful Gate' of the Temple, and an explanatory sermon by Peter delivered in 'Solomon's Colonnade' (3:11) on the east side of the outer court of the Temple area. What was behind it? Luke tells us it was the same jealousy and envy which provoked their hatred of Jesus himself (5:17; cf. Matt. 27:18). 'They were greatly disturbed because the apostles were teaching the people and proclaiming in Jesus the resurrection of the dead' (4:2), and they were determined to put a stop to it.

In this chapter we will examine the message by which Peter provoked the opposition of the Jewish leaders. It will again be our purpose to seek to discover the methods he used in proclaiming the gospel so that we might become more effective in our communication of the precious truth concerning Christ, His death and resurrection, and the hope of eternal life through faith in him. As we compare the message given in 'Solomon's Colonnade' with the one delivered on the Day of Pentecost, we will discover (ironically) that in some ways the sermon which landed the apostles in trouble with the Jews was less outwardly offensive than the one that won three thousand converts! We are reminded by this – and this point will be confirmed again and again throughout our study of the sermons in Acts – that preaching is a divine as well as a human activity. As preachers we are called to do our very best to follow biblical precepts and examples for effective preaching, so that we may fully discharge our responsibility as faithful stewards of God's message (1 Cor. 4:1-2). On the other hand, we preachers are 'fellow workers with God' (1 Cor. 3:9). We are servants to whom the Lord has assigned a task (v. 5). In our preaching we plant the seed, we water it, but the results come from God (v. 6). 'So neither he who plants nor he who waters is anything, but only God, who makes things grow' (v. 7). The results of preaching can be positive or they can be negative. Sometimes people will be moved by your message to a humble brokenness before God, turning to Christ in true faith. Other times your hearers will be critical, even hostile to your message – and to you! Sometimes you will find people responding in both ways to the very same message.

All men by nature have evil, unbelieving hearts (Heb. 3:12), and they cannot receive the things of the Spirit (1 Cor. 2:14), unless they are first transformed by the regenerating power of the Holy Spirit

(John 3:3). Thus, as Paul explained to the Corinthians (and we shall have occasion to remind ourselves of this passage several times in the chapters ahead), the same preaching of the gospel is at once 'the fragrance of life' to some, and to others 'the odor of death' (2 Cor. 2:15-16). Behind the human act of preaching is the *divine* act of converting and hardening sinners.

Personally, I have never been able to see how any pastor who faithfully does his work of preaching, pleading with men from the Scriptures Sunday after Sunday, can fail to be impressed by the reality of the sovereignty of God – whatever his theological convictions may be. How else can one explain the wondrous and sometimes bizarre responses of your people to your preaching. Certainly Paul is right when he declares, 'God has mercy on whom he wants to have mercy, and he hardens whom he wants to harden' (Rom. 9:18). Luke himself tells us as much. Speaking of the impact of Paul's sermon in the synagogue in Antioch upon the local Gentiles, he writes: 'And when the Gentiles heard this, they were glad, and glorified the word of the Lord: and as many as were ordained to eternal life believed' (Acts 13:48, KJV).

Only the sovereign, discriminating work of God can explain the phenomena you observe every week after the Sunday morning worship, as you meet people and hear from their own lips about the impact of the sermon on their hearts and lives. You know that in the last analysis, it was not your great preaching – or your poor preaching – which made the difference. It was God. Who is equal to such a task? Only men who are willing to work as hard as they can to do their part in the preparing and delivering good sermons to their congregations, and who will at the same time seek the face of God who alone by His almighty power can bring about the conversion of the hearts of sinners according to His sovereign will.

As a result of Peter's preaching in Solomon's Colonnade, many more believed in Christ (Acts 4:4) and Peter and John got arrested. The sovereign God at work! Let's look more closely at the message.

'An Outstanding Miracle'

Peter's sermon recorded in Acts 3:12-26 was precipitated by a miracle of healing, performed by Peter and John in the temple at the time of the evening sacrifice (v. 1). A man, who had been crippled from birth, was begging alms near the 'Beautiful Gate' of the Temple. When he saw Peter and John approaching, he asked them for money (v. 3). Peter replied with the now famous words: 'Silver or gold I do not have, but what I have I give you. In the name of Jesus Christ of Nazareth, walk' (v. 6). Helped to his feet by Peter, the man's feet and ankles became strong, and he began to walk – and then jump! – as he went with them into the Temple courts praising God (vv. 7-8). The effect of the miracle upon the surrounding crowd was electric! This lame beggar was well known to the people of Jerusalem who regularly went up to the Temple to worship. Since he had been lame from birth, and was now over forty years old (cf. 4:22), it is very likely that he had been a fixture at the 'Beautiful Gate' for years! Many of the pious would have contributed alms to his support as they passed by him on their way to worship. Thus they readily recognized him and knew his former condition. Now seeing him not only walk, but jump, 'they were filled with wonder and amazement' (v. 10). 'While the beggar held on to Peter and John, all the people were astonished and came running to them in the place called Solomon's Colonnade' (v. 11). 'The audience' – as they say – 'was listening'.

Your Appeal to Your Audience
Both of Peter's first two recorded sermons constituted explanations of a miraculous display of supernatural power before the assembly which was to hear the sermon. On the Day of Pentecost it was the descent of the Holy Spirit upon the disciples, the tongues of fire, and the miraculous speaking of the mighty acts of God in various languages that provoked the wonder of the crowd (2:1-12). Peter preached in answer to the question, 'What does this mean?' (v. 12). On this occasion it was the healing of the crippled beggar that caused the amazed people to run together, crowding around Peter and John (3:11). Again Peter spoke in answer to a question (i.e., Peter 'answered' the people, v. 12) which, though Luke does not record it for us (it may have been unexpressed by the people), must have been something like, 'How did these men make the beggarman walk?' We can easily imagine the crowd that pressed in upon the apostles buzzing with questions and opinions about the answer.

Peter further stimulated the interest of the audience by posing some questions of his own: 'Men of Israel, why does this surprise you? Why do you stare at us as if by our own power or godliness we had made this man walk?' (v. 12). The first question suggests that they should have already known how the miracle took place; but how could they? They have to think about this. The second question indicates that the majority opinion of the crowd – that Peter and John themselves must be somehow responsible for the miracle – is wrong.[2] The source of the miracle cannot be found in either the power or the godliness of Peter or John. Peter directs their attention away from the human instruments toward God, the source of all healing and salvation.[3]

Peter's words here remind us how vital it is for all preachers to create interest in their audience as they introduce their messages. Too much sermon listening is unfruitful (as is much personal Bible study) because it is not driven by important questions. The Bible has the answers, but as preachers you have to help your people ask the right questions. Questions in the minds of the audience provoke a deeper interest in the subject. Sometimes the preacher (wrongly) assumes that his congregation will be interested in the sermon just because the preacher is. This is frequently not the case. It has been said that every sermon ought to be an answer to a question in the mind of the audience. That means that most of the time you will have to raise the question and then answer it. Seldom do people come to church with the question in mind that you intend to answer. Furthermore, you will not have the benefit of some miraculous intervention by God to raise the question as the apostles did.

Good introductions create the mental and emotional hunger which the sermon is designed to fulfill. You will remember the frequency with which Paul, to take but one example, punctuates so many of the discourses in his letters of questions. Take out a few of your old sermon outlines. What kind of introductions do they have? Do they pose questions which the sermon then answers? Something like this:

> Are you a worrier? Have you ever prayed for peace and found that it didn't come? Have you tried to turn off that worry but couldn't find the switch? Yes? Well, let's take a fresh look at Philippians 4:6-9 to see if we can discover what has gone wrong.[4]

You want to get your people thinking. They come to the sermon with virtually no preparation – they are cold and you need to get them warmed up. Questions start the wheels turning. As we study the sermons in Acts, take note of the various ways in which the preachers stimulate the interest of the hearers. I won't be able to point out all of them, but you'll be able to pick them out if you pay attention. For now, make a note of this – when you are introducing your messages, follow Peter's example here by raising questions – and perhaps exploring possible answers – in order to prepare the soil for the sowing of the good seed of the Word for a fruitful harvest.

It is also good to note that Peter begins with his audience – building a bridge from where he finds them to the things he wants to say in his message. Often preachers simply begin the sermon with little or no consideration of the audience, and the hearers are left to 'jump on the train' as best they can. Many don't make it. Remember that you have carefully studied and understood the passage; you have an idea of what you wish to accomplish by your exposition; you are excited by the edifying message from the Lord it contains. You are ready to preach it! But your people are not equally ready to hear – in fact, they may not be ready at all! They have 'prepared' by racing around to get the children dressed and fed, looking for a lost earring, and narrowly avoiding a fender-bender on the way to church. Sitting down in the quiet of the auditorium is the first calming thing they have done in two hours. And now you want them to get on board a train that is racing through the station!

As you prepare your sermon outline imagine yourself in their shoes and ask, 'What would it take to get me ready to pay attention to and take to heart what God is saying in the passage we are studying today?' Then build into your introduction those steps which will take them from where they are to where they need to be to make the most of the Word of God you want them to hear. In some ways this is the most important part of your sermon preparation. What good is a rich exposition and thoughtful application of Scripture if you fail to engage your people at the outset? By the time you get to the really good stuff, their minds are long gone, and they may not even hear you. You need to spend much more time helping your people keep up with the sermon, starting with the first sentences you speak. Peter did: 'Men of Israel, why does this surprise you? Why do you stare at us as if by our own power of godliness we had made this man walk? The God of Abraham, Isaac and Jacob, the God of our fathers, has glorified his servant Jesus...' (vv. 12-13).

The God of Our Fathers in Action
We may outline Peter's sermon as follows (and as we do you'll notice that the outline is about as long as the printed sermon, reminding us

again that Luke has given us summaries of the messages sprinkled with key words and phrases, not full texts):

I. *This miracle has been performed in your presence by the God of our fathers – through the Name of Jesus, though you sinfully put God's Servant to death (vv. 13-16).*
   A. The God of our fathers has glorified Jesus of Nazareth by raising Him from the dead.
      1. Jesus was the 'Servant of the Lord,' 'the Holy and Righteous One' promised of old by the prophets.
      2. You denied His messianic claims and had Him killed.
      3. God raised Jesus from the dead and we (the apostles) are his witnesses.

   B. This miracle has been performed by the power of the Name of Jesus, a sign of God's approval upon Him.

II. *Your actions have unwittingly fulfilled the words of the prophets (vv. 17-18).*
   A. You acted in ignorance.
   B. Even though all the prophets predicted the sufferings of the Christ.

III. *Therefore, repent and receive the refreshing salvation of the Lord, for God has sent this message to bless you by turning you from your wicked ways (vv. 19-26).*
   A. Your sins may still be wiped away if you turn to Christ today.
      1. If you repent, Jesus will bring times of refreshing to you now.
      2. And He will bring restoration to all creation when he returns from heaven.

   B. Moses, Samuel, and all the prophets spoke of these days.
      1. Moses told of a coming Prophet, who is Jesus.
      2. You must listen to Him.
      3. If you do not, you will be cut off from covenant blessings, and (implied) those blessings will be given to others.

C. As the 'sons of the prophets and of the covenant,' God has sent the good news of the resurrection of Jesus the Messiah to you Jews first.

D. Indeed, 'all the families of the earth' will be blessed with salvation through the gospel of Christ.

There are several features of this sermon that we want to explore briefly. First, since Peter is preaching to a Jewish audience, the emphasis falls upon the action of the 'God of our fathers.' Having discounted the opinion that the healing miracle was accomplished through his own power or virtue, Peter directs the attention of his audience to 'the God of Abraham, Isaac and Jacob' (v. 13), a familiar liturgical identification[5] which he shortens to 'the God of our fathers.' It was this God who prepared for the coming of Jesus by predicting the sufferings of the Messiah (v. 18). It was this God – 'YHWH God' – who told Moses of the coming of the great 'Prophet,' which is Christ (v. 22). It was this God who glorified his Servant Jesus by raising him from the dead (vv. 13, 16). It was this God – the God who made his covenant with Abraham – who now, in fulfillment of the promise of that covenant, has sent his servant to the Jews to bless them (vv. 25-26). Peter was not preaching a new God or a new faith. Far from it. He was proclaiming nothing less than the final fulfillment of the ancient hope of Abraham and all his faithful descendants. There could be no legitimate charge of novelty against the apostle's message.[6]

Note also, from a practical preaching perspective, the effective rhetorical use of repetition by the Apostle Peter. Peter could have simply made his point didactically (as he did in v. 13), and left it at that. But by making God the subject of several of the following sentences throughout the sermon, he drove home his point – the familiarity created by repetition reinforced his point concerning the familiarity of the message of the messianic hope fulfilled in the ministry of Jesus.

Peter also makes dramatic rhetorical use of contrast in this sermon. He begins by contrasting God's exaltation of Jesus with the Jews' disowning of their appointed Messiah before Pilate (vv. 13-14). Next, Peter contrasts the fact that they killed the author of life with the fact that God raised him from the dead (v. 15). Later, Peter contrasts the ignorant actions of the Jews with God's fulfilling what he had foretold through all the prophets (v. 18). If they repent they will be 'refreshed' (v. 19). Heeding the message of God's great Prophet is contrasted with failing to listen – one brings blessing, the other a curse (v. 22-23). God raised up his Servant, and sent him, not to condemn, but to bless by turning each one from his wicked ways (v. 26). The sermon is a study in the use of contrast.

Peter's Use of the Old Testament Prophets

Peter points out that the death and resurrection of Christ fulfilled the words of the prophets, though he quotes the prophets much more sparingly in this sermon than in his Pentecost message. In the sermon on the Day of Pentecost, Peter began with a citation from the prophet Joel, and went on to quote and comment upon texts from Psalm 16, 110 and 132. The entire message was developed around these Old Testament quotations. In this sermon, however, Peter alludes in more general terms to 'all the prophets' (v. 18), 'his holy prophets' (v. 21), and 'all the prophets from Samuel on' (v. 24). But specific Old Testament citations are limited: the words of Moses in Deuteronomy 18:15, 18 (blended with a phrase from Lev. 23:29) are quoted in verses 22-23, and the promise to Abraham from Genesis 12:3. That is all.

Thus Peter here relies more upon the familiarity of his audience with the general thrust of the message of the prophets taken as a whole, rather than the citations of particular scriptural 'proof texts,' to establish his case that Jesus is the Messiah. In preaching to a biblically 'literate' audience (e.g., your regular Sunday morning audience), you too may rely upon their general grasp of certain biblical truths in developing a particular theological or ethical argument. You need not always cite long lists of 'proof texts' – which can sometimes break the flow of your message – to make your point. Sometimes it is in order to look closely at specific supportive passages to establish a point; at other times you may refer to corroborative biblical themes in more general terms, as Peter did in this sermon. And note again that Peter, by means of this significant repetition, makes clear that he is not proclaiming a new message, but the fulfillment of the single ancient message of the prophets, which flowed from God's seminal promise to Abraham which he finally quotes: 'Through your offspring all peoples on earth will be blessed' (v. 25; cf. Gen. 12:3; 18:18; 22:18; 26:4).

Peter's Witness to the Resurrection

This sermon contains a clear witness to the resurrection of Jesus and its redemptive significance: 'You killed the author of life, but God raised him from the dead. We are witnesses of this' (v. 15). Peter, John, and the others appointed by Christ to be his witnesses shared a dual authority. They were eyewitnesses, and thus could provide the most compelling human testimony to the events of Jesus' life and ministry: 'We did not follow cleverly invented stories when we told you about the power and coming of our Lord Jesus Christ, but we were eyewitnesses of his majesty' (2 Pet. 1:16). Beyond that, they were witnesses appointed by God himself – even as he had appointed the prophets of old – and therefore the apostolic witness is a *divine witness*, a point which Peter will emphasize later before the Sanhedrin (cf. 5:32).

In bearing witness to the resurrection, Peter emphasizes the *meaning* of the resurrection more than the *fact* of the resurrection. He does not enter into any attempt to 'prove' the resurrection really happened, beyond his and John's word as eyewitnesses. There was no need. Rather the apostle draws attention to the resurrection as the 'glorification' of Jesus, the 'Servant of the Lord,' by the God of Abraham, Isaac, and Jacob (vv. 13, 16). The resurrection is evidence of the previous divine 'appointment' of Jesus as Messiah (v. 20). The concluding claim that God 'raised up' his Servant (v. 26) is resonant with meaning – not only did God raise him up in the flow of redemptive history (cf. 13:33),[7] but he also raised him up from the dead (cf. 5.30)[8] – and thus the sermon comes full circle: 'The God of our fathers has glorified his servant Jesus.'

On the eve of his ascension, Jesus had told his disciples:

> This is what is written: The Christ will suffer and rise from the dead on the third day, and repentance and forgiveness of sins will be preached in his name to all nations, beginning at Jerusalem. You are witnesses of these things (Luke 24:46-48).

Here Peter is fulfilling that commission in precise terms. He bears witness to the sufferings, death, and resurrection of Jesus, and on that basis calls his audience to repent and receive the forgiveness of sins through faith in Christ.

You killed the author of life, but God raised him from the dead. We are witnesses of this.... Repent, then, and turn to God, so that your sins may be wiped out,... When God raised up his servant, he sent him first to you to bless you by turning each of you from your wicked ways (Acts 3:15, 19, 26).

Throughout Acts, as we shall see, the apostolic witness to the resurrection leads to a call to repentance, and the promise of forgiveness to everyone who believes – Jews and Gentiles alike. We will have a little more to say about this below.

Preaching Theology

Luke's outline of the sermon evidences a rich theological content in Peter's sermon – particularly in its Christology. John Stott has remarked,

> The most remarkable feature of Peter's second sermon, as of his first, is its Christ-centredness. He directed the crowd's attention away from both the healed cripple and the apostles to the Christ whom men disowned by killing him but God vindicated by raising him, and whose name, having been appropriated by faith, was strong enough to heal the man completely. Moreover, in his testimony to Jesus, Peter attributed to him a cluster of significant titles. He began by calling him 'Jesus Christ of Nazareth' (6), but went on to style him God's 'servant' (13), who first suffered and then was glorified in fulfillment of Isaiah 52:13 ff. (*cf.* 18 and 26; 4:27, 30). Next, he was 'the Holy and Righteous One' (14) and 'the author [or pioneer] of life' (15), while in the concluding part of the sermon Peter called him the 'prophet' foretold by Moses (22) and before the Sanhedrin the rejected stone which has become the capstone (4:11). Servant and Christ, Holy One and source of life, Prophet and Stone – these titles speak of the uniqueness of Jesus in his sufferings and glory, his character and mission, his revelation and redemption. All this is encapsulated in his 'Name' and helps to explain its saving power.[9]

From the very beginning, apostolic preaching (as evidenced in the two sermons of Peter in Jerusalem) was richly and profoundly theological.[10] Peter was able to draw from the words of the Old Testament prophets a definitive Christology, which needed only to be explicated in terms of its fulfillment in Jesus of Nazareth.

> Looking back over Peter's Colonnade sermon, it is striking that he presents Christ to the crowd 'according to the Scriptures' as successively the suffering servant (13, 18), the Moses-like prophet (22-23), the Davidic

king (24) and the seed of Abraham (25-26). And if we add his Pentecost sermon, and glance on to his speech before the Sanhedrin (4:8 ff.), it is possible to weave a biblical tapestry which forms a thorough portrait of Christ. Arranged chronologically according to the events of his saving career, the Old testament texts declare that he was descended from David, (Ps. 132:11 = 2:30); that he suffered and died for us as God's servant (Isa. 53 = 2:23; 3:18); that the stone the builders rejected has nevertheless become the capstone (Ps. 118:22 = 4:11), for God raised him up from the dead (Isa. 52:13 = 2:25 ff.), since death could not hold him and God would not abandon him to decay (Ps. 16:8 ff. = 2:24, 27, 31); that God then exalted him to his right hand, to wait for his final triumph (Ps. 110:1 = 2:34-35); that meanwhile through him the Spirit has been poured out (Joel 2:28 ff. = 2:16 ff., 33); that now the gospel is to be preached world-wide, even to those afar off (Isa. 57:19 = 2:39), although opposition to him has been foretold (Ps. 2:1 ff. = 4:25-26); that people must listen to him or pay the penalty of their disobedience (Deut. 18:18-19 = 3:22-23); and that those who do listen and respond will inherit the blessing promised to Abraham (Gen. 12:3; 22:18 = 3:25, 26).[11]

Now let me ask you a question. Is your preaching loaded with that kind of meaty theology? or have you fallen in step with the 'practical' (which is to say 'a-theological') temper of the times? Doctrinal preaching has fallen into disuse in many churches in our day. In reaction to what has been seen as dry, abstract 'theologizing,' pastors have opted for more 'relevant' and 'practical' messages. But there is a serious problem with the movement away from doctrine in favor of the practical – the 'practical' doesn't work any more! If in the past preachers have been guilty of preaching a theology abstracted from life, today many are guilty of preaching sermons which are full of technique and method (e.g., 'Ten Steps to a More Successful Marriage,' 'Seven Ways to Relate Effectively to Your Teen,' etc.), but lack power because they are not grounded in the truth of God's redemptive work in Christ.

Doctrine – that dreaded word! – is the food of faith, and faith alone gives power to Christian living. If preachers neglect instruction in sound doctrine (Titus 1:9) in favor of more 'practical subjects' they will be guilty of encouraging God's people to try to attain by human effort ('the flesh') a goal which they began to pursue 'in the Spirit' – which is to say, 'by faith.' Paul earnestly warns us against such a misguided effort (cf. Gal. 3:3). Like the apostles you must be careful to preach a rich and robust theology, and then take care to apply that doctrine concretely in practical ways. Over one hundred years ago, Bishop J. C. Ryle penned these words – which remain as timely in our day as they were in his – about the importance of doctrine to successfully fighting the 'fight of faith:'

> A religion without doctrine or dogma is a thing which many are fond of talking of in the present day. It sounds very fine at first. It looks very pretty at a distance. But the moment we sit down to examine and consider it, we shall find it a simple impossibility. We might as well talk of a body without bones and sinews. No man will ever be anything or do anything in religion, unless he believes *something*....
>
> As for true Christians, faith is the very backbone of their spiritual existence. No one ever fights earnestly against the world, the flesh and the devil, unless he has engraven on his heart certain great principles which he believes. What they are he may hardly know, and may certainly not be able to define or write down. But there they are, and, consciously or unconsciously, they form the roots of his religion. Wherever you see a man, whether rich or poor, learned or unlearned, wrestling manfully with sin, and trying to overcome it, you may be sure there are certain great principles which that man believes.[12]

Pastor, you may have puzzled over the reason your carefully crafted practical sermons bear so little lasting fruit in true godliness in the lives of your people. Consider, are you trying to plant the flowers of dedication and service in your people without first filling their hearts with the rich soil of sound Christian teaching – about God, and human nature, and sin, and the work of Christ and his Spirit? Any gardener will tell you that won't work. In expounding Scripture from the pulpit, pay attention to *both* theology and application. If you do 'you will save both yourself and your hearers' (1 Tim. 4:16).

A Message of Hope and Refreshment from God

In this sermon Peter preaches an eschatology of restoration. We noted in our discussion of his sermon on the Day of Pentecost that Peter understood that the 'last days' of messianic fulfillment had dawned with the coming of Christ.[13] The era of salvation blessing, which the prophets foretold, was now upon Israel (Acts 3:24), and they were being called to participate in its blessings by turning to Christ.

> Repent, then, and turn to God, so that your sins may be wiped out, that times of refreshing may come from the Lord, and that he may send the

Christ, who has been appointed for you – even Jesus. He must remain in heaven until the time comes for God to restore everything, as he promised long ago through his holy prophets (vv. 19-21).

In this sermon Peter explains the miracle by which the crippled man was wonderfully healed in terms of the 'refreshing' and 'restoration' that are the characteristics of Messiah's reign. 'He will be like rain falling on a mown field, like showers watering the earth. In his days ... prosperity will abound ... he will deliver the needy who cry out, the afflicted who have no one to help. He will take pity on the weak and the needy and save the needy from death' (Ps. 72:6-7, 12-13). Dennis Johnson has pointed out that Luke uses five different words for 'healing' in the larger context of Peter's sermon here and before the Sanhedrin in the next chapter (3:16; 4:9, 10, 14, 22, 30).[14] 'Salvation' as proclaimed by Peter in the Name of Christ is holistic – it includes both salvation from sin and physical restoration (cf. 4:9, 12). The healing of the crippled man in the Temple is but a token of the 'restoration of all things' which will one day take place (3:21; cf. Rom. 8:19-23). This comprehensive salvation is manifested in stages – it was *inaugurated* with the death and resurrection of Christ, and will be consummated when he returns in glory at the end of history. Peter's promise is of 'refreshment' now and full 'restoration' in the future.[15]

When we compare Peter's sermon here with the one he preached on the Day of Pentecost, we may notice the difference in his approach to his audience. In the Pentecost sermon Peter took his cue from Joel's prophecy, which was fulfilled in the outpouring of the Holy Spirit and the miraculous signs that accompanied it. Joel's vision of impending judgment – 'the great and dreadful day of the LORD' (Joel 2:31) – lent urgency to Peter's call to repentance in view of the death and resurrection of Jesus. The Jews had wickedly murdered the Lord's Messiah, and judgment was coming. The crowd's initial wonder at the miraculous signs was turned into fear by Peter's message until his audience was cut to the heart and cried out to Peter and the other apostles, 'Brothers, what shall we do?' (Acts 2:37).

This sermon too begins with the amazement of the crowd, prompted by the miracle of healing at the 'Beautiful Gate' (3:11), but here Peter sounds the note of *hope* rather than fear. The healing of the crippled beggar is, as Peter proclaims the 'good news', the harbinger of 'times of refreshing' (v. 20), indeed the 'restoration of all things' (v. 21). While Peter is still very clear about the sinful responsibility of the Jews in disowning the Servant of the Lord before Pilate, and putting to death the Author of Life (vv. 13-15), he focuses their attention upon God's gracious provision for physical and spiritual healing through the Name of the risen Messiah (v. 16). Even the judgment which will certainly come upon those who do not listen to the great Prophet (v. 23) is overshadowed in Peter's appeal by the fact that God sent his risen Servant to the Jews to bless them by turning them from their sins (v. 26).

Thus we see the way in which the same preacher can approach the same basic message from two angles and, without cutting out any part of the important message, strikes a different tone in each. At Pentecost Peter called men to faith in Christ against the background of coming judgment; here he invites his audience to turn to Christ in the hope that God will bless and refresh his people with salvation. These ideas are not mutually exclusive, but each may receive more emphasis depending upon the audience, situation, purpose of the message, etc. Not all audiences are alike, and not every preaching situation is the same. Good preachers are sensitive to these differences. At some times men need to be driven by a healthy fear of God to turn from their sins to him, while at other times you want to win your audience with a positive, hopeful appeal. Like Peter you must consider carefully how you may most effectively motivate your hearers on any given occasion, and adapt your presentation of God's message in such a way as to best reach them for Christ.

A Hint of Things to Come

In the conclusion of his sermon Peter alludes to the promise of God to Abraham: 'Through your offspring all peoples on earth will be blessed' (v. 25; cf. Gen. 12:3). In so doing the apostle hints at things to come as the gospel moves from the Jews to the Gentiles. Indeed Peter himself will soon carry the good news into the Gentile household of Cornelius. Peter acknowledged that the Jews enjoyed a position of priority in the redemptive plan of God – God sent his Servant Jesus first to the Jews (v. 26). With this the Apostle Paul agrees. The gospel is a message of salvation 'first for the Jew' (Rom. 1:16). The clear implication of this statement, however, is that the good news is also for the Gentiles.

As the narrative of Acts develops, the good news of Christ is carried more and more to a willing audience of Gentiles. At Pisidian Antioch Paul acknowledged that it was right that the gospel message be preached to Gentiles, especially in view of the hardness of heart on the part of the Jews: 'We had to speak the word of God to you first. Since you reject it and do not consider yourselves worthy of eternal life, we now turn to the Gentiles' (Acts 13:46). Indeed, Christ had called Paul for that very reason – that he might carry the message to the nations (9:15; 22:21; 26:17; cf. Rom. 15:8-17). At the close of the Book of Acts, Paul again declares the propriety of his mission to the Gentiles: 'Therefore I want you to know that God's salvation has been sent to the Gentiles, and they will listen!' (28:28).

Though Luke highlights the growing hostility of the Jews to the gospel as the reason for the spread of the gospel from the Jews to the Gentiles, Peter here grounds that transition in the original promise of God to Abraham (3:25). God's mercy to all nations was not an afterthought necessitated by the hostile reaction of the Jews to the messianic claims of Jesus. Far from it. Such 'gospel universalism' was anticipated and announced clearly from the very beginning. Through the promised 'Seed' (Gal. 3:16) 'all the families of the earth would be blessed.' Paul comments elsewhere: 'For I tell you that Christ has become a servant of the Jews on behalf of God's truth, to confirm the promises made to the patriarchs so that the Gentiles may glorify God for his mercy' (Rom. 15:8-9). It is true that Jewish hostility to the apostolic message was the commonest historic dynamic that prompted this transition, but fundamentally the preaching of the gospel to the Gentiles was the fulfillment of prophecy. The complaints of the Jews regarding the inclusion of the Gentiles was in reality a complaint against the gracious covenant promise of God.

This serves as a good reminder to us that the gospel is a message for all kinds of people in all kinds of places. Though for the most part we no longer face problems between former Jews and Gentiles in our churches, we do frequently have problems with 'insiders' versus 'outsiders'. Many churches get very comfortable with the status quo and want to keep things 'just the way they are'. They may resist efforts (by the pastor or others) to reach out to those who need to hear the gospel of Christ, but who do not fit the cultural (or racial) composition of the congregation. Outreach can be very inconvenient – it takes a lot of time to teach people who know nothing about the

Bible, to disciple in fundamental Christian obedience people who lack even common social graces, to deal with the unruly children of those who have little understanding of the nature of biblical family life, etc. Do you really want a former thief and drug addict possibly 'casing' your church property on Sunday? We may sing the glories of gospel outreach,

> Pity the nations, O our God,
> Constrain the earth to come;
> Send your victorious Word abroad,
> And bring the strangers home.[16]

But the actual practice is very demanding, and too many Christians – pastors included – shrink from it. Even if untainted by xenophobia or racism, it is much easier for churches to stay with what is familiar than take the risks which are necessary to bring the gospel to strangers, and 'bring the strangers home.'

Preaching Repentance
Finally, we should note that Peter calls his fellow Jews to a response of repentance and faith in Jesus the Messiah. Peter is well aware of the fact that for the Jews to come to Christ in faith they must first redirect (by the grace of God) the whole direction of their thought and life. Peter tells them, 'Repent, then, and turn to God, so that your sins may be wiped out,...' (Acts 3:19). In the apostolic preaching of the gospel, forgiveness of sins requires 'repentance' and 'turning'.

There is a marked contrast between the attitude of many evangelicals today toward repentance, and that of the Bible itself. For many moderns repentance is 'bad news' – a disheartening and embarrassing doctrine which gets in the way of reaching men with the 'good news' of Christ. They prefer to preach to men in such a way as to invite them to 'accept Christ' without ever having to face the realities of their natural, sinful way of thinking and living. Repentance smacks too much of traditional 'hell-fire-and-brimstone' preaching which is considered hopelessly out of step with the modern sensibility. Modern men must be approached more 'positively'. Thus the apostolic call, 'Repent, then, and turn to God, so that your sins may be wiped out,' has been replaced in many pulpits with the appeal, 'Give Jesus a place in your heart, and you will finally find true fulfillment.'

On the other hand, the Bible in general, and the Book of Acts in particular, has a much more 'positive' view of repentance. It is called 'repentance unto life' (11:18). Even a superficial scanning of the apostolic sermons in Acts will point up the centrality of repentance to the preaching of the gospel by Christ's appointed ministers. The apostolic message highlighted the importance of repentance, because it was the fulfillment of the message of Jesus himself. Jesus announced the nearness of the Kingdom of God with an emphatic call to repentance: 'The time has come,... The kingdom of God is near. Repent and believe the good news!' (Mark 1:15; cf. Matt. 4:17).[17] When Jesus sent out his disciples to preach, while he was still carrying out his own public ministry, we read that 'they went out and preached that people should repent' (Mark 6:12).

The apostles preached repentance because they had been commissioned by Christ to do so, explicitly. After his resurrection from the dead, Jesus told his disciples,

> This is what is written: The Christ will suffer and rise from the dead on the third day, and repentance and forgiveness of sins will be preached in his name to all nations, beginning at Jerusalem. You are witnesses of these things. I am going to send you what my Father has promised; but stay in the city until you have been clothed with power from on high (Luke 24:46-49).

The Book of Acts unfolds from this Lukan statement of the 'Great Commission.' Thus the message of the apostolic preachers is one of 'repentance and forgiveness of sins.' We have already heard Peter conclude his great Pentecost sermon with the call, 'Repent and be baptized, every one of you, in the name of Jesus Christ for the forgiveness of your sins. And you will receive the gift of the Holy Spirit' (Acts 2:38). Forgiveness of sins and the gift of the Holy Spirit were given to everyone – and only to those – who repented of their sins. Soon Peter will tell the Sanhedrin that Jesus is that 'Prince and Savior' whom God exalted to his right hand so that 'he might give repentance and forgiveness of sins to Israel' (5:31). Note that both forgiveness and the repentance which alone receives it are 'gifts' given by God to men in his mercy. Nor is this call restricted to Jews only. Paul told the Athenian intellectuals that though God overlooked their ignorance in the past, he now 'commands all people everywhere to repent' (17:30). Paul summarized his ministry and message in this way to the Ephesian elders: 'I have declared to both Jews and Greeks that they must turn to God in repentance and have faith in our Lord Jesus' (20:21; cf. 26:20).

If you would be faithful to these apostolic models in your own preaching today, you too must give renewed emphasis to God's call to repentance. What then is repentance? It is not (as too many view today) simply nasty 'name calling' – telling men and women they are 'damnable sinners.' Rather it is calling men to change their way of thinking[18] and consequently their way of life. 'Repentance is a rethinking of one's behavior, attitudes and beliefs. It is coming to a different opinion or viewpoint, one so different that it calls for different thought patterns and a different lifestyle.'[19] You must call men to such a radical rethinking as part of your preaching of the good news to them. There is hope for a sinner, but only if he repents.

The Apostle John highlighted the fundamental importance of repentance in the form of confessing and forsaking our sin.

> If we claim to be without sin, we deceive ourselves and the truth is not in us. If we confess our sins, he is faithful and just and will forgive us our sins and purify us from all unrighteousness. If we claim we have not sinned, we make him out to be a liar and his word has no place in our lives (1 John 1:8-10).

Man is naturally self-deceived – he claims he has not sinned (cf. Prov. 30:20). As long as he continues in that state, the truth can have no place in his life. Repentance comes when he sees his sinful condition and turns from it, wholeheartedly, towards Christ. C. John Miller has identified two problems facing the twenty-first century men and women to whom you preach.

> First, many who call Jesus their Savior are loaded down with pretense and evasion, and have no heart for confessing and forsaking their ways as God commands them (Prov. 28:13; 1 John 1:8-10). Secondly, many others have an awareness of their guilt but do not know how to go to Christ and rid themselves of their dark blots.[20]

If he is right – and I believe he is – your task as a preacher includes helping men and women face their 'pretences and evasions' and showing them how to 'go to Christ' for forgiveness. In short, Miller is calling us to do what the apostles did in their preaching – call men to repentance towards God and faith in the Lord Jesus.

In the sermon before us, Peter presses the Jews to change their way of thinking about Jesus of Nazareth. At best they considered him no more than a prophet; at worst, a lying messianic pretender. But Peter tells them that Jesus was the 'Holy and Righteous One' (Acts 3:14), God's appointed 'Servant' (v. 13). He calls them to rethink their involvement in Jesus' death. Far from being innocent bystanders at the crucifixion, they had 'disowned' God's Servant before Pilate, asking for a murderer to be released in his place – a grave insult to the majesty of the God of Abraham, Isaac and Jacob – and they had 'killed the author of life'. How overwhelming must have been the guilt of those whose minds the Holy Spirit opened to understand, finally, what they had done in putting Jesus to death! Most of all, they had to rethink their present relationship to this Jesus, for he was not safely dead and buried – God had raised him from the dead (v. 15). You see, for them to 'receive Christ' required a complete turn around in their way of thinking about him (vv. 19-20), but Christ had been sent to them – through the apostolic preachers – for that very purpose: 'to bless [them] by turning each of [them] from [their] wicked ways' (v. 26).

If you are going to lead men and women into an authentic relationship with Jesus Christ as Lord and Savior, you must make repentance from sin a prominent theme in your sermons, as the apostles did. In expounding and applying the Scriptures you must help your audience see itself as God does. Men and women must be brought to the realization that they are 'undone' in their sins before a holy and majestic God (Isa. 6:5). But this is part of the good news, for 'the sacrifices of God are a broken spirit; a broken and contrite heart, O God, you will not despise' (Ps. 51:17). 'He who lives forever, whose name is holy' not only inhabits 'a high and holy place', but he also dwells 'with him who is contrite and lowly in spirit, to revive the spirit of the lowly and to revive the heart of the contrite' (Isa. 57:15). The call to repentance, under the blessing of the Holy Spirit, is far from depressing – it opens the door to Christ and to life! It brings the joy of a clear conscience and a deepening fellowship with Christ.[21]

The Apostles Face the Sanhedrin
According to Luke, this second message by Peter was again blessed by the Holy Spirit with powerful converting success: 'But many who heard the message believed, and the number of men grew to about

five thousand' (Acts 4:4). Many Jews were won for Christ as they found in him the fulfillment of their hope. As far as the two apostles were concerned, however, the sermon won them an overnight stay in jail. The Jewish leaders (the Sadducees in particular) were upset 'because the apostles were teaching the people and proclaiming in Jesus the resurrection of the dead' (v. 2), and therefore had the captain bring the temple guard to arrest Peter and John (vv. 1, 3). The preaching of the gospel brings Christ's witnesses before the Sanhedrin for the first time since that same body condemned the Lord Jesus himself. It would not be the last time.[22] Luke's roll call of those present indicates that the composition of the council was essentially the same as it had been when Jesus appeared before it: 'Annas the high priest was there, and so were Caiaphas, John, Alexander and the other men of the high priest's family' (v. 6). Since so many of the leading figures were present, the Sanhedrin was taking serious note of the preaching that had taken place in the Temple area.[23]

Peter and John are questioned about the power or authority by which they performed the miracle (v. 7). It is interesting to note that no attempt is made to discount the miracle, indeed the leaders know that it cannot be denied (v. 16). A work of God has taken place (cf. John 3:2). The question is what specific authority was claimed by the preachers as the warrant for their miracle. Peter is 'filled with the Holy Spirit' (v. 8) and gives his answer. Later, following the release of the apostles from custody, the church gathers to pray for further boldness in preaching Christ (v. 29), and the Spirit 'fills' them again, with the result that they 'spoke the word of God boldly' (v. 31). We have discussed the relationship between the filling of the Holy Spirit and the boldness of the apostolic witness in an earlier chapter.[24]

Peter addressed his audience formally, 'Rulers and elders of the people!' (v. 8) and pointed up, ironically, that it appears that it is for an 'act of kindness' (*euergesia*) shown to a cripple that they have been arrested. Despite the seriousness of the circumstances, Peter was willing to prod his opponents – but it is not gratuitous sarcasm. These were the same leaders (at least from the same class) who attributed the miracle-working power of Christ to Beelzebub (Matt. 12:24), thus committing the unpardonable sin of blasphemy against the Holy Spirit (v. 31). They should have known the answer to their own question, but for their deliberate hardening of their hearts against the messianic claims of Christ – a theme to which Peter will soon turn. That Peter and John should be arrested for 'healing' a man and preaching the good news of 'salvation' (vv. 9, 12)[25] is an indication of the depth of the spiritual 'inversion' of the Jewish leadership – they 'call evil good and good evil' (Isa. 5:20). Jesus himself had posed a similar sarcastic question to the same Jewish leaders at one point during his public ministry when they took up stones to put him to death: 'I have shown you many great miracles from the Father. For which of these do you stone me?' (John 10:32). The Lord 'mocks proud mockers' (Prov. 3:34), as he does here through his servants. But at the same time he 'gives grace to the humble' – the apostles are humble before God and therefore can be bold and confident before men.

Peter identified Jesus of Nazareth as the One by whose authority (in whose Name) this miracle had been performed – the same point he made to the crowd in Solomon's Colonnade (Acts 3:16). Again he set forth the contrast between the sinful crucifixion of the Christ by the Jews and God's raising him from the dead (v. 10), but here he immediately interpreted these facts with a familiar citation from Psalm 118:22, 'The stone the builders rejected has become the capstone' (v. 11). Jesus had appealed to the same text at the conclusion of his parable of the vineyard (Mark 12:10-11; cf. Luke 20:17), in which he predicted his own death, and indicted the Jews for their rejection of both the prophets and the Messiah. Peter's use of the passage is perfectly in line with the Master's – he is confronting the Sanhedrin with the enormity of their crime against God.

Peter concluded climactically with the memorable words: 'Salvation is found in no one else, for there is no other name under heaven given to men by which we must be saved' (Acts 4:12). God's exaltation of Christ had opened the door of salvation for men everywhere. Just as the crippled man had been healed through faith in the Name of Jesus, so any man who turned from his sin and trusted in Christ could receive the gift of salvation in its fullest sense.

Peter, in contrast to his sermons to the general populace of Jerusalem, does not conclude here with an appeal to the members of the Sanhedrin to repent and believe in Christ. Peter had implied in his message both the necessity of repentance and the hope of grace for those who did repent, but he did not make an overt invitation. God's special purpose at this point in dealing with the Jewish leadership was not to call them with the gospel, but to indict them with it. As Jesus himself had pointed out earlier, God was fulfilling the words of Isaiah:

In them is fulfilled the prophecy of Isaiah: 'You will be ever hearing but never understanding; you will be ever seeing but never perceiving. For this people's heart has become calloused; they hardly hear with their ears, and they have closed their eyes. Otherwise they might see with their eyes, hear with their ears, understand with their hearts and turn, and I would heal them' (Matt. 13:14-15; Isa. 6:9-10).

Neither Peter, Stephen nor Paul offered a gospel invitation to the Sanhedrin. For every stubborn unbelieving heart there will come an end to the pleading of God. The invitations will end. The door of the ark will be closed and locked. Let men who sit under the preaching of the gospel not delay – 'Now is the time of God's favor, now is the day of salvation' (2 Cor. 6:2).

'We Cannot Help Speaking About What We Have Seen and Heard'

The response of the council was one of surprise and bewilderment. These were common, uneducated men, and yet they spoke with such bold confidence that the priests and others in the Sanhedrin were taken aback. 'They took note that these men had been with Jesus' (Acts 4:13).[26] There was no denying the miracle – the healed man was right there before them (v. 15). They did not even attempt to disprove the resurrection of Jesus.[27] So they dismissed the apostles while they conferred together about what to do with these men (vv. 16-17). Since they could not discredit the miracle or these messengers, they determined they must prohibit any further preaching in the Name of Jesus, which they did.

The bold response of Peter and John has become a clarion call for the liberty of the individual conscience over against the unlawful decrees of men. Commentators have pointed out the parallel with the words of Socrates when condemned by the rulers of Athens several centuries earlier.[28] Much has been written about these verses in discussions of civil disobedience. But we should note carefully just what the apostles say here. They do not say (here) 'We must obey God rather than men' (that phrase appears in 5:29). Here Peter and John say, 'Judge for yourselves whether it is right in God's sight to obey you rather than God. For we cannot help speaking about what we have seen and heard' (vv. 19-20). In the first place they call upon the Sanhedrin to make a judgment as to the propriety of obeying men rather than God. The Jews knew full well that the commandments of

God took precedence over the commandments of men. Peter and John were not articulating a novel principle here (especially in post-Maccabean Palestine!). Secondly, by contrasting the decree of the council with the will of God the apostles offer another indictment of the lawlessness of the Jews and their leaders.[29] Finally, Peter and John lay emphasis upon their obligation to bear witness concerning the things which they had seen and heard. This is more than the obligation we all have to obey the will of God, even in difficult circumstances. Peter and John are alluding to the same sense of necessity that Paul described when he wrote to the Corinthians: 'Yet when I preach the gospel, I cannot boast, for I am compelled to preach. Woe to me if I do not preach the gospel!' (1 Cor. 9:16; cf. Rom. 1:13-14). The apostles had been called by the risen Christ to be witnesses of his resurrection glory, and that calling placed them under the deepest obligation to preach. They were constrained by the love of Christ and the fear of the Lord to persuade men (cf. 2 Cor. 5:11, 14). In a sense, there was no force in the threats of the Jews because the apostles had no choice – the decision had been made for them when Jesus called them away from their fishing nets and made them 'fishers of men' (Luke 5:10). When Jesus arose from the dead, and showed forth his saving power and glory, the apostles had to tell about it! There was no other way.

Would that God would give you and me that same sense of obligation, of compulsion. Too many pastors preach simply because it is expected of them, and it shows in the way they prepare, pray over, and deliver their sermons. And when the fear of men arises, they back off. Not so Peter and John. Not so any man truly called of God to proclaim the glorious riches of Christ Jesus. 'We cannot help speaking about what we have seen and heard.'

Worthy to Suffer Disgrace for the Name

Peter and John were released, largely because of the Sanhedrin's fear of public opinion (v. 21). Upon reporting what had happened to the rest of the brethren, they prayed for sustained boldness, and it was given with a renewed filling of the Holy Spirit (vv. 23-33). The believers continued to meet in Solomon's Colonnade and the apostles performed many miraculous signs and wonders among the people (5:12). Through the apostolic preaching of Jesus the Messiah more and more men and women were converted and were added to the church (v. 14). Crowds of people even came in from the towns around Jerusalem, bringing their sick and those tormented by evil spirits, and all of them were healed (v. 16). Peter and John and the other apostles were obviously not complying with the order of the Sanhedrin.

As a result of the progress of the gospel in Jerusalem, the high priest and all his associates, who were Sadducees, were filled with jealousy, and again had the apostles (all of them this time) arrested and put them in the public jail (vv. 17-18). But as Gamaliel would later point out, it was futile to fight against the work of God (v. 39), and during the night an angel of the Lord opened the doors of the jail and brought them out (v. 19). The apostles returned to the Temple courts under orders from the angel to 'tell the people the full message of this new life' (v. 20). 'All the words of this life' is an interesting descriptive designation for the gospel. Jesus alone had the 'words of eternal life' (John 6:68). He alone is 'the Life' (14:6). Jesus has been given authority over all people whereby he might give eternal life to all those given him by the Father (17:2). 'Eternal life' consists in knowing the only true God and Jesus Christ, whom the Father has sent (v. 3). Thus the message of the gospel is nothing less than 'all the words of this Life'.

At daybreak the apostles resumed their teaching to the people in the Temple area, as commanded (Acts 5:21). Meantime the Sanhedrin assembled, only to find the apostles escaped from custody, though the doors of the jail were securely locked, with the guards standing at the doors (vv. 21-23). Soon a report was received that the apostles were back in the Temple courts, teaching (v. 25).[30] The captain was sent to fetch the apostles again, but peaceably for fear of the reaction of the crowd (v. 26). The apostles were brought before the Sanhedrin (a second visit for Peter and John) to be questioned by the high priest (v. 27).

The high priest, probably addressing Peter (both as the spokesman for the other apostles and as the one to whom the previous order of the council had been directed), accuses him of disobeying the Sanhedrin's order and filling Jerusalem with their teaching concerning Jesus of Nazareth (v. 28). Note that the Sanhedrin is clearly aware of the implications of the apostolic message – it makes the Jews 'guilty of this man's blood' (v. 28).

To this accusation Peter and the other apostles replied: 'We must obey God rather than men!' (v. 29) – echoing their previous stand against the unlawful decree of the council. In just a few words Peter rehearses the points he had made so clearly in his previous messages to the Jews. The prime actor in the drama of the ministry, death, and resurrection of Jesus of Nazareth is 'the God of our fathers' (v. 30). The Jews were guilty of a terrible insult to Abraham's God by shamefully hanging the Lord's Anointed on a tree (v. 30). And finally, 'God exalted [Jesus] to his own right hand as Prince and Savior that he might give repentance and forgiveness of sins to Israel' (v. 31). Peter again describes himself and the other apostles as 'witnesses of these things,' and emphasises the fact that they are witnesses together with God, for it is the Holy Spirit himself who also bears witness to these things (v. 32; cf. John 8:13-18). Here Peter reveals his understanding of the teaching of Jesus (at the Last Supper) concerning the interrelationship between the witness of the Spirit and the witness of the disciples: 'When the Counselor comes, whom I will send to you from the Father, the Spirit of truth who goes out from the Father, he will testify about me. And you also must testify, for you have been with me from the beginning' (John 15:26-27). Thus it was that Peter had been 'filled with the Spirit' in giving his defense previously before the Sanhedrin (Acts 4:8). Since the Holy Spirit is given 'to those who obey God,' the Jewish leaders would recognize Jesus if they were obedient to God, but they are not.

This time the response of the high priests and elders was no longer cautious: 'They were furious and wanted to put them to death' (v. 33). They were restrained only by the wise counsel of Gamaliel, the much respected Pharisee and teacher of the law (v. 34; cf. 22:3), who advised the council to leave the apostles alone, indeed to let them go. Gamaliel reminded the leaders, 'For if their purpose or activity is of human origin, it will fail. But if it is from God, you will not be able to stop these men; you will only find yourselves fighting against God' (v. 39). God used the caution of Gamaliel to protect and deliver the fledgling church in Jerusalem. The apostles were severely flogged, but they were released with another order not to speak any more in the name of Jesus (v. 40).

Luke concludes his narrative: 'The apostles left the Sanhedrin, rejoicing because they had been counted worthy of suffering disgrace for the Name. Day after day, in the temple courts and from house to house, they never stopped teaching and proclaiming the good news that Jesus is the Christ' (vv. 41-42). The spread of the gospel under the protecting hand of the risen Christ was unstoppable. The Jews would continue to try – putting to death some of the leaders of the church, attempting to kill others – but ultimately they would fail. This indeed was the work of God.

Conclusion

We have seen how Peter preached Christ to the Jews. Later we will study the preaching of Paul to the same audience, and note the similarities of theme and approach. For many of us the elements of Peter's 'Jewish apologetic' may not be directly relevant to the content of our preaching, but certainly the manner and method is. You must imitate the boldness of Peter in confronting your audiences with God's clear indictment of their sinfulness before God, and with equally clear promises of salvation and eternal life for every one who turns from his sin and commits himself to Christ by faith. This boldness will be yours as you cultivate a deepening awareness of the fact that you have been called to preach by Christ, and that the Holy Spirit bears his powerful, converting witness through your proclamation of the gospel. This compelling sense of calling will come by means of your careful study and thoughtful meditation upon the Word, and your constant prayerful communion with the risen Christ. Only so will you be able to say, 'I cannot help speaking about what I have seen and heard.' Only so will your ministry manifest the irresistible working of God.

12

Stephen Before the Sanhedrin:
The 'Aroma of Death'

Stephen was one of seven men appointed by the apostles to help with the daily distribution of food within the hard-pressed congregation in Jerusalem (Acts 6:1 ff.). He was chosen from among the Grecian Jews (i.e., Jews born outside Palestine who spoke Greek and were influenced by Hellenistic culture) as indicated by his Greek name (vv. 1, 5). He and his companions were chosen because they distinguished themselves among the saints as those who were 'full of the Spirit and wisdom' (vv. 3, 5). Stephen is further described by Luke as a man 'full of God's grace and power' (v. 8). In these attributes we see evident the kind of spiritual qualifications for ministry which are essential to the preacher and pastor, as well as (in Stephen's case) to the 'deacon.' We have already discussed the 'filling of the Holy Spirit' in relation to biblical preaching in detail (ch. 5). The Spirit himself is that source of 'grace and power' so evident in the ministry of Stephen, and in yours as well.

An Irrefutable Witness
Soon after his ordination (v. 6), Stephen began his ministry – it was not confined to 'waiting on tables' (v. 2). His service in the church apparently included considerable preaching activity. Luke tells us that Stephen's labors were accompanied by 'great wonders and miraculous signs' which authenticated his ministry as apostolic (v. 8; cf. the 'signs of the apostles', 2 Cor. 12:12). His ministry was so effective that it quickly provoked opposition from a group of Jews who had formerly been slaves – the so-called 'Synagogue of the Freedmen' (v. 9). Such was Stephen's wisdom – manifest in both his preaching and debating – that, according to Luke, his opponents 'could not stand up against his wisdom or the Spirit by whom he spoke' (v. 10). What a testimony to the effectiveness of this man's work! Would that our preaching and debating would be attended with such convicting power!

No one could 'stand up against his wisdom or the Spirit by whom he spoke' (Acts 6:10). Can you recognize here an echo of the promise

Jesus made to his disciples concerning his special blessing upon the
testimony of his witnesses (Luke 21:14-15)? As we have discussed
at an earlier point,[1] Jesus had promised to attend the apostles' ministry
with his personal presence, even to the end of the age (Matt. 28:20).
He would not leave them as orphans, but would come to them (John
14:18). The Spirit would bear witness to Christ, even as the apostles
bore witness (15:26 f.). Thus when Christ promised to equip his
disciples with all they needed to bring an invincible witness to men, it
is primarily the presence of the Spirit of whom he is speaking. Of that
Spirit, Jesus said, 'When he comes, he will convict (*elenchei*) the
world of guilt in regard to sin and righteousness and judgment' (John
16:8). The Spirit is the source of this effective, convicting testimony,
and thus Stephen, though not himself an apostolic organ of special
revelation, yet 'full of the Holy Spirit' found himself irrefutable as he
proclaimed the Word of God and the testimony of Jesus. Thus no one
could stand up against Stephen's wisdom, for he spoke the very words
of the Spirit of God.

This truth should be an encouragement to you who preach today
as well. God has promised to place this very same benediction to your
ministry. Though, like Stephen, you are not an apostle, you do share
the fullness of the same Spirit. If you are faithful in your proclamation
of the Word from Scripture – which is the Word of the Holy Spirit (1
Pet. 1:11; 2 Pet. 1:21) – you can expect the same grace and power to
manifest themselves to the conviction of the consciences of men.[2]
'We preach Christ crucified: ... the power of God and the wisdom of
God' (1 Cor. 1:23 f.). Such power in Stephen was irresistible! Such
wisdom in you will be irrefutable!

Falsely Accused

But bearing an irresistible and irrefutable testimony does not mean
you will win every argument – especially if the other side cheats!

> Then they secretly persuaded some men to say, 'We have heard Stephen
> speak words of blasphemy against Moses and against God.' So they
> stirred up the people and the elders and the teachers of the law. They
> seized Stephen and brought him before the Sanhedrin. They produced
> false witnesses, who testified, 'This fellow never stops speaking against
> this holy place and against the law. For we have heard him say that this
> Jesus of Nazareth will destroy this place and change the customs Moses
> handed down to us' (Acts 6:11-14).

Here Luke sets the stage for Stephen's defense, which is at the same time a sermon, delivered before the Jewish Council. Stephen faces some formidable opponents. The Jewish leadership has already shown itself hostile to the apostles, having already forbidden Peter and John to preach or teach in the Name of Jesus (4:18; 5:40), so Stephen faced a Council already committed to that precedent. As he entered their midst he was guilty until proven innocent, and vindication before this court was all but impossible.

This problem was compounded by the fact that this was the very group of leaders that had condemned Jesus himself (Matt. 26:57-66), and handed him over to Pilate for execution (John 18:28-31). Unless these men were ready to admit their guilty lawlessness in the trial and execution of Jesus, they were not at all likely to give Stephen a fair hearing. And if the deck was not sufficiently stacked against this bold deacon at the outset, Stephen's antagonists added to his predicament by bringing in a number of false witnesses who were willing to testify against him.

A Bold and Confident Witness

Was not the situation facing Stephen hopeless? Yes. Humanly speaking it was. What was Stephen thinking as he looked at the stern faces of his judges? Can he have imagined that he would be able to win the day in the face of such hostile opposition? Probably not. Yet Luke tells us, 'All who were sitting in the Sanhedrin looked intently at Stephen, and they saw that his face was like the face of an angel' (Acts 6:15). An enigmatic comment. Stephen was obviously not cowed by his enemies. Rather his mind was turning in another direction, toward the heavenly court before which he was about to bear witness. He was the 'messenger' (*angelos*) of Christ, and the look on his face appeared to reflect that fact. Saul remembered it, and later passed this eyewitness detail on to Luke.[3]

Stephen had a clear sense of his mission. As a herald of the risen King Jesus, he was called upon by Christ to hold fast a good confession, even as Christ had done previously in the presence of these very men (Heb. 4:14; 1 Tim. 6:12 f.). This Council imagined that it was about to pass judgment upon Stephen, but in reality it was itself on trial. The man Jesus of Nazareth, whom they had wrongly condemned to death, was now risen from the dead. As Stephen was soon to see in a vision (Acts 7:55-56), the heavenly court had convened. God, the Judge of judges, is seated in glory on his throne, and Jesus Christ the Righteous is standing at his right hand. Stephen stands before the Council on earth to testify at the arraignment of the Sanhedrin (and the Jewish nation they represented) before the judgment seat of God. He will bring the charge in Jesus' Name against them (vv. 51-53), and their judicial murder of Stephen will certify the righteousness of God's condemnation of these stiff-necked and rebellious leaders.[4]

This incident calls to mind another one familiar from the Old Testament. There the words of three faithful and fearless servants of God, facing a similarly impossible situation, and called upon to speak their testimony before a hostile power threatening them with death, ring out:

> Shadrach, Meshach and Abednego replied to the king, 'O Nebuchadnezzar, we do not need to defend ourselves before you in this matter. If we are thrown into the blazing furnace, the God we serve is able to save us from it, and he will rescue us from your hand, O king. But even if he does not, we want you to know, O king, that we will not serve your gods or worship the image of gold you have set up' (Dan. 3:16-18).

So might solitary Stephen say to the Sanhedrin. His 'defense' is not really an act of self-defense, but a defense of the faith. It is a vindication of Christ who was crucified in weakness, raised in power, and ascended into glory to reign forever, 'King of kings and Lord of lords' (cf. 1 Tim. 3:16; Rev. 11:15).

The Contours of Stephen's Defense

Stephen's sermon is shaped by his perception of the hostility of the environment in which he is preaching, and the form of the accusations made against him (i.e., against the message he proclaimed). First, because he understands that this audience is very volatile, and any false step could mean his end, and because he wants to be able to bring his full testimony to bear against them, Stephen determines to save his confrontational admonition until the very end of his message. The body of the sermon is virtually free of interpretive comments or hortatory interjections. He will say nothing to needlessly inflame his adversaries until he is ready to do so, having laid the foundation of his full indictment. This is not a choice made out of fearfulness – an attempt to play down the offense of the gospel in an effort to win over his opponents. Stephen intends to sting them with a sharp confrontation over their hardheartedness. Faithfulness to Christ demands nothing less. But he puts that 'stinger' in the tail of his message, for when it strikes there will be nothing more to say.

The second factor to notice about the form of Stephen's message is that it follows the contours of the accusations made against him. He was accused of 'blasphemy against Moses and against God' (6:11), which was finalized before the Sanhedrin in the charges of 'speaking against this holy place and against the law' (v. 13). To speak against the Temple, by allegedly claiming that Jesus would destroy it (v. 14), was tantamount to speaking against God himself, and to call for a change in the customs of Moses (v. 14) was to speak against the law. One recognizes old confusion, as well as falsehood, in the accusations brought against Stephen:

> The chief priests and the whole Sanhedrin were looking for false evidence against Jesus so that they could put him to death. But they did not find any, though many false witnesses came forward. Finally two came forward and declared, 'This fellow said, "I am able to destroy the temple of God and rebuild it in three days" ' (Matt. 26:59-61; cf. 27:40; John 2:19).

But despite the fact that the charges against him were trumped up, Stephen chose to answer them by an extended rehearsal of Old Testament history, selecting the people and incidents he deals with on the basis of their relevance to the charges made against him and the gospel he preached.

An Audience Which Knows the Bible

Before looking at the guiding ideas and specific statements of Stephen's message, we pause to note that the kind of sermon Stephen crafted would only work well where the audience has a high degree of biblical literacy, and is accustomed to drawing conclusions from biblical examples as well as biblical precepts. In short, it is a message perfectly suited to the Sanhedrin, and to few groups besides. Stephen knows that the Pharisees, Sadducees, and scribes that make up his audience are the theological elite of Israel. The Torah is their life, and the exacting, detailed study of the Scriptures is their daily exercise. Let us not lose sight of the fact that the rebellion of the Jewish leaders was not based on ignorance, but on knowing and willful disobedience. Jesus observed about them: 'The teachers of the law and the Pharisees sit in Moses' seat. So you must obey them and do everything they tell you. But do not do what they do, for they do not practice what they preach' (Matt. 23:2f). Paul evaluated his former co-religionists in similar categories:

> Israel, who pursued a law of righteousness, has not attained it. Why not? Because they pursued it not by faith but as if it were by works. They stumbled over the 'stumbling stone' (Rom. 9:31-32).

> For I can testify about them that they are zealous for God, but their zeal is not based on knowledge. Since they did not know the righteousness that comes from God and sought to establish their own, they did not submit to God's righteousness. Christ is the end of the law so that there may be righteousness for everyone who believes (10:2-4).

Now it is true that there was a profound spiritual ignorance (blindness) beneath this rebellion. As the Jews, and especially their leaders and teachers, read their Scriptures there was a 'veil over their hearts' which is only taken away in Christ (2 Cor. 3:15 f.). But these rabbis and priests knew their Bibles. They were accustomed, by training and profession, to drawing conclusions not only from studying and comparing didactic portions, but they could also readily deduce theological and ethical principles from narrative and descriptive portions of the Old Testament. For that reason they were able to keep right on track with Stephen's discourse, even in the absence of interpretive comments by the preacher, and had already drawn the appropriate conclusions from Stephen's examples by the time he made his point explicit in his closing words.

Stephen's Defense

Since I consider that my readers are similarly sophisticated in their ability to use the Scriptures, I think we can now move through the sermon readily once we have noted its controlling ideas. According to Stifler there are four: (1) Old Testament history shows that God's saving acts move gradually and there is development throughout the course of his dealings with his people Israel; (2) the Temple, though holy, is not exclusively so, for that which makes it holy is the presence of God, and wherever God is present, there is the 'holy place;' (3) Israel characteristically rejected their rulers and redeemers, though they would sometimes listen to them on later occasions; and (4) the message itself makes constant use of Moses and the Scriptures to support Stephen's case.[5]

The high priest asks Stephen if the charges against him are true (Acts 7:1), and Stephen delivers his message uninterrupted in reply. Like Peter and Paul under equally formal circumstances, Stephen addresses his audience with dignity and respect: 'Brothers and fathers, listen to me!' (v. 2).

He begins his survey of Old Testament history by drawing attention to 'the God of glory' (v. 2). Jehovah, the Lord of the covenant, is the prime Actor on the stage of Israel's history, and he remains so to the very day Stephen is called upon to testify before the Sanhedrin – remember the reference to 'the glory of God' enthroned above in Stephen's subsequent vision (v. 55). Stephen takes this audience clear back to the beginning – to the call of God to Abraham when he was still in Mesopotamia among the pagans (vv. 2-3). His antagonists, who put so much stock in the Temple, are reminded that God was dealing with men long before there was a Temple, or even a land (vv. 4-5). God is not slow in fulfilling his promises, Stephen points out, for though it took 400 years, God kept his promise to Abraham to give him the land of Canaan (vv. 7, 17, 45).

Implicit in Stephen's argument is the fact that these Jews should not imagine, since it had been 400 years or more since the last of the prophets (as acknowledged by them), that God could not now, through John the Baptist and Jesus, move his plan of salvation forward in another bold step of prophetic fulfillment. God was ever leading his people forward, and the temptation facing them at each step of the way was to stall – to demand the maintenance of the status quo – and resist God's call to move forward. Abraham could not rest in Haran (v. 4), nor Israel in Egypt (v. 34), neither could the Jews rest short of the fullness God had revealed in Christ.

In moving on to tell of Joseph, Stephen introduces the theme, so easily recognizable throughout Israel's history, that God's people frequently rejected the leaders and deliverers sent to them by God. This is not a new concern. Jesus himself had emphasized the problem in his parable concerning the vineyard and the unrighteous tenants (cf. Matt. 21:33-41). When God sent his servants to collect his rents, they were rejected and often killed. The Son himself experienced the same rejection. This sad tradition goes all the way back to Joseph, says Stephen. Jealousy stood at the heart of this rejection (v. 9). It is reflected as well in the question put to Moses, as reported by Stephen, 'Who made you ruler and judge over us?' (v. 27).

Yet despite rejection by the people, these leaders had the blessing of God's presence with them (vv. 9 f.). Joseph was humbled in Egypt, but in due time God raised him up and he became the instrument of deliverance for his brothers who at first had rejected him (vv. 10-15). God, ever faithful to his promise and compassionate towards his people, again prepared a deliverer for Israel (vv. 17-19). This time it is Moses (vv. 20-22), the one whom the Sanhedrin so reveres; the one against whom Stephen is accused of blaspheming. Stephen will appeal to Moses as an example of the very rejection to which he is alluding (v. 35). Like Stephen, Moses was surprised to find that Israel did not recognize her God-sent deliverer. He 'thought that his own people would realize that God was using him to rescue them, but they did not' (v. 25).

After forty years in Midian, Jehovah, 'the God of Abraham, Isaac, and Jacob' revealed himself to Moses and sent him back to Egypt to save Israel from their bondage (vv. 33-34). In this encounter Moses learns that it is the presence of God that hallows any place where he may choose to reveal himself. 'Take off your sandals,' he declares, 'the place where you are standing is holy ground' (v. 33).

It is this very Moses who announced the coming of a Prophet – known to the Sanhedrin to be the Messiah – who would be 'like him' (v. 37).

I think you can see Stephen's method of 'elenctics' – i.e., his method of bringing his audience to a conviction of their sin[6] – emerging clearly from the sermon by now. He has not yet drawn any explicit conclusions nor made any specific applications from the historical narrative he has been rehearsing. But, for the biblically sophisticated audience he is addressing, the narrative has become heavily weighted with questions. Stephen dare not (and need not at this point) make them explicit. They are growing forcefully in the minds and hearts of his hearers.

Moses had been rejected by Israel when sent by God to deliver them. He predicted a coming Prophet 'like himself' – the Messiah. Would this 'likeness' include his also being rejected by the very ones he was sent to deliver? Israel, even after many displays of saving mercy – wonders and miraculous signs in Egypt (v. 36), the angel in the desert (v. 38), the living words passed on to them (v. 38) – continued to disobey Moses (v. 39). Jesus of Nazareth had claimed to be the Messiah, and the Sanhedrin had rejected him. Had they in this way treated Jesus in the same way as Israel had treated Moses in Egypt?

Stephen then reminds Israel's leaders of a most painful piece of the nation's history, where a failure of leadership was central.

> ... in their hearts [they] turned back to Egypt. They told Aaron, 'Make us gods who will go before us. As for this fellow Moses who led us out of Egypt – we don't know what has happened to him!' That was the time they made an idol in the form of a calf. They brought sacrifices to it and held a celebration in honor of what their hands had made (vv. 39b-41).

For this rebellious rejection of Moses and the Lord, the Scriptures themselves pronounced the certain coming of an 'exile beyond Babylon' (v. 43; cf. Amos 5:25-27). Rejection of the Lord's anointed deliverers was a dangerous courting of disaster.

There are more pressing, unspoken questions. What about the Temple? God established it in stages as well. There was the tabernacle in the wilderness (v. 44), which was brought into the land and remained through the time of David (v. 45). David, though desiring earnestly to build a dwelling place for God, was prevented and Solomon was the one to do the work (vv. 46-47). Where was God before his 'house' was built? Was he not sovereignly dealing with his people? Was not every place he met with them a holy place? In Mesopotamia and Egypt and the wilderness as well as in the land and in the Temple? Stephen does not ask any of these questions, but they cry out implicitly from his sketch of biblical history.

Stephen does however make an explicit, though incontestable, point, which echoes the words of Solomon on the occasion of the dedication of the Temple (1 Kings 8:27) – viz., that the Most High does not live in houses made by men. He cites another Scripture (Isa. 66:1-2) to the same effect as decisive authority.

What inescapable conclusion is Stephen forcing the Sanhedrin to face? If saying that God is not bound to the Temple (remember the accusation made against Stephen is 'speaking against the Temple'), then the great Solomon too spoke against the Temple. Even God himself spoke against the Temple, and that in the Scriptures! Stephen, without making his argument explicit, has confounded every accusation made against him or his gospel preaching.

Stephen, for his part, knows that in Jesus Christ both the presence of God (which is the glory and holiness of the Temple) and God's appointed deliverers (like Joseph and Moses) come together finally and perfectly. Beneath the confused charge of 'Temple destroying' was the true declaration of Jesus in which he identified the Temple with his own body (John 2:19-22).

Stephen's Indictment of the Jews

Stephen has finished his narrative of Old Testament history. Where has he brought his audience? Without ever making an explicit exhortation to them, he has prepared them to receive his closing *coup de grâce*. By the time Stephen reaches this point, it is certain that the Sanhedrin has begun to remember a similar exchange on the same subjects – the Temple, Moses, the prophets – that took place in their presence on that very spot not so very long before.

> The chief priests and the whole Sanhedrin were looking for false evidence against Jesus so that they could put him to death. But they did not find any, though many false witnesses came forward. Finally two came forward and declared, 'This fellow said, "I am able to destroy the temple of God and rebuild it in three days." ' Then the high priest stood up and said to Jesus, 'Are you not going to answer? What is this testimony that these men are bringing against you?' But Jesus remained silent. The high priest said to him, 'I charge you under oath by the living God: Tell us if you are the Christ, the Son of God.' 'Yes, it is as you say,' Jesus replied. 'But I say to all of you: In the future you will see the Son of Man sitting at the right hand of the Mighty One and coming on the clouds of heaven' (Matt. 26:59-64).

Perhaps it is with an unsettling sense of *déjà vu* that the Council hears the closing broadside of Stephen. He draws all the strands of his history lesson together in one bold and burning charge:

> 'You stiff-necked people, with uncircumcised hearts and ears! You are just like your fathers: You always resist the Holy Spirit! Was there ever a prophet your fathers did not persecute? They even killed those who predicted the coming of the Righteous One. And now you have betrayed and murdered him – you who have received the law that was put into effect through angels but have not obeyed it' (Acts 7:51-53).

Yet in delivering this charge it is not Stephen who speaks. This indictment comes from heaven – from Jesus himself. He who stood silent at his own trial – except for his brief, but damning, testimony under oath (Matt. 26:63-65) – now declares his charge against the

Jewish leadership. He speaks through the mouth of his witness, Stephen.

There is one pregnant moment when a question hangs in the air as Jesus comes before them a second time in the person of his witness, Stephen. Will the Sanhedrin listen? Will they receive him whom they rejected in jealousy the first time? God in grace and patience gives another opportunity. Will they take it?

Silence the Witness!

The moment passes and the die is cast for Israel as a nation. 'They were furious and gnashed their teeth at him' (v. 54). They reject Jesus the Messiah a second time in the person of his servant Stephen, and as a consequence are themselves rejected.[7] In a final statement, Stephen draws back the curtain, and shows them what they would have understood, if they had had hearts to receive it: 'Look,' he said, 'I see heaven open and the Son of Man standing at the right hand of God' (v. 56). The leaders will not look. They will not hear. 'They covered their ears and, yelling at the top of their voices, they all rushed at him' (v. 57). Stephen, the faithful witness, is dragged from the chamber, thrust out of the city, and stoned to death.

Richard B. Gaffin, professor of New Testament at Westminster Seminary in Philadelphia, closed a sermon on Hebrews 4:14, 'The Christ and Our Confession,' with this eloquent allusion to this passage:

Here we have an example of someone who has 'held fast his confession'. Stephen has given a good and faithful witness. And it's going to cost him his life. But we're told here, we're enabled here to see, the full dimensions of what is taking place. We're told that Stephen in this extreme situation looked into heaven, and there he saw Jesus Christ, the Son of Man, *standing* at the right hand of God. Everywhere else in the Scriptures, Jesus is described as the Son of Man who *sits* at the right hand of God. And here in this *one* instance is the Son of Man who *stands*. And what is the significance of that? The Son of Man who sits is in the position of rule. He is the Judge. But the Son of Man who stands is the one who leaves (as it were) that place of rule to plead, to intercede. And you see what's happening here – on earth things unfold, wind down to this sickening miscarriage of justice. Stephen will be stoned. But in the throne room of heaven, in that ultimate law court, where things *ultimately* and *finally* count, the Judge becomes the Advocate. Jesus Christ the King becomes the Intercessor. Stephen *stands up* for Jesus Christ, and so Jesus Christ *stands up* for Stephen. And we shouldn't be all that surprised at this for Jesus is simply making good, at least in one way, on the promise he had given his disciples: 'Whoever confesses me before men, I will also confess him before my Father in heaven.' That is what Jesus Christ, the High Priest in heaven, is doing. Jesus Christ ever lives to make intercession for those who draw near to God through him.[8]

Like his Master before him, Stephen in his dying prays for his murderers (v. 60), while a young man named Saul stood nearby looking on (v. 58; 8:1). Soon the Lord Jesus would answer Stephen's prayer in part, by calling Saul to faith and commissioning him as apostle to the Gentiles (Acts 9:1-16).

Learning from Stephen
The martyrdom of Stephen touched off a wave of persecution in Jerusalem (8:1b), which drove the disciples (but not the apostles) and, with them, the gospel out in the first great wave of missionary expansion (8:4 ff; 11:19 ff.). Stephen did not win the Sanhedrin by his testimony, but his witness was not in vain. Through Luke's record, Stephen, though dead, yet speaks. His message before the Council is a rich treasury of history and theology for the Church. And I trust our examination of it will also make it a fruitful source of imitation in your preaching.

To that end, let me close this chapter with a few observations for consideration in light of your preaching practices.

Preaching and Debating
We took note earlier in our discussion of the fact that Stephen's opponents 'could not stand up against his wisdom or the Spirit by whom he spoke' (Acts 6:10). God so powerfully blessed Stephen in his preaching and teaching, that when they led to open debates with the members of the Synagogue of the Freedmen who took offense at his message (v. 9), Stephen's arguments were irrefutable.

'Open debates?' Yes debates. Did you realize that your work of preaching will demand that you be an effective debater, as Stephen was? Skim a few chapters of the Book of Acts, and notice how often the preaching of the Word issues immediately in controversy and there-fore in debate. It is truly noteworthy how often this happens. Shortly after his conversion, as the Apostle Paul was ministering the gospel freely in Jerusalem, he was drawn into debates with the Grecian Jews (Acts 9:28-29). When Apollos began to speak boldly in the synagogue at Corinth, he too was drawn into public debate with the Jews who opposed his message. He refuted them effectively, 'proving from the Scriptures that Jesus was the Christ' (18:26, 28). And we can take Luke's report of Paul's early ministry at Ephesus as characteristic of much of what occurred when the gospel was preached in a new city.

> Paul entered the synagogue and spoke boldly there for three months, arguing persuasively about the kingdom of God. But some of them became obstinate; they refused to believe and publicly maligned the Way. So Paul left them. He took the disciples with him and had discussions daily in the lecture hall of Tyrannus (19:8-9).

And there are many other examples (cf. Acts 17:1-3; 18:1, 4, 19; 24:24, 25). Frequently the apostles are called upon to answer for what they are preaching, and to reason from the Scriptures to prove their point. Sometimes they succeed in convincing their audience, sometimes they do not, but they never fail for lack of trying.

Why is this? It is, of course, rooted in the native hostility of this world order to the things of God (1 Cor. 2:7-8). When confronted with the legitimate claims of God the 'natural man', the pretentious would-be 'god', rebels. He refuses to hear what God has to say. The more pointed and confrontational is the declaration of the Word of God, the more hostile his reaction is likely to be (Rom. 8:7-8). The exact character of an individual's response to your proclamation of the Word will differ from person to person. It will range from polite disregard, to sullen silence, to angry scowls, to belligerent questioning, to contradiction and debate, to insults and abuse, to physical violence. I'm certain that, like me, you have experienced many of these responses to both your preaching and your personal and pastoral dealings with people, inside and outside the church.[9]

To be sure, in our week-by-week ministry to a local congregation, we pastors are not likely to face the kind of vociferous opposition faced in those early days by the apostles, or today by the missionary or evangelist who carries the gospel into an openly hostile cultural environment. In most of our polite congregations, church going protocol forbids hostile public reactions to the preacher. People may not come back to church again, but they don't often stand up and argue with you in the service.

This is a difference of degree and nothing more. All bold and effective preaching will lead to debate (inwardly or outwardly). If you are a faithful preacher, you should expect it – if not during the service, at least at the door following the service, or in the week following on the phone. The true herald of God should not take offense, or get his feelings hurt, when someone challenges his teaching. It's not a personal insult, or at least you shouldn't take it as one, though it may be couched in very personal terms. People usually don't know how to separate the man from the message; such opposition to God's Word is not surprising.

You should expect it, and prepare for it. When faced with opposition to the truth (from the pagan or the heretic), we should be ready to win the argument by honest reasoning from Scripture and by winsome persuasion. What a tragedy when errorists are more effective polemicists than the champions of the true faith. Peter gives us this command:

> Always be prepared to give the reason for the hope that you have. But do this with gentleness and respect, keeping a clear conscience, so that those who speak maliciously against your good behavior in Christ may be ashamed of their slander (1 Pet. 3:15-16).

As a preacher this is not optional for you. If you are not able or willing to engage in debate in defense of the faith, you are not qualified to be a minister of the gospel. Titus 1:9 reminds us that as ministers of the Word, we are called upon, and must therefore be equipped and able, 'by sound doctrine both to exhort and to convince the gainsayers' (AV). There is both a teaching side and a debating/convincing side to your ministry as a preacher.

The verb *elenchō* (variously translated 'convict,' 'convince,' 'rebuke,' or 'reprove') means to bring one to conviction. This term is sometimes used in a legal setting to mean to pursue a case against another so far that he is convicted of the crime of which he was accused (the related noun *elenchō* means 'proof' or 'inward conviction,' cf. Heb. 11:1). Thus the term refers not merely to a rebuke or reproof, but to an effective rebuke or reproof.[10] We are told in the Old Testament that God himself uses such convicting rebukes in his training of his children (cf. Prov. 3:12; Job 5:17 LXX). As we come into the New Testament, both Jesus (Rev. 3:19; Jude 15) and the Holy Spirit (John 16:8) engage in this same work of bringing conviction to the hearts of men. The term also appears in 2 Timothy 3:16 to describe one of the purposes of Scripture. Therefore, we who are sent by Christ and empowered by the Spirit to proclaim the Word of God must be able and willing to work to bring men to conviction by effective rebuking. It is an integral feature of your work of preaching, teaching, counseling, even informal witness bearing. Thus we see it demonstrated clearly in Stephen and the other apostolic witnesses. As a debater, Luke says, Stephen was unbeatable.

In a day like ours, when churches are more and more eager to *avoid* controversy, sometimes at any cost, we need to be reminded that, as Christians, but especially as ministers, we are 'to earnestly contend for the faith which was once delivered to the saints' (Jude 3, AV). It is a responsibility over which we ought to take great pains (cf. 1 Tim. 4:15 f.). A pastor whose preaching is not stirring up controversy, and who is not willing to involve himself in doctrinal and ethical debate for the purpose of bringing the opponents of the gospel to conviction, is failing to fulfill the responsibilities of his calling and office from God.

Please remember (since this is often misunderstood), I am not talking about controversy *for its own sake*. We pastors are not to be pugnacious or argumentative, 'spoiling for a fight' (1 Tim. 3:3; 2 Tim. 2:24). But neither are we to seek peace and consensus at the expense of clarity with regard to the truth. If the gospel is truly 'weakness' and 'foolishness' as far as this world is concerned, as Paul testifies (1 Cor. 1:18-25), then we ought to expect that our preaching, if consistent in proclaiming 'Christ crucified', will get us into intellectual, moral, and perhaps even physical scrapes from time to time. Jesus' preaching did. Paul's did. Stephen's did. What makes you think you are immune?

Students of church history know that the Church's understanding of biblical doctrine has often taken great steps forward through controversy.[11] Look what gains were made in the life of the Church through the Jew-Gentile controversy of the New Testament period (Acts 15). Essential aspects of the gospel were defined through Paul's controversy with the 'Judaizers' in Galatia (Gal. 3). The Arian controversy of the fourth century led the Church to a clearer grasp of the biblical doctrine of the Trinity and the person of Christ. The Pelagian controversy gave us a more profound understanding of the nature of sin and grace. Theology grows – the Church grows – in part through controversy.

So valuable were these spiritual, intellectual, and moral struggles in clarifying the Church's appreciation for biblical truth, that at times formal theological 'disputations' have been institutionalized as an accepted part of the Church's life. When confronted with Luther's early teachings, the natural thing for Rome to do was to arrange a disputation to confront and (they thought) refute the heretic. The 'Leipzig Disputation' backfired on the forces of Rome, but it clarified and propagated the 'Protestant' cause, and the truth won out again. I truly wonder if the modern evangelical church is better off for the tacit decision to 'agree to disagree' over such important issues as the nature of God's work in salvation (e.g., Arminians vs. Calvinists), the subjects of baptism (e.g., adult baptists vs. infant baptists), or eschatology (premils, postmils, amils, 'panmils').

In our churches such debate should be polite and civilized. But even there we prefer to call them 'discussions,' to avoid any hint of contention. Our worship services have evolved to the point where even asking questions of, let alone entering into debate with, the preacher is considered a serious breach of decorum. In a way that is too bad. Instead, today, when people disagree with the preacher, it is much more likely that they will 'roast him' (behind his back) over Sunday supper, or will simply leave and look for another church (or another preacher) that they do agree with. This is commonly accepted as the loving, caring way to handle disagreements in churches. Few, it seems, are willing to take the time and trouble, and risk the vulnerability, required to persuade, or be persuaded, by discussing and debating issues – where everyone concerned seriously wrestles with the Scriptures – until proper conclusions are reached and agreed upon.

It is important, of course, that everything in our worship be done 'with decency and good order' (1 Cor. 14:40, cf. v. 33). But it is too bad that even Berean-style inquiry (Acts 17:11) cannot find a place for exercise in many of our assemblies. Perhaps adult Sunday school would provide a good setting, but I suspect that in many churches the preacher is not required (by himself or by his board) to make himself available for questions and discussion of his sermons (much less critique or evaluation of his preaching in light of Scripture). The old cliché about 'preaching to the choir' draws our attention to the hazards of never having to answer for our teaching to our people or to our peers through questioning and theological debate. Since we all tend to draw the conclusion that, if we are not challenged, we must be correct, having developed an atmosphere in the Church where such things as controversy and debate are not encouraged (or even tolerated), we are in danger of allowing for the unchecked growth of serious error. One need not look far on the contemporary Church scene to find evidences of this very problem.

Stephen was a great preacher and a powerful controversialist, and we who are preachers today would do well to learn from his example in both areas. The Church will be the healthier for it.

Preaching to the Biblically Illiterate
The Sanhedrin was the most biblically sophisticated assembly on the face of the earth in Stephen's day. We have already noted that Stephen was able to take full advantage of the extensive knowledge of the Bible in delivering his indictment against them. The more your audience knows about the content and structure of the Bible, the more freedom you will have in preaching to them. You will be able to cite or allude to events in biblical history, or refer to the example of characters in both the Old and New Testaments, etc., without having to turn to them or extensively explain the reference. This serves to enrich your exposition and application of the passage from which you are preaching, and allows you to connect various passages, events, people, and themes in a biblical matrix for your hearers.[12] This is not possible when in every sermon you must review again and again the elementary teachings about Christ, laying again the foundation of repentance and faith (Heb. 6:1).

Yet as biblical literacy declines in our culture, this is exactly what many preachers are forced to do. We do not enjoy the same freedom that Stephen had in preaching to the Sanhedrin, or even a general Jewish audience. This problem arises, in part, from the fact that more and more people who visit our churches these days know next to nothing about the Bible. Though this has not been the case in past generations, where there has been a 'Christian memory' even on the part of the unchurched, it is still not unusual from the standpoint of the Book of Acts. We encounter unchurched people every day who are ignorant of the content of the Bible, as the Gentiles of the first century were.

The real problem arises when pastors operate on the assumption that their hearers know the Bible, or when they fail to support their pulpit ministry with a systematic program of education which has as its purpose providing church members with a growing, comprehensive knowledge of the content of the Scriptures. Preachers too often preach on the assumption that people have a background of understanding that they do not have. Many modern evangelistic methods do not require the presentation of much in the way of biblical content, and thus 'converts' may enter the church still largely ignorant of the Bible. They struggle to keep up with the preaching and are often embarrassed to ask questions; after all, everyone else already knows these things. Their spiritual growth is stunted for lack of knowledge and they don't know how to help themselves. Some eventually lose heart and drift away.

You must support your preaching with education. Many adult Sunday school classes are devoted to relational and problem-solving issues, when more should be teaching adults the basics of the Bible. It may strike some as 'childish' but it is absolutely necessary to lay out a base of information upon which your preaching can build. In addition you must encourage your people to read the Bible, not 'devotionally' (for a feeling), but broadly for information and understanding. Church members who struggle with illiteracy with respect to the Bible will be just as thankful as many of those adults in our society who cannot read when someone finally breaks the silence and helps them get the information they need and so desire, but are afraid to request.

It's Not Over Till It's Over

Stephen made no explicit indictment of his audience until his message was nearly finished. When he finally declared, 'You stiff-necked people, with uncircumcised hearts and ears! You are just like your fathers: You always resist the Holy Spirit!' (Acts 7:51), he had the full force of his whole message behind the rebuke.

In this respect Stephen's method was like that of Nathan the prophet in confronting King David with his dual sins of adultery and murder. Recognizing that David was guilty, the prophet had to find a way to bring the full force of the king's offenses against his conscience so that he would be broken before God and repent. To begin his message with the accusation of David's crimes might well have been to bring down the wrath of a defensive king upon his head. So Nathan determined to save the charge for the end, and begin rather with a parable. The story of the stolen ewe lamb so incensed the king, so provoked his moral outrage, that when Nathan finally concluded his message with the words, 'You are the man!' (2 Sam. 12:7), David was completely undone.

Likewise, for Stephen to begin his message with the indictment against the Jewish leaders (which he planned all along to bring) could well have brought an immediate end to his sermon. Stephen, therefore, wisely decided to lay out his case in full before drawing his conclusion, so that the 'elenctic force' of his survey of Jewish history could be brought to bear fully through the closing accusation. The Jews were convicted even if they were not convinced.

This is a wise approach to presenting controversial material when preaching to a hostile audience. Ordinarily it is not wise to follow this procedure in your sermons, for people need to know where you are taking them as a means of organizing and understanding the body of your sermon. If the audience is required to ask very often 'Where is this going?' you will lose them. There are some exceptions, however, and a preaching situation like that faced by Stephen is one of them. You will be required at times to set before your congregations things that they may not wish to hear – doctrines they don't agree with, ethical demands they are unwilling to submit to. You will face the danger of 'turning them off.' Many preachers 'solve' this problem by simply refusing to preach on 'controversial' subjects. This is a serious mistake, and unfaithfulness to your calling to preach the whole counsel of God (Acts 20:27). Rather you must, like Stephen, present the material in such a way that the case is fully made before you call upon the congregation to change their way of thinking or living. Use the weight of scriptural argument to establish beyond question the point at issue, then call upon your people before God to repent. You may not always convince or persuade them, but your preaching can convict them, and your method of presenting the material will ensure that they will not leave you before you have made your case.

Biblical History from Memory

One final note before we conclude. It is important to remember that Stephen and the other preachers in Acts make use of the Scriptures (i.e., the entire Old Testament) *from memory*. They did not carry their Bibles with them, much less notes of significant points and passages they wished to refer to in the course of their sermons. The Word they used was in their minds. In Stephen's sermon he was able to range broadly over Old Testament history, because he had a fluent grasp of the content of the Scriptures. He had treasured up the Word of the Lord in his heart.

We discussed earlier the special promise of the Lord Jesus to the effect that the Holy Spirit would help the apostles remember the things which Jesus had taught them, indeed would teach them more about the importance of the work of Christ (John 16:12-15).[143] I do not think that Stephen's recall of Old Testament history in this sermon is an example of the direct fulfillment of that promise. Rather, I believe Stephen's knowledge is the result of careful and continual exposure to the Scriptures (reading and especially memorization of the Word) over many years. It is evident that all of the apostolic preachers have a vast grasp of the content of the Scriptures from memory. That is perhaps not surprising in someone like Paul who had the best rabbinic education available in his day. But it was equally true of Peter and John, common fishermen. To be sure the Holy Spirit especially blessed their recall, but you cannot 'recall' that which is not hidden in the mind in the first place.

We have discussed above the decline of biblical literacy in our culture and in the church. Educators have been discounting the value of memorization for many years now. Even Christian families neglect daily Bible reading in the home, and few children are taught to memorize Scripture beyond the limited demands of a Sunday school class. This has had a devastating impact upon pastors as well as on church members. Ministerial candidates are drawn from the same pool. Many men who believe themselves called to the ministry are largely ignorant of the content of the Bible. They lack the broad background in Scripture necessary to provide a context for their specialized studies. In recent years many seminaries have had to require entrance exams and even introductory survey classes in English Bible in order to give students sufficient background to be able to do their work. Once engaged in a seminary program students are often required to spend more time reading dead German liberal theologians than they are the prophets of God.[14]

Once in the pastorate there are many other demands upon one's limited reading time, and if you have not mastered the disciplines of extensive Bible reading and memorization of important passages, you will remain largely ignorant of the content of God's Word. It is not neglectful parishioners alone who spend more time each day reading the newspaper and magazines – or surfing the internet – than they do the Bible. They are often led by negligent pastors who, if they are honest, would have to admit they do the very same thing. I'm convinced that so much preaching is so 'thin' because the preacher simply cannot bring a rich understanding of Scripture to his work of sermon preparation, and he cannot 'cram' sufficiently in a week to compensate for his underlying ignorance.

If you are going to preach like Stephen, you must know your Bible well. You must become familiar with its content through extensive reading. Dr. Bruce Waltke once told of a young rabbi with whom he roomed while studying in Jerusalem. It became apparent during their time together that this young man knew much of the Scriptures from memory. Upon questioning it came out that the rabbi knew the entire Pentateuch and the Psalter verbatim. Dr. Waltke asked the rabbi if he would be willing to recite them for him, which he did as Dr. Waltke followed along in his Hebrew Bible. It seems apparent that the apostolic preachers had that kind of grasp of the Scriptures. Their messages are rich with quotations from and allusions to the Old Testament, and all without benefit of concordance and cross-reference systems! You should strive for that kind of mastery if we want to be effective preachers. As Jesus said, 'Therefore every teacher of the law who has been instructed about the kingdom of heaven is like the owner of a house who brings out of his storeroom new treasures as well as old' (Matt. 13:52).

13

Peter's Sermon to the Household of Cornelius: The Gentiles Prepared for the Good News

Have you ever preached a sermon that was so favorably received by your congregation that you thought they must have been specially prepared for it by God? This was exactly the right sermon to the right people at the right time! It is a wonderful experience for a pastor. But it doesn't happen very often. Your customary experience in preaching is to have some of your people respond to your message with faith and obedience, while others are polite but seem unimpacted by the sermon.

Jesus told the 'parable of the sower' (actually of the seed and the soils) in Matthew 13:3-9, pointing out that the gospel falls upon the hearts of men in various stages of receptivity. In his explanation of the parable, our Lord pointed out that some people hear the message about the kingdom but do not understand it, and Satan comes and snatches away the Word that was sown in their hearts (v. 19). Those are the people who lose the impact of your sermon over coffee during the fellowship time after morning worship on Sunday. Others have an immediate joyful response upon hearing the Word, but that happy reaction soon fades away in the face of trouble or persecution (vv. 20-21). These folks remember your message until about Tuesday, when they are back into the daily grind and other problems eclipse the Word of God in their minds. Still others find the Word 'choked out' and rendered unfruitful in their lives because of their worldly anxieties or self-deceptive greed (v. 22). These men and women can't seem to bring themselves to use Scripture as the controlling factor in daily decision-making. It gets in the way of their pursuit of their own desires, and so they forget the Word you have preached.

But Jesus said there were also those whose hearts were like 'good soil', men and women who hear the Word of God and understand it, and then go home and put it into daily use in fruitful Christian living (v. 23). The presence of these hearers in each congregation make the preaching task worthwhile. Knowing that God's Word is having a powerful, life-changing effect upon some of your members keeps you working hard to feed them good spiritual food so that they will continue to grow (1 Pet. 2:2).

Well, when Peter went to the home of Cornelius, the Roman centurion from Caesarea, and found the room full of the Gentile's extended family and friends, God gave him the opportunity of a lifetime – to sow the seed of the gospel on a field which appeared to be composed entirely of 'good soil'! Peter had been chosen by God to present the gospel for the first time to an entirely Gentile audience, and God had graciously prepared the hearts of the hearers so that the Word of Christ was received with eagerness. With this message Peter uses the 'keys' entrusted to the apostles by Christ (Matt. 16:19)[1] to open the Kingdom of Heaven to the Gentiles, and as a result of this sermon (and others like it which would follow) the history of the world was forever changed.

God's Preparations for the Gospel

Stifler comments concerning this section of Luke's narrative in Acts, 'The idea which runs through this section from beginning to end is preparation.'[2] Luke emphasizes this point by the repetition in the narrative of those divine preparations – both on Cornelius's end and on Peter's.

Cornelius and his family were prepared for the gospel of Christ both (in a general way) by their spiritual pilgrimage toward Judaism – 'He and all his family were devout and God-fearing; he gave generously to those in need and prayed to God regularly' (Acts 10:2)[3] – and (more immediately) by the vision he was given by the Lord. One day at about three in the afternoon he had a vision in which an angel of God told him to send for Simon Peter in Joppa (vv. 3-6). Cornelius responded to this vision in faith, and sent his servants for Peter as instructed (vv. 7-8). Cornelius later rehearsed this vision for Peter in explaining why the apostle had been sent for (vv. 30-33). Peter also alluded to Cornelius's vision when he was informing the Jerusalem apostles about the events in Caesarea (11:13-14), adding that Cornelius was told in the vision that Peter would bring him 'a message through which [Cornelius] and all [his] household would be saved' (v. 14).

Peter was also prepared by the Lord for his encounter with the Gentiles. As a Jew he knew the ancient promise of God that the covenant mercies shown toward Abraham and his descendants would also be extended to the Gentiles (Gen. 12:3; etc.). He had even preached about this point in an earlier message (3:25-26).[4] What's more, Jesus had sometimes alluded to the inclusion of the Gentiles in Kingdom blessings during his public ministry. For example, in response to the faith of another Roman centurion, Jesus had said, 'I say to you that many will come from the east and the west, and will take their places at the feast with Abraham, Isaac and Jacob in the kingdom of heaven' (Matt. 8:11).[5] Jesus had also anticipated the abolition of the old covenant ceremonial dietary regulations – one of the chief hindrances to Jew-Gentile fellowship (Mark 7:14-23). Some commentators point to Peter's staying in the house of a tanner (a ceremonially unclean profession) while in Joppa (Acts 9:43; 10:6) as an indication that Peter may have learned to be less scrupulous about some ceremonial considerations by this point.[6] Despite this background, it took a vision to prepare Peter to accept Cornelius's invitation when it came.

While Cornelius's emissaries were en route to Joppa, Peter was on the roof of Simon's house praying (10:9). Peter 'fell into a trance and saw heaven opened and something like a large sheet being let down to earth by its four corners. It contained all kinds of four-footed animals, as well as reptiles of the earth and birds of the air' (vv. 11-12). Three times Peter was commanded by a heavenly voice to 'Kill and eat' (v. 13). Three times he protested (though he apparently recognized the voice as that of the Lord), 'Surely not... I have never eaten anything impure or unclean' (vv. 13-14). Three times the Lord remonstrated, 'Do not call anything impure that God has made clean' (v. 15). As Peter pondered the meaning of the vision, the men sent by Cornelius arrived at Simon's house looking for Peter (vv. 17-18). Peter was instructed by the Holy Spirit not to hesitate to go with Cornelius's men, for they had been sent by him (vv. 19-20). Peter understood. He immediately invited the men into the house to be his guests, and the next day he set out with them for Caesarea, accompanied by six brothers from Joppa (v. 23; cf. 11:12). Later Peter told Cornelius, 'God has shown me that I should not call any man impure or unclean' (v. 28).

As I mentioned above, Luke lays great stress on these preparations – repeating the account of the visions given to Cornelius and Peter three times in chapters 10–11. For the purpose of Luke's redemptive-historical narrative of the spread of the gospel, this event – the passing of the gospel into the Gentile world – is most significant, and its importance is underlined by these repetitions. This was a huge step for Peter, and a huge step for the Church.

For our purpose as pastors and evangelists studying the preaching of the apostles, this supernatural preparation of both preacher and audience serves to remind us that God is always sovereignly at work in preparing us, and our congregations, for the delivery and receiving of the Word of God we proclaim. Though God no longer uses these extraordinary 'sign' methods of preparation (i.e., special revelations of the Spirit given through visions and voices[7]), Christ does providentially prepare us in more general ways, even as he did Peter and Cornelius. Our study and meditation upon the Word, our daily communion with Christ in prayer, our lifelong experiences in putting the Scriptures into practice in daily living, our growth in grace and maturing faith: all these serve to prepare us for each sermon. On top of that, of course, is the specific preparations we make for each message. On the other side, God uses the same factors in the lives of our people to make them attentive and faithful hearers of the Word. We'll say a little more about what makes a good listener later in our discussion.

Common Vessels, Glorious Treasure
When Peter and his companions finally reached Cornelius's home, they found a large gathering of people (v. 27). As Peter entered the house, Cornelius paid homage to him by falling at his feet, but Peter refused the honor, reminding him, 'I am only a man myself' (vv. 25-26). Soon afterwards, however, Cornelius acknowledges that he, his family, and friends were all gathered 'here in the presence of God to listen to everything the Lord has commanded you to tell us' (v. 33). God's servant, the preacher, is only a man, but he is *God's* messenger. The pastor must always be aware of these two things – he is but a man, but he is God's man. The dignity of the office we hold, and the importance of the message we proclaim, can, if we are not careful, lead to a proud haughty spirit. God's people are willing enough to put their pastor on a pedestal, and too often we are willing to be thus exalted. Like Diotrephes, we can learn to 'love the first place' (3 John 9). May the spirit of Peter, and Paul (cf. Acts 14:15), be ours. May we conduct ourselves in ministry with humility as did John the Baptist declaring, 'Jesus must increase, I must decrease' (John 3:30). As Jesus himself said, 'Whoever wants to become great among you

must be your servant, and whoever wants to be first must be slave of all' (Mark 10:43-44), and in him we find the perfect example of such humility in service (cf. John 13:13-17). At the same time we must not let the common weakness of the messenger detract from the glory of the gospel we proclaim. Paul warned Timothy not to let anyone look down on him because of his youthfulness (1 Tim. 4:12). You may be mere men, but before your pulpit week after week men and women gather 'in the presence of God to listen to everything the Lord has commanded you to tell [them].' Paul rightly pointed out that 'we have this treasure in jars of clay to show that this all-surpassing power is from God and not from us' (2 Cor. 4:7).

'God Is No Respecter of Persons'

Peter asked Cornelius, 'May I ask why you sent for me?' (Acts 10:29), and after receiving the centurion's answer, Peter began his sermon. Luke introduces Peter's words with a formula which highlights the importance of what the apostle is about to say: 'Peter opened his mouth and said:...' (v. 34).[8] Peter took his starting point from the profound change which God had so recently brought about in his own point of view regarding God's attitude toward Gentiles.[9] 'I now realize how true it is that God does not show favoritism but accepts men from every nation who fear him and do what is right' (vv. 34-35, cf. v. 28). The truth that God is willing to receive Gentiles when they turn to him through faith in Christ has been powerfully impressed upon Peter by his recent experiences, and now he will proclaim the implications of that lesson to Cornelius's family and friends. Later in Acts, the Apostle Paul will also use his personal testimony to underline the transition that God was bringing to pass in his redemptive purposes by sending the gospel to the Gentiles (e.g., 22:1-21).

The note of racial and national 'universalism' in God's saving purpose is highlighted throughout Peter's message. Whoever fears God and does what is right is acceptable to God, regardless of the nation from which he comes (v. 35). Christ is identified as the 'Lord of everything' (v. 36),[10] who will one day be the Judge of all the living and the dead (v. 42). Again the promise of forgiveness through faith in his name is extended to 'everyone who believes' (v. 43).

Peter adapts his message wonderfully to his Gentile audience by showing them again and again that God's mercy is for them. Until he had the vision four days earlier, the pious Cornelius[11] could have hoped for no greater spiritual blessing than that which was already available to him in the Jewish synagogue.[12] He could worship and pray, hear the Scriptures expounded, and devote himself to good deeds. But he must always stand at a distance from God. His acceptance with God was 'provisional'. But now for the first time he was hearing from Peter a new and better hope. Now a door was being opened for him and his family – entry through faith in Christ into the fullness of redemptive privilege and blessing. That was indeed good news!

Peter had spoken of those who 'fear [God] and do what is right' (v. 35). In this statement he was no doubt reflecting what he had learned of Cornelius from the reports of the angelic words which attended the Gentile's dream. The Lord had told Cornelius through the angel, 'Your prayers and gifts to the poor have come up as a memorial offering before God' (v. 4). The centurion had later reported to Peter the angel's words, 'Cornelius, God has heard your prayer and remembered your gifts to the poor' (v. 31).

Some have confused this description with works righteousness, as if Cornelius were somehow being commended before God on the basis of his own good works. This is not the case, however. The words of the angel of the Lord and of Peter simply reflect the language of faithful covenant keeping in its Old Testament idiom. Micah had summed up the life of faith for the old covenant saint with the words: 'He has showed you, O man, what is good. And what does the LORD require of you? To act justly and to love mercy and to walk humbly with your God' (Micah 6:8). 'Fearing God' and 'walking humbly with God' entailed the realization that hope for salvation rested in the gracious provision of the Lord, embodied in the sacrificial provisions of the Law of Moses in particular. 'Turn to me and be saved, all you ends of the earth; for I am God, and there is no other' (Isa. 45:22). 'Doing what is right' (i.e., acting justly) and 'loving mercy' – as Cornelius had – were the fruits of faith. Paul makes the same point in Romans 2:6-11:

> God 'will give to each person according to what he has done.' To those who by persistence in doing good seek glory, honor and immortality, he will give eternal life. But for those who are self-seeking and who reject the truth and follow evil, there will be wrath and anger. There will be trouble and distress for every human being who does evil: first for the Jew, then for the Gentile; but glory, honor and peace for everyone who does good: first for the Jew, then for the Gentile. For God does not show favoritism.

Paul is not proposing a hypothetical self-justification here. Rather, he is saying that those who are covenant keepers – Jew or Gentile – will receive God's gracious promise of eternal life, while those who are covenant breakers – Jew or Gentile – will receive what they deserve, God's wrath and anger. Covenant-keeping Jews came to faith in Christ, the fulfillment of their old covenant expectation, upon hearing the gospel concerning his death and resurrection (Acts 2:37-38; 3:19-26). Covenant-keeping Gentiles – like the 'God-fearer' Cornelius and his family – also put their faith in Christ upon hearing the gospel. 'For God does not show favoritism.'

Cornelius was already a 'believer' – before Peter made his visit. God in his mercy sent Peter to make known to Cornelius the fulfillment of that hope which he had embraced in Judaism. For that reason Peter's sermon to these Gentiles (unlike those which Paul will later bring to totally pagan Gentiles) is very much like the messages he preached to the Jews in Jerusalem.

'You Know What Has Happened'

Central to Peter's message is an overview of the earthly ministry of Jesus of Nazareth. The gospel message is the 'good news' concerning the Person and saving work of Jesus Christ (cf. Rom. 1:2-4; 1 Cor. 15:3-8). It is the same message you must preach today. This message is encapsulated in Luke's summaries of the apostolic sermons, and elaborated in the Gospels and epistles of the New Testament. Peter calls it 'the good news of peace' (Acts 10:36; cf. Isa. 52:7; Luke 2:10-14). That the message of 'peace with God' was of special significance to Gentile audiences is evident from the words of Paul to the Ephesians:

> But now in Christ Jesus you who once were far away have been brought near through the blood of Christ. For he himself is our peace, who has made the two one and has destroyed the barrier, the dividing wall of hostility, by abolishing in his flesh the law with its commandments and regulations. His purpose was to create in himself one new man out of the two, thus making peace, and in this one body to reconcile both of them to God through the cross, by which he put to death their hostility. He came and preached peace to you who were far away and peace to those who were near. For through him we both have access to the Father by one Spirit (2:13-18).

Unlike in his earlier messages, which focused primarily upon Jesus' death and resurrection, Peter here begins his rehearsal of Jesus' redemptive work with his baptism by John at the beginning of his public ministry.[13] The apostle alludes to the fact that Cornelius was no doubt somewhat aware of the events of Jesus' life: 'You know what has happened throughout Judea, beginning in Galilee after the baptism that John preached...' (Acts 10:37). Peter again drew upon the firsthand knowledge of his audience (2:22), which served as a persuasive independent testimony confirming the truthfulness of what he was reporting.

Jesus had been anointed by God as his 'Servant' (cf. Isa. 61:1; 42:1; 11:1-5) at his baptism, a point to which Luke also drew attention in his gospel narrative (cf. Luke 4:14-21). 'He went around doing good and healing all who were under the power of the devil, because God was with him' (v. 38). Peter even names the places – Judea, Galilee, Jerusalem. This is not mythology, but real 'space-time' history (as Francis Schaeffer used to emphasize). Finally this review[14] comes to its climax with a reference to Jesus' death and resurrection. Peter again contrasts the deeds of men – 'they killed him by hanging him on a tree' (v. 39) – with the action of God – 'but God raised him from the dead on the third day' (v. 40).

Now that we have studied several of Peter's messages it might be instructive to note the way he addresses this particular issue before the several audiences to which he preached.

- To a general Jewish audience he says: 'This man was handed over to you by God's set purpose and foreknowledge; and you, with the help of wicked men, put him to death by nailing him to the cross' (2:23).
- To another general Jewish audience he says: 'You disowned the Holy and Righteous One and asked that a murderer be released to you. You killed the author of life, but God raised him from the dead. We are witnesses of this' (3:14-15).
- To the Sanhedrin he says: 'Then know this, you and all the people of Israel: It is by the name of Jesus Christ of Nazareth, whom you crucified but whom God raised from the dead, that this man stands before you healed' (4:10).
- Again to the Sanhedrin he says: 'The God of our fathers raised Jesus from the dead – whom you had killed by hanging him on a tree' (5:30).

In each instance the accusation is boldly and directly confrontational. But when speaking to Cornelius and his family, Peter shifts perspective. He says '*they* killed him by hanging him on a tree' (v. 39). Though all sinners are 'responsible' for the death of Jesus the sin-bearer, yet Peter is sensitive to the differences in his audiences. On this occasion he distances himself and his audience from the Jews who were directly involved in the murder of Jesus. We might compare this with Paul's words to another Jewish audience (which included 'God-fearing' Gentiles) which was far removed from Palestine. To the congregation of the synagogue in Pisidian Antioch, Paul declared,

> The people of Jerusalem and their rulers did not recognize Jesus, yet in condemning him they fulfilled the words of the prophets that are read every Sabbath. Though they found no proper ground for a death sentence, they asked Pilate to have him executed. When they had carried out all that was written about him, they took him down from the tree and laid him in a tomb. But God raised him from the dead... (13:27-29).

Paul shares the same awareness of the differences in his audiences and makes his sermonic points in a manner appropriate to those differences. You too must be careful to 'read' your audience accurately, and frame your presentation of scriptural teaching in a way that will be most relevant and persuasive to a particular audience.

We Are Witnesses

Peter does not cite any particular passages from the old covenant Scriptures in preaching to Cornelius' household, as he had done on previous occasions, though he could have expected his audience to be familiar with them. He does make a general reference to the Old Testament at the conclusion of his sermon: 'All the prophets testify about [Christ] that everyone who believes in him receives forgiveness of sins through his name' (v. 43). He leaves his audience to consider which prophets and which passages in particular he has in mind. Certainly they had enough background in the Scriptures to confirm the accuracy of Peter's general statement.

What does receive emphasis in this message is the 'witness' of the apostles to the ministry of Christ. We have seen that the apostolic 'witness' is central to the preaching in Acts (1:8; 2:32; 3:15; 5:32; 13:31). Ordinarily that witness is focused upon the resurrection of Jesus from the dead. But in this message Peter makes a point of the fact that the apostolic witness extended to 'everything [Jesus] did in the country of the Jews and in Jerusalem' (10:39). After his resurrection, Jesus was seen 'not ... by all the people, but by witnesses whom God had already chosen' (v. 41), alluding to the fact that Jesus had selected those who would be his witnesses long before his death and resurrection. This is consistent with what we learn from the opening chapter of Acts concerning the qualifications for an apostle, when a replacement for Judas was to be chosen. On that occasion Peter said: 'Therefore it is necessary to choose one of the men who have been with us the whole time the Lord Jesus went in and out among us, beginning from John's baptism to the time when Jesus was taken up from us. For one of these must become a witness with us of his resurrection' (1:21-22). Thus the 'witness' of the apostles was to encompass the whole of Jesus' public ministry, culminating in his death and resurrection. His post-resurrection appearances – the apostles 'ate and drank with him after he rose from the dead' (v. 41) – served to confirm and explain the events of Jesus' earthly ministry (cf. John 12:16), and confirm his messianic claims.

The commission to the apostles, as summarized by Peter here, was 'to preach to the people and to testify that he is the one whom God appointed as judge of the living and the dead' (v. 42). As stated by Peter, the audience for the apostolic witness was 'the people' – the Jews. But the fact that obedience to that very commission had now brought Peter to the 'God-fearing' Gentiles of Cornelius' household was a clear indication that the definition of 'the people of God' was expanding, and would soon encompass men and women from all over the Roman world.

> Consider Abraham: 'He believed God, and it was credited to him as righteousness.' Understand, then, that those who believe are children of Abraham. The Scripture foresaw that God would justify the Gentiles by faith, and announced the gospel in advance to Abraham: 'All nations will be blessed through you.' So those who have faith are blessed along with Abraham, the man of faith (Gal. 3:6-9).

The mention of Jesus as the appointed Judge of the living and the dead, reflects the teaching of the Savior (John 5:22, 27), and is a point which Paul later emphasizes in preaching to the Gentiles of Athens (Acts 17:31; cf. 1 Pet. 4:5; 2 Tim. 4:1). All men live under the shadow of the coming Judgment Day. Though that day does not arrive until the end of human history, individuals are set for judgment at the time of their death.[15] Thus there is a grave urgency about the preaching of the gospel and for men to respond to the message of Christ by faith. If men do not embrace him now as Savior and submit to him as Lord, they will, on that day, face him as their Judge.

> 'When the Son of Man comes in his glory, and all the angels with him, he will sit on his throne in heavenly glory. All the nations will be gathered before him, and he will separate the people one from another as a shepherd separates the sheep from the goats. He will put the sheep on his right and the goats on his left.
>
> 'Then the King will say to those on his right, 'Come, you who are blessed by my Father; take your inheritance, the kingdom prepared for you since the creation of the world....
>
> 'Then he will say to those on his left, "Depart from me, you who are cursed, into the eternal fire prepared for the devil and his angels..."'
> (Matt. 25:31-34, 41).

The Gentile Pentecost

The sermon was cut short by the miraculous descent of the Holy Spirit upon all who were in the house listening to the message (v. 44). No more dramatic confirmation of God's willingness to receive Gentiles into his Kingdom can be imagined. Peter's companions drew exactly that conclusion (v. 45). The same 'signs' of the Spirit's presence which accompanied his coming upon the disciples in Jerusalem – 'speaking in tongues and praising God' – were present among the family and friends of Cornelius (v. 46). Unlike those who responded to Peter's preaching on the Day of Pentecost, however, these Gentiles received 'the gift of the Holy Spirit' before receiving the outward sign of water baptism (v. 47; cf. 2:38). Though there is no explicit mention of repentance and faith as the response of Cornelius and the others, it is implied in Peter's words in v. 43 – 'Everyone who believes in him receives forgiveness of sins through his name' – and his later report to the Jerusalem apostles – 'So if God gave them the same gift as he gave us, who believed in the Lord Jesus Christ, who was I to think that I could oppose God?' (Acts 11:17, cf. v. 18). At the Jerusalem council in AD 50, at which the apostles and elders discussed the relationship between Jews and Gentiles in the church, Peter spoke of the fact that God 'made no distinction between them and us, for he purified their hearts by faith' (15:9). Cornelius and the other Gentiles in his house turned wholeheartedly in faith to Jesus as Messiah, for whose coming they had been prepared by their acquaintance with Judaism, and whose message of peace they had heard from the lips of Peter.

Upon returning to Jerusalem, Peter was questioned about his conduct in Caesarea: 'You went into the house of uncircumcised men and ate with them' (11:3). The apostle explained carefully everything that had happened, including his vision and that of Cornelius (vv. 4-14). When he told of the coming of the Holy Spirit on the Gentiles, just as he had come on the disciples in Jerusalem at the beginning (vv. 15-17; cf. 2:1-4), the apostles 'had no further objections and praised God, saying, "So then, God has granted even the Gentiles repentance unto life"' (v. 18).

'Their objections ceased; their praise began.'[16]

Good Listeners Make Good Preachers

We noted at the beginning of our discussion of this message the emphasis upon God's preparation of the audience for this sermon. 'Peter could have had no better-prepared and eager audience than this.'[17] Before we move on in our study, it might be helpful to consider a little further the question: 'What makes a well-prepared audience?'

When Luke narrates Paul's visit to Berea in chapter 17, he briefly characterizes the members of the Berean synagogue with the now-famous words which have made 'Bereans' synonymous with diligent students of the Bible and eager hearers of sermons ever since: 'Now the Bereans were of more noble character than the Thessalonians, for they received the message with great eagerness and examined the Scriptures every day to see if what Paul said was true' (v. 11). As important as preparing and preaching sermons is, it is equally important – perhaps more important – to have listeners who are able and willing to get the most out of the preaching they hear.

If you have been preaching for long, you have probably heard the complaint from some, 'I'm not being fed.' And of course if you are not taking care about what and how you 'feed' your flock, then you need to take this complaint to heart. But sometimes it is not a matter of 'feeding' but of 'eating.' There are many poor preachers, but there are also many poor listeners. In his helpful little book, *A Consumer's Guide to Preaching*, Jay Adams has written:

Too many laymen speak about the preaching event as if it were a one-way street, as if responsibility for what transpires when the Bible is proclaimed rests solely on the shoulders of the preacher. But that's not so! Effective communication demands competence from all parties.[18]

Scripture says more about the listener's responsibility to hear, understand, apply, and obey God's message than about the pastor's responsibility to preach it. While God holds his ministers accountable for their preaching, he also expects his people to admit and deal with their own deficiencies in listening and responding to God's Word. Too often church members think their only responsibility is to criticize and complain about the preaching they hear. Your congregation can use some practical, biblical advice on how to get more out of preaching. You must preach from time to time about how to listen to preaching. Becoming a 'good listener' takes instruction and practice.

The first thing to notice about the Bereans is that they responded to the preaching of the apostles as if it were the very Word of God – which it was.

Preaching is a form of the Word of God.[19] Not only is the content of your sermon to be comprised of Scripture – the exposition and application of the written Word of God – but preaching as a form constitutes the authoritative, God-appointed method of presenting the message of the Bible to men. 'For since in the wisdom of God the world through its wisdom did not know him, God was pleased through the foolishness of what was preached to save those who believe' (1 Cor. 1:21). 'And how can they hear without someone preaching to them' (Rom. 10:14). In the words of the *Westminster Shorter Catechism*, Q.89, 'The Spirit of God makes the reading, but especially the *preaching*, of the Word, an effectual means of convincing and converting sinners, and of building them up in holiness and comfort, through faith, unto salvation' (emphasis added).

If you are going to train your congregation to be good listeners, you must constantly remind them of the nature of preaching, so that they will characteristically respond as the Bereans, or even as Thessalonians, who apparently, as good as they were, were not as good at this as the Bereans! They received the apostolic preaching 'not simply with words, but also with power, with the Holy Spirit and with deep conviction' (1 Thess. 1:5). They 'accepted it not as the word of men, but as it actually is, the word of God, which is at work in you who believe' (2:13).

Two things in particular characterized the 'Berean spirit' – eagerness and thoughtfulness. On the one hand, they couldn't get enough of the Word. They loved to dig in whenever the opportunity presented itself. On the other hand, they were discerning. They listened to the Word in connection with their regular searching of the Scriptures 'to see if what Paul said was true.' This characteristic is in line with the commandment: 'To the law and to the testimony! If they do not speak according to this word, they have no light of dawn' (Isa. 8:20).

Preaching and personal Bible study go hand in hand. But that has been forgotten by many evangelicals today. Though the Reformers rediscovered and promoted the ministry of preaching, the heirs of the Reformation have lost sight of the centrality of preaching to the life of the Church and personal spiritual growth. The problem which results is that there is a failure to emphasize preaching – and with it the faithful and receptive hearing of preaching – as the principal means by which the Holy Spirit promotes the spiritual growth in the Christian.

> It is my contention that one reason why people are not growing as they should is that instead of encouraging Christians to drink deeply of the Word, as preached, preachers set their flock on a course of pseudo self-sufficiency that often deceives them into thinking they are sufficient interpreters of Scripture, when they are not. This kind of thinking makes believers critics of preaching rather than listeners and learners, and that confuses people about the true place of Bible study and the priesthood of all believers.[20]

Thus you need to encourage in your people a healthy balance between their eager receptivity under the preaching of the Word, and their personal study of the Word (and the checking of sermons thereby) as part of one's faithful response to the preaching ministry of the Church. This is not easily done. You must challenge your people to take the time and put forth the effort necessary to become more skilful and proficient listeners to the preaching of God's Word. Such effort will help them grow under good, mediocre, and even poor preaching (though you will also make sure they don't have to grow under poor preaching!).

In his *Consumer's Guide*, Adams points up some of the commonest problems in the pew affecting the reception of the Word as preached. First, he speaks of a controlling assumption that the preacher should do a good enough job that communication happens automatically (i.e., without effort by the listener).[21] Secondly, there is the problem of a lack of faith (and faithfulness) in listening (cf. Heb. 3:19; 4:2).[22] Hearing is fundamentally a spiritual and ethical issue. As Jesus repeatedly cautioned: 'He who has ears, let him hear' (Matt. 13:9; cf. Rev. 2:7, 11, 17; etc.). Jesus' disciples were frequently cautioned: 'Consider carefully how you listen. Whoever has will be given more; whoever does not have, even what he thinks he has will be taken from him' (Luke 8:18; cf. Mark 4:24; Matt. 13:12-15). Carefully listening to the Word is essential to being changed and made fruitful under the preaching of the Word. Further, true and faithful hearing of God's Word involves obedience: 'Therefore everyone who hears these words of mine and puts them into practice is like a wise man who built his house on the rock' (Matt. 7:24, cf. v. 26). Or as James reminds us:

> Do not merely listen to the word, and so deceive yourselves. Do what it says. Anyone who listens to the word but does not do what it says is like a man who looks at his face in a mirror and, after looking at himself, goes away and immediately forgets what he looks like. But the man who looks intently into the perfect law that gives freedom, and continues to do this, not forgetting what he has heard, but doing it – he will be blessed in what he does (Jas. 1:22-25).

Thirdly, sermon hearers today are influenced by a cacophony of conflicting voices (aided and abetted by the exponential 'information explosion').[23] Religious instruction and practical advice for living – given from various perspectives, even within the broadly 'Christian camp' – are readily available to your people at the 'click of a mouse'. Learning to distinguish and respond to the voice of the Good Shepherd, amidst the 'devilish din' which is contemporary pop culture, is difficult and takes discernment and discipline. The apostolic warnings are as relevant today as they were two thousand years ago: 'The Spirit clearly says that in later times some will abandon the faith and follow deceiving spirits and things taught by demons. Such teachings come through hypocritical liars, whose consciences have been seared as with a hot iron' (1 Tim. 4:1-2). John's caution should be taken to heart by every professing Christian: 'Dear friends, do not believe every spirit, but test the spirits to see whether they are from God, because many false prophets have gone out into the world' (1 John 4:1). Finally, there are physical hindrances to receptive listening to the

Word of God: 'The spirit is willing but the flesh is weak' (Matt. 26:41).[24] The facility in which your congregation worships may pose problems for attentive listening. I have preached during the winter in meeting places which were so cold as to present a serious distraction from worship. It has been said that the mind can only absorb what the bottom can endure. The harder the pew, the shorter the attention span of the congregation. (This is not strictly true as you will know if you have ever read a Puritan sermon and visited a Puritan church building or, conversely, sat on hard benches at a football stadium!) More to the point is the physical and mental condition of the listener. Too many Christians – especially young people – believe they can stay up late on Saturday evening and still be able to get something out of worship on Sunday morning. It didn't work when I was a teen (so many years ago) and it still doesn't work! Your people must make adequate physical preparation for listening to the sermon.

What can be done about these problems? Let's consider a few suggestions you can pass on to your congregation – if you have not already done so. Falling asleep during the sermon is usually a combination of a failure to prepare your body for worship and bad habit. Jesus gives the command to 'Keep watch!' – i.e., 'Stay awake!' (Matt. 24:42; 25:13). Adams suggests:

> Instead of making Saturday night a time to go out, or stay up late watching videos, we might consider it the beginning of the Lord's Day, a time to prepare for worship. It would become a time for the family to relax after the week's activities and go to bed at a respectable hour. Some coffee and fresh air before church may be helpful if you are prone to sleepiness, but adequate sleep the night before is the only sure cure.[25]

What can one do to break the habit of sleeping in church? He can move to a different location in the auditorium. If one is really serious one will move to the front row! When one sits in the back rows it is very hard to feel a part of what is going on in worship, and that is the beginning of boredom and sleepiness. Your drowsy listener can sit with someone who is a Berean and ask him to give a nudge when necessary until the habit is broken. Eating an adequate breakfast is also helpful – the brain needs food in order to stay alert and active.[26]

It is also important that your people plan ahead and get ready for worship early enough to be on time without rushing. In my judgment the indifference of Americans – at least the Southern Californians I know best – to being punctual for worship is scandalous! If our members were preparing for an important job interview, they would not dream of showing up as late as they routinely do for church – and in as poor condition! We are drawing near to meet the Lord of glory; how dare we be late and unprepared.

On the spiritual level, the most important thing to remind your people is that good listeners are converted people.[27] No amount of pulpit skill on the part of the preacher will compensate for a dead-hearted listener (cf. 1 Cor. 2:13-15). Some church members, like Herod, may be merely curious about preaching (cf. Mark 6:20), but if they are unconverted your preaching can be nothing to them but 'the odor of death' (cf. 2 Cor. 2:16). 'There is no way for you to benefit from preaching unless you trust in Jesus Christ as Saviour, believing the Good News of his redeeming death and resurrection.[28] Beyond that, the 'spiritual discernment' we spoke of earlier comes only as a result of the 'new birth,' without which one cannot 'see the Kingdom of God' (John 3:3), and the indwelling presence of the Holy Spirit. One must become Spirit-motivated and -controlled and God-oriented in order to get the most out of preaching. The Spirit of God is both the revealer of truth in Scripture, and the One who makes us receivers of the truth inwardly.[29]

Yet, even for the converted, old habits may remain that can hinder their ability to receive the truth of God through the preaching of the Word. Your people must be encouraged to work hard to overcome those hindrances. They can start by taking immediate steps to prepare for the preaching they will hear from you next Sunday by praying that God will increase their faith, and nurture it further through the preaching of the Word. According to the Book of Hebrews, the good news of the Word of God was of no value to the generation of Jews in the wilderness 'because those who heard did not combine it with faith' (Heb. 4:2). Your people should also be encouraged to study ahead. If you preach your sermons in series, or announce your topics in advance, they can do a little preparatory study the week before. This will help make them more alert listeners. Adams suggests that they familiarize themselves with the passage by reading it from several versions (or several times from one version), consulting a commentary if they wish.[30] They should note problems and questions that arise from their reading of the passage. They may also find it helpful to give some preliminary thought to possible applications of the passage.

Encourage your people to pray regularly for every element which impacts your preaching ministry – from your preparation to their listening and doing. Who can tell how much 'great preaching' is really 'great hearing' which has resulted to a large degree from 'great praying'? Remember James' words: 'You do not have, because you do not ask God' (Jas. 4:2b). So 'ask and it will be given to you; seek and you will find; knock and the door will be opened to you' (Matt. 7:7).

Finally, teach your people to be regular in their attendance upon the preaching of the Word. There can be no substitute for consistency in receiving the ministry of God's Word through preaching. Nothing will build their faith as effectively. The regular weekly exposition of Scripture by a faithful preacher with even moderate gifts will do a Christian more good than a multitude of special conferences sitting under the 'big names' of the pulpit. Some of the social distractions that hinder people from being good listeners result from irregular attendance (e.g., self-consciousness, guilt, evasions, etc.). And if – despite their best efforts – they miss a sermon (especially within a series) make it possible for them to get a tape so they can listen to it the following week in order to fill in the gap. (Using a tape for a second listening is very helpful as well.)

'Like newborn babies, crave pure spiritual milk, so that by it you may grow up in your salvation, now that you have tasted that the Lord is good' (1 Pet. 2:2). *The Westminster Shorter Catechism*, Q.90 asks, 'How is the Word to be read and heard, that it may become effectual to salvation? The answer is, 'That the Word may become effectual to salvation, we must attend thereunto with diligence, preparation, and prayer; receive it with faith and love, lay it up in our hearts, and practice it in our lives.' How much time, money, and effort do your people spend in providing, preparing, and consuming wholesome food for their physical health? Can you persuade them to spend even half that time and effort in seeking the nourishment of the Word of God from your preaching for their spiritual health and growth in a fruitful Christian life? If you do, you will vastly multiply the effectiveness of your pulpit ministry – the glory of God and the blessedness of your people.

14

Paul at the Synagogue at Pisidian Antioch: Jews and God-fearers Take the Next Step

The second great apostolic preacher highlighted by Luke in his narrative of the founding and spread of the church is Paul. He was probably present at the trial of Stephen and heard the bold defense of the faith presented before the Sanhedrin, but he is mentioned first at the execution – he took charge of the cloaks of those who did the stoning (Acts 7:58). Saul heartily approved of the decision to silence the witness (8:1), and he became involved in the move to suppress the fledgling church (8:3; cf. 1 Cor. 15:9; Gal. 1:13). It was while on his way to Damascus to arrest some Christians there that he met the Lord and was converted (9:1-20).

Paul, by his own testimony was a Jew's Jew – 'circumcised on the eighth day, of the people of Israel, of the tribe of Benjamin, a Hebrew of Hebrews; in regard to the law, a Pharisee; as for zeal, persecuting the church; as for legalistic righteousness, faultless' (Phil. 3:5-6). He had received the best education in the faith and traditions of his fathers available in his day (Acts 22:3). He knew and understood the mind of the Jew, and the zealous opposition the pious felt for Christ and his gospel (Rom. 10:2; Acts 22:4). When this man was converted to the cause of Christ he brought to the preaching of the gospel a brilliant mind, broad education, habits of careful reflection on matters of faith and practice, and consuming dedication to the service of him whom Paul came to recognize as the Messiah promised by God, the fulfillment of the hope of his fathers.

We have already looked at Paul's commission in an earlier chapter.[1] To review briefly, the risen Lord outlined the course of Paul's ministry through the words of the prophet Ananias recorded in Acts 9:15, 'This man is my chosen instrument to carry my name before the Gentiles and their kings and before the children of Israel.' And so he did. Luke has recorded eight messages (sermons or speeches) from the lips of the apostle which show him in action bringing the gospel 'first for the Jew, then for the Gentile' (Rom. 1:16). The first is that which he delivered during the Sabbath service in the Jewish synagogue of Pisidian Antioch, to which we now turn.

Preaching in the Synagogue

For Jews living outside the land of Palestine, the synagogue was the center of religious life. Here the Jews gathered regularly on the Sabbath to hear the Law and Prophets read and expounded for the edification of the faithful (Acts 13:27; 15:21), and to respond with their prayers and praises. When Paul and Barnabas arrived in Antioch of Pisidia[2] they entered the synagogue on the Sabbath, intent on bringing the good news of Christ to their brothers according to the flesh.[3]

It is especially helpful for us, as contemporary preachers of the gospel, that Paul's first recorded sermon was delivered in the synagogue setting. While many of Paul's sermons were given in settings and circumstances very different from ours, this one most closely approximates what we do week by week in preaching to our congregations. Though Paul was speaking to Jews, while we address Christians, he was speaking to *believing* Jews who were initially receptive to what the apostle had to say. Further, they were acquainted with the Scriptures, in fact, they probably knew them better than most of the people in our congregations today.[4] Paul's example, then, in preaching to a congregation of Jews, fully prepared to hear the message of the fulfillment of their expectations, can be very helpful to us as we learn to become more effective preachers of the good news.

Gentiles Too

As indicated by Paul's opening address to the synagogue congregation (Acts 13:16), there were not only Jews present, but Gentile proselytes (cf. v. 43) and 'God-fearers' as well. The gospel had already been taken to the Gentiles by the Jerusalem apostles when Peter proclaimed the message of Christ to Cornelius and his family in Caesarea (Acts 10).[5] It is now for Paul to open the same 'door of faith' to the Gentiles in Asia Minor (14:27). William Ramsay argues that no city in the region was better suited to such an occasion, due to the 'friendly relations' between Jew and Gentile in that city, resulting from a 'general sympathy of spirit that existed between Anatolians and Jews.'[6] This, he believes, accounts both for the presence of a significant number of Gentiles in the synagogue service, and for the fact that later so many Gentiles came to hear Paul's further discourse (v. 44). 'We should not expect that in an ordinary Graeco-Roman city, almost the whole population would gather to hear a Jew preach to them in the atmosphere of a Synagogue.'[7]

These 'God-fearing Gentiles' were not full proselytes to Judaism, but had been attracted by the monotheism, the simple worship, and the ethical ideals of Judaism. They had grown to respect the teachings of the Scriptures as they were expounded week by week in the synagogue. But they were unwilling to separate decisively from their culture by receiving the sign of circumcision. Because these Gentiles were 'new to Judaism' they were often more open to the preaching of Christ as the fulfillment of old covenant expectation than were the more traditional Jews. Further, Adams points out that the Jews of 'the Diaspora' (the Jews living outside Palestine in the Graeco-Roman Mediterranean world) were more pious and exhibited a more vital and inquiring faith.[8] Thus in the synagogue at Pisidian Antioch, with its combined audience of Jews and 'God-fearers', Paul had as promising and receptive an audience as could be hoped for.

Of this sermon Ramsay comments that 'from first to last it includes the Gentiles in its clearly expressed scope.'[9] If you compare Paul's three direct addresses to his audience in this message, you will notice the progression of his inclusion of the Gentiles. At first (v. 16) he says, 'Men of Israel and you Gentiles who worship God, listen to me!' Later Paul addresses the congregation in these terms: 'Brothers, children of Abraham, and you God-fearing Gentiles, it is to us that this message of salvation has been sent' (v. 26). Both the Jews and the God-fearing Gentiles are addressed as 'brothers.' Finally, in his conclusion, all distinction is lost. 'Therefore, my brothers, I want you to know that through Jesus the forgiveness of sins is proclaimed to you' (v. 38). Though Paul has gone to the synagogue in search of his fellow Jews, he is every bit as concerned to win the Gentiles to Christ as the sequel demonstrates (vv. 43-46).[10] Thus 'Luke places the speech at the beginning of Paul's work among the Gentiles as a typical example of the way in which Judaism and the promises of God were made universal by him.'[11]

A 'Word of Exhortation'

When Paul and Barnabas arrived in Pisidian Antioch, they entered the synagogue on the first Sabbath day and sat down (v. 14).[12] Farrar gives us a portrait of the unfolding of the early part of the synagogue service.

> After the prayers followed the First Lesson, or *Parashah*, and this, owing to the sanctity which the Jews attached to the very sounds and letters of

Scripture, was read in Hebrew, but was translated or paraphrased verse by verse by the *meturgeman*, or interpreter. The *chazzân* or clerk of the synagogue, took the *Thorah*-roll from the ark, and handed it to the reader. By the side of the reader stood the interpreter, unless he performed that function for himself, as could be easily done, since the Septuagint version was now universally disseminated. After the *Parashah*, was read the short *Haphtarah*, or what we should call the Second Lesson, from the Prophets, the translation into the vernacular being given at the end of every three verses. After this followed the *Midrash*, the exposition or sermon. It was not delivered by one set minister, but, as at the present day any distinguished stranger who happens to be present is asked by way of compliment to read the *Thorah*, so in those days the *Rosh ha-Keneseth* might ask anyone to preach who seemed likely to do so with profit to the worshippers.[13]

We are not told how the invitation came to be extended to Paul and Barnabas. Perhaps it was because of where they sat in the synagogue, or because of some distinctive dress, or perhaps they had already become known in the Jewish community of Antioch. In any case, they were invited to speak and Paul quickly accepted the invitation. It was the custom in the Palestinian synagogues to stand to read the Scriptures and sit to preach (cf. Luke 4:20). Here Paul follows the Greek custom of standing to deliver his sermon – either from the *bema* or pulpit[14] or from the place where he had been sitting.[15] He gestured with his hand for the attention of the audience and began his message.

The phrase used to describe the sermon is 'a word of exhortation' (*logos parakleseōs*), which F. F. Bruce suggests might have been a current designation for a synagogue sermon.[16] The phrase also occurs in Hebrews 13:22, where it seems to be used as a designation for the whole Book of Hebrews. A 'word of exhortation' was a homily based upon one or more of the biblical texts which had been read during the synagogue service. The purpose was pastoral – both to inform and to urge the congregation to greater faith and fidelity in view of the relevance of the biblical texts to their lives. The message could strike a note of comfort and encouragement (v. 32) or admonition (vv. 40-41).

The sermon in most instances, as in the case of our Lord's address at Nazareth, would naturally take the form of a *Midrash* on what the congregation had just heard in one or other of the two lessons. Such seems to have been the line taken by St. Paul in this his first recorded sermon. The occurrence of two words in this brief address, of which one is a most unusual form, and the other is employed in a most unusual meaning, and the fact that these two words are found respectively in the first of Deuteronomy and the first of Isaiah, combined with the circumstance that the historical part of St. Paul's sermon turns on the subject alluded to in the first of these chapters, and the promise of free remission is directly suggested by the other, would make it extremely probable that those were the two chapters which he had just heard read. His sermon in fact, or rather the heads of it, which can alone be given in the brief summary of St. Luke, is exactly the kind of masterly combination and application of these two Scripture lessons of the day which we should expect from such a preacher.[17]

Paul, then, takes as his starting-point for his sermon the passages read as part of the regular service of the synagogue. He expounds the old covenant Scriptures in terms of their fulfillment in Christ, and applies the message with encouragements and admonitions to the audience to trust in Jesus as the Lord's Anointed, the one in whom the hope of Israel (and the nations) finds its fulfillment.

Paul's Approach to Winning the Jews

Paul begins laying the groundwork for his proclamation of the gospel with a brief survey of some important elements of Old Testament history: the choice of the patriarchs by God, the Exodus, Israel's taking possession of the land of Canaan and the tumultuous period of the judges, and finally the choice of David as king following the rejection of Saul, the people's choice (vv. 17-22).

In proceeding in this fashion, Paul had both a *rhetorical* (persuasive) and a *theological* purpose. Rhetorically, it was his concern to lay a firm foundation for what he was going to say about Christ – the 'new' element in his message – by setting forth from the Scriptures the very familiar account of God's historical preparation for the coming of David. An audience is much more likely to accept new ideas if they are firmly tied to others which are familiar and commonly believed.[18] We noticed above that Paul had reason to hope that his audience of devout Jews and 'God-fearing Gentiles' would prove receptive to his message. His sermon is perfectly adapted so as to make the most of the opportunity. Paul begins on very familiar ground, with Old Testament historical highlights. His audience is accustomed to hearing this material, and is thus put at ease as Paul treads the old paths. So far, nothing very different from what they might expect from any rabbi preaching to them in the synagogue.

It is interesting to contrast the opening section of Paul's sermon with Peter's on the day of Pentecost. Peter begins by immediately bringing Jesus to center stage: 'Men of Israel, listen to this: Jesus of Nazareth was a man accredited by God to you by miracles, wonders and signs, which God did among you through him, as you yourselves know' (Acts 2:22). Even though the Jews in Jerusalem are potentially much more hostile than those in Pisidian Antioch, Peter does not adopt an indirect approach. He confronts them head on (as we have seen).[19] Did Peter make a serious tactical error in his approach? Does Paul furnish us with a more sophisticated and useful example? I'm convinced that when we take into account not only the audience, but also the circumstance and purpose of the messages, we will discover that both approaches were proper. As important as 'audience adaptation' is to the effectiveness of the preaching of the apostles, it is only one factor among several to be taken into account.

The two audiences were very much alike. In Jerusalem, Peter spoke to 'God-fearing Jews' from all over the Roman world who were in town for the great festivals of Passover and Pentecost (2:5).[20] Here Paul speaks to an audience of Jews and Gentiles who are committed to the faith of Abraham and Moses. But the similarities end there. A further step in audience analysis discloses that though they are all Jews, their *circumstances* are quite different. Peter confronts his audience as those directly responsible for the rejection and death of the promised Messiah (2:23, 36). Paul, on the other hand, though he recognizes the racial and religious solidarity of all Jews, approaches those in Pisidian Antioch as distinct from the Jews of Jerusalem. 'The people of Jerusalem and their rulers did not recognize Jesus, yet in condemning him they fulfilled the words of the prophets that are read every Sabbath. Though they found no proper ground for a death sentence, they asked Pilate to have him executed' (13:27-28). The clear implication of Paul's words is that the Jews he was addressing had yet to make a choice about Jesus' claim to be the Messiah. He pled with them not to make the same mistake as their brethren and reject Jesus the Messiah.

There is a further difference between the immediate *purpose* of Peter and Paul in their respective messages. Of course both desire the conversion of their fellow Jews, but Peter is also playing a direct role in the fulfillment of the predictions of the Lord Jesus regarding the Jews of Jerusalem.[21]

> Therefore I am sending you prophets and wise men and teachers. Some of them you will kill and crucify; others you will flog in your synagogues and pursue from town to town. And so upon you will come all the righteous blood that has been shed on earth, from the blood of righteous Abel to the blood of Zechariah son of Berekiah, whom you murdered between the temple and the altar. I tell you the truth, all this will come upon this generation. 'O Jerusalem, Jerusalem, you who kill the prophets and stone those sent to you, how often I have longed to gather your children together, as a hen gathers her chicks under her wings, but you were not willing. Look, your house is left to you desolate' (Matt. 23:34-38).

Peter's purpose was to bring an indictment against those Jews who had murdered their Messiah in light of God's vindication of Jesus through his resurrection from the dead. By so doing he hoped to make them understand what they did not understand a few weeks earlier when they consented in Jesus' crucifixion (Luke 23:34). And as we have seen, the Holy Spirit who led Peter thus to confront the Jews (Luke 21:15), blessed his sermon to the conversion of many (Acts 2:37-41).[22] Later, Peter used virtually the same approach to another crowd of Jews in Jerusalem (3:12-26). We are not told what effect it had, beyond getting the apostles arrested (4:1-3). When Peter took the same line with the Sanhedrin, they were hardened in their unbelief and wanted to kill him (5:30-33).

Thus we learn that Peter's confrontational approach was dictated by his audience, the circumstance, and the specific purpose of his sermon. So it was with Paul in Pisidian Antioch. He addressed Jews, to whom Jesus had been sent as their promised Messiah (Acts 13:23,26), but these Jews were far removed from the events in Jerusalem, and Paul takes that into account (v. 27). Paul's purpose for this sermon does not include bringing the same kind of strong indictment against these Jews that Peter did. Rather, Paul's purpose was to persuade them, and the Gentiles who had joined themselves to the synagogue (if not fully to Judaism), to receive Jesus of Nazareth as the Messiah. Paul knows that his audience has every historical and scriptural reason to do so. Thus Paul preaches in such a way as to point that out – gently and carefully, but clearly – so that, if possible, by the Holy Spirit's blessing, he may win his brothers.

The Scriptures Point to God's Choice of Christ

It is not possible to explore in depth the rich details of Paul's sermon there. I'll have to leave that for your further study.[23] But I do want you to notice something about the *theological* purpose of Paul's introductory survey of Old Testament history. Paul emphasized the sovereignty of 'the God of the people of Israel.'[24] His mention of Old Testament events is bracketed by God's choice of the patriarchs (v. 17) and his selection of David as king (v. 22). Blessings came upon Israel in accordance with God's good choices for them – he 'exalted' (*hupsōsen*) them in Egypt, and 'sustained' them[25] in the wilderness, and gave them the good land of Canaan as their inheritance (vv. 17-19). When God chooses, Israel is blessed.

The mention of David, however, is prefaced by a reference to a bad choice by Israel – 'the people asked for a king, and he gave them Saul' (v. 21). Paul does not elaborate the point. There was no need. The people's desire for a king was declared at the time (by Samuel, who is also mentioned, v. 20) to be an act of willful rebellion, rejecting God's program for his people (cf. 1 Sam. 8). The history of Saul's reign proved God's prophet right. It was a disaster. When Israel chooses, in defiance of God, trouble follows. But God in his mercy delivered Israel (again) by removing Saul and appointing David king in his place (v. 22). Of David, the Lord said, 'I have found David son of Jesse a man after my own heart; he will do everything I want him to do.' God's choice restores his people to the place of blessing.

Paul then jumps from David directly to Jesus.

> 'From this man's descendants God has brought to Israel the Savior Jesus, as he promised. Before the coming of Jesus, John preached repentance and baptism to all the people of Israel. As John was completing his work, he said: "Who do you think I am? I am not that one. No, but he is coming after me, whose sandals I am not worthy to untie" ' (vv. 23-25).

Paul identifies Jesus simply as 'the Savior' who was 'promised' by God to Israel, relying upon the messianic expectations of his audience to fill in the picture. He does not labor at this point to prove that Jesus was the Messiah, he simply identifies him as such. As the Lord had identified David as the man of his choice ('a man after my own heart'), so he had declared that Jesus was his chosen One through the testimony of John the Baptist. The introduction of John is a persuasive move by the apostle, for John had come to be acknowledged as a true prophet by the Jews. His testimony was weighty. Further, some thought at the time of his ministry that he himself might be the Messiah, an error he soon corrected (John 1:20, 25; 3:28-31; Luke 3:15-17). It is to that testimony that Paul alludes here. John was not the expected Messiah, but the one sent by God to announce his coming.

Paul has set up his audience to face the same choice that Israel has faced so many times in the past. Will they act as seems right to them – as they did during the days of the Judges (Judg. 17:6; 21:25) and in their election of Saul as king? Or will they acknowledge God's chosen King, Jesus, the Son of David? It is a very effective persuasive device to formulate an issue in dispute in terms of another issue which is not controversial. No one in Paul's audience would have been prepared to argue that the choice of Saul was a good idea (at least not in retrospect). David was obviously the king chosen by God, and Israel was right to own his appointment by God. Now Paul has developed his argument in such a way that, both formally and materially, the acknowledgment of Jesus as Messiah is similarly the right choice. Choosing Jesus is formally parallel to choosing David. Materially, choosing Jesus is (in a sense) choosing David again, for Jesus is the 'Son of David.'

What Choice Will You Make?

Now Paul presses his argument a further step. Again he addresses his audience formally (including both the Jewish and Gentile components), underlining the importance of what he is about to say: 'Brothers, children of Abraham, and you God-fearing Gentiles, it is to us that this message of salvation has been sent' (Acts 13:26). He persuasively commends faith in Jesus in the most positive terms. Again in contrast to Peter in Jerusalem, who first confronts the crowd with the murder of Jesus, and only later offers them the hope of salvation through faith in him (2:23, 38), Paul reverses the order. Jesus is the Savior promised to Israel (13:23). Paul's sermon in the synagogue is a 'message of salvation' (v. 26). Paul then goes on to speak of the crucifixion of Jesus:

> The people of Jerusalem and their rulers did not recognize Jesus, yet in condemning him they fulfilled the words of the prophets that are read every Sabbath. Though they found no proper ground for a death sentence, they asked Pilate to have him executed. When they had carried out all that was written about him, they took him down from the tree and laid him in a tomb (vv. 27-29).

All the elements of the historic account are mentioned, as they were by Peter at Pentecost, but the 'sharp edge' of direct indictment is again softened by Paul in this instance. Here the ignorance of the Jews in Jerusalem is emphasized (in contrast to their overt wickedness, cf. 2:23). They did not recognize that Jesus was the Messiah promised by the old covenant Scriptures ('the words of the prophets'), though they knew very well, by repeated exposure, what the prophets had promised ('that are read every Sabbath', v. 27). The implication, of course, is that Paul's audience too knows very well the words of the prophets, for they have just heard their words read again in the very service in which Paul is preaching. Because of that ignorance they condemned Jesus and asked Pilate to have him executed. Paul alludes to the fact that Pilate, the Gentile, found no reason to condemn Jesus to death, but did so anyway (cf. 4:27). Yet, ironically, the effect of the Jews' ignorance and the Romans' injustice was to fulfill the words of the prophets and carry out all that was written about him (vv. 27, 29)!

Paul is not suppressing the 'negative elements' of the condemnation and death of Christ, as if it were a 'no fault' affair. But he is framing the sinful actions of men in the context of the larger purpose of God, purposes of salvation and grace, upon which his emphasis falls.

We have already noted above that Paul addresses his audience of Jews and Gentiles in Pisidian Antioch in such a way as to distinguish them from the 'people of Jerusalem and their rulers'. In so doing he wants his hearers to consider 'objectively' (rather than as Jewish partisans) the events which took place in Jerusalem. This 'objectivity' is aided by their geographical and temporal remove from those events. He does not want his auditors to feel obliged to join in the error of the Jerusalem Jews, just because they too are Jews. The God-fearing Gentiles in Paul's audience have even more reason to distance themselves, if they will, from the errors of the people of Jerusalem and their rulers. Paul, by his presentation of the gospel, is making it as easy as possible for these Jews and Gentiles in Asia Minor to 'break ranks' with their co-religionists, and receive and acknowledge Jesus of Nazareth as their Messiah. He then clinched his argument with the proclamation of the good news of the resurrection of Jesus.

Paul Proclaims the Resurrection of Christ
Paul, in common with the other apostolic preachers, uses the resurrection of Jesus of Nazareth from the dead as the great

confirmation of his messianic claims, and as the glorious display of God's power to save. 'We tell you the good news: What God promised our fathers he has fulfilled for us, their children, by raising up Jesus' (vv. 32-33). In turning now to the resurrection, and making use of it to convince a Jewish audience, Paul proceeds very much in the same manner as Peter did before him. Both Peter and Paul point up the eyewitness testimony to the fact of Jesus' resurrection (2:32; 13:31), but the emphasis lies (for both apostles) upon the resurrection as the fulfillment of 'what God promised our fathers' in the Old Testament – in particular those made to David. Paul proclaimed the resurrection of Jesus as the ultimate fulfillment of Psalm 2:7, 'You are my Son; today I have become your Father' (v. 33).[26] God's promise to David included the 'adoption' of David's sons as 'sons of God' in their official role as kings: 'I will be his father, and he will be my son' (2 Sam. 7:14). Accordingly, in Psalm 2 the day of the new king's accession to the throne ('I have installed my King on Zion, my holy hill,' v. 6) is the day of his 'adoption' – the king becomes the 'son of God'. According to Paul, this type was finally fulfilled in the resurrection of Jesus – which (with his ascension) was the exaltation of Jesus to the place where he was to begin his reign.[27] In this way God 'raised up' Jesus as the Messiah.[28]

Both Peter and Paul also made use of Psalm 16:10. Peter quoted the context in full (2:25-28) while Paul made a briefer allusion and citation (13:34-35). Paul, in the manner of rabbinic exegesis,[29] links Psalm 16:10 with the 'the holy and sure blessings promised to David' (v. 34), a reference to the Davidic covenant (Isa. 55:3). He does so by the repetition of the adjective 'holy'. The 'holy blessing' promised David and the 'Holy One' who will not see decay are one and the same – namely, Christ.

> The promises made to David and his posterity could not have been realized apart from the resurrection of the crucified Messiah. Centuries after the promises were made to David himself, God renewed them ... by assuring his people that he would yet give them the pledged tokens of his 'steadfast, sure love for David' (Isa. 55:3). One of these pledged tokens – indeed, the greatest of them – was the resurrection of the Son of David, in accordance with the assurance of Psalm 16 (LXX 15:)10, quoted in the same sense by Peter on the day of Pentecost (cf. 2:27): 'You will not let your holy one see corruption.'[30]

Paul has taken perfect account of his audience and the situation by using very familiar Old Testament passages in a very familiar way to prove his point that Jesus of Nazareth is indeed the promised and long-expected Messiah.[31]

Paul's Appeal

In his peroration Paul again addresses his audience directly: 'Therefore, my brothers, I want you to know that through Jesus the forgiveness of sins is proclaimed to you' (v. 38). Within the setting of the synagogue, any distinction between the Jews and God-fearing Gentiles has now fallen away. They are all Paul's 'brothers' (in that they share his ancestral faith), and he calls upon them to become his 'brothers' in turning to Jesus as the fulfillment of the hope of Israel.

Paul's appeal emphasized the hope of the forgiveness of sins and free justification.[32] In this connection Paul mentioned the Law of Moses. The accusation of speaking against the Law of Moses had been brought against Stephen (6:13) and would later be raised as a charge against Paul (21:28). Paul's allusion to the fact that the Law could not justify is not a criticism of the Law, but rather an acknowledgment that the Law was never intended by God to serve as a means of justification. Paul later elaborated this same point in his letter to this and other churches in the region of Galatia:

> What I mean is this: The law, introduced 430 years later, does not set aside the covenant previously established by God and thus do away with the promise. For if the inheritance depends on the law, then it no longer depends on a promise; but God in his grace gave it to Abraham through a promise. What, then, was the purpose of the law? It was added because of transgressions until the Seed to whom the promise referred had come. The law was put into effect through angels by a mediator. A mediator, however, does not represent just one party; but God is one. Is the law, therefore, opposed to the promises of God? Absolutely not! For if a law had been given that could impart life, then righteousness would certainly have come by the law (Gal. 3:17-21).

Here Paul spoke as he did in full recognition of the fact that devout Jews were deeply zealous for the righteousness of God, though their zeal was not based on knowledge (Rom. 10:2). Gentiles also were drawn to the synagogue because of the distinctively ethical emphases of Judaism over against the immorality of pagan religions. In speaking of righteousness before God, Paul was striking a responsive chord in the hearts of his hearers. The problem was that 'they did not know the righteousness that comes from God and sought to establish their own,' thus 'they did not submit to God's righteousness' which was revealed in Christ (Rom. 10:3). Therefore, Paul called upon them to seek justification in the only place where it could truly be found. He urged them to trust in Jesus for 'through him everyone who believes is justified from everything you could not be justified from by the law of Moses' (Acts 13:39). Note the mention that 'everyone' – Jew or Gentile – who trusts in Christ will experience this great forgiveness (cf. 10:43; Rom. 1:16; 3:22; 4:11; 10:4, 11).

This appeal to find salvation in Christ, is balanced by a warning: 'Take care that what the prophets have said does not happen to you: "Look, you scoffers, wonder and perish, for I am going to do something in your days that you would never believe, even if someone told you"' (vv. 40-41, a quotation of Hab. 1:5 from the LXX). Habakkuk warned the people to beware of the impending invasion by the Chaldeans. Paul here alludes to the danger of rejecting God's offer of salvation. Those who will not receive Jesus as Messiah will face a certain judgment at the Lord's hands.

Tell Us More

The response of the synagogue congregation to Paul's message was very favorable. They were invited to 'speak further about these things on the next Sabbath' (v. 42). But Luke tells us that many of the Jews and worshipping proselytes did not want to wait until the next week. They followed Paul and Barnabas discussing further what had been taught concerning Jesus the Messiah. It appears that these inquirers made the transition, by faith, from the old covenant to the new by putting their trust in Israel's true Savior, and were urged to 'continue in the grace of God' (v. 43).

The full measure of the impact of Paul's sermon was seen the next Sabbath when, according to Luke, 'almost the whole city gathered to hear the word of the Lord' (v. 44).[33] The Jews – who had apparently been on generally good terms with the Gentiles of Antioch, and who seem to have sensed no difficulty with Paul's Jew–Gentile appeal in the synagogue the previous Sabbath – were disturbed by the magnitude of the Gentile response. 'Filled with jealousy' they began to 'speak abusively against what Paul was saying' (v. 45).

Sadly, the obstinate rebelliousness so characteristic of the leaders of Palestinian Judaism, had reared its head now in Asia Minor as well. It would set off the same pattern of persecution it had elsewhere (v. 50; cf. 8:1; 14:2, 5, 19). Later Luke goes on to note that 'the Jews incited the God-fearing women of high standing and the leading men of the city. They stirred up persecution against Paul and Barnabas, and expelled them from their region' (v. 50).

The reply of Paul and Barnabas to Jewish hostility is clear and bold: 'We had to speak the word of God to you first. Since you reject it and do not consider yourselves worthy of eternal life, we now turn to the Gentiles' (v. 46). Though Paul continued throughout his ministry to preach 'to the Jew first' (Rom. 1:16) the gospel began now to move definitively away from the Jews toward the Gentiles. To reject the message of Christ, graciously proclaimed by the apostles to their countrymen, was to consider oneself unworthy of eternal life. Jewish unbelief was self-condemning.[34] Upon leaving town, the apostles 'shook the dust from their feet' (v. 51), a sign of coming judgment against the unbelieving Jews commanded by Jesus himself (Luke 9:5; 10:11).

How different is the response of the Gentiles: 'When the Gentiles heard this, they were glad and honored the word of the Lord; and all who were appointed for eternal life believed. The word of the Lord spread through the whole region.... And the disciples were filled with joy and with the Holy Spirit' (vv. 48-49, 52). Indeed, as Paul and Barnabas later reported upon their return to Antioch in Syria, 'God ... had opened the door of faith to the Gentiles' (14:27). This joyful receptivity was fully in accord with the Scriptures, as Paul pointed out elsewhere in glorifying his ministry to the Gentiles:

> For I tell you that Christ has become a servant of the Jews on behalf of God's truth, to confirm the promises made to the patriarchs so that the Gentiles may glorify God for his mercy, as it is written: 'Therefore I will praise you among the Gentiles; I will sing hymns to your name.' Again, it says, 'Rejoice, O Gentiles, with his people.' And again, 'Praise the Lord, all you Gentiles, and sing praises to him, all you peoples.' And again, Isaiah says, 'The Root of Jesse will spring up, one who will arise to rule over the nations; the Gentiles will hope in him' (Rom. 15:8-12; cf. Ps. 18:49; Deut. 32:43; Ps. 117:1; Isa. 11:10).

Some Lessons

In this first recorded sermon of the Apostle Paul, we have a masterful example of his preaching ministry to an audience that knows and respects the faith of historic Judaism. The Jews and Gentiles gathered in the synagogue in Pisidian Antioch were alike committed to the God of Abraham, Isaac, and Jacob; they accepted the words of Moses and the prophets as the very Word of God; they believed the Scriptures to have a continuing relevance to the life of God's people throughout the ages; they embraced the messianic hope fostered by the promises of God made to David; and they were together seeking a right relationship with God. At the same time, they were far removed from the events which took place in Jerusalem several years before. They were not directly bound up in the opinions and actions of the Jewish leadership in Palestine. Paul took all of these things into account as he crafted and presented his gospel message.

By way of applying the example of Paul to our own work as preachers, we notice first of all the means by which Paul led his audience to take the transitional step from Judaism to Christianity. He was concerned to take every opportunity to identify himself with his audience – both the Jews and the God-fearing Gentiles.[35] He called them all 'brethren'. He speaks of the patriarchs as 'our fathers'. He tells them that the message of salvation had been sent to 'us'. Paul is not interested in setting forth the antithesis between Christianity and Judaism as much as the continuity between the latter and the former (cf. Acts 24:14 f.). Christianity is the 'natural' fulfillment of the promises of God in the history of redemption. The point being that devout Jews (and Gentile proselytes and adherents to the synagogue) should willingly embrace Jesus as the Messiah *for the same reasons* that they are committed to the faith of the old covenant.

When we address our messages to today's Christian 'synagogues' we, unlike Paul, have an audience that has already embraced Christ as the fulfillment of all the promises of God (2 Cor. 1:20). But discipling the people of God always involves persuading them to move forward in the faith, and in the obedience of faith, as the next step on the path of following Christ. Accordingly, we must appeal to them on the basis of what they already know of Christ. We must persuade them that the next step is the 'natural' continuation of what they have already believed and obeyed in the past. Paul's method is instructive in learning how to do this effectively. We capitalize upon the knowledge and

respect our people have for the Word of God in Scripture. We base
our instruction and exhortations on the Bible alone – only thus will
they be persuasive and convincing. We call them to meet new and
more difficult challenges against the background of previous obedience
to which, by reason of use, they have become accustomed (Heb.
5:14). As Paul writes elsewhere: 'Therefore, my dear friends, as you
have always obeyed – not only in my presence, but now much more
in my absence – continue to work out your salvation with fear and
trembling, for it is God who works in you to will and to act according
to his good purpose' (Phil. 2:12-13). Discipleship preaching is
'continuity preaching' – moving from the familiar to the unfamiliar,
from the routine to the challenging, from immaturity to maturity.

> Not that I have already obtained all this, or have already been made
> perfect, but I press on to take hold of that for which Christ Jesus took
> hold of me. Brothers, I do not consider myself yet to have taken hold of
> it. But one thing I do: Forgetting what is behind and straining toward
> what is ahead, I press on toward the goal to win the prize for which God
> has called me heavenward in Christ Jesus (Phil. 3:12-14).

Secondly, we have noted Paul's specific purpose in this message.
In general terms the purpose of the preaching of the gospel is always
two-sided (2 Cor. 2:15-16) – i.e., both creating faith and provoking
unbelief, both opening and hardening hearts of the hearers. That means
that the Spirit of God is always sovereignly at work applying the
message of the preacher effectively toward one of these two goals.
'God has mercy on whom he wants to have mercy, and he hardens
whom he wants to harden' (Rom. 9:18).

The preacher cannot read the heart, so that he is not aware
beforehand who will believe and who will reject the truth he is
preaching. But circumstances differ, and the preacher for his part
must take account of differing situations as he tries to determine his
specific purpose for a given message. In the discussion above I have
contrasted Peter's approach to the Jews in Jerusalem with Paul's to
the Jews in Pisidian Antioch. I was not suggesting that Paul's method
was better than Peter's (as some of my readers may have concluded).
Far from it. Both approaches are valid and were, with the blessing of
God's Spirit, equally effective. In Peter's situation, a direct, forceful
challenge to the wickedness of the Jews was the appropriate tactic to
use (remember, it was dictated by the Spirit of God himself). In the

setting of Paul's sermon, a more conciliatory, persuasive approach was dictated. Both men declared the truth. Both men called sinners to repent. Both saw men converted to Christ.

For most of you reading this, I would imagine, the setting of your preaching, and your audience, does not change much from week to week. The purpose of your message will usually be dictated in the first place by the passage from which you are preaching,[36] rather than the situation in which you are preaching (though even in a fixed congregation this must be taken into account). Some congregations are generally resistant to certain obligations of the Christian life (e.g., the racism that continues to characterize too many congregations in certain parts of the United States). Some passages, therefore, will require that you confront your audience forcefully with the truth of God and the obligations which flow from it. Other passages will set forth truths that your congregation is already disposed (on the basis of past instruction and experience) to believe and obey – i.e., their problem is ignorance rather than resistance. In these cases Paul's more winsome, persuasive approach will be in order.

As a preacher you are always called to weigh the meaning and purpose of your text, the nature of your audience, and the necessities of the circumstance in order to devise your tactics for preaching. A close reading of the apostolic sermons with these considerations in mind will help you in becoming a more effective minister of the Word. At the same time, we must always remember that it is God who gives the increase in our preaching, as it was in the preaching of Peter and Paul (1 Cor. 3:6).

One final matter to note before we move on is Paul's emphasis upon justification by faith in his sermon to the synagogue congregation at Pisidian Antioch. Rightly understood, Judaism was an expression of God's 'covenant of grace'. As such, it emphasized the redemptive work of God on the one hand, and the covenantal response of faith and obedience on the part of God's people on the other. As long as Israel remembered that her standing before God was a matter of grace and faith, then obedience to the Law of God remained an expression of gratitude and devotion to God. The Ten Commandments themselves set forth this proper balance. The 'preface' to the Ten Commandments reminds Israel that YHWH is her gracious redeemer: 'I am the LORD your God, who brought you out of Egypt, out of the land of slavery' (Exod. 20:2). Obedience to the Law, then, is not a means by which the favor of God might be earned. Rather, obedience was the response of the redeemed to the saving mercy of God. The commandments of God mark out the path of life in which Israel is to walk (cf. Deut. 30:16-20). Obedience is 'the obedience of faith' (Rom. 1:5; 16:26).

By the time we come to the first century, the Jews had seriously perverted the faith of the fathers. The Pharisees were singled out by Jesus for their gross hypocrisy (e.g., Matt. 23), adding to or taking away from the commandments of God by their traditions (cf. Mark 7:9, 13). Even devout Jews, as we have seen, were commended by Paul for their zeal, but indicted for their ignorance of the ways of God: 'Since they did not know the righteousness that comes from God and sought to establish their own, they did not submit to God's righteousness' (Rom. 10:3). The self-righteousness of the Jews was the chief stumbling-block to their receiving and resting in the work of Jesus the Messiah. When the Law of God was divorced from the redemptive accomplishment of God on behalf of His people, it was perverted from its original design and use.

Thus Paul made as the centerpiece of his appeal to the Jews and Gentiles in the synagogue of Pisidian Antioch the proclamation of the fact that 'through Jesus the forgiveness of sins is proclaimed ... everyone who believes is justified from everything you could not be justified from by the law of Moses' (Acts 13:38-39).

It is very important for you as a preacher to remember, and continually emphasize in your preaching, the centrality of the redemptive accomplishment of Jesus Christ through his death and resurrection. This may seem a strange thing to say, especially to evangelical Protestants. But it has been my experience that Christians, like the Jews before them, all too easily slip away from redemptive religion in favor of some form of self-justifying moralism. After beginning with the Spirit, it is too easy for Christians to try to attain their goal by human effort (Gal. 3:3). It happened in Pisidian Antioch (and elsewhere) – hence the need for Paul to write the letter to the Galatians to address this issue directly. It will happen in your congregation as well if you are not careful.

My church interviews men and women who wish to join the church before admitting them to membership. Perhaps your church does the same. Have you, like me, been disappointed at the kind of answers you get to the question: 'What does it mean to you to be a Christian?'

I would say (again, based on my experience) that it is by far the minority of professing Christians who, without prompting, identify the redemptive accomplishment of Christ as the basis of their acceptance with God. You will hear about (generic) 'faith', 'believing in God', and 'obeying God's will', etc. Too rarely do you hear, 'Christ Jesus came into the world to save sinners – of whom I am the worst' (1 Tim. 1:15). It's not that people don't believe in the atoning death of Christ. It's just that it does not burn at the center of their Christian consciousness. There is a 'Judaizer' asleep in the heart of every professing Christian, and it takes little to awaken him.

Churches which place a proper emphasis upon the Law of God; upon the 'obedience of faith' (Rom. 1:5; 16:26) may face a special danger in this regard. While the commandments of God are essential for mapping out the Christian life, they cannot empower obedience, nor can they provide pardon for disobedience. The Law must always operate in the Christian life in the context of the redemptive gospel. If not, our churches will soon decline into Pharisaism.[37]

In an earlier chapter I tried to warn you against the dangers of 'moralistic preaching'[38] – especially treating the biblical stories as if their main purpose were to inculcate moral values, rather than describe and explain the great work of redemption which God has performed in history. If congregations are subjected to a steady diet of this sort of preaching, then the story of redemption as it focuses in Christ will cease to be something to be trusted absolutely, and will rather be used only as an 'illustration' of how we should live.

Paul told the Jews and God-fearing Gentiles in Pisidian Antioch that they must ever seek forgiveness of sins and justification in Christ. You must tell your congregations the same. Faith is fundamental to Christianity as a redemptive religion. The work of Christ on the cross and in his resurrection is foundational to authentic Christianity. Obedience – as important as it is – must always be the obedience that flows from faith. It is your task in preaching constantly to 'placard' Jesus Christ as crucified before the very eyes of your congregation (Gal. 3:1), as Paul did, so that their faith might rest in him alone.

15

Paul and Barnabas at Lystra:
Putting the Brakes on Idolatry

As you confront the secular world of today with the gospel, you probably find that twenty-first century pagans come in two general types. Some nonbelievers are strongly committed to their anti-Christian views, though they have given very little thought to the reasons for their opposition. Their opinions have been formed by prejudice and distorted information about Christianity flowing through the mass media. Some have had unhappy personal experiences with Christians or the Church. Such people are often very hostile to the faith, making up in zeal what they lack in careful reflection. In a discussion they are likely to resort to shouting and name calling as they see their reasons for opposing the gospel melt away.[1]

The other kind of modern pagan is one who resists the claims of Christ and the Bible on the basis of a self-consciously chosen and (more or less) well-thought-out alternative worldview. He may be an Existentialist or a Marxist. He believes he has good and sufficient reasons for his atheism or agnosticism. He is convinced that in the modern scientific world there is no room for the ancient superstitions of Christianity. That he might actually be expected to convert to such an outmoded faith is unthinkable. On the other hand, he may be a devotee of another form of 'spirituality' – that of an Eastern religion like Hinduism or Buddhism, or he may be exploring the many expressions of 'New Age religion'. He may be fully satisfied with the religious experiences he enjoys within that religious context.

Such people are usually willing to discuss religion with you, sometimes over extended periods of time. They will listen politely to what you have to say, and counter with their own arguments. They will seek to persuade you to convert to their philosophical or religious perspective. It will all be very civilized. The conversations usually end inconclusively. As Bob Dylan sang, 'Most likely you'll go your way and I'll go mine.'

In the Book of Acts, Luke records two incidents where the gospel encounters these two sorts of pagan audiences. The first is the experience of Paul and Barnabas in Lystra, a frontier town in Asia Minor, on the first missionary journey. Here Paul addresses briefly an audience of hotheaded, superstitious pagans who respond vigorously to the miraculous sign performed by Paul and Barnabas in the healing of the lame man. It was quite a day – at first Paul and Barnabas were almost worshipped as deities, but by the end of the day Paul was lying in his own blood, having been stoned by the same people at the instigation of Jews who pursued him from Antioch and Iconium.

The second incident is Paul's visit to Athens on his second journey, where he preached in the marketplace and later before the council of the Areopagus. With these two paradigmatic incidents, the Holy Spirit illustrates for us some of the principles we must keep in mind as we preach 'the unsearchable riches of Christ' (Eph. 3:8) to modern day pagans. Because of the considerable overlap in the substance of Paul's preaching in these two settings, we will look briefly at the incident in Lystra in this chapter, noting the unique features at play there, and reserve our fuller discussion for the next chapter where we will discuss Paul's preaching ministry in Athens.

A Frontier Town

Lystra was at the opposite end of the Roman military road which began in Antioch 100 miles to the northwest.[2] The original town had been fortified and garrisoned by the Romans in AD 6 as a colony and military outpost in the province of Galatia. In addition to the Roman *coloni*, who constituted the upper class of the city, there were some Greeks and Jews (cf. Acts 16:1), though apparently not enough of the latter to make up a synagogue.[3] The crowd that Paul addressed was made up of the lower classes of the city – the native Anatolians who were less educated and more superstitious.[4] They spoke a native dialect (v. 11), while the cultured and business classes would have spoken Greek.

The city was located in a valley formed by the collapsed top of a large volcano. Though there was a stream in the area, the surrounding plain was arid, and the city had to depend upon rainfall for most of its crops and water supply. Commerce with the other cities of the region brought further supplies of 'the good things of life' (cf. v. 17).

'The Gods Have Come Down to Us!'

In this city, Paul and Barnabas encountered a man who had been crippled from birth (Acts 14:8).[5] As Paul began to preach the gospel of Christ, this man responded by faith. We are not told by Luke what Paul was saying at this early stage in his proclamation, but presumably he was telling the people of this town about the earthly ministry of Jesus of Nazareth, and the many wonders which he performed (cf. 2:22). In any case, the lame man heard something that made him pay careful attention. Then 'Paul looked directly at him, saw that he had faith to be healed and called out, "Stand up on your feet!" At that, the man jumped up and began to walk' (14:9-10).[6]

The crowd was galvanized by the miracle. In their pagan superstition they drew the obvious conclusion, 'The gods have come down to us in human form!' (v. 11). In particular, they assumed the visitants were Zeus and Hermes (v. 12) who, according to a local legend preserved in Ovid's *Metamorphoses* (VIII, 636 ff.), had once before visited the region, but were unrecognized by the whole population. An elderly couple, Philemon and Caucis, nevertheless showed the gods hospitality and were rewarded for it. Apparently the common people of Lystra were not willing to overlook such a divine visitation a second time.

The priest (or priests, according to the Bezan text) of Zeus set about busily making preparations to offer sacrifices to these gods – Zeus (Barnabas) and Hermes (Paul).[7] The latter were apparently unaware at first what was afoot, due to the unknown dialect used by the people. The local temple of Zeus was 'before the city gates' (v. 13) and the sacrifices were to be offered there. When it finally became apparent to Paul and Barnabas what was about to take place, they were horrified! They tore their clothing – the response of a pious Jew to blasphemous words or actions (cf. Mark 14:63) – and rushed into the crowd in an effort to put a stop to the proceedings. Obviously, Paul did not have time to prepare a careful message for the people of Lystra under these conditions. Providentially, events had overtaken him. A grave evil was about to be done. Thus his primary purpose in speaking was to put an end to the idolatrous sacrifice which was about to be offered.[8]

Paul's Strong Reaction to Idolatry

Paul's message is brief and urgent. Rushing into the crowd, perhaps gesturing wildly to get their attention, he and Barnabas shout loudly,

'Men, why are you doing this?' (Acts 14:15). The crowd, intending to offer religious worship to these two visiting 'gods', are startled by their reaction. Rather than receiving their worship in serene silence, these 'gods' are protesting, halting the procession and the sacrifice! What can this mean? Paul explains, 'We too are only men, human like you' (v. 15). Paul must begin by forcefully contradicting the opinion of the crowd (cf. 2:15). The visitors are not gods as the people suppose, but mere men. To worship them would be an abomination.

Notice that Paul's faithfulness to God will not permit him to capitalize upon a situation in which he has the respect and attention of the audience. They would receive any word from him at this point as a divine oracle. With a sudden verbal 'slap in the face' Paul tries to bring them to their senses. Jay Adams asks the question, '[Was] it ethically (or religiously) necessary to destroy good will by such a violent reaction?'[9] He suggests that Paul lost his composure, and by his overreaction lost his rapport with the audience, thus crippling his opportunity to call the Lycaonians from their idols to the living and true God. Yet he admits that under the circumstances there was little else Paul could do.[10] 'There are times when Audience Adaptation, sermons and all else must be forgotten. Here was one.'[11]

We cannot know on the basis of Luke's summary of the message (received secondhand from Paul) just how much the apostle actually said. Perhaps his message was brief. Perhaps he was permitted to speak at some length after having dissuaded the crowd from their intention. It is impossible to know how much time elapsed between the end of Paul's sermon and the events described in verse 19.[12] It must not have been a long time since 'the crowd' was apparently still gathered by the time the Jews from Antioch and Iconium arrived.[13] On the other hand, there is no suggestion that the Lystran crowd had become hostile to Paul and Barnabas simply on the basis of the sermon. Disappointed, yes. But murderously angry? Probably not. The crowd had to be 'persuaded' (*peithō*) by the Jews to attack Paul.[14] This suggests that it took some effort to convince the disappointed townspeople that there was malice in Paul's actions. Certainly there was none evident in his manner (no matter how intense) or message. The balance of the evidence does not seem to demonstrate that Paul's strong reaction and abrupt introduction to his message 'lost his audience'.

Paul's Message to the Gentiles

What is remarkable in Paul's performance here is that he not only succeeded (with difficulty) in preventing the blasphemous sacrifice (v. 18), but also was able to set forth, however briefly, the outlines of his 'gospel to the Gentiles'. Despite the enormous pressure upon him – temporally (he had to think and act quickly) and emotionally (he was faced with a religiously horrifying situation) – Paul was able to gather his thoughts and set forth a faithful witness to the true and living God.

The 'body' of Paul's sermon is simply outlined.

I. *We are bringing you good news of the true and living God, calling you to turn from these worthless idols to him.*
A. He is the Creator of all things.
B. He shows his kindness by supplying you with good things.

II. *The time for delay is past; now is the time to repent.*

As has been frequently pointed out, this summary corresponds very closely to the first section of Paul's message to the Areopagus (17:24-26). Though the two situations and the approach of the apostle in each differ significantly, the Athens address is generally considered a fuller exposition of the same themes contained (in seed form) in the message at Lystra. Accordingly, we will save our discussion of these themes for the next chapter. But for now let us note a few details with respect to this message.

Paul addresses the crowd with the call, 'Men!' He then goes on to identify himself with them as a man of the 'same feelings' or nature as them (*homoiopatheis*, v. 15; cf. James 5:17). When one considers the several approaches that Paul could have chosen to try to make the priests of Zeus stop their sacrifice, it is noteworthy that the apostle chose the one he did. He does not distance himself from his audience, but rather fully identifies himself with them. This is not a denunciation of idolatry as much as an urgent, heartfelt explanation of why it is inappropriate. Divine honors must be paid to God alone – the God whom Paul will identify as the Creator and Sustainer of all things. Paul was like the Lystrans. Though a Jew, he knew what it meant to be a blasphemer; to act in ignorance and unbelief (1 Tim 1:13). In the press of the moment, Paul is careful not to alienate his audience any more than absolutely necessary.

Biblical Ideas If Not Biblical Words

In addressing a Gentile audience (here and at Athens), Paul does not make explicit use of the Old Testament Scriptures. They were unknown to these people, and had no authority for them. Pagan religions are 'nature religions' – they pay special attention to times and seasons, the cycles of growth and dormancy, weather patterns, etc. Thus Paul declares to them the true and living God who is revealed in the natural world around them. His key themes are Creation and Providence. The unbeliever is exposed to the evidence of God's existence and character in the created world around him: 'For since the creation of the world God's invisible qualities – his eternal power and divine nature – have been clearly seen, being understood from what has been made, so that men are without excuse' (Rom. 1:20). Yet because he willfully and wickedly 'suppresses the truth' (v. 18), the natural man misinterprets the information he receives from 'general revelation'. The purpose of the 'special revelation' which came to the Gentiles of Lystra in the form of Paul's preaching was to make clear the true meaning of their experience of life. They knew all about 'rain from heaven and crops in their seasons,' and about the food that filled their hearts with joy (Acts 14:17) – perhaps an allusion to the festive meal that might have been part of the anticipated sacrificial ritual.[15] What they did not know and understand was that these good things were 'provided' by God the Creator of all things as a demonstration of his kindness, even to those who refuse to acknowledge him (cf. Matt. 5:45).

Nevertheless, though Paul makes no explicit appeal to the Scriptures, his explanation of 'general revelation' is expressed in language largely drawn from the Old Testament.'[16] He alludes to Exodus 20:11 in his description of God as the one 'who made heaven and earth and sea and everything in them' (Acts 14:15, cf. 17:24). He describes the Gentiles' idols as 'worthless things' (*tōn mataiōn*), a term frequently used by the prophets of the old covenant to describe the idolatry of Israel and the nations (Deut. 32:21; 1 Kgs. 16:13, 26; 2 Kgs. 17:15; Ps. 31:6; Jer. 2:5, 8, 11; 8:19). The reference to God's gifts of rainfall and plentiful harvests echoes Psalm 148:8 (cf. Gen. 8:22; Jer. 5:24). The joy which is brought to the hearts of men by an abundance of good food and drink is another Old Testament theme emphasized by Paul here (cf. Ps. 4:7; 104:15; Isa. 25:6; Eccles. 9:7).[17] The significance of all this (as we will argue in more detail in the next chapter) is that

Paul adapts to his audience not by abandoning scriptural revelation for natural revelation, but simply by making a more 'transparent use' of the Scriptures when speaking to the Gentiles. Paul always reads the 'book of nature' (creation) through the 'spectacles' of Scripture.[18] I will say more about this subject as it applies to our preaching in the next chapter.

What Happened to the Resurrection?

Among the sermons and speeches in Acts, this one is unique in that it contains no reference to Jesus or to his resurrection. Paul's message before the Areopagus, which so closely parallels this one, contains a closing reference to the resurrection of Christ (Acts 17:30), but here there is none. How do we account for such an omission? Perhaps Luke simply chose to exclude any reference to Christ's resurrection from his summary. This seems unlikely, given the central importance of the resurrection to the apostolic witness. If Paul had mentioned it, Luke would have. It is more likely that – given the purpose of Paul's message (i.e., to put an end to the idolatrous sacrifice about to take place) – he said little more at this time than was required to accomplish that goal. Incidentally, it is a tribute to the authenticity and accuracy of Luke's record (questioned by so many scholars[19]) that he does not take it upon himself to fill the gap, and make Paul's sermon more complete than it was.

Did Paul preach Christ and his resurrection at Lystra? We have noted above that there was some preaching done in the city before the miracle of the healing of the crippled man (14:9).[20] In this earlier preaching the full outline of the life, death, and resurrection was no doubt covered, so much so that the crippled man was able to put his faith in Christ as One who could heal him at Paul's word. It is quite likely that many in the crowd of would-be worshippers of Paul and Barnabas had heard the earlier instruction. Perhaps they were beginning to grasp the importance of the person and work of Christ when the miracle in a sense 'derailed' them, and they returned to their superstitious ways. Paul had to stop them so that he could 'get them back on track' with the central message he had come to proclaim. He wanted the inhabitants of Lystra, like those later in Thessalonica, to turn to God from their idols and to serve the living and true God (1 Thess. 1:9). It was Paul's concern to call them to faith in Jesus Christ, the Son from heaven, whom God had raised from the dead (v. 10). Jesus would rescue them from the coming wrath.

Paul's strategy in every city was to give the people enough information about Christ and his saving work to make such a turning from idols to God possible. But in those situations where he spoke to the same general audience on a number of occasions, he may not have believed it necessary to include all the elements in his presentation in each message. He could build his case from sermon to sermon. Perhaps that is what he was doing in Lystra in his earlier preaching. Then the miracle threw all into confusion. Another agenda temporarily came to the fore, so Paul adjusted his message accordingly. He is adapting to new circumstances without losing sight of his overall goal.[21]

Strategy and Tactics in Preaching

Most of you reading this book probably preach to essentially the same group of people Sunday after Sunday – the members of your local church and visitors to the congregation. I would be surprised if each of your messages was a carbon copy of the one before it. You have an overall strategy[22] for edifying and discipling those in the congregation who have committed themselves to Christ, and for reaching those who have not with the good news that by faith in Christ they can find a new life. At the same time you must make 'tactical' decisions[23] about your preaching in view of the variables of congregational life and experience.

If every Sunday morning message is essentially the same three-point evangelistic sermon with an altar call at the end, you may reach your visitors, but your members will soon become wearied by the repetition, and will be unchallenged for the lack of biblical variety and depth in your preaching. On the other hand, if you orient your preaching exclusively to those who know the Lord and are growing in him, the members may be well fed, but there will be nothing for the visitor (who knows little or nothing of Christ or the Bible) to lay hold of for the saving of his soul.

You also need to be able to respond with flexibility to the changing circumstances of congregational life. If you are an experienced pastor, especially of a small or medium-sized congregation, you know how the character of a congregation can change over time with the coming and going of members. Median age changes. You may have a church full of families with teens at one point, and a few years later a 'baby-boom'. The level of spiritual maturity may change dramatically with an influx of 'unchurched' people. You know very well how things can change. In addition, certain events in the life of the congregation can collectively affect your people in dramatic ways. These and other considerations must be kept in mind as you make tactical decisions about your preaching. Your choices of what books of the Bible to preach through, topics or themes to highlight, how to approach each passage in view of congregational needs, etc. all must be in line with your overall strategy for your pulpit ministry, but they must also reflect a healthy flexibility.

As we follow Paul from town to town, audience to audience, and situation to situation we can discover in concrete terms how Paul made short-term preaching decisions in view of his long-term goals for spreading the news of Christ. Even in situations, like at Lystra, which called for quick responses, Paul did not merely become reactionary. He accomplished his immediate goal without sacrificing his ability to pursue his larger strategy. At the same time, it is important to note – as you also well know – you are not in total control of circumstances. You are not always able to fulfill your longer term plans. The Lord who commissioned you for your preaching task is the sovereign Lord of history. Every circumstance comes to pass in accordance with his will (Eph. 1:11). He rules in the lives of men, in detail (Matt. 10:30). In Acts Luke records instances when the apostles were not permitted to carry out their plans: 'Paul and his companions traveled throughout the region of Phrygia and Galatia, having been kept by the Holy Spirit from preaching the word in the province of Asia' (Acts 16:6). Paul told the Roman believers, 'I do not want you to be unaware, brothers, that I planned many times to come to you (but have been prevented from doing so until now)' (Rom. 1:13).

You must make your strategic plans for your ministry in accordance with Christ's program set out in Scripture (Matt. 28:19-20). You must adapt your tactics and adjust your ministry in terms of the variables you encounter in the providence of God. But having done all that, you must recognize that sometimes you will not be able to accomplish what you thought you could and should. We cannot say what Paul's ministry in Lystra would have been like had he not healed the crippled man and thus set off the idolatrous reaction of the priests and people. Luke tells us what did happen, and how Paul adapted to the new circumstance. By the blessing of Christ he handled it well, and left us an example to follow of *purposeful flexibility*.

A Stoning and A Church

As we noticed, Paul was finally successful in keeping the crowd from offering their sacrifice, though it was difficult to calm the crowd and dissuade them (Acts 14:18). Whatever further ministry Paul might have had in Lystra was cut short by the arrival of hostile Jews who had followed Paul's trail from Antioch and Iconium (v. 19). By means unrecorded by Luke, the Jews incited the crowd to stone Paul and drag him outside the city, thinking he was dead. Christ was not yet finished with his servant – not by a long shot – and so 'after the disciples had gathered around him, he got up and went back into the city' (v. 20).[24]

It is often pointed out that the results of Paul's ministry in both Lystra and Athens were meager, and this observation is sometimes used to buttress the claim that Paul's method in those places was somehow inadequate.[25] But does the evidence bear out this conclusion? It is true that Paul and Barnabas left for Derbe the very next day, where they preached the gospel to good effect, winning 'a large number of disciples' (v. 21). Soon they returned to Lystra (and later returned to Iconium and Antioch as well). What did they find in Lystra – the results of their preaching ministry there but a short time before? They found a church (v. 23)! That is, they found sufficient Christian believers assembling together to be constituted a church. What's more, there were among these new Christians men of sufficient character and commitment to be appointed elders to continue to teach and lead the people (v. 23; cf. 1 Tim. 3:1-7; Titus 1:6-9).[26] Indeed, it is apparent from a later point in Luke's narrative, that Paul's trusted disciple and co-laborer Timothy arose from this very congregation (cf. Acts 16:1-2).[27] This hardly sounds like 'meager results'.

What a powerful testimony to the effectiveness of the gospel as preached by Paul in Lystra! From that crowd of ignorant, superstitious idolaters a church was born of the Holy Spirit. The crippled man who trusted Christ was joined by others of his countrymen in professing faith in Jesus Christ and (presumably, though Luke does not mention it) receiving baptism. In a very short period of time, the Holy Spirit used the instruction that Paul and Barnabas had given to raise some of the Lystran men to a level of spiritual maturity sufficient to become leaders of the congregation. And all this in the context of persecution!

When Paul told them 'We must go through many hardships to enter the kingdom of God' (v. 22, cf. Matt. 11:12), they all knew what he was talking about. Paul bore in his body 'the marks of Jesus' (Gal. 6:17), and his brothers had tasted the same suffering. But the Kingdom of God had come to Lystra, and men were entering into it.

16

Paul and the Greeks:
Facing the 'Cultured Despisers'

Friedrich Schleiermacher's first major book bore the title *On Religion: Speeches to Its Cultured Despisers*. Though I cannot recommend the book, or Schleiermacher's version of Christianity, he did come up with an apt description of many in our day who reject Christianity, allegedly on the basis of reason and science – 'cultured despisers'. In our last chapter we noted that modern-day pagans, like their counterparts in the first century, can be either ignorant or well educated, violently hostile to or urbanely uninterested in the claims of Christ and the gospel. Paul encountered the former in Lystra, the latter among the philosophers of Athens. We observed earlier that there was some overlap in the themes of these two messages. Let us look in detail at Paul's proclamation and defense of the gospel before its 'cultured despisers' among the first century Greeks.

Intellectualism and Idolatry

The Apostle Paul came to Athens after he was driven from Thessalonica and Berea by Jewish opponents who dogged his steps from one Macedonian city to the next (Acts 17:13). He sent word that Silas and Timothy, who had stayed behind, should join him in Athens as soon as possible (vv. 14-15). While waiting for them, Paul began to explore the city and observe carefully its temples and religious shrines (cf. v. 23). Paul became greatly distressed because of the prevalence of idolatry in Athens (v. 16).

The idolatry of Athens was known to all. The Roman poet Petronius, in his *Satyricon*, claimed it was easier to meet a god in Athens than a man. According to Pausanias, there were more statues of gods and heroes in Athens than in all of the rest of Greece combined. This idolatry not only fed the gross superstitions of the masses, but in Athens it also coexisted with the intellectual and artistic pursuits for which the city had been historically famous. By the time Paul visited the city, however the intellectual life of the city was moribund. Farrar writes:

The whole city, indeed, was not unlike one of our University towns at the deadest and least productive epochs of their past. It was full of professors, rhetors, tutors, arguers, discoursers, lecturers, grammarians, pedagogues, and gymnasts of every description; and among all these Sophists and Sophronists there was not one who displayed the least particle of originality or force. Conforming sceptics lived in hypocritical union with atheist priests, and there was not even sufficient earnestness to arouse any antagonism between the empty negations of a verbal philosophy and the hollow profession of a dead religion.[1]

We are used to being told that 'enlightenment' – reason, science, and education – stands at the opposite extreme from 'religious superstition' (including Christianity). But this is not so. All men are inescapably religious, and the rejection of Christianity does not lead to 'no religion', but to another, idolatrous religion. Recent studies of American higher education have charted the growth of paganism, witchcraft, and other superstitions under the banner of 'scientific' secularism.[2] The intellectual and spiritual distance between the modern Western world and ancient Athens is not that great.

Instruction Borne of a Zeal for God's Glory
Paul did not observe the idolatrous practices of the Athenians with the detachment of a modern sociologist or museum browser. He was deeply distressed by what he saw. The verb with which Luke describes the apostle's reaction is a strong one.[3] It is significant that the same term is used in the LXX to describe God's anger against the idolatry of Israel (Deut. 9:18; Ps. 106:29; Isa. 65:3; Hosea 8:5; Deut. 29:25-28). Thus the term is not selected to describe the degree of Paul's agitation, but rather its meaning. When confronted with the idols of men, Paul shares the same repulsion and holy anger as his Lord. He may outwardly express this outrage in different ways. As we have seen, at Lystra he let it break forth in order to restrain the offering of pagan sacrifices to himself and Barnabas. Here at Athens, under different circumstances, his outward behavior was more restrained. But it is important to note that Paul was motivated in each case by the same burning zeal and jealousy for the Lord's glory.

What a rebuke the apostolic example is to you and me who have become so jaded to idolatry and other evils that we can dispassionately absorb the news of almost any horror! Most of us are capable of profound agitation, and even (at times) violent outbursts of anger, but it is seldom provoked by a holy zeal for the honor of Christ. If we are personally insulted or otherwise harmed, if our ministry is not gratefully received, if our families are somehow threatened, we can become very angry. But can it be said of us, 'Zeal for your house consumes me, and the insults of those who insult you fall on me' (Ps. 69:9)?

Paul's provocation brought him out of retirement. As he had done in other cities, the apostle began to preach and 'reason' with the Jews and the God-fearing Greeks who were to be found in the synagogue (Acts 17:17). Beyond that, he began 'taking the gospel to the streets' as he spoke in 'the marketplace' day by day with those who happened to be there. This is the first record of Paul engaging the Gentiles 'on their own turf'.

We are reminded by historians that the marketplace in Athens was the locale where the great philosopher Socrates had brought his teaching to the people in the fifth century BC.

> It was in the marketplace of Athens – the very Agora in which Socrates had adopted the same conversational method of instruction four centuries before him – that he displayed his chief activity in a manner which he seems nowhere else to have adopted, by conversing daily and publicly with all comers. His presence and his message soon attracted attention.[4]

The 'attention' Socrates attracted eventually led to his arrest, trial, and condemnation. Paul too was soon called to answer (albeit less formally) for his views before the Areopagus.

Paul's teaching in the marketplace was 'dialogical'[5] – his proclamation of the gospel led to repeated interchanges with the passers by who were willing to listen. Frequently in the Book of Acts Luke uses this term to describe Paul's method of apostolic teaching.

> Every Sabbath he reasoned in the synagogue, trying to persuade Jews and Greeks.... They arrived at Ephesus, where Paul left Priscilla and Aquila. He himself went into the synagogue and reasoned with the Jews (18:4, 19).

> Paul entered the synagogue and spoke boldly there for three months, arguing persuasively about the kingdom of God. But some of them became obstinate; they refused to believe and publicly maligned the Way. So Paul left them. He took the disciples with him and had discussions daily in the lecture hall of Tyrannus (19:8-9).

> On the first day of the week we came together to break bread. Paul spoke
> to the people and, because he intended to leave the next day, kept on
> talking until midnight.... Paul talked on and on (20:7, 9).

Paul apparently had extensive opportunities for preaching and teaching
in the agora in Athens. His instruction provoked questions, which Paul
would answer, and perhaps the expression of counter-opinions and
arguments which led to debate. Like the peripatetic philosophers,
Paul's concern was not simply to announce the truth, but to educate
his audience. Thus he engaged them in personal conversation in an
effort to persuade them of the truth.[6]

Formal Opposition to the Gospel Arises

Eventually, Paul's interchanges with the common people in the
marketplace drew the attention of some of their philosophers, who
gathered nearby. Luke writes, 'A group of Epicurean and Stoic
philosophers began to dispute with him' (17:18). The 'man on the
street' in Paul's day was no doubt like his counterpart today whose
'worldview' is a patchwork of information, opinion, and conjecture
derived from a variety of sources. For the most part he has not thought
carefully or systematically about what he thinks about life, or why he
believes what he believes. That does not mean that he does not put
forth his beliefs forcefully, or fails to hold on to them tenaciously. It
does mean that engaging such a person with the gospel involves both
clarifying what he believes (and why), and setting it in contrast to the
Word of God so as to show the weakness and insufficiency of his
opinons over against the truth of God.

When the 'official philosophers' showed up, however, it is not
hard to imagine them monopolizing the conversations with Paul and
moving them in the direction of more formal debate. Paul now had to
deal with the more self-consciously philosophical worldviews of the
Epicureans and Stoics.

Much has been written about these philosophical schools, which I
will not reproduce here. You may check the commentaries and other
expositions of the Areopagus address.[7] For our purposes here we
need only note that both philosophical schools shared in common: (1)
a denial of the transcendence of God, (2) a denial of the personal
involvement of God in the life of men, (3) a denial of a final judgment.
Paul discusses all three of these points in his address to the Areopagus.
We should also note that both the Epicureans and the Stoics were

tolerant of popular idolatry.[8] Paul later used this point to show up the inconsistency of the Greek position.

As Paul interacts with the Greeks, either in the marketplace or before the Areopagus, he is not particularly concerned to discuss the fine points upon which they differ, but to set all pagan thought over against the revelation of the true and living God through the resurrection of Jesus Christ.[9] Luke tells us that in the marketplace 'Paul was preaching the good news about Jesus and the resurrection' (v. 18). Paul was not engaging in philosophical discussion. Just because he was talking to philosophers, that did not lead him merely to 'philosophize'.[10] Here, as elsewhere, he was busy fulfilling his calling – to preach the good news of Christ (*euangelizomai*). Paul did not allow himself to get sidetracked by his audience or his situation. His eye was firmly fixed upon his calling. He was not a 'proclaimer' (*katangeleus*) of just any message; he was a preacher of the gospel of Christ. Here as elsewhere he determined to know nothing but Jesus Christ and him crucified (1 Cor. 2:2).[11]

When You Can't Win the Argument

You often hear people – Christians and non-believers alike – celebrating the intellectual glories of the 'marketplace of ideas'. Men and women come together for a free exchange of views, characterized by mutual respect and open honesty. Through this dispassionate intellectual process the best opinions prevail for the mutual benefit of all. Sounds great. But I have never seen it work that way. Have you? Nobody likes to be shown up to be wrong. People change their minds very reluctantly. What's more, according to God, all men (being sinners) 'suppress the truth by their wickedness' (Rom. 1:18). In a world of sinners, Luke's account of the marketplace in Athens is more true to life than the idealized 'marketplace of ideas'.

Presumably, as in the case of Stephen so in the case of Paul, the Greeks 'could not stand up against his wisdom or the Spirit by whom he spoke' (Acts 6:10). Not being able to win the argument, the philosophers resorted to the two commonest responses of unbelieving intellectuals – mockery and intimidation.

Some resorted to ridicule: 'What is this babbler trying to say?' they asked (17:18). They show their contempt by calling the apostle a 'seed-picker' of ideas.[12] They cannot defeat his arguments so they try to call into question his credentials. The fact that he was probably better educated than all of his opponents did not make any difference. 'Jewish education' was not intellectually respectable. He was a stranger. He was not an acknowledged member of one of Athens' philosophical 'schools'. 'Where did this bumpkin get his Ph.D. anyway?' they might ask. 'No need to pay any attention to someone who so obviously lacks accredited academic qualifications.'

Surely this experience is (in part) what Paul had in mind when he wrote later of the hostility of the 'wise men' of this world to the gospel (1 Cor. 1:18-29). The message of the cross is foolishness to the 'wise man', the 'scholar', and the 'philosopher' of this age. (You can hear them boasting their credentials!) Unbelieving intellectuals claim to look for 'wisdom', but they find the message of Christ 'foolishness'. Paul reminds us that the accusations often made against us by secular mockers are true. Of those of us who have been called to faith in Christ, 'not many ... were wise by human standards; not many were influential; not many were of noble birth' (v. 26). No matter how we may court worldly intellectual respectability, we are not recognized as credible. But it does not matter. 'God chose the foolish things of the world to shame the wise.... he chose the lowly things of this world and the despised things – and the things that are not – to nullify the things that are so that no one may boast before him' (vv. 27-29).

When you enter the 'marketplace of ideas', expect to be mocked. Even if you have spent thousands of dollars and years of your life accumulating a string of initials after your name (so much so that you impress all your Christian friends and colleagues), it will count for nothing to those who despise your message. No Ph.D. degree will make respectable to the world a message which they find supremely foolish. In fact, the more effective you are in making that message known, the more certain you can be that the unregenerate will mock and reject it. If your academic studies make you a substantively better exegete, theologian, and preacher – wonderful. But don't get your feelings hurt when your degrees cannot buy you intellectual respectability. Like Paul, if you are faithful to the message of Christ, you're nothing more than a 'seed-picker' to the wise men of this world. No matter. God is pleased 'through the foolishness of preaching to save those who believe' (v. 21).

Mockery was not the whole story. Others in the crowd were ready to intimidate Paul with the accusation of 'advocating foreign gods'.

This was a potentially serious accusation. It was very similar to the charge lodged against Socrates:

> Accusing Paul of being a propagandist for new deities was an echo of the nearly identical charge brought against Socrates four and a half centuries earlier.... As introducing foreign gods, Paul could not simply be disdained; he was also a threat to Athenian wellbeing. And that is precisely why Paul ended up before the Areopagus council.[13]

Notice again that the unbelieving are not interested in a 'free exchange' of ideas. When they are unsuccessful in refuting Paul, they want his message officially supressed.

History is replete with examples of attempts on the part of governmental and institutional authorities to silence the preaching and teaching of Christianity, even in allegedly free and democratic societies. In our own day one need only think of the manner in which the principle of 'separation of church and state' has been used to suppress the teaching or free expression of Christianity, while permitting (and even encouraging) occultism, goddess worship, animism, 'New Age' mysticism, etc. Further, some of you have no doubt been asked at one time or another to offer an 'invocation' in certain public settings, and if your prayer included (as it should) an acknowledgment of the sovereign lordship of the Triune God alone, an honest confession of sin, and an explicit reference to the mediatorial work of Christ – rather than the generic slogans of 'civil religion' – you probably did not get invited back.

Satan is not hesitant to use the 'powers of this world' against the Lord who ordained and sustains them (Rom. 13:1-7). When the gospel makes significant inroads into any society or institution, the ungodly will fight back, and they won't fight fair. It may be an unconverted husband who tells his wife, 'I don't want you talking about your religion to our friends.' It may be a manager firing his Christian employee for 'wasting too much time talking' (about the gospel) at work. Or, as here, calling the Christian minister to answer for his teachings before the local authorities.

Paul Meets the Council

'Then they took him and brought him to a meeting of the Areopagus, where they said to him, "May we know what this new teaching is that you are presenting? You are bringing some strange ideas to our ears, and we want to know what they mean" ' (Acts 17:19-20). Paul is brought before the Areopagus council, probably now meeting near the marketplace in the Royal Portico,[14] for an informal hearing during which his ideas would be reviewed.

> The Council was a small but powerful body (probably about thirty members) whose membership was taken from those who had formerly held offices in Athens which (due to the expenses involved) were open only to aristocratic Athenians. This Council was presently the dominating factor in Athenian politics, and it had a reputation far and wide.... They exercised jurisdiction over matters of religion and morals, taking concern for teachers and public lecturers in Athens ... one way or another, the Council would have found it necessary to keep order and exercise some control over lecturers in the agora. Since Paul was creating something of a disturbance, he was 'brought before the Areopagus' for an explanation (even if not for a specific examination toward the issuance of a teaching license).[15]

'Paul appeared before the Areopagus Council for a reason that probably lies somewhere between that of merely supplying requested information and that of answering to formal charges.'[16] Luke indicates that the reason for the inquiry was as much a result of the proverbial curiosity of the Athenians (v. 21) as the formal lodging of charges.[17]

It was clear to the Athenians that Paul was preaching something radically different from what they were used to: 'You are bringing some strange ideas' (v. 20). Paul was not, in fact, an eclectic, borrowing ideas from other philosophies and blending them into a 'new' mixture. Rather, he was proclaiming a message that stood over against the Greek philosophies in a radical antithesis. The good news of the resurrection of Christ, which Paul had been proclaiming from the outset in Athens, required a context of understanding, and it was that which Paul intended to give in his speech before the council. Paul's purpose is not primarily to defend the fact of the resurrection, but to explain its meaning (cf. v. 31).[18]

Next, in an aside which is anything but irrelevant to Paul's situation, Luke describes the Athenians (and their foreign visitors) as those who 'spent their time doing nothing but talking about and listening to the latest ideas' (v. 21). Here Luke punctures the intellectual pretentions of the most famous of Greek institutions, highlighting instead their lack of moral and intellectual earnestness. The intellectualism of Athens current in Paul's day was but a shadow of its legendary past. According to Farrar:

Athens had been in all ages a city of idlers, and even in her prime her citizens had been nicknamed Gapenians, from the mixture of eager curiosity and inveterate loquacity which even then had been their conspicuous characteristics. Their greatest orator had hurled at them the reproach that, instead of flinging themselves into timely and vigorous action in defence of their endangered liberties, they were forever gadding about asking for the very latest news; and St. Luke – every incidental allusion of whose brief narrative bears the mark of truthfulness and knowledge – repeats the same characteristic under the altered circumstances of their present adversity. Even the foreign residents caught the infection, and the Agora buzzed with inquiring chatter at this late and decadent epoch no less loudly than in the days of Pericles or of Plato.[19]

Similar characteristics have been discerned in the modern university where ideology has replaced ideas as the driving interest of professors and students alike.

Paul's Address

Let's sketch the outline of Paul's address to the Athenians. In this outline I have made explicit what Paul leaves largely implicit in his delivery. This will help you see more clearly the evangelistic (as well as the apologetic) concern of the apostle's message. A little later we will discuss his 'indirect' approach in the actual delivery of the message.

CONCLUSION (vv. 22-23): 'I see that in every way you are very religious.... I even found an altar with this inscription: TO AN UNKNOWN GOD.' I am here to tell you about the God you admit you do not (and cannot) know.

I. *Your ideas about God are in error – you are 'groping' in the 'darkness' of an ignorance you partly admit (vv. 24-28).*
   A. God is your transcendent Creator and Sustainer (v. 24a). He gives life and breath and everything else to all men (v. 25b). Therefore,
      1. He cannot be contained in manmade temples (v. 24b).
      2. Nor can he be served by human hands as if he needed anything (v. 25a).
   B. This transcendent God orders your lives (v. 26) so that you might seek the meaning and purpose of existence in him (v. 27a), yet,

    1. You are 'groping' in the darkness of ignorance (v. 27a) though,
    2. God is not far from each one of you (v. 27b). To this your own poets bear witness (v. 28).

II. *Therefore, your practice of idolatry is a guilty rebellion against the God who is there (v. 29), for,*
  A. We are God's 'offspring' – we were made in his image (v. 29a).
  B. Therefore, for you to make God in the image of man (or other creatures) is an act of (sinful) inversion (v. 29b).

III. *You must repent of your idolatrous ignorance, and turn to the true and living God whom I am proclaiming to you (vv. 30-31).*
  A. In the past God overlooked man's (sinful) ignorance (v. 30a), but now he has come to you with the good news of salvation.
  B. He has set a day when he will judge the world with justice (v. 31a).
    1. The resurrection of Jesus from the dead proves that such a day of judgment is 'set' and certainly coming (v. 31a).
    2. The resurrection of Jesus from the dead proves that he himself is the man who will be your Judge (v. 31b, c).

CONCLUSION (implicit): Therefore, you ought to turn from your idols to the living and true God (whom I represent), and wait for his Son Jesus, who can (and will, if you believe) rescue you from the coming wrath (1 Thess. 1:9-10).

This is the most formal of Paul's speeches. Its subtle argumentation, allusions to Greek authors, and elevated style fit perfectly the occasion, setting, and audience. Paul is again adapting well to the circumstances into which the Holy Spirit has placed him. He was called to give an answer (cf. 1 Pet. 3:15) before the Areopagus, but was also aware of the bystanders' presence (cf. Acts 17:34). His manner is bold, confident, yet respectful: 'Men of Athens! I see that in every way you are very religious.'[20] As Farrar has noted, 'It is possible to be "uncompromising" in opinions, without being violent in language or uncharitable in temper.'[21] Accordingly, he adopts a method of *indirection*, leaving most of his hortatory points unsaid, but driving his hearers to draw certain conclusions by means of his exposition.

Paul describes the Athenians as very 'religious' (*deisidaimonesterous*). Most commentators are unsatisfied with the King James' rendering, 'superstitious'. While the term can have that connotation, it is more likely that Paul deliberately chose this term for its ambiguity – it is a term which can offer a compliment without implying commendation. Stifler renders the phrase, '[You are] more reverential to the gods than others.'[22] Behind Paul's use of this term is his theological understanding (explained in Rom. 1:19; 2:15) that man, as a unique creature made in the image of his Creator, is inherently a religious being. But that religious instinct has been twisted by sin. Thus man's religious impulse cannot be taken at face value (i.e., complimenting them for being 'very religious'), but neither is it to be discounted (by calling it mere 'superstition'). Perhaps his hearers noted the ambiguity, and made them begin to ponder his words carefully at the outset.[23]

The 'Unknown God'

Paul masterfully finds his point of contact in the experience of his audience (as Peter had done in Acts 2:22). He tells his audience, in a way that would no doubt have won their approval, that he had made a careful and thorough inspection of their many notable religious shrines (v. 23). After all, their city was noted the world over for these things. Paul did not dismiss them outright, not having even taken the time or effort to look at them. He spoke to the Greeks as one who had seen and considered their point of view.

While reviewing their 'objects of religious devotion' (*sebasmata*), Paul says, 'I even found an altar with this inscription: TO AN UNKNOWN GOD' (v. 23). This comment brings immediate recognition by his audience. This altar (or others like it) was well known in Athens.[24] Paul has made his point of contact. The apostle 'show[s] himself to be a masterful public speaker in his ability to arrest attention by linking his message with features of his listeners' own experience.'[25] From the recognition of this altar to an 'unknown god' Paul introduces his theme: 'Now what you worship as something unknown I am going to proclaim to you.'

In a sense the purpose of this message is 'pre-evangelism.' Paul must, through his preaching, lay a foundation of understanding within which the proclamation of the historical message of Christ's incarnation, atonement, and resurrection will make sense to a Greek audience. This may in part explain the absence of references to the death of Christ in Luke's summary of the message. Paul's clear announcement of the fact of the resurrection of Jesus at the conclusion of the message shows plainly that Paul was not adopting a neutral, 'philosophical' approach to this 'pre-evangelistic' task – he is ever the herald of the resurrected Christ – but Paul's primary concern was to dispel the ignorance of his audience so that they might be prepared to truly understand the message of the cross.

Therefore, Paul takes for his starting point the self-confessed ignorance of Athenian worship (*eusebeō*, genuine piety).[26] 'Paul did not attempt to supplement or build upon a common foundation of natural theology with the Greek philosophers here. He began, rather, with their own expression of theological inadequacy and defectiveness. He underscored their ignorance and proceeded from that significant epistemological point.'[27] It is not the apostle's intention to fill out their imperfect monotheism. Rather he wants to expose the underlying skepticism and irrationalism of all pagan thought and worship.

We discussed in an earlier chapter the authoritative stance taken by the apostles as 'heralds' of the risen Christ.[28] We might have expected, however, that in this unusual setting, Paul would adopt a less 'dogmatic' stance – reasoning with the Greeks on a more neutral basis. That Paul does not intend anything of the sort is indicated by the word he uses to describe what he here intends to do – he will 'proclaim' (*katangellō*, i.e., official proclamation) the truth to the Athenians. This same term is used to describe the ministry of the apostles in various settings with many kinds of audiences (Acts 4:2; 17:3b; 13:38; cf. Col. 1:28). Paul is speaking here by the authority of Christ, as he did in every other place. He is not going to step down to a 'level playing field' and debate the mere possibility of the gospel of Christ being true. Adaptation to the audience never meant for the apostles the abandoning of their authoritative stance.[29]

Paul's Use of Scripture to a Pagan Audience

Much has been made of Paul's differing approaches to Gentile as opposed to Jewish audiences, especially with respect to his use of the Scriptures. It is true that Paul could, and did, make a more direct appeal to the old covenant Scriptures when addressing Jews, for whom they were a well-known and acknowledged authority. But is it true that in speaking to Gentiles he moved from special to general revelation as the basis of his argument and appeal? Did he preach 'revealed theology' to Jews and 'natural theology' to Gentiles? Not at all. Rather Paul simply makes a *less explicit appeal* to the Scriptures while continuing to use them as the subtext for his messages to biblically illiterate pagans. The fact that Gentiles did not acknowledge the authority of the old covenant Scriptures did not induce Paul to abandon them as the basis of his proclamation. Acknowledged or not, the Scriptures remain 'God-breathed' and for that reason they are 'useful for teaching, rebuking, correcting, and training in righteousness' (2 Tim. 3:16).

Paul believed that God's 'general' and 'special' revelation were ultimately one, and so he could find numerous parallels between what the Scriptures said and what nonbelievers, who are ignorant of the Scriptures, nevertheless know by nature. He did not proclaim a 'natural theology,' but rather a biblical theology which is evident (though distorted through man's sinful misperceptions) in man's own created nature and surrounding environment. Paul set forth his understanding of the natural man's relationship to God's revelation in the opening chapter of Romans. When the nonbeliever shows some awareness of the truth as revealed by God (within himself or in the world around him) – as the Greeks here did by means of their 'agnostic' altar – Paul draws attention to it as an evidence that the unbeliever knows God and is without excuse since he wickedly supresses that truth (Rom. 1:18-20). But Paul always interprets that 'natural' revelation through the spectacles of special revelation (as Calvin put it[30]). 'Unlike some later apologists who followed in his steps, Paul does not cease to be fundamentally biblical in his approach to the Greeks, even when (as on this occasion) his biblical emphasis might appear to destroy his chances of success.'[31]

This sermon is full of scriptural allusions, even though no direct appeal is made to the old covenant documents. The United Bible Society's edition of *The Greek New Testament*[32] lists the following:

Ps. 146:6; Isa 42:5; 1 Kings 8:27 in Acts 17:24
Ps. 50:12; Isa. 42:5 in v. 25
Deut. 32:8 in v. 26
Isa. 55:6; Ps. 145:18; Jer. 23:23 in v. 27
Gen. 1:27; Isa. 40:18-20; 44:10-17 in v. 29
Ps. 9:8; 96:13; 98:9 in v. 31

To take a particular instance, Greg Bahnsen has pointed out the formative role played in Paul's argument to the Athenians in verses 24-25 by Isaiah's indictment of Israel's idolatry as set forth in Isaiah 42:

> In the Isaiah pericope, the prophet goes on to indicate that the Gentiles can be likened to men with eyes blinded by a dark dungeon (42:7), and in the Areopagus address Paul goes on to say that if men seek after God, it is as though they are groping in darkness (i.e., the sense for the Greek phrase 'feel after him,' 17:27). Isaiah's development of thought continues on to the declaration that God's praise ought not to be to graven images (42:8), while Paul's address advances to the statement that 'we ought not to think that the Godhead is like unto gold, or silver, or stone, graven by the art and device of men' (17:29). It surely seems as though the prophetic pattern of thought is in the back of the apostle's mind.[33]

The apostles were always men of the Word of God written. They knew and understood that the coming of Christ represented the supreme and final revelation of God (Heb. 1:1-2; John 1:18; etc.). Consequently, they preached on the premise that all of God's revelation has to be explained from the perspective of its fulfillment in Christ. Thus 'general revelation' was explained by 'special', scriptural revelation, and Old Testament scriptural revelation was explained by the new covenant revelation which had been made in Christ. This explains their approach to the use of the Scriptures before various audiences. Where the Old Testament was known they used it explicitly and they expounded it as pointing to Christ. When the Old Testament was unknown (as here) the Apostle Paul simply used it without making explicit reference to it, focusing on those themes which are also evident in God's general revelation to mankind.

The God Whom Paul Knows and Proclaims

Paul begins to raise questions about the adequacy of the Greek world view by setting their 'unknown god' over against the God he knows – the Creator and Sustainer of all things. 'The God who made the world and everything in it is the Lord of heaven and earth and does not live in temples built by hands' (Acts 17:24). The God of the Bible whom Paul is proclaiming is 'the Maker of heaven and earth, the sea, and everything in them' (Ps. 146:6). He is the one 'who created the heavens and stretched them out, who spread out the earth and all that comes out of it, who gives breath to its people, and life to those who walk on it' (Isa. 42:5). This is not the 'unknown god' of the Greeks – both the Epicurean and Stoic philosophers might well have taken offense at Paul's portrayal of God. Paul's biblical doctrine of creation contradicted both the materialism of the Epicureans and the pantheism of the Stoics. 'Against naturalistic and immanentistic views Paul proclaimed supernatural transcendence.'[34]

What's more, Paul declares that this transcendent God 'does not live in temples built by hands' (Acts 17:24), an echo of Solomon's words recorded in 1 Kings 8:27. It is noteworthy that here Paul made the same point before a skeptical Gentile audience as did Stephen in his defense before the Jewish Sanhedrin (cf. Acts 7:48), though for a somewhat different reason. This point would have been less objectionable to the Greek philosophers, and thus Paul puts them into an intellectual bind. He ties the claim that God cannot be contained in a stone building (with which they agree) to the proclamation of his absolute transcendence (which they strongly deny). They cannot have it both ways. To this Paul adds the further point that God 'is not served by human hands, as if he needed anything, because he himself gives all men life and breath and everything else' (Acts 17:25). This too is an echo of the Old Testament (Ps. 50:12), and an idea with which even the Epicureans would have agreed. Paul is building up the intellectual tension in the minds of his thoughtful hearers by exploiting the contradictions inherent in their religious opinions.

Paul moves on in his argument:

> From one man he made every nation of men, that they should inhabit the whole earth; and he determined the times set for them and the exact places where they should live. God did this so that men would seek him and perhaps reach out for him and find him, though he is not far from each one of us. 'For in him we live and move and have our being.' As some of your own poets have said, 'We are his offspring' (Acts 17:26-27).

Paul continues to use an indirect method of bringing conviction to the hearts of his auditors, pressing home his point that the Greek's ignorance is a guilty ignorance, which results from their supressing the truth in unrighteousness (cf. Rom. 1:18).

According to Deuteronomy 32:8, 'When the Most High gave the nations their inheritance, when he divided all mankind, he set up boundaries for the peoples according to the number of the sons of Israel.' It is to this reality that Paul is here alluding. Further, according to Job, the Lord 'makes nations great, and destroys them; he enlarges nations, and disperses them' (Job 12:23). Paul's point is clear: the transcendent God whom he has come to proclaim to the Greeks sovereignly orders their lives and is not far from any of them.

Paul hereby presses the fundamental contradiction in the pagan worldview. The Greek philosophers denied that the gods had any direct involvement in the lives of men, and yet their poets declared that men live and move and have their being in God. Which is true?

Paul again exposes, without making a direct indictment, the ignorant 'darkness' in which they are 'groping' (*psēlaphaō*[35]) for answers, yet finding none. How much this groping differs from the invitation which God extends to sinful men: 'Seek the LORD while he may be found; call on him while he is near' (Isa. 55:6). 'The LORD is near to all who call on him, to all who call on him in truth' (Ps. 145:18). The difference is between groping in darkness and calling upon the Lord in truth. Men need not remain in the darkness and shadows, unless they 'loved darkness instead of light' (John 3:19).

Paul's Use of the Pagan Poets

There has been much debate among Christian apologists concerning the significance of Paul's quotations from the pagan poets Aratus of Cilicia and Cleanthes. We cannot enter that debate here. We are concerned with the homiletical purpose of Paul's citations.

Most scholars agree that Paul was well versed in the learning of the Greeks.[36] Paul must have long before noted the formal parallels between the quotation from Aratus and the pervasive teaching of Scripture: ' "Am I only a God nearby," declares the LORD, "and not a God far away?" ' (Jer. 23:23). 'For this is what the high and lofty One says – he who lives forever, whose name is holy: "I live in a high and holy place, but also with him who is contrite and lowly in spirit, to revive the spirit of the lowly and to revive the heart of the contrite" ' (Isa. 57:15). Thus the apostle can couch the truth of the biblical revelation in the language of the Greek poets. Thereby he builds another bridge to his audience. Paul is not, however, basing his point about the immanence of God the Creator on the insights of the poets, but on the fact that their words confirm (at least formally) what the Bible itself consistently teaches. But Paul knew full well that the poet was speaking of the Zeus of Stoic pantheism – an idol. He was far from equating that idol with the God and Father of the Lord Jesus Christ!

Paul uses the poets because they are familiar to his audience. Their mention will evoke a response of recognition and assent. Further, the poets had an acknowledged authority for the Greeks – they were considered prophets. In earlier days the poets claimed divine inspiration. Though the philosophers to whom Paul was speaking would have been skeptical about such claims, the poets nevertheless enjoyed the authority of tradition, and when they aphoristically set forth what was taken to be self-evident, as in the case of these two citations, they would have elicited a knowing nod from the audience.

Finally, Paul is using the words of the poets *against* the opinions of those who claim to acknowledge the insights of the poets. According to Bahnsen:

> Paul appealed to the distorted teachings of the pagan authors as evidence that the process of theological distortion cannot fully rid men of their natural knowledge of God. Certain expressions of the pagans manifest this knowledge as suppressed. Within the philosophical context espoused by the ungodly writer, the expressions were put to a false use. Within the framework of God's revelation – a revelation clearly received by all men but hindered in unrighteousness, a revelation renewed in writing in the Scriptures possessed by Paul – these expressions properly expressed a truth of God. Paul did not utilize pagan ideas in his Areopagus address. He used pagan expressions to demonstrate that ungodly thinkers have not eradicated all idea, albeit suppressed and distorted, of the living and true God.[37]

Again Paul is exploiting the inherent contradictions within the Greek mind set. Paul is pointing out that his teaching is more consistent with their poets than their own pantheism and materialism are.

Paul draws his conclusion in Acts 17:29, 'Therefore since we are God's offspring, we should not think that the divine being is like gold or silver or stone – an image made by man's design and skill.' We can again see the restraint which is evident in Paul's method. In his *heart* the apostle burns with the conviction that it is wicked rebellion against the true and living God, deserving of eternal condemnation, to make and worship an idol (remember he tore his clothes in Lystra!). But what he *says* to the Athenians is much more reserved – that men should not imagine that the divine being is like a piece of skillfully crafted gold or silver or stone. 'Thus far, then, with a considerateness which avoided all offense, and a power of reasoning and eloquence to which they could not be insensible, he had demonstrated the errors of his listeners mainly by contrasting them with the counter truths which it was his mission to announce.'[38]

The Call to Repentance

Paul has taken a reserved, dispassionate approach to his subject thus far (in contrast to his speech at Lystra). But that does not mean that he is willing to let his audience go without a challenge to repent and believe. As he moves to the final 'point' of his message, the exhortation to repent and believe becomes more explicit, yet he continues to couch it in the more 'objective' third-person language of a lecture: 'In the past God overlooked such ignorance, but now he commands all people everywhere to repent' (Acts 17:30).

As Paul points out elsewhere (Rom. 3:25), God 'in his forbearance ... left the sins committed [by the Gentile nations] beforehand unpunished.' This is not an indication that the Gentiles escaped the judgment of God beforehand, as some would suggest. Rather, Paul is declaring that by not calling them to repentance they were left in their lostness. But now, through the preaching of the message of Christ, God calls 'all people everywhere to repent' (cf. Luke 24:47). God's provision of salvation in Christ for men of every nation (Rom 3:29-30) now puts them under obligation to repent. The door of salvation is swung open at Athens, the free offer of the gospel is made. But entry must come by way of repentance. These Greeks may receive God's merciful blessing, but to do so they must abandon their idolatry[39] – they need a complete and radical turn around, a total change of thinking (*metanoeō*). Surely Paul had this kind of appeal in mind when he later told the Ephesian elders: 'I have declared to both Jews and Greeks that they must turn to God in repentance and have faith in our Lord Jesus' (Acts 20:21).

The question which always arises in the mind of the unbeliever when the preacher of the gospel calls him to repent is, 'Why should I repent – and why *now*?' The fact of man's sin – a personal offense to a holy Creator – establishes man's liability to punishment. Implicit in all Paul has said thus far is the fact that the idolatry of the Athenians is just that sort of offense. Paul now creates a sense of urgency by putting his call to repentance in the context of a certain coming day of judgment: 'For he has set a day when he will judge the world with justice by the man he has appointed' (17:31a).[40] Peter had done the same thing on the Day of Pentecost (cf. Acts 2:16, 20). Paul's language speaks of the certainty of divine appointment. The coming judgment is not Paul's 'best guess' about an unknown (and unknowable) future, nor is it a philosophical 'limiting concept' necessary only to ensure right conduct by men in this life. Rather, it is a certainty – God has appointed it, and Paul has been sent to reveal it to the Athenians. God is no longer overlooking their sinful idolatry; he has come through his messenger to call men from it to Christ.

Only now, at the conclusion of his message, does Paul introduce the subject of the resurrection, about which he had originally been invited before the Areopagus to speak (Acts 17:19). And when he finally speaks of Christ's resurrection, it is to make a particular point – God has appointed the Judge and has certified that appointment by raising him from the dead (v. 31b). Paul introduces the resurrection, not as a bare 'fact' in need of proof (though such proof exists in the eyewitness testimony of the apostles and others, cf. 1 Cor. 15:4-9), but as a fact which, within the worldview defined by God's transcendence and his creative and providential works in history (outlined by Paul in his sermon), itself proves the reality of coming judgment and identifies the Person who is to be the Judge – Jesus Christ. It is the meaning of the resurrection as much as the reality of the resurrection that is important to Paul.

Paul identifies Jesus as a man. He is not setting forth 'strange gods' (in the speculative sense in which the Greeks would have understood that idea). He is declaring the truth about space-time history. Christianity is not another 'trip' (as Francis Schaeffer used to say). It is rooted in day-by-day reality. That which God has done in our world by raising Jesus from the dead demands that we change our way of thinking about the nature of reality and act in a new way toward God. The reality of the resurrection of Jesus requires that men believe. To withhold such faith is to compound one's former ignorant blindness with a further culpable act of supression. Paul deals with the Athenians as men and women knowing the truth (Rom 1:21).

Don't Call Us, We'll Call You
Notice how Paul brings his whole indictment of Greek religion (and philosophy) together in this final statement. Early on in his message Paul had proclaimed the transcendence of the true and living God, the Creator and Sustainer of the universe, over against the pantheism of the Stoics and the atheism of the Epicureans. The materialistic,

deterministic presuppositions of both schools led them to deny any involvement of the gods in the affairs of men, the reality of a personal existence beyond death, and any notion of future judgements or rewards.[41] In proclaiming the resurrection of Jesus as the proof of a coming day of judgment, Paul is refuting all of those assumptions at once. God *is* taking note of the lives of men in this world against a day of final reckoning. There *is* a life beyond the grave – even a bodily resurrected life (cf. 2 Cor. 5:10; Rom. 14:10; John 5:28-29). Each of Paul's hearers *will* one day face as their Judge this Jesus whom Paul is proclaiming. 'No one can be confronted with the fact of the Christ and of his resurrection and fail to have his own conscience tell him that he is face to face with his Judge.'[42]

With this powerful *coup de grâce* Paul drops a bomb on the intellectual playground of the Greeks. They cannot approach his message – as they have every one before his – with a bemused curiosity (Acts 17:21). The message of Christ demands that they act. The pressure is too much for them. 'When they heard about the resurrection of the dead, some of them sneered, but others said, "We want to hear you again on this subject" ' (v. 32).

Was Paul's message cut short by the reaction of the audience? No. According to F. F. Bruce, 'There is no ground for supposing that the ridicule with which some of his hearers received his reference to Jesus' rising from the dead seriously curtailed the speech he intended to make.'[43] Were they simply brushing off the apostle? Perhaps that was the reaction of the members of the Areopagus. But what of the bystanders who had also heard Paul's message? J. S. Steward expressed this opinion:

> I used to think this was just polite evasion, the eternal refuge of the procrastinating spirit. I am not so sure of it now. I think they were really touched and moved by the dramatic kerygma. This Resurrection message – righteousness vindicated, captivity led captive, death and the demons defeated – they wanted to believe it. For that pagan world was in the grip of fear. Neither philosophy nor mythology, neither astrology nor mystery cult, had been able to roll back the dark shadow of irrevocable fate. The race was in bondage to a destiny decreed and fixed for ever in the unfriendly stars, and the terror of a hostile cosmos held the human spirit in thrall. So these men at Athens resolved to hear the apostle again; for wistfully they hoped his message might be true.[44]

The audience cannot be reacting simply to Paul's statement about Jesus' resurrection. After all, that is what Paul had been proclaiming in the marketplace from the beginning (vv. 17-18). He was called before the council to discuss precisely that subject. They were curious about what a 'resurrection' might be. But they are not prepared to come to grips personally with this message, as if it has something to do with them. The other philosophers they had heard set forth their ideas, and perhaps even attempted to persuade people to adopt their ideas. But after all was said and done, it was a matter of each man doing what seemed wisest to himself. Paul was not interested in theorizing in the abstract about the possibility of bodily resurrection. For him, resurrection was a reality (based both on the resurrection hope of Judaism and the resurrection of Christ) that carried with it a life-and-death implication. It is the significance of the resurrection as proclaimed by Paul which brings the philosophers up short. It is the idea of final judgment at the hands of the risen Christ that makes them balk.

Some mock (*echleuazon*, 'sneering'), others temporize (cf. 24:25). What a telling response! Luke here exposes the moral paralysis which so often infects intellectuals. They are willing to hear and discuss new ideas (v. 21), but they are incapable of responding to Paul's call to action (v. 30), even if their eternal destiny depends upon it. They cannot even bestir themselves to the level of response that their predecessors had when they condemned Socrates for (on the basis of their pagan presuppositions) far less radical ideas.

The Results

Was Paul's message a failure? Some have argued that it was – even to the point of suggesting that Paul radically altered his method of presenting the gospel following his experience at Athens.[45] This hardly seems to be the case. On the basis of his statement in verse 21, it is not likely that Luke (or Paul) was expecting the Areopagus to be a group of morally earnest seekers after the truth. At this stage in his missionary career, Paul could have had no illusions about his audiences. Nevertheless, some who heard Paul preach became believers as a result of his message (v. 34). In particular Luke names Dionysius, a member of the Areopagus itself, and Damaris, a woman who must have been listening from the gallery. And he says there were 'others'.

The gospel was a message with a double effect (2 Cor. 2:15-16).

By his speech Paul accomplishes the purposes for which he was commissioned as a preacher. He bore witness to the resurrection of Christ, and in the process he brought to nothing the wisdom of this world (1 Cor. 1:19-20). God was the one who gave the increase, by graciously granting repentance and a knowledge of the truth to some (1 Cor. 3:6; 2 Tim. 2:25). As Paul wrote elsewhere, reflecting upon his ministry of the gospel among the Greeks,

> For the message of the cross is foolishness to those who are perishing, but to us who are being saved it is the power of God. For it is written: 'I will destroy the wisdom of the wise; the intelligence of the intelligent I will frustrate'.... For since in the wisdom of God the world through its wisdom did not know him, God was pleased through the foolishness of what was preached to save those who believe. Jews demand miraculous signs and Greeks look for wisdom, but we preach Christ crucified: a stumbling block to Jews and foolishness to Gentiles, but to those whom God has called, both Jews and Greeks, Christ the power of God and the wisdom of God (1 Cor. 1:18-24).

'Taking it to the streets'

As we conclude our discussion of Paul's Areopagus address, let's consider some lessons for our preaching from the apostle's example.

The first thing which impresses the preacher reading this chapter is the fact that Paul met the unbelieving Gentiles 'on their own turf'. Paul would 'go to church' (i.e., the synagogue) to preach to one kind of audience – those who were already believers or who had sufficient interest in biblical religion to attend the synagogue services. But this group was only a minority of those who needed Christ, and whom Paul wanted to reach. Therefore, he had to take his message into the marketplace. If he was going to reach the 'unchurched,' he had to go where they could be found, and that was not around the synagogue door.

For too many preachers today, 'outreach' doesn't really mean reaching out at all. It means devising ways by which we can get the unconverted and unconcerned to visit the church so we can preach to them! Heeding the Master's call (Luke 14:23) to 'go out to the roads and country lanes and make them come in' – to the Kingdom, not the church building – is rarely obeyed by pastors in local churches today. That's what missionaries are supposed to do.

In recent years there has been considerable controversy over the so-called church growth movement. Some have argued that the Sunday worship services of the church have to be made more 'user-friendly' in order to attract the 'unchurched'. Services have been made more 'upbeat' and interesting (entertaining) through the use of contemporary music, drama, and dance; sermons have been shortened, simplified, and expurgated of offensive doctrines; 'divisive' elements like the celebration of the Lord's Supper have been relegated to Sunday evening (or a midweek service), etc. Others have reacted strongly to this 'downgrading' of worship.

What is of great interest, however, is the premise that the 'unchurched' must be drawn into the church (its buildings and services) in order to be reached with the gospel. This assumption is rarely even examined, let alone evaluated biblically. Paul's example in Athens (and elsewhere) raises serious questions about the propriety of such an idea. Paul did not wait for the 'unchurched' Gentiles of Athens to come to the synagogue so he could preach to them. He certainly did not propose a modification of the synagogue worship in order to accommodate such a plan! No. In the synagogue he spoke to those who already had an interest in the God and Scriptures of Judaism (Jews and 'God-fearers'), but then he *left* the synagogue for the marketplace to reach the rest of the Greeks.

As uncomfortable as it may be to contemplate (for the author as well as for you), as preachers we cannot escape the Savior's call to take the message to men where they live. You may not wait for them to come to you. You must plan to include in your ministry times when you go to the marketplaces, the college campuses, the neighborhoods, etc. where the 'unchurched' live, and speak to them of Christ and his resurrection, as Paul did. 'Street preaching' in our day has a very bad name, for it has been abused by many kooks with Bibles, but we ought not to conclude that this method of reaching the lost is therefore of no value. In days gone by it was one of the most effective ways of reaching the lost with the gospel (e.g., John Wesley and George Whitefield). In many parts of the world today it is still very effective. We ought not assume that modern mass communication has rendered it untenable in our society. It has to be carefully and wisely planned, but it may still be used by God to great effect.

You should also look for regular opportunities to speak for Christian groups on college and university campuses. Members of those groups are frequently engaged in personal evangelism with classmates, colleagues, and roommates, and often are successful in getting them to attend the campus meetings of the club. What's more these groups are often looking for pastors who are willing and able to bring challenging messages full of solid biblical content to their discipleship meetings. It is a golden opportunity to reach a mixed multitude on their own ground. You might even set aside some time to accompany these believers into the quad for some more individual conversations with unbelieving students. This will be a great way for you to refine your skills in reasoning from the Scriptures (Acts 17:2) and refuting those who oppose the gospel (Titus 1:9).

If pastors spent as much time going to the marketplace as they spend dreaming or planning ways to get the marketplace to come to them, they might be more successful in doing the work of an evangelist as the Lord has commanded (2 Tim. 4:5).

Beware the Seductions of Academia

As you study Paul's speech before the Areopagus, you come to realize that the apostle does not let the intellectual sophistication and philosophical interests of his audience deflect him from his primary concern to bear witness to the resurrection of Christ, and to call men to repentance and faith in terms of that historic reality and the coming judgment it entails.

You may not be as immune to the seductions of academia. Many of us would like to be 'deep thinkers,' and even if we are not, we sometimes would like to act like one. Intellectual pride is a powerful temptation for men of learning, and many pastors are men of learning. They have taken the classes, read the books, written the papers and dissertations, and received the degrees. Then they go off to churches where those qualifications are of little significance. Few people respect them because of their academic achievements. They care more about his 'people skills' than his intellectual prowess. So when this pastor is drawn back into an academic setting (perhaps for a debate with the resident atheist professor), he may be tempted to play the intellectualist's games rather than fulfill his calling. He may be drawn away from his commitment to the absolute authority of Christ and his Word by the expectation that all ideas are equally valid (at least at the outset of discussion). He may surrender the certainty of the gospel to the possibilities and hypotheticals of intellectual discourse. He may adopt a posture of dispassionate 'distance' from his subject in place of radical personal commitment. In these ways and more he may lose sight of his goal – to proclaim Christ and call men to decision.[46]

Paul was not willing to be sidetracked by his audience. Though (as we have seen) he adapted his message in a way suitable to the occasion, he never lost sight of his purpose in speaking to them. He was not there to engage in a philosophical 'joust' – an intellectual exercise. Rather it was his concern to call the Athenians away from their ignorant worship of idols – for which they would be condemned to hell (a word you rarely hear in academic circles) – to the Way, the Truth, and the Life which is Christ Jesus.

When you are called upon to face Christianity's 'cultured despisers' your goal must not be merely to win the debate (though you must strive to do that), but to win the hearts of men for Christ.

Using an Indirect Approach

We have noticed in our study of Paul's message, that he uses a less direct approach to his audience in Athens than elsewhere. In an earlier chapter, we noted that the sermons in Acts were characteristically addressed to the audience in a pointed and personal way.[47] Many pastors need to correct their preaching in favor of a more direct appeal, couched in the second person. But there are times when it is appropriate to be less directly confrontational – to lay out the message more fully before calling men to repent and believe. Stephen saved his pointed admonition to the very end of his message because of the bloody hostility of his Sanhedrin audience. We will see Paul exercise the same care in his defenses in the closing chapters of Acts.

The point to note and remember is that direct, personal appeals in preaching *will evoke a response from your audience*. As we have argued, if you never use that approach you will miss a very important element in effective preaching. But, by the same token, that ability to draw a reaction from your audience should be used tactically. When and how do you want to call for a response? There are times – most of the time when speaking to believers – when you want them responding throughout the message to the truths of God's Word you are bringing to them. But there are also times when you want them to hear all that you have to say before they are called upon to respond, as when you are introducing material from God's Word which is new to them, or with which they might be inclined at first blush to disagree. There will be times when you must call your people to repentance for sins that are so common and deeply engrained that they will be resistant unless you lay adequate groundwork for your admonition. Depending on the specific purpose of your sermon, you need to be able to judge wisely when and on what basis to make your direct, personal appeal to them to respond, for when you do, they will.

Knowing and Using the Poets of the Age

Every age has its 'poets' – cultural spokesmen who are acknowledged authorities and familiar voices. In some ages and cultures these poets are considered authorities in and of themselves. More often they bear the authority of tradition or consensus – they say (in the apt phrase of Alexander Pope) 'what oft was thought, but ne'er so well expressed.' It behooves the preacher to be able to make use of these 'voices' (where appropriate) just as Paul used his knowledge of pagan Greek and Roman literature to build bridges to his audience.

In order to do that, the preacher must seek wide exposure to the culture in which he ministers. You have to read, listen to, and watch what the poets of our age are saying. If you rely for your quotations or illustrations largely on an encyclopedia of '10,000 Handy Sermon Illustrations for Every Occasion', your citations will lack the affective pungency that comes from knowing not only what, but why the poets say what they say. On the other hand, some pastors sprinkle their sermons so freely with quotations that the message becomes an exercise in name-dropping rather than biblical exposition. Erudition for its own sake is no virtue in preaching.

The great advantage of such quotations or allusions is that they are *familiar* to your audience. Appeal to them has the force of confirming your words in the experience of your hearers. A biblical truth which can be paralleled by a statement from a popular rock singer does not thereby gain authority (or explication), but rather is made to strike a familiar, responsive chord in the mind of the young person who knows those lyrics by heart. For example, a few years back, when singer-songwriter Bruce Springsteen was 'the Boss' for millions of young people, I found it very effective to point out in speaking to them that Springsteen's songs frequently wrestled with the problems of sin and atonement, but with no real answers. The poet's expressions touched a deeply resonant chord in the minds of the young people, and the gospel provided the answer 'the Boss' could not.

Use of the poets of the age is also a means of building credibility with a hostile audience. It helps persuade the audience that the preacher is willing to listen honestly to, and consider, the ideas that are held by the audience. Too often preachers come across to an unbelieving audience as dismissive of their own ideas. As a matter of fact, that is what many object to when they complain of being 'preached at'. To be sure, false ideas about God, man, society, sin, and redemption must ultimately be rejected in favor of the Bible's teaching, but it is important in speaking to 'the children of this age' that we let them know that we understand their position, have considered carefully their view, and have been compelled to turn from them to Christ, not out of prejudice but for good and sufficient reasons.

Such credibility is the very opposite of the effect we sometimes witness when notable Christian spokesmen will publicly denounce a humanistic book, film, or other cultural artifact that they consider godless (and which usually is), but it emerges in an interview that none of them have even read the book or seen the movie about which they are so vigorously expressing an opinion. The effect of such an admission is immediate – the opinion is discounted and the Christian speaker dismissed with contempt. It is not even a question of whether the Christian view is true or accurate (you don't have to swim in a sewer to know it's a sewer). Rather the question is one of the *credibility* of the witness.

As we have seen Paul's view of the Athenian's idolatry was clear (Acts 17:16), but he did not lay himself open to the criticism of being an ignorant, prejudiced opponent of Greek ideas. He had done his homework – 'as I walked around and looked carefully at your objects of worship' (v. 23). Paul's later use of the quotations from the Greek poets had the same effect. It built credibility. Your understanding and judicious use of the cultural expressions of today can have the same effect when you address a secularized audience.

Don't Drop Your Weapon

When Paul preached to the Athenian philosophers, as we have seen, he did not abandon 'special', biblical revelation in favor of 'general revelation' alone (or 'natural theology'). His references to God's works of Creation and Providence were fully informed by the teaching of the Scriptures of the Old Testament. What he did do was preach from the Scriptures *without citing the Scriptures*. Paul knew very well that the Greeks did not accept the authority of the Scriptures, but that did not induce him to turn from them to another source of authority more acceptable to the philosophers (e.g., reason, experience, history, etc.). He continued throughout his message to stand fully upon the unique authority of the Word of God written. Paul did accommodate himself to their skepticism regarding the Scriptures by refraining from citing chapter and verse. An overt appeal to the Scriptures would simply have raised an issue that did not need to be raised. He set forth ideas which corresponded to the experience of the audience, but he set them forth in a thoroughly biblical way. No objection was raised.

We need to remember afresh today that the denial of the truth and authority of the Bible by nonbelievers is irrelevant to our use of them. Too often Christians (individual believers and their pastors) have been driven from the high ground of biblical truth into the swampy speculations of vain philosophy by the mere objection of non-Christians to the authority of the Bible. Gary DeMar has written an amusing, but telling 'parable' to warn us against such a critical strategic error.

> It's ten o'clock at night. You're just leaving the library building. This is the third night this week that you've had to work on your research paper. You begin to walk toward your dorm. Out of the shadows of the alley behind the library building a man appears. He attempts to block your path. He appears to be about six feet, four inches tall, and probably weighs nearly two hundred fifty pounds. He's holding a knife with a ten-inch blade. He starts to walk toward you. The campus is deserted. Screaming for help would be fruitless. You know he wants to run you through. He's not after money. He wants your life.
>
> You panic for a moment. But you remember that you're armed with a .45 service automatic. The instructor at the survival school warned you there would be nights like this.
>
> Your sweat-drenched hand reaches into your coat to grasp the handle of the gun. The campus menace is just a few feet away. You shout to him in a weakened but confident voice:
>
> 'Stop! If you take one more step, I'll shoot!'
>
> He laughs. Your calm turns to panic. Fear descends on you like a thick cloud. He shouts back to you, 'I don't believe in guns. And I certainly don't believe in .45 service automatics.'
>
> Fear has now gripped you like a vise. You put the gun down and allow the brute to slash you to pieces.
>
> Of course, this student's reaction is absurd. Nobody in his right mind would cease to believe in the effectiveness of his weapon just because some brute didn't believe in it....

How many times have you been confronted by someone who said he didn't believe in God, the inerrancy and infallibility of the Bible, the divinity of Jesus Christ, miracles, the resurrection, and a whole host of other Bible doctrines? And when you were confronted with such unbelief, how many times were you cut to pieces because you acted as if the Bible were not true unless you could convince the skeptic of its truthfulness? How often do you in practice deny the faith or its power because a skeptic did not believe the Bible?[48]

When you are called upon to address an audience that knows nothing (and perhaps cares nothing) for the Bible, you need not abandon it in an attempt to fight the fight of faith on some 'neutral ground'. Simply refrain, as Paul did, from making explicit references to 'the Bible says ...' and keep right on preaching from the Bible! If you draw special attention to those biblical teachings of which your audience is well aware by virtue of the fact that (despite their denials) they are made in God's image and live in God's world, you may well be able to carry them much further than they would otherwise be willing to go. Although, as Paul discovered, eventually you must tell them things that they will not agree with (apart from the regenerating work of the Holy Spirit), and at that point your audience too may say, 'Don't call us, we'll call you.'

Providing a Context for Understanding for the Gospel
Paul's concern in his message to the Areopagus and the Athenian people was 'pre-evangelistic'. He set forth an historical and theological context for understanding the message of Christ and the meaning of his resurrection, without which his audience might consider the resurrection no more than a remarkable 'freak of nature'.[49] In our day as well, it is of little value to speak to skeptical moderns, who do not know much about the content of the Bible (and what little they may have been taught hopelessly distorted), about being 'sinners' in need of a 'Savior', when those ideas are virtually meaningless, or subject to a wide range of interpretations.

In his book, *The Gagging of God*, D. A. Carson advocates the importance of setting the good news in the context of 'biblical theology' in our preaching so that it will make sense to biblically illiterate modern men who are deeply committed to religious pluralism.

What I am arguing is that without this kind of structure [of the biblical narrative of Creation and Fall] the gospel will not be rightly heard. The doctrine of Creation establishes the grounds of our responsibility before God: he made us for himself, and it is the essence of our culpable anarchy that we ignore it. The doctrine of the Fall establishes the nature of our dilemma: by nature and choice we are alienated from God, deceived, justly condemned, without hope in the world, unless God himself delivers us. All of our ills trail from this profound rebellion. Solutions that do not address our alienation from the personal/transcendent God who made us are at best superficial palliatives, at worst deceptive placebos that leave us to die. In this framework, the philosophical pluralist is not on the vanguard of progress, but an idolater.

In a similar way we could work through all the major turning points of redemptive history to establish the framework which alone makes the good news of Jesus Christ coherent. Perhaps I should mention in passing that this insistence on establishing a biblical/theological framework does not in itself dictate the style of approach, or the point of entry.[50]

Carson argues that this basic biblical framework has been largely lost even among the 'thoroughly churched', not to mention the biblically illiterate and philosophically pluralistic public. If we are not careful, as Paul was, to place the gospel in the setting of the biblical worldview, which alone gives it meaning and urgency, we will be guilty as preachers of empty sloganeering, and will be ineffective in leading men to an authentic experience of Christian faith.

Faithfulness Versus Results

Too often we judge our success as preachers by the short-term results. Many scholars have felt bad about Paul's 'lack of success' at Athens. But as we have noticed, there is no indication that Paul himself was discouraged with the outcome of his message. It was his task to be faithful to his calling – to bear witness to the resurrection of Christ and his exalted, saving glory. This he was. The preaching of God's powerful Word never fails to accomplish its purpose (Isa. 55:10-11), and Paul's preaching was effective at Athens. 'For we are to God the aroma of Christ among those who are being saved and those who are perishing. To the one we are the smell of death; to the other, the fragrance of life' (2 Cor. 2:15-16; cf. Rom. 9:18).

Our task as preachers is to remain faithful to our calling and our message. God will bring the results as he sovereignly ordains: 'I planted the seed,... but God made it grow. So neither he who plants nor he who waters is anything, but only God, who makes things grow' (1 Cor. 3:6).

17

Paul at Miletus:
Comfort to the Faithful

When Paul, while upon his return trip from Greece to Jerusalem in AD 57, summoned the elders of the church(es) at Ephesus to meet him at Miletus (Acts 20:17 ff), he was setting the stage for one of the most powerfully moving of the sermons recorded for us in Acts.

The Uniqueness of the Sermon

As I mentioned in the first part of this study, this sermon to the Ephesian elders is the only example Luke gives us of preaching directed toward an already converted Christian audience. Thus it is the only sermon that approximates what most of us, as pastoral preachers (rather than evangelists or missionaries), do week after week during our Sunday pulpit ministry. Yet the circumstances of this sermon are such as to make it unique as well, so that it is in many ways still quite dissimilar to our usual task in preaching. It has been called Paul's 'Farewell Discourse', and so it is, for as he himself says (vv. 25, 38), he does not expect to see these men face to face in this world ever again.

These ominous circumstances notwithstanding, this sermon has a great deal to teach the thoughtful preacher about what and how he ought to preach to his congregation – even when he fully expects (God willing) to see them again the next week! This sermon is 'pastoral' in the fullest sense – preached by a pastor to other pastors – and its themes, its methods, and its language can be very instructive to us, if we would become more effective in the pastoral ministry of the Word from our pulpits.

The Purpose of Paul's Message

Paul's purpose in this message is to comfort, warn, and encourage his fellow elders in light of his imminent (and final) departure from their midst, and in consideration of their own ongoing task of shepherding the flock of God, entrusted to them by the Holy Spirit.

Obviously, Paul's startling news hit his listeners like a bombshell. Luke tells us that at the conclusion of the sermon the elders wept a great deal, 'especially grieving over the word that he had spoken that they weren't going to see his face any more' (vv. 37-38). Because of their deep respect and affection for Paul, as well as their very specific reliance upon him as colleague and leader during the time of their ministry together for three years as elders at Ephesus (v. 31; cf. Acts 19:1-10), they are deeply troubled with the thought that he will no longer be among them – directing their work, challenging and correcting them, encouraging them to perseverance.

Knowing this in advance Paul, like Jesus before him, makes the most of an opportunity to speak to them that will be *momentous* – taking advantage of the situation to add weight to his words thus giving them a more powerful and lasting effect. In the press of his hurry to reach Jerusalem, the Apostle Paul had already decided to bypass Ephesus and the province of Asia Minor (20:16). He could have simply sent word to the Ephesian elders by messenger informing them of recent developments in his ministry, and in this way convey the news that he would not be returning to the area of their ministry again. It would have been personally disappointing, of course, but perfectly understandable under the circumstances. Certainly a written communication would have been adequate to meeting the specific ministry needs of those elders. Paul had worked with them and had trained them for several years. They knew what to do and would do it. He had little more to give them in the way of further instruction.

But by sending for the elders so that they would meet with him face to face at Miletus, Paul was not only showing his personal interest in seeing these brothers from Ephesus one last time, but he was also setting up a situation where, in his sermon, a brief reminder of his former words and example before them would have maximum impact.

If you think about the upper room discourse of Jesus (John 13–16), you will see something very similar happening. Jesus takes the occasion of his imminent trial, suffering, and crucifixion to create a situation of heightened poignancy in order to drive home his message of hope, warning, and comfort to his bewildered disciples. He tells them what will happen in advance, so that when it happens, they will believe rather than stumble (16:4, cf. v. 33). Taking full advantage of all the emotional resources at play in the circumstances – personal affection, fear, and longing – Jesus brings them all to bear powerfully in reinforcing his message to them on that occasion. Paul is adopting the same procedure at Miletus in preaching for the last time to his co-laborers in the eldership.

Paul's Use of Personal Example

Paul begins by alluding to his personal example in the conduct of his ministry (Acts 20:18-21). He calls for confirming testimony from his auditors as eyewitnesses of the way in which he labored in the gospel among them. This is very similar to the way Peter calls for the confirming eyewitness testimony from his hearers in the course of his sermon on the Day of Pentecost (cf. 2:22).[1] Paul's purpose in using himself as an example is not to exalt himself, but to point his hearers to a concrete embodiment of the kind of pastoral attitude and ministry which he wants them to continue. As an effective preacher, he prizes the specific over the general, and the concrete over the abstract. He could have given them a handful of general directives for pastoral ministry in the local church (as we might be inclined to do), but he does not. He gave them a man in ministry – and that man is himself. In so doing he used their love and respect for him personally to bind their hearts tighter to the work they shared with him. What a persuasive argument from example! And heightened by the uniqueness of the occasion.

What sort of ministerial conduct does Paul's personal example commend? Ministry which was first of all diligent: 'You know how I lived the whole time I was with you, from the first day I came into the province of Asia' (20:18). Service marked by humility and tenderness: 'I served the Lord with great humility and with tears' (v. 19a). Perseverance in the face of trials, i.e., the 'plots of the Jews' (v. 19b). An all-around ministry: teaching 'publicly and from house to house' (v. 20). A ministry of the Word that is comprehensive and balanced: 'I have not hesitated to preach anything that would be helpful to you ... I have not hesitated to proclaim to you the whole will of God' (vv. 20, 27). For all of these sermonic 'points' there is but one illustration, and it stands before them – Paul himself.

There is but one single goal – one holy aspiration – toward which Paul would drive his fellow elders. One goal which he himself seeks with every breath. 'I consider my life worth nothing to me, if only I may finish the race and complete the task the Lord Jesus has given me – the task of testifying to the gospel of God's grace' (v. 24). His testimony – confirmed by their own observation of his conduct in ministry – is that he was 'innocent of the blood of all men' (v. 26; cf. Ezek. 3:18), having fully and faithfully discharged his responsibilities as a herald and pastor (v. 26). He did not desire anyone's money (v. 33) – a most telling testimony in light of today's ecclesiastical scandals – but on the contrary he labored with his own hands to pay his way, as again they themselves can attest (v. 34). His working, producing, and giving (v. 35, cf. Eph. 4:28) were but one way in which he showed them that pastoral ministry must be guided and controlled by the Lord's principle: 'It is more blessed to give than to receive' (v. 35b).

Do you see what Paul is doing in this sermon? He knows the elders have come to see him in person because of their affection for him and appreciation of his ministry to them and with them. While with him they learn that they will never see him again. This last visit with Paul thus makes Paul's person and Paul's ministry the most impressive means by which to drive home the warnings and challenges he wishes to give these elders. His appeal to his own example, therefore, and their eyewitness testimony concerning his conduct among them, is a masterstroke of powerful, persuasive preaching.

Paul did not have to offer a disclaimer regarding his personal example, as most of us might, for he had lived and served in an exemplary way with the Ephesian elders. He may well have told them during his time of service in Ephesus, 'Follow my example, as I follow the example of Christ' (1 Cor. 11:1). And here Paul can use the hortatory force of his own example to great effect. As he stands before his fellow elders and friends at Miletus, he wants to take full advantage of the ties that bind them to him (in Christ and in the ministry), so he calls upon them to remember and imitate his attitude and service.

You and I might, on occasion, use ourselves as an example in preaching, but we might also mitigate its effectiveness by believing it necessary to qualify it. A pastor who is sensitive to his own soul will always be on the alert to guard against spiritual pride and moral smugness. On the other hand, he may find it all too easy to adopt a kind of false humility. To be sure, our lives do not present an unqualified example of holiness or faithfulness in service. Nor did Paul's. He knew better than we just how far short of the glory of God he fell. That is why he articulates the general principle which controls his use of himself as an example – where he faithfully imitates Christ, he calls God's people to imitate him.

What does that mean for us as preachers? First, it is appropriate to use yourself as a sermon illustration on occasions that particularly warrant it. It should not be your ordinary practice. Most pastors would say that they do not prefer to use themselves as illustrations in sermons. Yet, in practice, they may do so all too frequently – either out of an unconscious self-centeredness or, perhaps, a lack of imagination in the development of illustrative material. Paul deliberately chose himself as the prime illustration in this sermon because the uniqueness of the situation demanded it, and for that reason it was most effective in persuading and motivating the elders to continue in the work set before them. There will be times in your preaching ministry when the personal ties that unite you to your people, and they to you, will be in the forefront of everyone's attention. For example, when you leave a pastoral charge, or when you have recovered from a serious illness, or when you preach at the ordination of an elder whom you have personally discipled and prepared for ministry, etc. Often on these occasions your concern will not be so much to instruct – in the sense of imparting new material – but rather to remind and motivate. In that setting the judicious use of self-example can be a most effective means of persuading or challenging others to greater faithfulness and perseverance. You ought to be sensitive and alert to such occasions and, like Paul, take full advantage of them in reliance upon the Spirit of God who opens the heart.

Second, you must be ready to count the cost of using yourself as such an illustration. You are an example to the flock whether you want to be or not, whether you are worthy of emulation or not. To use yourself as a concrete illustration of Christian faith, life, or ministry is a call to be as diligent as Paul in commiting yourself to 'complete your ministry', and faithfully living out that commitment. Pastors sometimes err in comparing themselves to their people, concluding that it is 'safe' to use themselves as an example by virtue of the relative superiority of their faith or obedience. This sometimes backfires, however, in that the people of God can see the inconsistencies with painful clarity, and will judge the pastoral example, not by how it compares to them, but how it compares to the Word of God – in Christ and in the Scriptures. That is as it should be, so we preachers need to examine ourselves to see if we 'measure up' to the standard we are preaching. So, you must be discerning enough to know when to put yourself in the sermon (as an example), and when to leave yourself out!

A Warning and a Challenge

The apostle comes to the heart of his exhortation in Acts 20:28, 'Keep watch over yourselves and all the flock of which the Holy Spirit has made you overseers. Be shepherds of the church of God, which he bought with his own blood.' This is always the duty of the leaders of the congregation, but here it is given a heightened sense of urgency by the warning Paul goes on to make, 'I know that after I leave, savage wolves will come in among you and will not spare the flock. Even from your own number men will arise and distort the truth in order to draw away disciples after them' (vv. 29-30).

Notice the directness of Paul's warning. Perhaps the apostle knew, by means of special revelation, who among the Ephesian elders these destroyers would be, even as Jesus knew who would betray him (John 13:26). But that is not necessarily the case. His warning may have been based on a general understanding of fallen human nature, and of the specific temptations which regularly befall church leaders (e.g., the 'Diotrephes syndrome' in 3 John 9). In the course of his ministry he had observed others abusing their office and making shipwreck of their faith (e.g., Hymenaeus and Alexander in 1 Tim. 1:19-20). Thus he puts his caution to his fellow elders in a very pointed way – a way designed to make them wonder, 'Is it I?' – in order to drive them to some serious soul-searching and mutual accountability.

Against this immediate background he reminds them again that he spent three years – night and day – continually counseling (*noutheeton*) each one of them (Acts 20:31). The point, of course, is that they must continue to counsel one another in the same way, with the same diligence and care, if they expect to protect themselves, and one another, from the defections that may come from within their own ranks. Paul is counseling the elders here in his sermon, and, by means of his sermon, he is encouraging the elders to an ongoing work of pastoral counseling as an integral ministry in overseeing and shepherding the flock entrusted to their care by God the Holy Spirit. I want to return to this matter of preaching and counseling again a little later.

A Closing Word of Encouragement

Paul concludes his sermon with a word of comfort and hope.[2] There has been a lot of bad news for the elders to digest in the course of this brief sermon. Paul is facing greater hindrances to his freedom to preach the gospel and intensified persecution (vv. 22-23). The elders are facing the prospect of continuing their ministry without the help and encouragement of Paul's presence (vv. 25, 38), while at the same time a dangerous internal threat will make itself known (vv. 29-30). What are they to do?

Paul, who has so far used his presence as a key element in his message, now uses his impending absence to underscore what he is about to do. As he parts from them for the last time, Paul commends the elders to God (v. 32). Paul must leave them, and so he hands them over to the One who will never leave them nor forsake them. Now it is true that God alone is the source of our strength, and we should depend upon him wholly even when he gives us other earthly helpers. But it is a fact of experience that too often our sense of our need for God is diminished as we rely upon the helpers he sends. It must have been so with Paul and his colleagues at Ephesus. No doubt he regularly urged them to trust in God alone and serve in the strength he alone provides, but he also knows that now he must leave them they will feel especially alone, bereft of help. So they must learn to live without the presence of Paul, and for that reason Paul calls upon them to rely more completely upon the One who said, 'Surely I am with you always, to the very end of the age' (Matt. 28:20). It is not Paul whom they need in order to continue their work, it is God and his Word.

This moment at the close of Paul's sermon is at once deeply touching and profoundly instructive. As he would later do with his disciple and colleague Timothy (2 Tim. 4:1-8), here Paul (in a sense) breaks the ties that bind the elders to himself, and thereby binds them the more closely to the Savior's side.

God is with them, says Paul to his brethren, and has given them his Word, 'which can build you up and give you an inheritance among all those who are sanctified' (Acts 20:32). In the last analysis that is all they need. If they will heed Paul's exhortation and follow his example then they too, like Paul, will 'finish the race and complete the task the Lord Jesus has given' them (v. 24). That is Paul's deepest desire for his brethren. For that reason he worked with them, and for that reason he now must leave them. And in leaving them he crafts a sermon full of truth and brotherly love, which lives on to bless us as it did those who first heard it. It is personal and pastoral preaching at its finest.

Some Lessons You Can Learn

Paul's emotional leave-taking of his friends and co-laborers in the Ephesian church was (according to the narrative of Acts) a once-in-a-lifetime incident for Paul. You may share an experience like this a few times in your ministry as you move from one church to another. Are there other things we may learn from Paul's preaching here that will help us be more effective in our ministry of the Word to our congregations?

Occasion, Emotion, and Preaching

We noted above how Paul took full advantage of the significant occasion in this sermon. Are you able to recognize those times when in the providence of God your people are readied with a special receptivity to the Word you are preaching? Do you take full advantage of them? Some preachers lack the flexibility and courage to make full use of those occasions. Since they often arise suddenly, it may require that you change your plans, and your sermon, with little time to prepare. You should never be so tied to your announced topic and your prepared sermon that you cannot respond to those situations when your congregation may be especially prepared to hear a particular word from your lips. Events that profoundly affect the life of your congregation, or significant congregational changes, are occasions that you should be ready to take advantage of in your preaching ministry to them. 'Preach the Word; be prepared in season and out of season' (2 Tim. 4:2), this is your charge.

One of the commoner (though still unusual) occasions where strong emotions may play an important role in the frame of mind of the congregation you address with your preaching is the funeral. You usually are able to plan to some extent for these occasions. Yet the very power of the emotional setting under these circumstances sometimes inhibits the preacher. Raw and open emotionalism, especially grief, is embarrassing and that can hinder the preacher from saying things that may add to the emotional upset. In its most dangerous form, such reticence can cause a preacher to fail to confront the issues of sin and judgment head on in the face of the reality of death. Consequently, he may not be able to offer the true consolation and hope of the gospel of Christ's redemptive work as he should. This is especially true in the case of a funeral for a non-believer. Your hearers do not want to face the lostness of the lost in such an emotional time. Thus the preacher may instead opt for a kind of sermon *cum* eulogy that (he imagines) will be easier for the grieving family and congregation to receive. He may believe that such an approach will bring more immediate comfort. But he may also have opted for the superficial rather than the profoundly life-transforming impact of the gospel message. It is at just that time when we stand 'in the valley of the shadow of death' that the message of the Cross speaks with most power to the living! It is then that Jesus promises that the Holy Spirit will convict men about sin, righteousness, and judgment (cf. John 16:8-11). A faithful pastor and preacher needs to pray and prepare himself to have the boldness to take full advantage of the opportunity afforded by the openness of the hearers caused by their emotional vulnerability under such circumstances.

There is, of course, need for a word of caution here as well. Many preachers over the years have been guilty of deliberately manipulating the emotions of their hearers to achieve a desired effect. That has caused other ministers (including you, I hope) to be very reluctant to press an emotional advantage in preaching. Emotion is no substitute for conviction arising from a knowledge of the truth. In fact, strong emotion can sometimes get in the way of the true conviction of the Spirit by encouraging men to rest in a superficial feeling rather than in the genuine moving of conscience under the Word of God.

Having acknowledged that danger, however, let us not forget that we are whole people, and that the emotions have a legitimate role to play in our learning and doing of the truth. Our 'affections' (as the Puritans called them) should not be considered unimportant, any more than they should be considered of primary importance. There are times when God sensitizes strong emotions so that the impact of his Word upon the heart will register outwardly (emotionally) as well as inwardly (morally and spiritually). That was certainly the case in the upper room, as we have noticed, and it was also true at Miletus. Where motivation is of particular concern in a sermon, as it was for Paul before his fellow elders, this conscience–emotion matrix can be very important.

Preaching and Counseling

For many years there has been a growing interest among Bible-believing ministers and elders in the work of pastoral counseling – a counseling which is 'biblical' in that it is firmly and exclusively rooted in the Word of God in Scripture.[3] In light of this interest in biblical pastoral counseling, one of the most frequently asked questions is, 'What is the relationship between preaching and counseling?' Adams has pointed out that both preaching and (effective) counseling are ministries of the Word of God, properly performed as a life calling by elders, called and set apart through ordination to shepherd the people of God.[4] How then do preaching and counseling fit together? How do they depend upon each other? How do they strengthen each other in the context of pastoral ministry within the local church? It is worth our taking a few moments at this point in our discussion to note the interrelationship between these two important ministries.

As we have already noticed, Paul alludes in this message to his daily practice of public and private preaching and teaching (Acts 20:20), including 'counseling' (*nouthetōn*, v. 31). This sermon itself had a pastoral counseling purpose – to prepare Paul's fellow elders for his final departure from their company. He is counseling them in sermonic form by comforting, encouraging, and exhorting them.

We have already noted a verse in which Paul (in another context) links the preaching and counseling ministries directly: 'Preach the Word; be prepared in season and out of season; correct, rebuke and encourage – with great patience and careful instruction' (2 Tim. 4:2). In general there is a significant overlap among the terms used to describe preaching and counseling in the New Testament. The sermon recorded by Luke in Acts 13 is called 'a message of encouragement' (v. 15).

> Whatever speaking is carried on in the church after it has assembled, though never divorced from the gospel message, is *didaskalia*, or 'teaching' (cf. 1 Tim. 4:16; 5:17). It also may be called simply 'speaking' (*lalia*) as it is in 1 Corinthians 1:5. Both *didaskalia* and *lalia*, among other things, include *paraklesis* ('aid, assistance, advice, exhortation, encouragement, urging'), *paramuthia* ('comfort, cheer'), and *nouthesia* ('counsel, admonition') as well as instruction (cf. Titus 2:15).[5]

This close relationship between preaching and counseling arises from the character of the 'Great Commission' that governs them both, and the nature of the Scriptures, which forms the only proper content for both. Christ's commission charges the Church with the task of discipling the nations through baptizing and teaching obedience (Matt. 28:18-20). Teaching cannot be done properly in isolation from pastoral concerns, including counseling. The office of elder, to whom these tasks are given as life callings, has as its purpose the building up of the Church by 'equipping the saints for works of service' (Eph. 4:12). The Scriptures themselves preach and counsel in the form of teaching, rebuking, correcting, and training in righteousness (2 Tim. 3:17).

Both preaching and counseling are essential elements in the ministry of the Word committed by God to the pastor-teacher (elder). To do one without the other is not only unbiblical, but will bring about significant failure in whatever side remains neglected. The preaching ministry of any pastor will benefit greatly from the practice of biblical counseling. The problems of the congregation, uncovered through the personal contact afforded by (formal and informal) counseling, will greatly assist the preacher in directing his preaching to real, timely, flesh-and-blood needs. Preaching, when informed by pastoral counseling will be more immediate and personal. Rebukes and corrections included in a sermon can be more effectively given if the preacher understands (from his counseling) the kind of barriers and objections that might be raised in the minds of his hearers. The practical emphasis on real change, which forms the heart of biblical pastoral counseling, will influence preaching with a salutary concreteness and practicality.[6]

On the other hand, pastoral counseling can be strengthened immeasurably by a powerful pulpit ministry. For a counseling preacher, behind each individual encounter with church members in a counseling setting will stand the rich background of his balanced pulpit ministry in which both biblical doctrine and ethics are systematically expounded and applied. The exegetical and theological skills that make for good preaching are also of invaluable assistance to the work of counseling. Pastoral counseling can provide the opportunity for the sort of structured accountability needed in order to consistently implement the 'how-to's' raised from the pulpit. And finally, effective preaching and counseling together will enrich the whole congregation's experience of worship through the involvement of an increasingly sanctified and committed people, ready and able to offer worship to God that is truly acceptable.[7]

Paul was an effective preacher, and an equally effective counselor. The sermon at Miletus is a powerful example of both. You are called upon by him, as were the Ephesian elders, to use both of those skills to 'keep watch over yourselves and all the flock of which the Holy Spirit has made us overseers' (Acts 20:28).[8]

'Preaching the Gospel'

I suppose that as long as men have been preaching the gospel there have been debates over what it really means to 'preach the gospel'. Too often this phrase is used as a nice-sounding slogan and is treated as if it were self-defining. We speak in resonant tones of being under compulsion to preach the gospel: 'Woe to me if I do not preach the gospel!' (1 Cor. 9:16). But what does it mean to 'preach the gospel'?

It is an important question. God has ordained that through the preaching of the gospel men are to be saved (1 Cor 1:21) and the church built up (3:10-15). Therefore, lives are hanging in the balance. You had better know what you are doing!

Some of you may have received criticism from your people in the form of the accusation that you are *not* 'preaching the gospel'. Ministers have been asked to leave their churches for failing to 'preach the gospel'. Yet often when it is asked, 'What do you mean by that?' the answers are very vague and confused.

What do preachers say 'preaching the gospel' is? In our own day there are heated discussions between theological points of view and ecclesiastical denominations over this question. Some, who lay particular emphasis on the evangelistic purpose of preaching, would say that 'preaching the gospel' is preaching man's need of salvation (due to sin) and setting forth the salvation accomplished in the atoning death of Christ. That is the 'good news'. Such sermons should be followed by an invitation and challenge to 'receive Christ' as one's personal Savior.

Others, out of concern to stress the importance of discipleship to the preaching task, would say that preaching the gospel is teaching men how to live in accordance with God's will. The 'good news' is that God not only saves sinners, but he has a word of direction for every area of their lives.

Still others, pointing up the 'worldview' dimensions of the Christian faith and preaching, would say that preaching the gospel is explaining every word that proceeds from the mouth of God by which men are to live (Deut. 8:3). The 'good news' is that God both saves sinners and teaches them how to live in accordance with his will personally and calls them to seek his Kingdom and righteousness in every area of their lives (Matt. 6:33). He has given man a revelation that enables him to make sense of all human thought, relations, and institutions by means of the whole system of biblical truth.

Which group is correct? Do we have to choose one rather than another? I think not. I believe Paul's sermon, which we have been examining together and is itself an example of 'preaching the gospel' (Acts 20:24-25) sheds some helpful light on an answer to this question. Let me draw your attention to the three (parallel) phrases Paul uses in this message to describe his ministry among the people of Ephesus.

First, Paul can describe his ministry as 'declar[ing] to both Jews and Greeks that they must turn to God in repentance and have faith in our Lord Jesus' (v. 21). Here he focuses our attention on the gospel as the particular call of God – carried through preaching – to men who are lost, dead in their transgressions and sins (Eph. 2:1). It is a call to turn from their rebellious independent self-reliance, and commit themselves in grateful trust to the Savior. This was the message Jesus preached while upon the earth (Mark 1:14), and it is the message he continued to proclaim through the apostolic witnesses. Thus it must be your message as well.

This means that your preaching must seek and find men where they are. You must study your congregation with the same diligence you use in searching the Scriptures. You must know those in your congregation who have not yet made a commitment to Christ, and you must speak to them pointedly. You must be aware of those whose 'faith' is more nominal than real, and you must call them to a true, fruitful repentance. Your preaching must help those who are struggling with besetting sin and despair of the grace of Christ to bring them through.

Your preaching must clearly set before men Christ crucified (cf. 1 Cor. 2:2; Gal. 3:1). Does that mean that every sermon must be atonement-centered? No. But it does mean that all your preaching must aim at the conversion of men – both the initial conversion to saving faith, and the ongoing conversion of daily repentance and faith which constitutes Christian discipleship (cf. Luke 9:23). Such a focus will keep your sermons from becoming abstract or diffuse. It will also preserve a powerful hortatory character in your preaching.

It is not only the 'evangelistic sermon' which must contain the call to conversion – every sermon (to one degree or another) should. Your hearers should never sense that your expositions of Scripture are given on a 'take it or leave it' basis. You have not done your work if you have not pled with men to come to Jesus Christ and put their trust in him.

This is hard for preachers to learn. It is easier to command than to beg, but Paul calls you to follow his example of begging with tears (Acts 20:19, 31). Some of you may not have begged for anything in your life. Begging is humiliating. But love has no pride when it is calling out to sinners to be reconciled with God (2 Cor. 5:20).

Second, Paul says that he was busy in his ministry teaching what would be 'helpful' or 'beneficial' (*sumpherontōn*, Acts 20:20) to his hearers. This draws attention to the *practical usefulness* of Paul's instruction – both in his public preaching and in private by other means. No vain theoretician building castles in the air, Paul was concerned to instruct the churches in the practical implications of the message of Christ. This practical concern arises from the nature of the preaching office and the purpose of the Word being preached.

In Ephesians 4:11-12, Paul explains that the risen Christ gave pastors and teachers to build up the church by equipping God's people for works of service. This means that one of the central purposes of your preaching ministry is to equip and train believers for their service to Christ. Your preaching must strive always to be beneficial by applying the teachings of God's Word holistically to the lives of your listeners – intellectually, ethically, relationally, vocationally. The practical, ethical concern of preaching the gospel must not be minimized: 'The truth ... leads to godliness' (Titus 1:1). As the *Westminster Shorter Catechism* reminds us, 'The Scriptures principally teach what man is to believe concerning God, and what duty God requires of man' (Q/A 3). Man's duty can be understood in terms of the two great summary commandments given by our Lord Jesus – we are to love God and love our neighbor as ourselves (Matt. 22:37-40).

Your preaching can accomplish this purpose, because the Scriptures we preach are eminently suited to that task. In 2 Timothy 3:16, Paul tells his young disciple that the God-breathed writings have as one of their main purposes to direct, equip, and enable men and women to keep those two 'great' commandments: 'All Scripture is God-breathed and is useful for teaching, rebuking, correcting and training in righteousness.' You must follow Paul's example by incorporating the Scripture's own method of teaching, rebuking, correcting, and training in righteousness in your sermons. You 'teach' by clearly setting forth the truth of the passage from which you are preaching. You 'rebuke' by pointedly identifying the sinful aberrations by which your people miss the biblical norm and calling them to repentance. You 'correct' by showing them in specific ways how to return to God and to the paths of righteousness through godly change. And you 'train' them by directing your people in repetitious self-discipline and practice until new, godly character traits are established. If your preaching regularly does these things, it will be useful, even as Paul's was.

Finally, you must preach the 'whole counsel of God' (Acts 20:27). Paul did not have a narrow view of the purpose of his preaching. He knew that all Scripture is profitable. That man is to live by every word that comes from the mouth of God. Thus he was concerned to introduce his hearers to the broad scope of biblical teaching, to the 'systematic theology' of the Bible. What's more, he understood (as too few preachers understand today) that we are engaged in a cosmic warfare in which everything is at stake:

> For though we live in the world, we do not wage war as the world does. The weapons we fight with are not the weapons of the world. On the contrary, they have divine power to demolish strongholds. We demolish arguments and every pretension that sets itself up against the knowledge of God, and we take captive every thought to make it obedient to Christ (2 Cor. 10:3-5).

If your people are going to meet the challenges of the twenty-first century and the rise of New Age paganism[9] you must take pains to introduce them to the broad scope of biblical teaching. They need to learn what the Bible teaches about everything from the question of human authority, to sexuality, to the role of the civil government in the lives of individuals. The pagan movers-and-shakers have an ideological answer to all these questions, and we need to equip our people to counter them from the Word of God.

Therefore, your preaching ministry must have both comprehensiveness and balance. We discussed balance in preaching earlier.[10] Let me say a word here about comprehensiveness. Appreciating the *breadth* of biblical truth will insure that you will always have plenty to say to your people throughout their lives under your care and throughout your preaching career.[11] You will have good food for them which will feed their continued growth in grace and in the knowledge of the Savior. They should never have to face the shallow repetitiousness into which some preaching ministries fall.

From these few comments I trust you can get a clear picture of Paul's own understanding of his public preaching ministry and his more private instruction 'from house to house' (Acts 20:20) – what he calls 'testifying to the gospel of God's grace' (v. 24). As you can see, it is a broad and rich conception. Paul had a sense of the breadth of his preaching task, but never lost sight of its particular focus and practical purpose. Your preaching will have the same powerful usefulness if you follow his example.

18

Paul to the Jews in Jerusalem:
The Final Confrontation

As we have seen in our study thus far, Paul, as he carried the gospel through the Roman world, customarily preached it first to a Jewish audience wherever possible – in the synagogue (Acts 14:1) or in a place of prayer (16:13). It was his personal desire to see his brethren according to the flesh saved (Rom. 9:3), and it was the will of God that the gospel be preached 'to the Jew first' (1:16). The response of the Jews to Paul's preaching was (in general) growing hostility. They rejected the message and sought to eliminate the messengers (Acts 14:5; 20:3). Though Paul turned more and more to Gentile audiences (13:46), he nevertheless continued to appeal to the Jews with the message of Jesus the Messiah and the fulfillment of their ancestral hope. In the larger narrative of Acts, Luke paints for us a vivid picture of the 'hardening' that was taking place among the people of Israel (Rom. 11:25) – especially among their leaders. The hostility of the Jewish leadership against Jesus, so evident in the gospel of Luke, continues in the story recorded for us in Acts.[1] The Holy Spirit is describing the descent of Israel into judgment for their final acts of covenant breaking, the rejection and murder of their Messiah (Zech. 11; Luke 20:9-18; cf. Matt. 21:33-45).

The two streams of opposition – that of the Jews of Jerusalem to Peter, John, Stephen and the others, and that of the Jews of the Dispersion to Paul and his companions – merge climactically in Paul's final confrontations with the Jews, which took place in Jerusalem, and are recorded for us by Luke in Acts 21–23. There the apostle preached publicly one last time to the Jewish crowds of the city, and made a brief deliverance to the Sanhedrin, sealing the judgment of God prepared for them. The account is a dramatic one, and we turn to study it now.

Paul's Return to Jerusalem
Paul returned to Jerusalem at the end of his third missionary journey in AD 57. Though the prophet Agabus had warned that the Jews of

293

Jerusalem would bind him and hand him over to the Gentiles (Acts 21:11; cf. 20:22-24), and though his friends pled with him not to go, the apostle's resolution was firm: 'I am ready not only to be bound, but also to die in Jerusalem for the name of the Lord Jesus' (21:13). It was Paul's purpose in going to Jerusalem to demonstrate, in a tangible and dramatic way, the fruitful gospel harvest which the Spirit had sovereignly granted among the Gentiles.[2] The offering for the relief of the poor saints in Jerusalem, which Paul had collected in the churches of Macedonia and Achaia, was, in Paul's mind, a token of the Gentiles themselves. The Gentiles had shared in the Jews' spiritual blessings, Paul thought, therefore they owed it to the Jews to share with them their material blessings (Rom. 15:27). In bringing their offering to Jerusalem, he was bringing them as an offering to God! As he had explained to the Corinthians:

> This service that you perform is not only supplying the needs of God's people but is also overflowing in many expressions of thanks to God. Because of the service by which you have proved yourselves, men will praise God for the obedience that accompanies your confession of the gospel of Christ, and for your generosity in sharing with them and with everyone else. And in their prayers for you their hearts will go out to you, because of the surpassing grace God has given you. (2 Cor. 9:12-14).

Thus, despite the warnings of danger, Paul pressed on toward Jerusalem. The visit was very important to him. He also explained to the Romans how this visit fit into his overall missionary strategy: 'So after I have completed this task and have made sure that they have received this fruit, I will go to Spain and visit you on the way.... Pray that I may be rescued from the unbelievers in Judea and that my service in Jerusalem may be acceptable to the saints there, so that by God's will I may come to you with joy and together with you be refreshed' (15:28, 31-32).

New Troubles in Jerusalem

When Paul arrived in Jerusalem, he met with James and the leaders of the Jerusalem church (Acts 21:17-18). He reported to them in detail about this successful ministry among the Gentiles (v. 19). The elders rejoiced in this good news of the spread of the gospel (v. 20). But there was a problem. James informed Paul of the rumors which had spread within the Jerusalem church (among the brethren who were 'zealots for the law') that Paul allegedly taught all the Jews who lived among the Gentiles 'to turn away from Moses, telling them not to circumcise their children or live according to our customs' (v. 20). This twisted report of his views and practices can have come as no great surprise to the apostle, given his experience with the Jews of the Dispersion on his travels. While James and the elders, for their part, had no suspicions about Paul, they were concerned that Paul's reputation be rehabilitated among the brethren in general who would soon know of his visit to Jerusalem (v. 22). They had a plan, which F.F. Bruce explains as follows:

> There was, however, a way in which Paul himself could give the lie effectively to those disturbing reports. If he were seen to take part publicly in one of the ancestral customs, it would be realized that he was, after all, an observant and practicing Jew. Therefore, in their *naïvete*, they put a proposal to him. Four of their number had undertaken a Nazirite vow: if no time limit was specified, their vow would last for thirty days. During that period they would abstain from wine and strong drink, would avoid any defiling contact (e.g., with a corpse), and would leave their hair uncut. At the end of the period they would present an offering in the temple, and their hair, which they had now cut, would be consumed in the sacrificial fire. Another Israelite might associate himself with Nazirites by defraying the cost of their offering; this was regarded as a pious and charitable action. The elders' proposal, then, was that Paul should associate himself with the four Nazirites when they discharged their vow in the temple and pay their expenses.[3]

Bruce calls the suggestion naïve, because it did not take into account the potential hostile reaction of the *unbelieving* Jews in Jerusalem. Paul nevertheless agreed to the suggestion. 'The next day Paul took the men and purified himself along with them. Then he went to the temple to give notice of the date when the days of purification would end and the offering would be made for each of them' (v. 26). That decision precipitated the crisis which brought Paul into his final confrontation with the Jews of Jerusalem.

When Paul was recognized in the Temple by some Jews from the province of Asia (v. 27), a riot ensued. Paul was accused (falsely, as Luke explains, v. 29) of bringing Greeks into the Temple area and thus defiling the 'holy place' (v. 28). 'The whole city was aroused, and the people came running from all directions' (v. 30). Having Paul in their clutches, they began beating him, intent on killing him (vv. 31-

32). Paul's life was only spared by the intervention of the commander of the Roman cohort and his men, who took the battered apostle into custody, placing him in chains (v. 33). When the commander inquired as to Paul's offense, he could not get a clear answer from the enraged crowd (v. 34). In frustration he ordered that Paul to be taken into the barracks (in the Fortress of Antonia, adjacent to the Temple).

Preaching Is Your First Task

Put yourself in Paul's sandals. If you had been mobbed and beaten by a murderous multitude, and then snatched from the jaws of death, would you not have been eager to be carried away to safety as quickly as possible? As the soldiers surrounded you and lifted you to be carried up the steps out of harm's way, would you not have breathed a deep sigh of relief and a prayer of thanksgiving for your deliverance? I would. But not Paul. Having explained himself briefly to the commander (vv. 37-39), Paul requests permission to face the crowd again and speak to them!

In his later letter to Timothy, Paul commanded, 'Preach the Word' (2 Tim. 4:2). He went on to advise his young colleague in the ministry, 'be prepared in season and out of season.' One wonders if Paul remembered this occasion in Jerusalem (as well he might) as a time when he had been called upon by Christ to preach 'out of season'. There he stood, his body aching from the blows of the violent mob, perhaps wiping the blood from his eyes, his heart pumping hard with adrenalin, the deafening shouts of the crowd ringing in his ears, and trying to collect his reeling thoughts so that he might call his brother Jews once more to faith in Jesus Christ.

Of all the astonishing events in the ministry of an astonishing man, this has to impress the preacher who reads it as much as any other detail of Paul's life. If you are a preacher, you know how last minute distractions can unfit you for your pulpit ministry. How Satan loves to provoke an argument in your family as you drive them to church on a Sabbath morning – 'Why can't she (your wife) save her criticism for another time?' 'Why can't the kid's behave? I have to preach!' Last minute details in the preparation for the worship service can break your concentration. A parishoner who buttonholes you on the way into the sanctuary with a tearful report of a personal crisis can lead your mind far away from the preaching task at hand. Try as you might, these and a thousand other hurdles have to be jumped on your way to the pulpit. At other times you may be called upon to preach when you are not prepared, and often in an unusual and difficult circumstance – you are called at the last minute to fill in at a funeral for a person you hardly know. But few of us will ever be called upon to preach 'out of season' as Paul was that day on the steps of the Fortress of Antonia!

This was a time when the single-mindedness of Paul's commitment to his mission as a preacher, and his vast experience in preaching,[4] enabled him (with the sustaining help of God) to preach when everything within him cried out, 'Just relax – keep quiet – stop the bleeding – and get into the barracks – you'll be safe.'

Paul once wrote the Corinthians: 'For Christ did not send me to baptize, but to preach the gospel' (1 Cor. 1:17). Elsewhere he wrote, 'Yet when I preach the gospel, I cannot boast, for I am compelled to preach. Woe to me if I do not preach the gospel!' (9:16). These and other texts evidence for us Paul's single-minded commitment to his calling to preach the gospel. Certainly he performed other pastoral tasks as he planted churches throughout the Roman world, but above all else he was a preacher. There is good reason to suppose that he preached most every day (Acts 20:20), and he was eager to preach it in every place (Rom. 1:15).

I wonder if that is so for you pastors who are reading this? You have many duties included in your 'job description' as a local pastor in addition to preaching – you are a counselor, an administrator, an ecclesiastical judge (i.e., in the conduct of church discipline[5]), a youth leader, a consultant on interior decoration, a hospital visitor, a handyman, etc. No doubt you would say, in theory, that preaching is your most important task. But, in practice, is it? If your pastoral week is like mine, many duties crowd out the time and attention you can and must give to the preparation (technical and spiritual) of sermons and their delivery. The phone rings all the time. Everybody wants to talk with you. When do you find time to study and pray for the Sunday message? You don't find it – you must make it. For many pastors, preaching is pushed down the list of priorities by the seeming urgency of other demands upon your time and attention.

You may even have imbibed the spirit of the age, which has infected Evangelicalism with the notion that preaching is not the most effective way of building up the church. Developing and administering programs has replaced preaching as the primary duty of many pastors today.

Furthermore, most local pastors only preach a couple of times a week at most (and may in addition prepare one or two Bible studies for Sunday School and midweek classes). If you are a minister on the staff of a larger church, your specific duties may not even include regular preaching. In times past – when the church flourished under the outpouring of the Holy Spirit's reforming and reviving blessing – pastors preached several times each week, sometimes daily – and even more than once a day![6] Preachers today, I believe, are significantly handicapped by the relative infrequency with which we preach.

For these and other reasons, you might not share (though you might wish to) Paul's single-minded sense of purpose. It is hard to be 'prepared in season and out of season' if you are not thinking about preaching all the time, and too many pastors do not think enough about their preaching. You know enough to get the job done. You have the skills; you can put a sermon together. Your people are (for the most part) receptive, and usually don't realize when you enter the pulpit insufficiently prepared (at least they don't mention to you that they notice).

If you are a pastor who has slipped into the pattern of 'just getting by' in your preaching, buried under a multitude of other pressing duties, let me tell you I've been there many times myself. We all have. May I encourage and challenge you to rethink your priorities. As important as your other duties may appear, they are secondary. Preaching comes first. Effective pastoral work flows from the preaching of the Word, and if your counseling, visitation, and church discipline are to be effective, they must be an extension of your ministry of the Word from the pulpit.[7] Indeed, if you preach well, a great deal of counseling, and even church discipline, goes on from the pulpit.

'Preach the Word; be prepared in season and out of season; correct, rebuke and encourage – with great patience and careful instruction.' You and I must daily reaffirm our commitment to the task of preaching to which Christ has called us. Because Paul had, he was able to preach to that hostile crowd in Jerusalem. If you are humbled and convicted by his example, as I am, then let us turn again to the Lord and pledge again to make that our first and most important work.

All Things To All Men

Another detail we ought to note before looking at Paul's message to the Jewish mob, is the vivid, though brief, illustration we have of his principle of 'becoming all things to all men' in the interchange between the apostle and the Roman commander.

> As the soldiers were about to take Paul into the barracks, he asked the commander, 'May I say something to you?' 'Do you speak Greek?' he replied. 'Aren't you the Egyptian who started a revolt and led four thousand terrorists out into the desert some time ago?' Paul answered, 'I am a Jew, from Tarsus in Cilicia, a citizen of no ordinary city. Please let me speak to the people.' Having received the commander's permission, Paul stood on the steps and motioned to the crowd (vv. 37-40).

Paul expressed his principle of accommodation to the Corinthians: 'Though I am free and belong to no man, I make myself a slave to everyone, to win as many as possible.... I have become all things to all men so that by all possible means I might save some' (1 Cor. 9:19-22). When Paul makes his request of the Roman commander to speak to the Jewish crowd, we see this principle at work in miniature. Paul addresses the Roman in the Greek language, establishing a vital communication link. This takes the officer by surprise. At the same time, by so doing, the apostle virtually dispels the commander's suspicion that he is an infamous Egyptian terrorist. Paul goes on to speak of his background – he is a Jew (not an Egyptian) and a Jew of the Dispersion – a detail designed to impress the Roman, who was bound to be especially prejudiced against local Palestinian Jewry. Paul goes on to make reference to his citizenship in Tarsus in Cilicia, 'no ordinary city'.[8] This is especially interesting in that when Paul next addresses the crowd of Jews, as we will see in a moment, he emphasized his 'Jewishness' (e.g., he shifts languages from Greek to Aramaic, Acts 21:40) and his close ties to Jerusalem (more than Tarsus, 22:3).

By these means Paul secures his object. We can learn how to implement Paul's principle, by following even this small example. With a few well-chosen words (designed to establish rapport with the Roman commander), the apostle persuaded him to allow him to speak to the crowd. No doubt the officer had his own strong reasons to get Paul out of reach (and earshot) of the mob in the Temple area, but by appealing to him in terms most appropriate to a Roman's point of view, Paul 'wins' him – if not to faith in Christ (which was not his object here) – at least to permitting the delivery of the message which follows.

The Apologetic Task of the Preacher

Each of Paul's messages is called – in his own terms – a 'defense' (*apologia*). Strictly speaking, it is not a sermon. There is no exposition and application of the Scriptures. It is more of an extended personal testimony. The emphasis falls not upon the resurrection itself as much as the post-resurrection appearance of Christ to Paul on the Damascus road. The purpose of Paul's testimony is 'apologetic', that is, he is attempting to give a reason for his present course of life, and thus 'defend' his faith in Christ, which so radically transformed him.

In 1 Peter 3:15-16, Paul's fellow apostle gave these instructions to the church concerning their apologetic task:

> But in your hearts set apart Christ as Lord. Always be prepared to give an answer [*apologia*] to everyone who asks you to give the reason for the hope that you have. But do this with gentleness and respect, keeping a clear conscience, so that those who speak maliciously against your good behavior in Christ may be ashamed of their slander.

Paul's defense before the mob in Jerusalem is the first of several textbook examples Luke gives us of Peter's principles in action. We have already discussed the fact that Paul was 'always prepared' to preach or to defend the faith. Indeed, he could style his whole ministry as one of 'defending and confirming the gospel,' for which at other times (as here) he had been imprisoned (Phil. 1:7,16). The defenses he was called upon to offer could be both informal (1 Cor. 9:3) and formal (2 Tim. 4:16). Those recorded for us by Luke in the closing chapters of Acts are of both kinds. The speech before us at present is an informal defense against the hostile reaction of the crowd and their shouted accusations against him. Soon Paul will be called upon to answer more formally before the Sanhedrin, the Roman governor Felix, and the Jewish King Agrippa.

Jude called the church to the defense of the faith: 'Dear friends, although I was very eager to write to you about the salvation we share, I felt I had to write and urge you to contend for the faith that was once for all entrusted to the saints' (Jude 3). In particular, skill in defending the faith is an essential qualification and duty of the pastor and preacher – he must be able to 'encourage others by sound doctrine and refute those who oppose it' (Titus 1:9). Though a detailed discussion of Christian apologetics – the theological 'science' of defending the faith – would take us beyond the scope of this study,[9] the fundamental point mentioned above needs to be emphasized in our day, as ministers become less and less adept at, and less and less inclined to engage in, apologetic controversy with unbelievers. Many of you readers who are seminary-trained pastors probably were required to take at least an introductory course in Christian apologetics as part of your education. Depending upon your 'philosophical inclinations', your background exposure to philosophy and logic, and your professor, that study may have been more or less valuable. I attended a seminary that was defined to a large degree by its contribution to the study of apologetics, and we studied with 'the master', yet several of my classmates found apologetics difficult and boring, and (in their view) of little practical relevance to the work of a pastor. And they were not very good at it. Many pastors let what little apologetic proficiency they gained in seminary dissipate during their ministry through lack of use. (The one exception might be apologetics aimed at refuting the false claims of 'cults' like the Jehovah's Witnesses and Mormons. But even there most men have to 'bone up' to meet the challenge.) They are not 'always ready' to give a reason for their hope, to refute those who oppose the gospel.

Some ministers even dispute the importance of the apologetic task, despite the words of Peter and Paul. It is objected that the gospel 'needs no defense'. Bahnsen responds to such a claim:

> ... it is obvious that God does not need our inadequate reasoning and our feeble attempts to defend His word. Nevertheless, the pious-sounding remark [to the effect that the gospel needs no defense] with which we began is still mistaken. It suggests that we should not concern ourselves with efforts at apologetics because God will directly take care of such matters Himself. The remark is just as mistaken as saying that God does not need us as evangelists (He could even make the stones to cry out, couldn't He?) – and therefore efforts at evangelistic witness are unimportant. Or, a person might misguidedly think that, because God has the power and ability to provide his family with food and clothing without 'help from us,' he does not need to go to work tomorrow.
>
> Thinking like this is unbiblical. It confuses what God Himself needs from us and what God requires of us. It assumes that God ordains ends,

but not means to those ends (or at least not the instrumentality of created means). There is no need for God to use our evangelistic witness, our daily work for a paycheck, or our defense of the faith – but He chooses to do so, and He calls us to apply ourselves to them. The Bible directs us to work, although God *could* provide for our families in other ways. The Bible directs us to evangelize, even though God *could* use other means to call sinners to Himself. And the Bible also directs us to defend the faith – not because God would be helpless without us, but because this is one of His ordained *means* of glorifying Himself and vindicating His truth.[10]

He concludes:

The necessity of apologetics is not a divine necessity: God can surely do his work without us. The necessity of apologetics is a moral necessity: God has chosen to do His work through us and has called us to it. Apologetics is the special talent of some believers, and the interested hobby of others; but it is the God-ordained responsibility of all believers.[11]

Paul fully understood this and thus, when prudence would have dictated another course, he turned again to face the crowd and offered them his defense.

Paul Speaks in His Own Defense

While there are many elements which make up a well-rounded and balanced apologetic approach,[12] in the speech before us Paul emphasizes only one – personal testimony.[13] The accusation made against Paul by the mob was essentially the same as that brought against Stephen some twenty years earlier: 'This is the man who teaches all men everywhere against our people and our law and this place' (Acts 21:28). Paul chose to defend himself against this charge by explaining to the mob how he came to be standing where he was, rather than where they were. Perhaps if they could be made to realize the powerful effect of the risen Christ in the life of Saul of Tarsus, the Christ-hating persecutor of 'the Way,' they could be persuaded to consider the gospel more carefully, even favorably. As Stifler writes, this defense is a 'narration of the facts of [Paul's] own history, but so arranged as to be a powerful plea for his course of life and for the truth of the gospel.'[14] Stifler goes on to summarize the points of Paul's message as follows:

I. His present beliefs and course of life could not have issued from an original difference between himself and his hearers, for there was none (xxii. 3-5).

II. In so far as any difference existed at the present time it was to be accounted for by God's immediate dealing with him (vv. 6-16).

III. As to his affiliation with the Gentiles, God directly sent him to them (vv. 17-21).

The sum of all this is that Paul could be and do no other without flying in the face of God. Or had his hearers been candid men some of them must have reflected that to persecute Paul was to oppose God.[15]

Paul recognized, on the basis of past experience (e.g., Acts 17:5), the precarious volatility of the mob. He would have to tread very carefully if he were to be given a full hearing. This speech is a masterpiece of tactfulness and care in approaching a hostile audience concerning a sensitive (even inflammatory) subject. Having motioned with his hand to quiet the crowd (Acts 21:40), he began to make his defense.

Paul Defends His Jewishness

We note first of all that Paul, who spoke Greek to the commanding officer of the Roman guard, addressed the crowd in their vernacular 'Hebrew dialect' (Aramaic). This surprised the mob into an even deeper silence (22:2). This man spoke their language! Further, despite the mob's rough handling, Paul addressed them in a respectful and conciliatory fashion: 'Brothers and fathers ...' (v. 1). The apostle is seeking by a 'gentle answer' to turn away their wrath (Prov. 15:1).

In the first section of his defense (vv. 3-5), Paul sought to convince his audience that by blood, by education and training, and by the zeal with which he held his religious convictions, he at one time was no different from them. He did this by emphasizing his ties to Jerusalem. Though born in Tarsus, he was raised in Jerusalem. What's more, he chose language designed to emphasize his identity with them, for example, far from speaking against the law, he refers to 'the law of *our* fathers' (v. 3). Later he mentions the Jews of Damascus as 'the brothers' (v. 5). He goes on to point out that his religious beliefs were shaped by the strict education he received under Gamaliel. The mention of Gamaliel, one of the foremost rabbinic scholars of the day, would surely have impressed his audience. Such a credential carried great weight of authority. Paul was no 'outsider' seeking to tear down that in which he had no real part. As he wrote elsewhere, he was a 'Hebrew of Hebrews' (Phil. 3:5).

As to his zeal for Judaism, Paul can well remember feeling a rage like that of the crowd welling up in his own breast (Acts 22:3), and 'breathing out murderous threats against the Lord's disciples' (9:1). The record of Saul of Tarsus as a fierce agent of Sanhedrin policy against the growing movement called 'the Way' was well known in Jerusalem, and could be easily confirmed (if any one of his hearers cared to) by inquiring of the Council itself (vv. 4-5). By these words Paul built a very strong case for his solidarity with his audience. He was 'one of them' in every way. Without directly, expressly contradicting their claim that he taught against the Jewish people or law (21:28), he is refuting the accusation.

Often when we are called upon to defend the gospel, or our confidence in it, the opposition is based on faulty information and prejudice. It is important for us to be able to help critics of the gospel to get their facts straight. Perhaps a person has formed a negative opinion about the Bible without even knowing what the Bible teaches. He may have heard others misrepresent what the Bible says, and may be passing on their opinion as his own. He may have seen or heard things from professing Christians which he took to be authentic Christian ideas or attitudes, which are in fact unbiblical. In many cases, the pastoral apologist needs to lay the foundation for his defense of the faith by simply explaining carefully, and from the Bible, what exactly the Christian faith is. This does not usually remove all disagreement – you will have to go on to argue in favor of the claims of Christ and the Scriptures – but it helps clear away a lot of debris, which will assist you in setting forth the reason for the hope you have in Christ. That is what Paul was doing with the crowd in Jerusalem. He began by correcting their mistaken impression of who he was and what religious convictions drove him.

It was a mission against the Christians which placed Paul on the road to Damascus where the encounter occurred which produced a dramatic and radical change in the zealous persecutor's life (vv. 5-6). An account of his vision of Christ and subsequent meeting with Ananias comprises the second point of Paul's defense.

Paul's Life Was Turned Around by God Himself

He recounts his vision of the risen Christ with a vivid immediacy, reproducing his dialogue with Jesus in direct address to convey that sense of immediacy to his listeners – he wants them to hear the exact words he heard. Paul heard a voice calling him, 'Saul, Saul, why do you persecute me?' (v. 7; cf. 9:4). He responded 'Who are you, Lord?' The voice replied 'I am Jesus of Nazareth, whom you are persecuting' (v. 8).[16] Paul mentions that his companions 'did not understand the voice of him who was speaking to me' (v. 9), and that he was instructed to go on to Damascus for further instructions concerning those things he had been 'assigned to do' (v. 10, 'must do', 9:6). Paul subtly strikes the note of divine appointment (cf. v. 14). Paul's passivity in all this is reinforced by his mention of his blindness: 'My companions led me by the hand into Damascus, because the brilliance of the light had blinded me' (v. 11).

The implications of Paul's encounter with Jesus are drawn out by means of his recounting the words of Ananias (vv. 12-16). Ananias was, according to Paul, 'a devout observer of the law and highly respected by all the Jews living [in Damascus].' Perhaps Ananias was known in Jerusalem as well. In any case, as a well-known, devoted observer of the Law, Ananias would hardly be one to vouch for a man who was a subverter of that very Law! Again, the credibility of Paul's witness in the eyes of his audience is very strong.

Ananias' explanation of Paul's conversion experience is a very Jewish one. Once the apostle's eyes were opened he received this oracle from Ananias: 'The God of our fathers has chosen you to know his will and to see the Righteous One and to hear words from his mouth' (v. 14). These words of Ananias are not recorded in the account in chapter 9, but Paul introduces this detail here for its relevance to this audience of Jews. The origin of Paul's experience is none other than 'the God of our fathers'.[17] According to Ananias, Paul was divinely appointed, 'chosen' by the God of Abraham – who could be expected to refuse God's will? Certainly none in the crowd would have seen himself resisting the divine will in a similar situation.

Paul's miraculous encounter on the Damascus road had also been the fulfillment of the purpose of God. Though he does not mention Jesus the Nazarene again here, Paul implies the identification of Jesus with 'the Righteous One', whom God had ordained he see and hear. The 'Righteous One' is a resonant Old Testament designation for the

Messiah (cf. Isa. 53:11; 52:13 [LXX]; 32:1; 2 Sam. 23:3; Zech. 9:9). It had been used climactically in referring to Jesus by both Peter and Stephen in their sermons (cf. Acts 3:13-14; 7:52). Yet here Paul mentions this messianic identification matter-of-factly and does not comment further. He is planting a seed.

Furthermore, Paul's commission too came from 'the God of our fathers' through his servant Ananias. 'You will be his witness to all men of what you have seen and heard' (22:15). In telling all men what he had seen and heard, Paul had become a witness of the Lord's Anointed, and thus of God himself. In Acts 9:15, the words to be conveyed to Paul from the risen Christ through Ananias are recorded as: 'Go! This man is my chosen instrument to carry my name before the Gentiles and their kings and before the people of Israel. I will show him how much he must suffer for my name.' Paul does not want to raise the inflammatory reference to 'the Gentiles' yet, so instead of mentioning them specifically, he broadens the reference to 'the Gentiles and ... the people of Israel' to 'all men.' Neither does he mention Jesus' reference to the suffering which Paul will undergo – indeed is undergoing – for the sake of Jesus' name. He continues to exercise great care in his choice of expression before this volatile mob. How remarkable under the circumstances! How often we 'say the wrong thing' when we are pressured or upset. Paul did not. The Spirit was truly giving him the words.

Ananias finally commands Paul to 'be baptized and wash your sins away, calling on his name' (22:16). Again there is nothing particularly un-Jewish about this command; there are, for example, similarities in it to the ministry of John the Baptist (Matt. 3:5-6). Thus, Paul's argument to this point may be summarized: 'It was God who had strikingly arrested Paul in his former course and a reputable Jew guided him to his present one.'[18] Paul has successfully negotiated the first two points of his message without losing his audience, and he has prepared them carefully for his climax.

Paul's Commission to the Gentiles

Paul brings his audience next to the very precincts of the Temple in which they stand.[19] 'When I returned to Jerusalem and was praying at the temple, I fell into a trance and saw [him][20] speaking' (vv. 17-18). Here Paul offers another implicit refutation of the accusation against him. When he entered the Temple for the first time after his conversion (as far as the crowd knew), he did not desecrate it. Rather, he used it for the purpose for which it had been built – prayer (cf. Isa. 56:7; Mark 11:17).[21] While devoutly praying in the Temple of his fathers, Paul had a vision of the Lord, who warned the apostle, 'Quick! ... Leave Jerusalem immediately, because they will not accept your testimony about me' (Acts 22:18). Did the crowd catch the irony in this statement? Their actions that very day in seeking to kill Paul confirmed the words of the risen Lord spoken years earlier. If the Jews did not, their immediate reaction to the next part of Paul's message would definitively confirm it.

Far from being eager to turn his back on his fellow Jews, Paul remonstrated with the Lord (vv. 19-20). He wanted to stay on in Jerusalem and preach the gospel to his brethren. This is hardly the attitude of one who allegedly 'teaches all men everywhere against our people' (21:29). F. F. Bruce writes:

> [Paul's] former anti-Christian activity in that very city, he argued, was fresh in people's minds, and many could remember the responsible part he had played in the martyrdom of Stephen. His point seems to have been that people who knew his former record would be the more readily convinced that his change of attitude must be based on the most compelling grounds.[22]

If this was the meaning of Paul's words to the Lord, then it prefigured exactly his apologetic method in the message before us. Paul emphasized his former way of life as a devout and zealous Jew, and detailed the circumstances of his conversion, in order to convince the crowd than nothing less than a direct calling from the God of his fathers – *their* God – could account for the change. Perhaps if they were convinced of this, the Jews would give Paul's gospel concerning Jesus the Messiah a fresh hearing.

But it was not to be. The hardening of the hearts of the Jews in Jerusalem, about which Jesus had warned Paul early on in his ministry, was virtually complete. When Paul reported the final words spoken to him by the risen Lord, the die was cast. Jesus had commanded Paul, 'Go; I will send you far away to the Gentiles.' Paul had waited until now to speak the dreaded 'G-word', but now it must be spoken. The crowd – which, due to Paul's skillful avoidance of inflamatory expressions, had listened carefully to him up to this point – now erupted again in renewed hostility. They raised their voices and shouted, 'Rid the earth of him! He's not fit to live!' (v. 22). They renewed their abusive shouting and were throwing off their cloaks and flinging dust into the air (v. 23). So far as we know from the New Testament record, Paul had spoken his last words to the general Jewish populace of Jerusalem. Like the Jews elsewhere, these too rejected the gospel, not considering themselves worthy of eternal life (cf. 13:46).

> What Israel sought so earnestly it did not obtain, but the elect did. The others were hardened, as it is written: 'God gave them a spirit of stupor, eyes so that they could not see and ears so that they could not hear, to this very day.' And David says: 'May their table become a snare and a trap, a stumbling block and a retribution for them. May their eyes be darkened so they cannot see, and their backs be bent forever' (Rom. 11:7-10).

Success or Failure?

Was Paul's message, after all, a failure? Not at all. We have noticed before the two-sided character of the preaching of the gospel – it is both a 'fragrance of life' and the 'odor of death' (2 Cor. 2:16). To those who are perishing the message of the cross is foolishness, but to us who believe it is the power of God unto salvation (cf. 1 Cor. 1:18; Rom. 1:16). The preacher must prepare and deliver his message as skillfully and carefully as possible, but that is only half of the equation. God must give the increase (1 Cor. 3:6). Those who are appointed by God to eternal life, believe (Acts 13:48).

Paul's message is an astonishing example of how a preacher should approach a hostile audience. The judiciousness of Paul's approach, under the most adverse of circumstances, is a testimony to both the power and wisdom of the Spirit speaking through him, and to the thoughtfulness and love of the apostle toward his brothers in Israel. Paul did everything he could do to win a hearing for the gospel among the Jews. No one would have blamed him for bypassing this occasion for preaching altogether. But he gathered his thoughts, and his courage, and faced the lions with a message as winsome as any in the Book of Acts.

He answered each of the malignant accusations made by the angry crowd. To the charge that he 'taught against the Law,' he answered that he had been trained in the Law as well as any Jew before him, and was devoted to it, but that his coming to Jesus as the Messiah was the fulfillment of that dedication to the faith of the fathers (cf. Rom. 10:4). To the false claim that he 'taught against the Temple,' he showed that his previous conduct in the house of God had been entirely appropriate, and that the Christ had met with him there. And as far as the calumny that he 'taught against his people' was concerned, he pointed to his desire from the first to preach 'to the Jew first' – indeed, his very message on this occasion was nothing less than an effort to bring his Jewish brothers to the realization of their fathers' hope.

You may never face such a hostile crowd in your preaching of the gospel. On the other hand, with the growing public opposition to the gospel we encounter in America today, you may be called upon to preach to such an angry group of unbelievers. If your message has been rejected and you are abused, you will be tempted to retaliate – to 'shake off the dust from your feet' too quickly. If you ever find yourself in that situation, remember that God has placed you there as a herald of his truth, a witness of his Son and his saving power, and be prepared to follow Paul's example in preaching with wisdom, care, and tact in hope that, by God's grace, you might win even the violent enemies of the gospel to faith in Christ.

Paul's Very Different Approach to the Jewish Leadership

Paul had one more audience to address in Jerusalem – the Jewish governing council, the Sanhedrin. You might be surprised, in view of the message we have just studied, to find that Paul takes a very different – much stronger – tack when he is brought before the Jewish leadership. As you read the Gospels and the Book of Acts, it becomes apparent that Jesus and his apostles view the Jewish leaders in a harsher light than the Jewish people as a whole. Indeed, all of the Jews were implicated in the terrible rejection of their Messiah, but the leaders clearly bear the greater responsibility. The harshness of Jesus in addressing them (e.g., Matt. 23:13-39) is contrasted with the gentleness and patience with which he approached the people (cf. Matt. 9:36; 11:28-30). The leaders were harder of heart and though some put their faith in Christ, they would not confess him openly because they were afraid that the Pharisees would have them put out of the synagogue (John 12:42).

Luke has mapped out for us the escalation in the opposition of the Jerusalem leadership to the gospel. In his gospel Luke sketched Jesus' trial before the Sanhedrin (Luke 22:66-71). Then in Acts he recorded the arraignment of Peter and John twice before the council (Acts

4:1-22; 5:27-41) as well as the condemnation of Stephen (6:15-8:1).
Now Paul must take his turn. But whereas Peter, John, and Stephen
attempted to bear witness to the leaders in their messages before the
court, Paul abruptly reduces the Sanhedrin to contention and chaos
by his words.

The events that brought Paul before the Sanhedrin are narrated
in Acts 22:23-30. We can only highlight them. Following the violent
reaction to Paul's mention of the Gentiles on the steps of the
Fortress of Antonia, the Roman commander had Paul taken into
the barracks, where the commander intended to beat information
out of Paul which would help him ascertain what had caused the
riot in the Temple precincts (v. 24). As the torture was about to
begin, Paul raised a question about Roman citizenship (v. 25). As
a result the commander asks Paul if he was, in fact, a Roman
citizen, to which Paul replies, 'Yes, I am' (v. 27). The Roman was
now fearful of having violated the civil rights of a fellow citizen
(v. 29) – one born to his citizenship at that! Paul's protestation
before the Jews that he was a faithful Jew meant nothing to them,
but one word of his Roman citizenship brings an immediate change
in his treatment by the Roman guard – he was released from his
bonds (v. 30). Again the Holy Spirit is indicting the hardheartedness
of the people of Israel by means of Luke's narrative. 'Luke shows
triumphantly how much better it is to be a Roman among the
heathen than to be a Jew among his fellow countrymen.'[23]

The Roman commander still needed to discover the reason for the
civil disturbance, and the accusations brought against Paul by the
Jews. He therefore convened the Sanhedrin the next day, and brought
Paul in to stand before them (v. 30).

Paul's Message Aborted

Paul was not intimidated by the Sanhedrin. He knew it well from his
previous days as their 'hit-man'. He had seen others in the dock
before himself. With bold confidence in Christ, he looked straight at
the assembled leaders of his people and without hesitation began to
address them, 'My brothers, I have fulfilled my duty to God in all
good conscience to this day' (23:1). Paul appears to have intended to
pick up his defense where he left off with the crowd in the Temple
(no doubt members of the Sanhedrin had been in Paul's audience
there).[24]

Paul begins with an appeal to conscience – he had fulfilled his calling before God with a good conscience. Paul wrote elsewhere of the importance of a good conscience before God: 'The goal of this command is love, which comes from a pure heart and a good conscience and a sincere faith' (1 Tim. 1:5, cf. v. 19). Not that he could be commended before God on the basis of his own righteousness, far from it (1 Cor. 4:4; cf. Phil. 3:8). But he had conscientiously fulfilled his calling before God, both as a Jew (Phil. 3:6) and as a Christian missionary. Even those evil things which he had done before his conversion in persecuting the church were done in ignorance and unbelief, not by acting against his conscience (1 Tim. 1:13). It was his testimony to his fellow elders from Ephesus that in the conduct of his ministry he was innocent of any man's blood, and further that he had coveted no man's silver or gold (Acts 20:26, 33-35). Later Paul would make a similar claim to a good conscience before Felix (Acts 24:16).

Paul's emphasis upon his having a good conscience[25] in the discharge of his duties before God is taken by the high priest as an insult to the Sanhedrin, whether Paul intended it as one or not. Ananias ordered those standing near Paul to strike him on the mouth, a particularly insulting action from one Jew to another.[26] Josephus reports that Ananias was known to have an insolent and quick-tempered character. What's more he had a reputation for greed and violence, was deposed from office once by the Romans (AD 58–59) and later restored, and eventually was killed by insurgents at the beginning of the Jewish War with Rome (AD 66).[27] No wonder he was offended at Paul's remark.

Paul's response was sharp: 'God will strike you, you whitewashed wall! You sit there to judge me according to the law, yet you yourself violate the law by commanding that I be struck!' (23:3). Like Jesus before him (John 18:21-23), Paul protested against the unlawful action of the court. He called Ananias a 'whitewashed wall' – a telling insult.[28] Was this simply an expression of the apostle's 'warm impetuousness?'[29] Did Paul lose his temper? Or was this an appropriate – even prophetic – indictment of this hypocritical priest?[30] The reference to a 'whitewashed wall' calls to mind the words of the prophet Ezekiel, whose indictment of the false priests of his day, and of the coming judgment of the Lord against them, and their people, is most significant for understanding Paul's actions before the Sanhedrin here. The prophet wrote,

Because they lead my people astray, saying, 'Peace,' when there is no peace, and because, when a flimsy wall is built, they cover it with whitewash, therefore tell those who cover it with whitewash that it is going to fall. Rain will come in torrents, and I will send hailstones hurtling down, and violent winds will burst forth. When the wall collapses, will people not ask you, 'Where is the whitewash you covered it with?' Therefore this is what the Sovereign LORD says: In my wrath I will unleash a violent wind, and in my anger hailstones and torrents of rain will fall with destructive fury. I will tear down the wall you have covered with whitewash and will level it to the ground so that its foundation will be laid bare. When it falls, you will be destroyed in it; and you will know that I am the LORD. So I will spend my wrath against the wall and against those who covered it with whitewash. I will say to you, 'The wall is gone and so are those who whitewashed it, those prophets of Israel who prophesied to Jerusalem and saw visions of peace for her when there was no peace, declares the Sovereign LORD' (Ezek. 13:10-16).

Just as Jehovah threatened to tear down the wall which the false priests had covered with whitewash, and spend his wrath against the wall and against those who covered it with whitewash, so he would soon bring down the high priest and the Sanhedrin in his fierce anger and overwhelming judgment. The ignominious death of Ananias at the beginning of the war with Rome would be but the beginning of the end for Jerusalem, which came in AD 70, according to the word of the Lord (Luke 21:5-6; cf. Matt. 24:1-2; 23:38).

This understanding sheds light on Paul's further response to being informed that he had 'insult[ed] God's high priest' (Acts 23:4). Paul said, 'Brothers, I did not realize that he was the high priest; for it is written: "Do not speak evil about the ruler of your people" ' (v. 5). Some commentators find in Paul's words a sincere apology. For example, F. F. Bruce writes,

> As soon ... as they pointed out to Paul that the man to whom he spoke so freely was God's high priest, he apologized to the official, if not to the man. And in the act of apology, he displayed his ready submission to the law which he was accused of flouting. 'I did not know he was the high priest,' he said, meaning that, had he known, he would not have called him a whitewashed wall, since the law of Moses forbade an Israelite to revile a ruler of his people (Exod. 22:28b).[31]

It seems most unlikely, however, that Paul would not have recognized the high priest. He was very familiar with Sanhedrin protocol. He would have known the high priest by his dress, or his position as presiding officer at the meeting, if not by sight. Some have suggested that Paul's eyesight was not good, and thus he failed to make the proper identification. Perhaps Paul was looking in the other direction when the high priest ordered him struck. But if so, how would Paul have known to direct his remark to the high priest in the first place?

There is a better solution to the problem. In keeping with his original remark about the hypocrisy of the high priest Ananias, 'Paul was speaking in bitter irony.'[32] In effect he was denying that one who acted in such a manner – and who had a reputation for living so notoriously contrary to the Law of God – could in reality be God's high priest.[33]

Thus, though we do not believe that Paul was sinless in all his actions, nor would it undermine his apostolic authority to believe that he may have reacted sinfully in his anger before the Sanhedrin, there is every reason to believe Paul's response to the high priest was more than an insulting quip, even as our Lord spoke the truth when he insulted Herod, calling him 'that fox' (Luke 13:32), or denounced the Pharisees as 'whitewashed tombs' (Matt. 23:27). If the sinless Jesus did not violate his own principle of 'turning the other cheek' (Matt. 5:39) by objecting to the insulting slap he received from this same court (John 18:23), then Paul may not have been violating his principle of 'not returning evil for evil' (Rom. 12:17) by prophetically condemning the false shepherds of Israel.

Strong Language in Preaching
In view of Paul's interchange with the high priest, it might be helpful for us to spend a moment considering the appropriateness of the use of strong, harsh, or so-called judgmental language in preaching. It may seem strange to some of you that I would even raise this question. You perhaps have always assumed that it is never proper for a preacher to speak of others in a derogatory or mocking way – certainly not in a sermon. But is that opinion biblical? What of the mockery contained in the preaching of the Lord's prophets? Elijah taunted the prophets of Baal on Mt. Carmel: 'Shout louder!... Surely he is a god! Perhaps he is deep in thought, or busy, or travelling. Maybe he is sleeping and must be awakened' (1 Kgs. 18:27). Or what about the satirization of idolatry by the prophet Isaiah?

All who make idols are nothing, and the things they treasure are worthless. Those who would speak up for them are blind; they are ignorant, to their own shame. Who shapes a god and casts an idol, which can profit him nothing? He and his kind will be put to shame; craftsmen are nothing but men. Let them all come together and take their stand; they will be brought down to terror and infamy. The blacksmith takes a tool and works with it in the coals; he shapes an idol with hammers, he forges it with the might of his arm. He gets hungry and loses his strength; he drinks no water and grows faint. The carpenter measures with a line and makes an outline with a marker; he roughs it out with chisels and marks it with compasses. He shapes it in the form of man, of man in all his glory, that it may dwell in a shrine. He cut down cedars, or perhaps took a cypress or oak. He let it grow among the trees of the forest, or planted a pine, and the rain made it grow. It is man's fuel for burning; some of it he takes and warms himself, he kindles a fire and bakes bread. But he also fashions a god and worships it; he makes an idol and bows down to it. Half of the wood he burns in the fire; over it he prepares his meal, he roasts his meat and eats his fill. He also warms himself and says, 'Ah! I am warm; I see the fire.' From the rest he makes a god, his idol; he bows down to it and worships. He prays to it and says, 'Save me; you are my god.' They know nothing, they understand nothing; their eyes are plastered over so they cannot see, and their minds closed so they cannot understand. No one stops to think, no one has the knowledge or understanding to say, 'Half of it I used for fuel; I even baked bread over its coals, I roasted meat and I ate. Shall I make a detestable thing from what is left? Shall I bow down to a block of wood?' (Isa. 44:9-19).

First the Lord mocks the idolaters through his prophet, then he destroys them. Then of course, in the wise Book of Proverbs, there is the unflattering portrait of the sluggard – we'd call him a 'couch potato' today – who is too lazy even to lift his food from the dish to his mouth (Prov. 26:13-16). In each of these instances, God uses strong, 'judgmental' language to describe the wickedness of the wicked.

Nor is this only an Old Testament phenomenon. Few can match Paul for the vividness of his language of condemnation. In Philippians, Paul denounces his Jewish opponents as 'dogs', and vilifies their religious ceremonies as nothing more than 'mutilation of the flesh' (3:2-3). To the Galatians he expresses his wish that they would 'emasculate themselves' (5:12). And yet this harsh language comes from a man who solemnly testifies (Rom. 9:3) that he would gladly see himself dead – even damned – if these 'dogs', these 'mutilators of the flesh' might be saved!

Is there a place in your preaching for such strong language? To answer that question we must ask what the purpose of such language would be? In brief, in Scripture such language is designed to elicit from the hearer or reader an emotional reaction – laughter, revulsion, terror, etc. – which corresponds to the spiritual nature of the thing being described.

Idolatry – spiritual adultery – is such an abomination to the Lord that at times he uses graphic, violent language to describe his judgment upon it. For the sorceries and witchcraft of Nineveh, God decrees the following startling punishment.

> 'I am against you,' declares the LORD Almighty. 'I will lift your skirts over your face. I will show the nations your nakedness and the kingdoms your shame. I will pelt you with filth, I will treat you with contempt and make you a spectacle. All who see you will flee from you and say, "Nineveh is in ruins – who will mourn for her?" Where can I find anyone to comfort you?' (Nahum 3:5-7).

Such language is used for its shock value. God does not want us to intellectualize sin. He wants to grip us on all levels – emotion and will as well as mind. He uses strong language to accomplish this purpose.

In the contemporary world, however, a different idea rules. 'Nice' is better than holy. 'Comfortable' is better than dedicated and devoted. Churches have become places for 'support' and flattery, not truth. To be shocked in church is virtually the unpardonable sin. As a consequence, sermons become so bloated with euphemisms that they no longer communicate the truth of God with sharpness and clarity. When many pastors are through with the Word of God it is no longer a 'sharp, double-edged sword' but rather a big foam pillow. Is it any wonder that our preaching is so often ineffective. Pastors even find themselves uncomfortable with the candor and power of Scripture itself! 'Let me see ... how can I say this so that it will not offend anyone?'

Paul was not that sort of man. Nor should you be. Love and truth are not contrary ideas. And truth must be delivered truthfully. That means that sometimes you will have to speak with a bluntness that may seem offensive to some, in order to faithfully elicit from your audience the kind of whole-being response that is required.

To be sure, Scripture uses this kind of strong language sparingly. So should you. If such language is overused it will lose the very effect it is designed to create: like a parent who yells at the kids all the time – what do they do when they have something really important to say? Such strong language should be used with care. You must calculate its potential effect in view of the purpose you have in mind for using it. But it should be used. You are called upon to communicate the Word of God to the whole man, and that means using language which will engage him as a whole person.

'A House Divided'

The purpose of Paul's meeting with the Sanhedrin now became clearer as he resumed speaking: 'My brothers, I am a Pharisee, the son of a Pharisee. I stand on trial because of my hope in the resurrection of the dead' (Acts 23:6). In the words of the psalmist, Paul was there to 'confuse the wicked' and 'confound their speech' (Ps. 55:9). He was to be the instrument in the hand of the risen Christ to complete the hardening of the Jewish leadership, so that judgment might fall upon them. The apostle knew the make-up of the Sanhedrin, 'that some of them were Sadducees and the others Pharisees' (v. 6), and that the Sadducees did not believe in the resurrection (nor angels or spirits), while the Pharisees acknowledged them all (v. 8).

By introducing the issue of the resurrection of the dead, he was not only being faithful to his apostolic calling, but he precipitated another riot! This time in the Sanhedrin itself, and this time deliberately. 'When he said this, a dispute broke out between the Pharisees and the Sadducees, and the assembly was divided.... There was a great uproar' (vv. 7, 9). Here, unlike in his speech to the Jews in the Temple area, Paul set aside any attempt to be tactful. He did not seek to avoid conflict. He chose rather to bring the meeting to an end by reducing it to confusion – and so he did. 'The dispute became so violent that the commander was afraid Paul would be torn to pieces by them. He ordered the troops to go down and take him away from them by force and bring him into the barracks' (v. 10).[34]

When judged in view of Paul's purpose, this message, though extremely brief, was successful. Paul pursued a very astute tactic of divide and conquer.[35] He did not want to allow the Sanhedrin an opportunity to pass any form of judgment upon him – whether invited to or not. Charges against him would have to be formulated another day in another way. Paul wanted the Sanhedrin as a body confounded and silenced. 'He knew the "enemy." He knew where his weakness was. And with one, smooth, well-aimed, stone he slew Goliath.'[36]

In the 'Sermon on the Mount' Jesus said, 'Do not give dogs what is sacred; do not throw your pearls to pigs. If you do, they may trample them under their feet, and then turn and tear you to pieces' (Matt. 7:6). In both personal witnessing and preaching the question sometimes arises, 'When are we "casting pearls before swine" – how do we know?' It would appear that in Paul's appearance before the Sanhedrin we have an example of an occasion when to preach would have been fruitless – even wrong. The Jewish leaders, despite years of opportunity, hearing the gospel from Jesus himself and from his apostles, remained adamant in their hatred of Christ and their rejection of the very Scriptures that spoke so clearly of him.[37] In approaching his meeting with them, Paul took into account the past history of the Sanhedrin (which he knew for many years as an 'insider'), as well as the reaction of the Jews elsewhere. He determined (rightly) that it would be foolish for him to enter into a further discussion with them of the gospel. They were intent on his destruction; he would not play into their hands.

There are occasions (in private or public) where we face men and women who, repeatedly and stubbornly rejecting the gospel, become ever more violent (verbally or physically) in the process. We are not under obligation to continue to bring the message of life to such as these. We may – with a clear conscience – turn our efforts elsewhere – to others who will listen (Acts 28:28).

'Well Done, Good and Faithful Servant'

Paul did not win many converts during his last visit to Jerusalem. Both speeches ended with violent riots, and Paul had to be extricated from life-threatening danger by the intervention of Roman troops. If we measure success by the number of people who are converted, we would have to judge Paul's efforts in Jerusalem a failure.

But we have learned by now to measure success in terms of the purpose of God, and of the preacher, in bringing a given message to men. Christ had a particular job for Paul to accomplish through these messages in Jerusalem. And judged in those terms, the apostle's messages – both to the general Jewish audience in the Temple area and to the leadership in the Sanhedrin – were very successful. This is borne out by the Lord's imprimatur. The night after the blowup in the Sanhedrin, the Lord Jesus came and stood near Paul to comfort and strengthen him. Jesus said, 'Take courage! As you have testified about me in Jerusalem, so you must also testify in Rome' (v. 11). The work in Jerusalem was well finished. Now it was on to Rome.

19

Paul's Defenses:
The Gospel Before Kings

Paul's last recorded speeches in the Book of Acts are delivered before
Roman governors and a Roman-surrogate Jewish king. In delivering
these speeches – in defense of his conduct in Jerusalem and, indeed,
his whole ministry – Paul was fulfilling the promise of Christ to his
apostles: 'You will be brought before kings and governors, and all on
account of my name' (Luke 21:12). Paul, in particular, was fulfilling
the commission given him by the risen Lord 'to carry [his] name
before the Gentiles and their kings' (Acts 9:15). In these defenses
Paul manifested great skill in maneuvering, as he answered the
accusations brought against him, but never lost sight of his primary
responsibility – to be a witness of the risen Christ and an evangelist.
In speaking with Felix and Drusilla, and later King Agrippa and his
wife, Paul made direct appeals to them to turn from their sin and
embrace Jesus Christ by faith as their only hope of salvation. Again
Paul provides us with an example of single-minded and clear-sighted
devotion to his primary calling as a preacher of the gospel, even in
very challenging and dangerous situations.

Paul's Hearing Moves to Caesarea

Luke sketches for us the events which brought Paul to Caesarea under
Roman guard in Acts 23:10-34. After the collapse of the meeting of the
Sanhedrin, Paul was returned to Roman custody in the barracks of the
Fortress of Antonia (v. 10), where the Lord himself in a vision (v. 11)
assured Paul that he would testify for him in Rome. Meanwhile the
angry Jews were conspiring to put Paul to death (vv. 12-15). The plot
was revealed to the Roman authorities (vv. 16-22), and as a result Paul
was sent by night to Caesarea under guard of seventy horsemen and
two hundred spearmen, so that he might be presented to the Roman
governor, Felix (vv. 23-24). After a stopover in Antipatris, Paul arrived in
Caesarea and he was delivered to the governor (vv. 32-33).

Claudius Lysias, the commander of the Roman troops in Jerusalem,
sent a letter along with Paul explaining (from his perspective) the

circumstances of the apostle's arrest in Jerusalem (vv. 26-30). In his letter, Lysias expressed the opinion that no charge made against Paul by the Jews deserved death or imprisonment as far as Roman law was concerned. The accusations involved no more than questions about Jewish law (v. 29). After reading the letter and inquiring as to Paul's home province (Cilicia), Felix determined to hear Paul's case as soon as his accusers arrived in Caesarea (v. 34). It didn't take long. 'Five days later the high priest Ananias went down to Caesarea with some of the elders and a lawyer named Tertullus, and they brought their charges against Paul before the governor' (24:1).

Paul Accused Before Felix

The attempt of the Jewish leaders from Jerusalem to secure a conviction of the Apostle Paul is a confused mixture of effort and error. On the one hand, they were willing to enlist the services of a professional rhetor, Tertullus (v. 2), to set forth their case before Felix, but on the other, they do not bring with them those witnesses who alone (according to Roman law) could bring convincing testimony against Paul (cf. v. 19). As one reads Luke's accounts (in his Gospel and in Acts) of the Jewish attempts to secure 'legal' condemnation of Jesus and his followers, one is impressed with the almost irrational intensity of the Jewish hatred. Repeatedly they are willing to try anything to secure a conviction, even when their case is extremely weak, as it often was. Even their suborning of perjury was a miserable failure (Matt. 26:59f.). However, when they had total control of the situation, as in the case of Jesus and Stephen, they were successful. But when they had to press their claims before an independent authority, like that of Rome, the weakness of their case was immediately evident. In his defenses before Felix, Festus, and Agrippa, Paul demonstrates his skill as a legal tactician as well as a theologian and preacher.

The formal charge against Paul was to be presented by Tertullus. It has been suggested that the use of a professional advocate was contrary to common Jewish practice, and thus an indication of the fact that the Jewish leaders themselves knew that their case against Paul was weak.[1] Roman law balanced the status of the accused against the status of the accuser, and the seriousness of the crime against the potential consequences of the verdict. Paul's accusers had imposing political, social, and economic credentials, which had to be balanced against Paul's Roman citizenship. The use of Tertullus may have been an effort to tip the scales in favor of the accusers.[2] 'Retaining him probably conferred an additional advantage because Tertullus was a familiar face to the governor. Tertullus would undoubtedly have represented other clients before Felix.'[3] Recognizing that they would have little influence in a Roman court (due to the deterioration under Felix of the relationship between the Jews and Romans), the high priest and elders entrusted their case entirely to their spokesman, only offering their confirmatory words following Tertullus' speech (v.9).

Tertullus began his presentation with the customary *captatio benevolentiae*, i.e., an introduction designed to win the goodwill of the judge.

> We have enjoyed a long period of peace under you, and your foresight has brought about reforms in this nation. Everywhere and in every way, most excellent Felix, we acknowledge this with profound gratitude. But in order not to weary you further, I would request that you be kind enough to hear us briefly (vv. 2-4).

Of Tertullus' opening statement Rapske writes:

> Far from being a rather artless and insincere attempt by Tertullus at flattering Felix ... it follows closely the conventional advice of the forensic handbooks. Winter concludes that Tertullus 'was an able professional rhetor, whose *captatio benevolentiae* was carefully linked to his accusations in the hope of mounting a formidable case against Paul'. Well schooled in rhetoric and sensitive to Roman provincial governance, he was perfectly fit to cross swords with Paul.[4]

There was, of course, flattery in Tertullus's words,[5] but there was a very serious point to the flattery. The advocate was laying a foundation for the charges he would next present to the governor. Tertullus's claims about Felix, it was hoped, would predispose the governor to act favorably on the accusations made against Paul. Again building on the work of Winter,[6] Rapske argues:

> Tertullus indicated ... his clients' general support for Felix's administration, praising him for the exercise of his *imperium* on behalf of the Jewish nation in the interests of public order and legal reform. Winter suggests that the first part of this praise would recall to Felix how he had recently quelled the rebellion of the Egyptian false prophet and his forces. The second part would affirm, in addition to his judicial competence, Jewish

appreciation of the helpfulness of Felix's legislative acts. Among them may have been Felix's inclusion in Judaean legislation of the specific provisions of the Claudian expulsion edict of 49/50 AD and the sanctions of the Claudian findings for the Alexandrian situation. Whatever the case, Tertullus accuses Paul of offending pragmatic and legislative efforts to maintain the peace, a matter concerning which Felix has a stake and thus will wish to act; i.e., to render a judgement favourable to the plaintiffs.[7]

Following his introduction, Tertullus sets forth the accusations against Paul. First, the apostle is called a 'pest' (*loimos*, v. 5), a 'troublemaker' (NIV) who stirred up riots (*stasis*) among the Jews all over the world. This was a very serious allegation. If it were proved true that Paul had habitually subverted public law and order all over the world, the Romans would have judged him guilty and deserving of death.[8] Secondly, Tertullus charges Paul with being 'a ringleader of the Nazarene sect' (v. 5). The charge of 'sectarianism' would have been of little interest to the Roman authorities, unless the sect in question could be clearly identified as subversive. By associating Paul's involvement with 'the Nazarenes' with the claim that he had stirred up riots all over the Roman world, Tertullus was certainly trying to imply that Christians were social revolutionaries. 'By calling Paul a ringleader, Tertullus ascribes to him full responsibility for the troubles.'[9]

The third and final charge was that Paul attempted to desecrate the Temple (v. 6). This charge was weak in that it is not supported by any specification. Felix knew only what Lysias had told him in his letter about the disturbance in the Temple, and that report gave no reason for the trouble. According to Lysias, Paul was seized by the Jews who wanted to kill him, but Lysias intervened with his troops and rescued him (23:27). At the time the Jews, supposing Paul to have taken Gentiles with him into the Temple, had accused him of actually desecrating the Temple (21:28-29), but here the charge of 'attempted' desecration is much weaker and more vague.[10]

No witnesses were produced, though the Jewish leaders lent what weight their authority warranted in confirming the statements of their spokesman (24:9). Tertullus closed his presentation by urging the governor to conduct a judicial inquiry in order to learn more fully the truth of the charges brought against Paul – a 'lame and impotent conclusion' by the prosecution which underlined the weakness of the case against Paul.[11]

Paul Replies to the Charges

Felix declined to take up Tertullus's suggestion by questioning Paul or the Jewish leadership. Instead, he motioned for Paul to speak (v. 10). Rapske comments: 'If Tertullus was an expert at forensic discourse, Paul's own defence showed him to be equally well equipped.'[12] Like his opponent, Paul introduces his defense with an appeal to the goodwill of the court. But his comments are more brief and less elaborate than Tertullus' were. Paul too knew Felix's background. He did not flatter the immoral and brutal governor, but rather highlighted the one detail in his background which was relevant to this case (v. 10). The governor had for some eight or nine years been involved in administrative posts in Palestine,[13] and thus he was familiar with the ideas and practices of Judaism. In mentioning this point, Paul was able to 'stroke' the governor and also alert him to the fact that his expertise would be helpful to his making a decision about Paul's case.

In his presentation of the charges, Tertullus had minimized their religious dimension and emphasized their political implications. In defending himself, Paul takes exactly the opposite tack – he focuses the governor's attention upon the religious character of the dispute. In so doing he was able to highlight the central issues of his faith, and at the same time exploit aspects which had been ignored by his accusers.

Paul flatly contradicts the first charge on factual grounds – facts which Felix himself could easily verify (v. 11). There was no proof of the charge against him (v. 13). Paul had gone up to Jerusalem no more than twelve days earlier – hardly enough time to foment a revolution! Besides, the purpose of his visit was not political – far from it. He went to Jerusalem to worship, as any devout Jew might be expected to do. Paul went on to say, 'My accusers did not find me arguing with anyone at the temple, or stirring up a crowd in the synagogues or anywhere else in the city' (v. 12). This claim, while true, is ironic since this would have been one of the few occasions when Paul was *not* engaged in presenting the gospel of Christ in public places and disputing with those who opposed the truth (cf. 17:17; 18:4). The purpose of Paul's visit to Jerusalem on this occasion was very limited, as he would later state (24:17), and he had not engaged in his usual evangelistic activities. Since there were no witnesses present who could testify to his ministry elsewhere (cf. v. 19), the claim that he was a 'troublemaker' could not be sustained (v. 13).

In moving to the second accusation, Paul admitted that he was in fact a follower of 'the Way' (v. 14) – he does not use the term 'the Nazarenes' – but as such he was simply following the faith of his fathers. Here the governor's background understanding of Judaism and 'the Way' (cf. v. 22)[14] was particularly useful, and was exploited by Paul. Felix could be expected to appreciate that 'the Way' was not a 'sect' in the sense implied by Tertullus. Paul's religious convictions were Jewish in that he worshipped the God of Abraham, Isaac, and Jacob according to the words of the Law and the prophets contained in the Scriptures (v. 14). Even his most distinctive conviction – 'that there will be a resurrection of both the righteous and the wicked' (v.15) – was not unique to himself, or to the followers of 'the Way'. It was shared by many of his opponents! Though Paul did not specifically mention the resurrection of Jesus, he took the opportunity to place the divine promise of the resurrection at the center of his defense, and would return to it again (cf. v. 22; cf. 23:6; 26:8).

If Paul was 'guilty' of anything, it must be of 'striv[ing] always to keep [his] conscience clear before God and man' (v. 16). Could his accusers (or his judge!) say as much? Nothing in Paul's summary of his beliefs and practices suggested any threat to Roman peace and order, and because of his own experience Felix would have readily recognized that fact.

Finally, Paul answers the third charge – that he attempted to desecrate the Temple – by pointing out the purpose for his presence there. 'After an absence of several years, I came to Jerusalem to bring my people gifts for the poor and to present offerings. I was ceremonially clean when they found me in the temple courts doing this. There was no crowd with me, nor was I involved in any disturbance' (vv. 17-18). Again, Felix would know enough of Judaism to appreciate that a Jew who was ceremonially clean and alone had done nothing to desecrate the Temple. What's more, the governor might well question why the Jews would find fault with Paul for bringing gifts to the poor, or presenting offerings in the Temple?

At this point Paul moved to the offensive. He offered an objection to the proceedings on judicial grounds. According to Roman law, plaintiffs must be present to accuse.[15] Therefore the case against him had not been advanced on the basis of 'best evidence'. The absence of the 'Jews from the province of Asia' who had initially charged Paul (v. 19; cf. 21:27-28) was grounds for a valid technical objection.[16] As far as the members of the Sanhedrin present were concerned, Paul rightly states that they could bear witness only to a crime committed by him when he stood before the council (v. 20) – and there had been none! Here the sagacity of Paul's strategy before the Sanhedrin is borne out – by raising the divisive question of the resurrection he disrupted and effectively ended the hearing before the council. Consequently, no judgment against him had been established. Thus here Paul could honestly allude to the fact that he had shouted as he stood before them: 'It is concerning the resurrection of the dead that I am on trial before you today' (v. 21). The doctrine of the resurrection was the issue then, and it was still the issue. And this question of Jewish theology was not one that Felix would likely wish to determine.[17]

After the Hearing

Felix decided he had heard enough. He adjourned the proceedings with the promise that he would decide the case after conferring with Lysias, the Roman commander from Jerusalem (v. 22). Because Lysias' letter had contained little helpful factual information, and because there were contradictory accounts of the events in Jerusalem, Felix decided he needed to talk to the Roman commander in person. 'Lysias was, from the Roman perspective, the only independent witness.'[18] Luke does not record whether or not Felix met with Lysias – though it is hard to imagine that such a meeting did not take place – nor are we informed of its outcome. While there was sufficient reason for Felix to dismiss the charges against Paul, he did not. He continued to hold Paul in custody, albeit under relaxed conditions (v. 23), for two more years (v. 27). Most scholars believe Felix, in keeping Paul in custody, was influenced by the potential threat of political trouble with the Jews rather than the merits of their case against the apostle.[19] Yet, in view of Paul's Roman citizenship, the governor was also not willing to condemn Paul on the basis of such flimsy evidence.

Paul had successfully fended off another attempt to put an end to his ministry (and his life!) by the enemies of the gospel of Christ. In his defense before Felix, Paul has shown us an example of his skill in using his knowledge of legal procedure to neutralize the case brought against him by the Sanhedrin. Most preachers today have but limited knowledge of the courtroom. Having to appear before a magistrate to answer charges levelled at your ministry may be the farthest thing from your mind. But don't make the mistake of assuming that 'it can't happen here.' The handwriting is already on the wall. As our society (and courts) gradually expand the definition of 'hate crimes', it is not hard to imagine a day – not so far in the future – when preachers may be arrested and tried for nothing more than faithfully preaching from the Bible against a growing number of social evils (abortion, homosexuality, etc.).[20] Indeed, calling men to turn from false religions and cults (Judaism, Islam, Mormonism, etc.) to the true gospel of Christ might soon be considered an act of 'religious genocide'. Paul's experience in the Roman court of Felix should serve as a 'wake-up call' to you. Start learning about how the legal system works, you may need to use it one day. May God grant you the ability to defend your ministry and your message before the magistrate as he did the Apostle Paul.

Righteousness, Self-control, and Coming Judgment
Luke adds one further note concerning Paul's ministry to the Roman governor Felix. Several days after the hearing Felix and his Jewish wife Drusilla sent for Paul – they wanted to hear more from this intriguing man. This time, freed from the demands of the law court, Paul reverted to his favorite subject and preached 'about faith in Christ Jesus' (v. 24). Now was Paul's opportunity to appeal to Felix and his wife as needy sinners, and they were needy indeed! Drusilla was the youngest daughter of Herod Agrippa I, and at the tender age of sixteen had been persuaded by Felix (with the help of Atomos, a Cypriot magician) to leave her husband, the king of Emesa, and marry him. This reputed beauty was the third wife of Felix.[21]

Luke gives us only the broadest summary of this private audience.[22] Before these two hardened sinners, 'Paul discoursed on righteousness, self-control and the judgment to come' (v. 25). The exposition of the summary of Paul's message here by the notable preacher from earlier in the twentieth century, Dr. Clarence E. Macartney, itself a nice piece of preaching, is worth quoting in full:

> As he stood before them he reasoned of righteousness and temperance and judgment to come. It was a great service that was held that day in the procurator's palace at Caesarea. No processionals, no preludes, no anthems, and a congregation of just two persons. Yet what a service and what a sermon! The sated Roman was expecting that Paul would have something to say about the distinction between Christianity and Judaism,

or upon the subject of predestination, or perchance the resurrection of the dead; and the brilliant Drusilla was hoping to hear something of a new cult, or a new philosophy, or some new interpretation of the Old Testament. They were looking for an hour's entertainment, but Paul gave them judgment and searching of heart.

Paul could preach a great doctrinal sermon when he wanted to, but he could also preach an ethical sermon when it suited the occasion, yet an ethical sermon, a sermon on conduct, based on the great redemptive facts of the Christian faith. He was not unfamiliar with the lives and characters of those who sat on the throne before him, and he preached a sermon that was eminently and painfully practical. Instead of flattering his aristocratic hearers, or avoiding any subjects which might have been interpreted as having a personal application, Paul reasoned with them of righteousness, temperance, and judgment to come.

The administration of Felix had been full of dishonesty, extortion and injustice, and Paul discoursed of righteousness and justice; how God would not overlook the acts of wicked injustice and would regard the cry of the poor and the oppressed and surely avenge them, and how righteousness and judgment are the habitation of his throne. Paul mentioned no places, repeated no names, gave no dates, but his sermon covered the past life of Felix. The Governor thought of the bribes he had paid or received; of the innocent men he had falsely charged and cast into prison; of the crowds of people in the street upon whom he had loosed his cruel soldiery; of the homes that had been laid waste and made desolate at his command. When he did these acts, he had no compunction of conscience, but now, under the preaching of Paul, that terrible past rose before him in fearful resurrection and accusation.

As Paul reasoned of self-control, temperance, chastity, Felix thought of those sins, common among high class Romans of that day, but of which today it would be a shame even to speak. And here Drusilla, too, began to show some uneasiness. She thought of her own shameful escapades; of the lover she had deceived, of the husband she had abandoned, and now her adulterous union with Felix. Perhaps she thought, being a Jewess, that Paul would have something to say about the new faith of the Nazarenes in its relationship to Judaism. But instead of that, he preached an old fashioned Hebrew sermon on the Seventh Commandment.

By the time Paul had reached the third head of his sermon, both Felix and Drusilla were very unhappy and both anxious for the preacher to come to a close. Paul in his preaching did not leave out, as so many do, the territory of life to come. He preached not only to the times, but to the eternities. His preaching had the power of the world to come in it. Like the preaching of Christ, who ever spoke as standing under the rule of another

world, Paul told Felix and Drusilla that this life is not all; that a man might
have his good clothes, his good times, his mistresses, chariots and villas,
and yet be cast into hell in the next world; and that all three of them, Paul,
Felix and Drusilla, must stand before the judgment seat of Christ and give
an account of the deeds done in the body.

Paul's message was so searching and convicting that even the
jaded Felix was afraid and said, 'That's enough for now! You may
leave. When I find it convenient, I will send for you' (v. 25). Macartney
concludes:

> No wonder Felix trembled. Never did preaching have a greater vindication
> or a preacher receive a greater tribute than when Felix, the hardened,
> withered, licentious despot, trembled. He was the last man in the world
> one would have expected to tremble. He had listened in his day to all
> sorts of orators and enthusiasts and philosophers, yet, of them all, this
> Jewish prisoner was the only one who had ever made him tremble ... Felix
> could break up the meeting and dismiss the preacher, but it was some
> time before he could still the storm of conscience that had arisen within
> his heart. Paul had started the bell to tolling, and Felix could not muffle it.
> Wherever he went, this preacher went with him....
>
> This sermon, like so many others, made a deep impression, but had
> little result. The preacher had brought Felix to the gates of the great
> opportunity. The voices of those within were crying to him, 'Come in,
> come in, eternal glory thou shalt win.' But Felix would not go in. Felix
> trembled, but he would not go in. He might have been a brand plucked
> from the burning. With all his crimes and wickedness, the blood of Christ
> could have made him a fit citizen of the City of the Redeemed; but he
> would not go in. God said, 'Today,' but Felix said, 'Tomorrow,' and
> tomorrow never came.[23]

Luke's closing comment points up the veniality of the Roman
procurator, who gave up his opportunity for true riches. Over the next
two years Felix frequently sent for Paul and talked with him, but now
the focus of his attention was elsewhere – 'he was hoping that Paul
would offer him a bribe' (v. 26). What will a man give in exchange
for his soul (Mark 8:37)?

Paul and Festus

In due course Felix was succeeded by Porcius Festus (Acts 24:27).
'The occasion of Felix's recall from his office was an outbreak of
civil strife between the Jewish and Gentile inhabitants of Caesarea, in

which Felix intervened with troops in such a way as to cause much bloodshed among the leaders of the Jewish faction.'[24] Apparently Festus was a reasonably good ruler, though his term in office was brief, for he died in office after only a few years of service in AD 62.[25] 'The change of administration brought no advantage to Paul ... the arrival of a new and inexperienced governor meant the reopening of the case in circumstances less favorable to Paul.'[26]

Shortly after arriving at the capital of the province, Festus traveled to Jerusalem to meet with the Jewish leaders (25:1-2). The Jews were eager to resume the trial of the hated apostle, this time in Jerusalem, or so they said to the new procurator, but in reality they were still seeking any means to kill him (v. 3). Festus proposed instead that the Jewish leaders again send representatives to Caesarea, 'and press charges against the man there, if he has done anything wrong' (v. 5, cf. vv. 15-16).

The Jews accepted the proposal, and probably accompanied Festus on his return to Caesarea several days later (v. 6). The next day the court was convened and Paul was once again surrounded by his accusers (v. 7). Luke does not bother to tell us the exact charges this time, they have become grimly familiar by now, but he does remark that the Jews were no closer to proving their accusations than they had been in the past. When Festus later reported the whole affair to King Agrippa, he said, 'When [Paul's] accusers got up to speak, they did not charge him with any of the crimes I had expected. Instead, they had some points of dispute with him about their own religion and about a dead man named Jesus who Paul claimed was alive' (25:18-19). Thus it appears that the Jews, in renewing their charges against Paul in the presence of Festus, included in their presentation the central issue of the messianic claim of Jesus of Nazareth, and the debate over Jesus' resurrection.

Paul again 'made his defense' – this time in a brief, summary fashion: 'I have done nothing wrong against the law of the Jews or against the temple or against Caesar' (v. 8). Note that Paul made very emphatic for the first time here what had been clearly implied in his defense before Felix – he had violated no law of Caesar's. That was Festus' only legitimate interest.

When the procurator proposed that Paul return to Jerusalem for trial, the apostle had had enough. His life had been on the line ever since he returned to Jerusalem. He had willingly submitted to the

hardships and imprisonment as long as he might complete the task the
Lord Jesus had given him (20:23-24). He had defended himself
successfully in every instance where specific charges had been
brought against him. Yet he was still in custody – all because the
Roman leaders were more sensitive to political pressure from the
Jews, or payoffs, than they were willing justly to administer Roman
law. Now he forcefully presses his point (v. 10): 'I am now standing
before Caesar's court, where I ought to be tried' – a rebuke to the
weakness of Festus in the face of Jewish pressure. 'I have not done
any wrong to the Jews, as you yourself know very well' – Festus
knew the details of the case. The burden of proof was upon his
accusers. They had not made their case in the past, and Paul is
confident they cannot make it now. Paul boldly reaffirms his innocence
(v. 11): 'If ... I am guilty of doing anything deserving death, I do not
refuse to die.' Finally, Paul twists the knife in Festus – if the procurator
will not act on behalf of a Roman citizen as a representative of Caesar
should, the apostle will take his case directly to the emperor: 'No one
has the right to hand me over to [the Jews]. I appeal to Caesar!'

Festus was no doubt shaken by Paul's appeal, and after conferring
with his advisors, the procurator declared: 'You have appealed to
Caesar. To Caesar you will go!' (v. 12).

While the apostle was still in Jerusalem, Jesus had appeared to
him in a vision and told him, 'Take courage! As you have testified
about me in Jerusalem, so you must also testify in Rome' (23:11). As
events developed in Caesarea, culminating in Festus' proposal to send
Paul back to Jerusalem, it must have become clear to the apostle that
the time appointed by the Savior had come, and thus he made his
appeal to Caesar. It is ironic that later King Agrippa told Festus what
the procurator must have already known: 'This man could have been
set free if he had not appealed to Caesar' (26:32). The injustices of
men were in the service of the Lord of Glory, who was determined to
bring his faithful witness before the most powerful ruler on the face
of the earth.

The Apostle and the King

Before Paul was sent to Rome, there was one last message he must
deliver in Caesarea. King Agrippa[27] and his sister Bernice came to
Caesarea on a state visit to pay their respects to the new procurator
(25:13). During the visit Festus reviewed Paul's case for the king (vv.

14-21), who seemed very interested and asked if he might hear from Paul in person. An audience was arranged for the next day (v. 22). Agrippa and Bernice appeared with great pomp, accompanied by an entourage of high-ranking officers and the leading men of the city (v. 23).

Festus introduced the apostle by mentioning the plea of 'the whole Jewish community' against Paul, calling for his death (v. 24). Festus then declared (surprisingly, since he did not mention it at the time), 'I found he had done nothing deserving of death' (v. 25). Though Agrippa had asked for the meeting with Paul, Festus expressed his hope that the king would be able to help him formulate a summary of the accusations against Paul, which could be forwarded with the prisoner to Rome (vv. 26-27).[28] Accordingly, the hearing proceeded with the king giving Paul permission to speak on his own behalf (26:1).

Seeking the Heart of the King

'It was a dramatic moment when the holy and humble apostle of Jesus Christ stood before this representative of the worldly, ambitious, morally corrupt family of the Herods, who for generation after generation had set themselves in opposition to truth and righteousness.'[29] Before this king Paul delivers his most dignified, polished, and lengthy address recorded in Acts.

> Here, in the calm and dignified setting of the governor's chamber at Caesarea, Paul delivered the speech which, above all his other speeches in Acts, may worthily claim to be called his *Apologia pro vita sua*.... The construction of the speech is more careful than usual, the grammar more classical, and the style more literary, as befitted the distinguished audience. The argument is designed to appeal particularly to the mind of Agrippa, who was reputed to be interested in Jewish theology, even if Festus found himself completely out of his depth after the first few sentences.[30]

Paul's defense is in many ways similar to that which he offered to the Jewish mob in Jerusalem. '[It] consists of another account of his conversion experience, in which he stresses that his Christian faith is in line with his Jewish beliefs as a Pharisee and that his commission from the risen Lord is to offer salvation both to the Jews and also to the Gentiles.'[31] Since no particular charges had been set forth, it appears that Paul was trying to explain to Agrippa the reason for the great and abiding hatred of the Jews against the apostle and his message. The question must have occurred to the king, 'Why is the whole Jewish nation crying out for the blood of this man?' (cf. 25:24; 26:21).[32]

In aiming his speech at Agrippa in particular, however, Paul was not interested in merely appealing to the king's interest in theology. He had a deeper purpose. He was seeking the heart of the king. The appeal to Caesar had been made and, come what may, Paul was going to Rome. In a sense, this meeting with Agrippa was merely a courtesy. Festus would have to draft his report to the emperor, with or without Agrippa's help. Thus, Paul used this occasion to try to win for Christ the great-grandson of Herod the Great who sought to end God's great work of redemption as soon as it had begun (cf. Matt. 2:1-18), the grandson of the king who had beheaded John the Baptist (cf. Mark 6:16), and the son of the man who killed the Apostle James and met a loathsome death for his blasphemy (cf. Acts 12:1-2; 12:21-23).[33] What a strategic victory for the cause of Christ that would be! If such a man were converted under the preaching of the gospel of Christ, would it not be true (as it was of Paul himself) that in Agrippa 'Christ Jesus might display his unlimited patience as an example for those who would believe on him and receive eternal life?' (1 Tim. 1:16). Stott has written:

> He wanted the king's salvation, not his favour. So he did not stop with the story of his own conversion; he was concerned for Agrippa's conversion too. Three times, therefore, Luke has Paul repeating the elements of the gospel in the king's hearing. First, he summarized Christ's commission to him to bring people into his light, power, forgiveness and new community (18). Secondly, he described his obedience to the heavenly vision in terms of preaching that people should repent, turn to God and do good works (20). Thirdly, he detailed his continuing mission 'to this very day', which was to testify that, as the Scriptures had foretold, Christ died, rose and proclaimed the dawn of the new age (23). Each time Paul thus repeated the gospel in court, he was in fact preaching it to the court. Festus might call him mad, as some had said of Jesus, but Paul knew that he was 'speaking the sober truth' (25, RSV). And when the apostle finally addressed the king directly, he was confident that he not only believed the prophets (27), but was also sufficiently familiar with the facts about Jesus (26) to be persuaded of his truth.[34]

Paul's Masterful Apology

After a courteous and deferential introduction (Acts 26:2-4), Paul proceeded to outline his early history emphasizing again his Jewish orthodoxy and his zeal in persecuting the name of Jesus the Nazarene (vv. 4-11). He then went on to recount, for the second time (cf. 22:6-11), his converting encounter with the risen Christ on the Damascus road (vv. 12-20). The climax of the message comes in vv. 21-23, where Paul explained that, as paradoxical as it may sound to Agrippa, he is hated by the Jews because he has embraced the hope of Moses and the prophets – Jesus the Messiah. After an interruption by Festus, Paul concludes his message with a pointed personal appeal to King Agrippa (vv. 24-27), which the king dismissed with a 'non-committal half-jest.'[35]

In his opening remarks to the king, Paul expresses his confidence that one so 'well acquainted with all the Jewish customs and controversies' (v. 3) will be readily able to make sense of his case and judge it rightly. He asks Agrippa for a patient hearing, for he intends to lay out the matter fully and in detail. It has been pointed out that in Paul's defense in Acts 22, on the steps of the Fortress of Antonia, he views his conversion, and his life before and after it, from a Jewish perspective, whereas here, before Agrippa, he sets forth those same events from a Christian perspective.[36] In Acts 22:3, Paul began by declaring, 'I am a Jew.' Here he is more careful to distinguish himself from the Jews, while still affirming his solidarity with them, especially before his conversion (e.g., Judaism is 'our religion', v. 5). Indeed, Paul's manner of life was well known to the Jews, going all the way back to his days in Tarsus, and later in Jerusalem (v. 4). That he had been a strict Pharisee, adhering faithfully to all the tenets of that sect, they themselves could bear witness, if they would (v. 5). For one like Agrippa, well acquainted with the theological controversies of the Jews, mention of the Pharisees would immediately bring to mind the issue of the resurrection of the dead, and Paul builds upon that knowledge. Paul declared emphatically (repeating the point in vv. 6 and 7b) that he was on trial for one thing, and one thing alone – the hope which was promised by the God of Abraham, Isaac, and Jacob, and in which all the twelve tribes put their trust – the hope of resurrection life (v. 8). By the way he expressed himself, Paul wanted the king to share his total astonishment that such a thing could take place.

Paul then moved on to explain to the king his zeal as a fanatical persecutor of the church (vv. 9-11). The name of Jesus the Nazarene is now introduced for the first time. Paul was convinced that it was his special calling to turn back to Judaism, or exterminate, all those who had devoted themselves to the messianic pretender, Jesus of Nazareth. Commissioned by the high priests (who now oppose him so vehemently) Paul had persecuted Christians (whom he now must call 'the saints', cf. 22:4-5) – both in Jerusalem and in foreign cities. As he now sees it, however, to force one to renounce one's faith in Jesus on pain of death was actually compelling them to blaspheme!

One day, on the road to Damascus, everything changed – Saul became Paul. The One who had blinded him with light, and was then speaking to him, was Jesus: 'Saul, Saul, why do you persecute me? It is hard for you to kick against the goads' (v. 14). In persecuting the church, Jesus explained, Saul had been persecuting him. Jesus was no memory, he was a living, *resurrected* Person. Paul's account of his meeting with the risen Christ focuses upon the commission he was given. Jesus said,

> Now get up and stand on your feet. I have appeared to you to appoint you as a servant and as a witness of what you have seen of me and what I will show you. I will rescue you from your own people and from the Gentiles. I am sending you to them to open their eyes and turn them from darkness to light, and from the power of Satan to God, so that they may receive forgiveness of sins and a place among those who are sanctified by faith in me (vv. 16-18).

Paul here summarizes all that was said to him by the risen Lord – directly or through Ananias. His point in telescoping the details is to emphasize the divine authority of the commission. The terms of Paul's call, echoing as they do the calling of the prophets of old (cf. Jer. 1:7-8; Ezek. 2:1, 3) and even the Servant of the Lord himself (Isa. 42:1-7), make it clear that Paul had no alternative but to obey. Paul was to become a 'witness' of what he had seen and would see of the resurrected Christ. The effect of his witness upon men – Jews and Gentiles alike – would be enlightenment, repentance, deliverance from the bondage of Satan, forgiveness of sins, and holiness.

For this reason Paul had been sent out as a preacher, and he had not been disobedient to this 'vision from heaven' (Acts 26:19). Throughout the world, to all kinds of men, Paul had preached the importance of a fruitful repentance towards God (v. 20). This was his *mission*, and God was graciously sustaining him in it (v. 22). Agrippa must understand that this too is why the Jews had seized him in the Temple courts and tried to kill him (v. 21). Why was Paul so hated? Because he believed in the resurrection spoken of by the prophets and Moses, and because he was faithful to his miraculous calling. In short, it was the ancient messianic promise – 'that the Christ would suffer and, as the first to rise from the dead, would proclaim light to his own people and to the Gentiles' (v. 23; cf. Luke 24:45-47) – for which Paul was suffering. This was the sum and substance of his *message*.

A Personal Appeal

Having reached this climax, Paul was now ready to put the question to Agrippa – 'Do *you* believe, O King, that the Jews are justified in their opposition to my message and ministry?' – but he is interrupted by Festus: 'You are out of your mind, Paul! Your great learning is driving you insane' (v. 24). Paul replied courteously to the flustered procurator,[37] expressing his confidence that King Agrippa knew full well what Paul was speaking about – so public had been the events about which he had spoken (v. 26). Then Paul turned his attention to Agrippa. To address a judge or king directly, as Paul did here, was unprecedented, but 'when opportunities to witness were given him, he seized them with confidence and courage.'[38] Paul asks, 'King Agrippa, do you believe the prophets? I know you do' (v. 27). The force of the question is not lost on the king. If he believes the prophets, and if the prophets predicted the suffering, death, and resurrection of Jesus, the Christ, then he too must 'become a Christian'. But the king is unwilling to be so quickly pressed to that conclusion, though it appears he was being forced in that direction by the cogency and power of Paul's argument. The outward call of the gospel was deflected with a jest: 'Do you think that in such a short time you can persuade me to be a Christian?' (v. 28).

Paul had made his play for the king's heart, but in the plan and purpose of God it was not to be. With a sincerity which is all the more striking in view of the one to whom the apostle is speaking, Paul replied to the king: 'Short time or long – I pray God that not only you but all who are listening to me today may become what I am, except for these chains' (v. 29).

Here is the apostle's heart. In any and every situation he proclaimed with boldness the reality of the resurrection of Jesus Christ, and the hope for poor lost sinners which was to be found through repentance and faith in him. It was his heart's desire that all who heard the gospel might be saved – Jew or Gentile, in Jerusalem or in Rome. For that he prayed, for that he preached, and for that he suffered, 'fill[ing] up in [his] flesh what [was] still lacking in regard to Christ's afflictions, for the sake of his body, which is the church' (Col. 1:24).

> Thank God for Paul's courage! Kings and queens, governors and generals did not daunt him. Jesus had warned his disciples that they would be 'brought before kings and governors' on account of his name, and had promised that on such occasions he would give them 'words and wisdom'. Jesus had also told Ananias ... that Paul was his 'chosen instrument' to carry his name 'before the Gentiles and their kings and before the people of Israel' (9:15). These predictions had come true, and Paul had not failed.[39]

'Nothing Worthy of Death'

Though Paul was not successful in winning Agrippa (or Festus) to Christ, his defense was most successful in convincing both of them that the charges against him were unsubstantiated. These two leaders – the Roman and the Jew – agreed that 'This man is not doing anything that deserves death or imprisonment' (v. 31). Agrippa even went so far as to say, 'This man could have been set free if he had not appealed to Caesar' (v. 32). That was the *just* verdict, even if it might not have been the *actual* one had Paul not exercised his right of appeal. Festus, new to the job and daunted by the power and influence of the Jews, may well have sent Paul back to Jerusalem. But God continued to keep his promise to his faithful servant: 'Never will I leave you; never will I forsake you' (cf. Heb. 13:5). Paul had completed his witness in Jerusalem and Caesarea, now he would bear witness in Rome.

Paul in Rome

Luke has left us no record of any sermons preached by Paul in Rome, nor do we have an account of his trial before Caesar. What we do have is a brief speech by the apostle to his fellow-Jews in Rome. His words sum up briefly the several defenses which we have studied in the last two chapters:

> My brothers, although I have done nothing against our people or against the customs of our ancestors, I was arrested in Jerusalem and handed

over to the Romans. They examined me and wanted to release me, because I was not guilty of any crime deserving death. But when the Jews objected, I was compelled to appeal to Caesar – not that I had any charge to bring against my own people. For this reason I have asked to see you and talk with you. It is because of the hope of Israel that I am bound with this chain (Acts 28:17-20).

Paul continued to maintain, as he had done time and again, that it was for the sake of the historic hope of Israel – the hope of the resurrection – that he was persecuted by the Jews and imprisoned by the Romans.

When Paul further 'explained and declared ... the kingdom of God' (v. 23) to the Jews of Rome, who were largely ignorant of his views (vv. 21-22), and 'tried to convince them about Jesus from the Law of Moses and from the Prophets,' the dual reaction was again typical. We have observed it wherever Paul preached – to Jews and Gentiles alike. 'Some were convinced by what he said, but others would not believe' (v. 24).

Though the Jews had become hardhearted and calloused to the promises of God as they came to fulfillment in Jesus, the Christ (vv. 25-27), there was nevertheless hope that the Gentiles, when hearing the good news of God's salvation, would listen (v. 28). And so Paul the apostle continued boldly to preach the kingdom of God, and taught all who would listen about the Lord Jesus Christ (v. 31).

Conclusion

'While Paul was waiting for them in Athens, he was greatly distressed to see that the city was full of idols' (Acts 17:16).

As we begin a new millennium, Western culture is becoming more overtly pagan than it has been at any time during its history. As the Christian elements of our traditional culture recede more and more into the background of our common life, new ideas and forces are stepping forward. Not only do we face the continued powerful influences of materialism and humanism, but non-Christian religions like Islam and Buddhism are experiencing phenomenal growth in the Western world. Through films and television, stars and other celebrities continue to promote their brand of 'spirituality'. At the same time, the oldness of this 'New Age' religion is becoming evident as its connections with ancient paganism are exposed. What's more, today's brand of 'religious pluralism' is not as tolerant as it might appear to be. Strong social and even political pressures are being brought to bear in an attempt to silence the message of Jesus Christ and the Bible. Every month there are a growing number of reports of Christians – pastors and laymen – being forbidden freedom of speech on behalf of the gospel. Laws are being promoted which would attempt to define historic Christian moral stances (e.g., the view that homosexuality is a freely chosen lifestyle that is condemned by God in the Bible as sin) as 'hate crimes'.

The Western world today looks more like the Greco-Roman world of the first century than ever before. And that will constitute an enormous challenge to the Bible-believing preacher who seeks to carry out his ministry faithfully in the years ahead.

We noted in the introduction to this study that there are those who believe that preaching has become an outmoded and unfruitful means of communicating divine truth in our day. Many more are too busy (or too lazy) to do the difficult work which is necessary in order to preach well and effectively. They allow themselves to become caught up instead with administrative and other duties that take time away from the study and the place of prayer where vital, life-transforming preaching must be rooted. Perhaps you have found yourself swept up in that current – but you don't like it.

If you have read through our study, perhaps the Spirit of the Lord – who is the Spirit *of preaching* – has convinced you afresh that preaching Christ is the only answer for the spiritually blinded and dying culture of our day – just as it was in the age of Peter and Stephen and Paul. Perhaps you have recaptured something of the vision for preaching that animated these first missionaries, evangelists, and pastors. Perhaps you again believe that preaching is the central work of the church, and indispensable both to reaching the lost and to the health and growth of the body of Christ.

As the world in which most of you conduct your ministry becomes more like that of the pagan Roman Empire, your willingness and ability to imitate the preaching of the apostles will become even more relevant to your receiving God's blessing upon your ministry.

Paul's advice to young Timothy has always been timely, and pastors have turned to it again and again for instruction and encouragement. But in light of the study of the preaching in Acts we have just completed together, it might be especially helpful to remind ourselves in closing of some of the wise words of the Spirit given to us through the apostle.

Paul opened his first epistle to Timothy by calling upon him to 'command certain men not to teach false doctrines any longer', and not to 'promote controversies rather than God's work' (1 Tim. 1:3). The ministry of the truth was rather to have as its 'goal ... love, which comes from a pure heart and a good conscience and a sincere faith' (v. 5; cf. 2 Tim 1:3). We are reminded of what we learned in our study about the relationship between the preacher's boldness in the ministry of the Word and his openness before the face of God. Purity of heart, sincerity, and a good conscience are essential prerequisites if you are going to preach the gospel of Christ with fearless confidence and clarity. The apostolic preachers of Acts were able to confront men with boldness because they looked upon God with 'unveiled faces' (2 Cor. 3:18), having 'renounced secret and shameful ways' (4:2). As I stated before, boldness is not a matter of technique or personality – it is a matter of holiness and nearness to God. If you would be the kind of preacher *God* wants, you must 'purify [yourself] from everything that contaminates body and spirit, perfecting holiness out of reverence for God' (7:1; cf. 1 Tim. 4:15-16). This is the path to biblical boldness – to preaching like the apostles.

Paul declared, 'I am not ashamed of the gospel' (Rom. 1:16), and he called his young colleague Timothy to share that same attitude toward his ministry of the Word of Christ – 'do not be ashamed to testify about our Lord' (2 Tim. 1:8). What intimidates you?

The intellectual sophistication of academics and intellectuals? Seemingly bold preachers have sometimes been reduced to purring kittens when called upon to address the wise men of this age. But Paul was not ashamed of the gospel when he addressed the Areopagus council in Athens. As he said to the Greeks of Corinth, 'Where is the wise man? Where is the scholar? Where is the philosopher of this age? Has not God made foolish the wisdom of the world? For since in the wisdom of God the world through its wisdom did not know him, God was pleased through the foolishness of what was preached to save those who believe' (1 Cor. 1:20-21).

The power of the law brought to bear in prohibiting the proclamation of Christ? Confident ministers have sometimes turned to jelly when arraigned before the judges of this world. Peter and John, however, were not ashamed to proclaim Christ to the Jewish Sanhedrin, thirsty for their blood. 'Judge for yourselves whether it is right in God's sight to obey you rather than God,' replied the apostles to the council's prohibition, 'For we cannot help speaking about what we have seen and heard' (Acts 4:19-20).

The anarchy of an angry mob? Most of you have never faced such an audience, and can only guess (and fear) how you might react. Rather than escape the mob's clutches in Jerusalem, Paul asked permission to speak to them, and one last time he proclaimed to them Jesus the Messiah. He rehearsed for them the commission he had received from the risen Lord: 'The God of our fathers has chosen you to know his will and to see the Righteous One and to hear words from his mouth. You will be his witness to all men of what you have seen and heard' (Acts 22:14-15). In the face of violent death, Paul continued to bear witness to his Jewish brethren.

Why was Paul unashamed? Why should Timothy and you be unashamed? Because the message you preach is 'the power of God for the salvation of everyone who believes: first for the Jew, then for the Gentile' (Rom. 1:16). As you preach the same message – the mighty redemptive acts of God in history, centered in the death and resurrection of Jesus – in the power of the same Holy Spirit, you can be equally unashamed, in every situation. 'For God did not give us a spirit of timidity, but a spirit of power, of love and of self-discipline. So do not be ashamed to testify about our Lord ...' (2 Tim. 1:7-8).

At the conclusion of his second letter, Paul gave Timothy a most solemn charge: 'In the presence of God and of Christ Jesus, who will judge the living and the dead, and in view of his appearing and his kingdom, I give you this charge: Preach the Word; be prepared in season and out of season; correct, rebuke and encourage – with great patience and careful instruction' (2 Tim. 4:1-2). If you are a minister of the gospel, you share that same charge. To be sure, there are many elements to an all-around pastoral ministry (cf. v. 5), but at the top of your list must be *preaching* (cf. 1 Tim. 4:13). You must be ready to preach in any and every situation – and we have learned from the sermons in Acts how diverse those situations can be. To all kinds of people in all kinds of circumstances you must be prepared to 'correct, rebuke and encourage – with great patience and careful instruction'. By studying these sermons as we have, I trust you will be better equipped to speak clearly and relevantly to the people to whom God will send you in the course of your ministry.

In George Frederick Handel's powerful oratorio, *Messiah*, there are many wonderful choruses. One of the brief and lesser-known, but nonetheless magnificent, comes in a section following the resurrection and exaltation of Christ, when librettist Jennens and Handel depict the sending forth of the gospel to the ends of the earth. Following a bass aria, 'Thou art gone up on high ...,' the chorus breaks forth in the words of Psalm 68:11 (AV), 'The Lord gave the word; great was the company of the preachers.' It is glorious!

Even as I write these words and hear that sound in my mind, I get goosebumps. Why? Because to me this chorus represents in musical terms the transcendent majesty and graciousness of the central message of God's Word – 'God raised Jesus Christ from the dead' (cf. Acts 3:15). And it captures the thrilling delight which should fill the heart of any man called by God to be a preacher – 'We are witnesses of this.' This awareness drove the apostolic preachers to turn the world upside down. It is this same conviction which will set the tongues of a new generation of preachers aflame as they proclaim to the world the glorious riches of Christ.

References

PART 1

Chapter 1. Apostolic Examples for Preachers Today

1. John A. Broadus, *Lectures on the History of Preaching* (New York: A. C. Armstrong & Son, 1899), p. 36.
2. Herman Ridderbos, *The Speeches of Peter in the Acts of the Apostles* (London: Tyndale Press, 1962), p. 7.
3. *Ibid.*, p. 9.
4. *Ibid.*, p. 5
5. 'When, therefore, we ask why Luke included speeches in his history, the answer must lie in the fact that preaching was a part of the activity of the early church and not in the fact of historical convention. It is thus likely that Luke incorporated speeches not primarily to express his own theological viewpoint but rather because preaching was an integral part of the activity of the early church, as he saw it.... In short, it is one-sided to look at the speeches in Acts merely as evidence for Luke's theology, they have a claim to be based on the practice of the early church' (I. Howard Marshall, *Luke: Historian and Theologian*, [Grand Rapids: Zondervan, 1971], p. 73).
6. Ridderbos, p. 6.
7. Martin Dibelius, *Studies in the Acts of the Apostles* (New York: Charles Scribner's Sons, 1951), p. 181.
8. F. F. Bruce, *The Speeches in the Acts of the Apostles* (London: Tyndale Press, 1943), pp. 7-9; cf. *Commentary on the Greek Text of the Book of the Acts* (London: Tyndale Press, 1951), pp. 18-20.
9. Ward Gasque, *A History of the Criticism of the Acts of the Apostles* (Tübingen: J. C. B. Mohr, 1975), pp. 223-34.
10. *Ibid.*, pp. 225-26.
11. *Ibid.*, p. 228.
12. 'In spite of all the similarities which exist among the speeches, the differences are also great. The layman who hears the suggestion that the speeches of Peter in the early chapters of Acts, the speech of Stephen, the Areopagus address of Paul at Athens, and Paul's farewell address to the Ephesian elders at Miletus are all the literary creations of a single mind may be tempted to scoff at the absurdity of the suggestion. This is not the impression which one has when one compares them. Although there is a basic unity of language and even of theology (as one would expect, if the picture the writer of Acts gives of the essential agreement of the early Church on basic issues is accurate), there are also striking differences.' (*Ibid.*, pp. 229-30)
13. *Ibid.*, p. 232.
14. *Ibid.*, p. 233.

15. Jay E. Adams, *Audience Adaptation in the Preaching of Paul* (Grand Rapids: Baker Book House, 1976), pp. 90-102.

16. Sir William Ramsay, the great nineteenth-century British New Testament researcher, began his studies of Acts convinced that Luke was not a reliable historical reporter. He was, however, forced during the course of his archaeological research to conclude that Luke was indeed a contemporary witness of the events of Acts, and that he set them down with unsurpassed accuracy. He wrote, 'It was gradually borne in upon me that in various details the narrative showed marvellous truth' (William Ramsay, *St. Paul the Traveler and Roman Citizen* [Grand Rapids: Baker Book House, 1949], pp. 7-10).

17. Adams, p. 93.

18. *Ibid.*

19. Ridderbos, pp. 9-10.

20. Adams, p. 96.

21. Donald Guthrie, *New Testament Introduction* (Downers Grove, IL: Inter-Varsity Press, 1970), pp. 742-43.

22. Ridderbos, p. 10.

23. Cited in Adams, pp. 97-9.

24. G. Kittel and G. Friedrich, eds., *Theological Dictionary of the New Testament*, One volumn edition, tr. Geoffrey W. Bromiley (Grand Rapids: Wm. B. Eerdmans, 1985), pp. 430-35.

25. *Ibid.*, p. 399.

26. Note also in this regard the qualification for Judas' replacement: 'Therefore it is necessary to choose one of the men who have been with us the whole time the Lord Jesus went in and out among us, beginning from John's baptism to the time when Jesus was taken up from us. For one of these must become a witness with us of his resurrection' (Acts 1:21-22). Because of this unique qualification, the apostles could serve as 'witnesses of everything he did in the country of the Jews and in Jerusalem' (cf. Acts 10:37-39).

27. Luke writes in Acts 1:1 f., 'In my former book, Theophilus, I wrote about all that Jesus began to do and to teach until the day he was taken up to heaven,' implying that Acts will be a continuation of the account of the doings and teachings of Jesus.

28. The form *en humin* meaning 'with' or 'by' is instrumental, i.e., 'by means of.'

29. John Calvin, *The Acts of the Apostles, 1-13*, John W. Frazer and W. J. G. McDonald (trans.), *Calvin's New Testament Commentaries*, David W. Torrance and Thomas F. Torrance, eds. (Grand Rapids, MI: Wm. B. Eerdmans, 1965, reprint 1979), p. 166.

30. J. M. Stifler, *An Introduction to the Study of the Acts of the Apostles* (New York: Fleming H. Revell, 1892), pp. 18-19.

Chapter 2. Surveying the Sermons

1. Though only one of the sermons comes from Stephen, it is a very important example of early apologetical preaching, and we will examine it carefully later in our study.

2. Since in Acts 20 Paul is preaching to other church leaders (ruling and teaching elders), this sermon is more precisely parallel to those times (usually rare) when you are called upon to preach to a gathering of ecclesiastical officers (e.g., a conference or governing assembly of the church). These are notoriously tough audiences to address, and most pastors find their local congregations much more receptive. In Paul's case the high emotion of the situation makes these brothers acutely responsive to what he has to say.

3. Rather than letting the weekly circumstances in which you preach – which can appear, and actually become, quite routine – proscribe your preaching, you should let the variety found in the apostolic preaching influence the goals which you set for yourself each Lord's day as a preacher.

Chapter 3. The Preaching in Acts is Bold Preaching

1. H. Schlier, 'parrhesia,' in eds. Gerhard Kittel and Gerhard Friedrich, *Theological Dictionary of the New Testament*, tr. Geoffrey W. Bromiley, One volume edition (Grand Rapids, MI: W. B. Eerdmans, 1985), pp. 794-95.

2. Gk., *hōs dei me lalēsai*, 'as it behooves me to speak' (v. 4).

3. Gk., *parrēsia*, 'boldly.'

4. Jay Adams, *Preaching to the Heart* (Phillipsburg, NJ: Presbyterian and Reformed Publishing Company, 1983), p. 32.

5. Mortimer Adler, *How to Speak, How to Listen* (New York: MacMillan, 1983).

6. Jay Adams, *Pulpit Speech* (Nutley, NJ: Presbyterian and Reformed Publishing Co., 1974).

Chapter 4. Preaching Before the Face of God

1. Since James is correct in warning us that 'anyone who listens to the word but does not do what it says is like a man who looks at his face in a mirror and, after looking at himself, goes away and immediately forgets what he looks like' (1:23-24), then is it not all the more true that any minister who does not 'practice what he preaches' will soon forget who he is as a preacher? To the extent that our manner of proclamation depends upon our understanding of who we are as servants of the risen Lord, we will also falter in our actual work of preaching. The unholy preacher is an ineffectual preacher.

2. Nathaniel Hawthorne, *The Scarlet Letter*, in Norman H. Pearson, ed., *The Complete Novels and Selected Tales of Nathaniel Hawthorne* (The Modern Library; NY: Random House, 1937), pp. 168-69.

3. This point was brought to my attention by one of my professors in seminary, the late Dr. C. John Miller, who was very influential in both my personal spiritual growth and preparation for the ministry.

Chapter 5. Preaching in the Fullness of the Spirit

1. 'This filling of the Spirit is not some second work of grace. Rather, it is an ongoing work in which the Spirit more and more controls each area of our lives. It is the sanctification (the gradual process of putting off sin and replacing it with righteousness) of the whole man. It is a matter of asking the Spirit to work in every area of life, and a willingness to be changed by Him in anything, no matter what it may be. This is what Paul prayed for the Thessalonians: "May the God of peace Himself sanctify you completely; may your entire being – spirit and soul and body – be kept blameless for the coming of our Lord Jesus Christ" (1 Thess. 5:23)' (Jay E. Adams, *Preaching to the Heart* [Phillipsburg, NJ: Presbyterian and Reformed Publishing Co., 1983], p. 13.)
2. *Ibid.*, p. 12.
3. *Ibid.*
4. John Calvin, *Institutes of the Christian Religion*, Ford L. Battles tr., Library of Christian Classics (Philadelphia: Westminster Press, 1960), vol. 2, p. 850.

Chapter 6

1. C. John Miller, *Evangelism and Your Church* (Phillipsburg, NJ: Presbyterian and Reformed Publishing Co., 1980), p. 19.
2. In recent years several writers have exposed the twisting of the biblical message by ostensible 'evangelicals', e.g. Michael Horton, *The Agony of Deceit* (Chicago: Moody Press, 1990).
3. Jay E. Adams, *Preaching to the Heart* (Phillipsburg, NJ: Presbyterian and Reformed Publishing Co., 1983), p. 9.
4. John Murray, *Redemption: Accomplished and Applied* (Grand Rapids, MI: Wm. B. Eerdmans, 1955), pp. 119-29.
5. *Ibid.*, pp. 109-15.
6. Adams, pp. 7-9.
7. When Jesus summoned Lazarus back from the dead, he did not issue his command, 'Lazarus, come out!' (John 11:43) because he assumed Lazarus had the power within himself to come forth from the tomb. On the contrary. Similarly, those today who believe in the sovereignty of God the Holy Spirit in conversion should not hesitate to command men to do what they know they are incapable of doing. For when the dead respond it will be evident that the life-giving power at work is of God.

Chapter 7

1. Jay E. Adams, *Audience Adaptation in the Sermons and Speeches of Paul* (Nutley, NJ: Presbyterian and Reformed Publishing Co., 1976). Hereafter *Audience Adaptation*.
2. *Ibid.*, pp. 6-8.
3. *Ibid.*, p. 68.
4. See, for example, Gary North, *Unholy Spirits* (Ft. Worth, TX: Dominion Press, 1986), and Peter Jones, *The Gnostic Empire Strikes Back* (Phillipsburg, NJ: Presbyterian and Reformed Publishing Co., 1992), and *Spirit Wars* (Milkiteo, WA: WinePress Publishing and Escondido, CA: Main Entry Editions, 1997).
5. Adams, *Audience Adaptation*, p. 69.
6. *Ibid.*, p. 69.
7. *Ibid.*, pp. 69-70.
8. For those who preach to virtually the same audience every week, this process becomes easier as we grow more intimately acquainted with our congregation over time. The preacher will have all the 'audience questions' in mind as he is working through his study and preparation from the biblical text, and will take them into account throughout his development of the sermon.
9. See our discussion of Paul's sermon to the Athenians in chapter 16.

Chapter 8. Preaching the Mighty Acts of God

1. C. H. Dodd, *According to the Scriptures* (London: Nisbet and Co., 1952), pp. 11-12.
2. Paul himself does so when he observes regarding events of old covenant history: 'These things happened to them as examples and were written down as warnings for us, on whom the fulfillment of the ages has come' (1 Cor. 10:11).
3. A seminary friend once pointed out this very problem in the words of the perennially popular evangelical hymn, 'He Lives!' The chorus of the song triumphantly poses the question, 'You ask me how I know He lives?' and answers, 'He lives within my heart.' My fellow student pointed out that the New Testament witnesses to the resurrection never say anything like that. While the believer's subjective experience of salvation is a very important feature of Christianity, it is not used in the New Testament to 'prove' that Jesus rose from the dead. For the apostolic witnesses, such proof was found in what they had seen with their eyes, looked at, and touched with their hands (1 John 1:1) in their encounter with the risen Christ (John 20:27 f.), and the fact that the God-given Scriptures promised that the Messiah would rise from the dead (1 Cor. 15:3 ff.). They point their audiences to these historic realities. Even when Paul uses his own personal conversion experience in his defense of his ministry (e.g., Acts 22:1-10), it

is because his transformation resulted from a post-resurrection appearance of Christ identical with that of the other apostles (1 Cor. 15:8). Our experience of the 'application' of redemption is a wonderful reality, but it is meaningless apart from the historic 'accomplishment' of redemption through the person and work of Christ.

Chapter 9. Standing With the Apostles – in the Twenty-first Century

1. For example, John R. W. Stott discusses the subject of 'preaching and bridge-building' in his book, *Between Two Worlds: The Art of Preaching in the Twentieth Century* (Grand Rapids, MI: Wm. B. Eerdmans, 1982), pp. 135-79.
2. Alfred Edersheim, *The Life and Times of Jesus the Messiah* (Grand Rapids, MI: Wm. B. Eerdmans, 1967).
3. Jay E. Adams, *Preaching With Purpose* (Phillipsburg, NJ: Presbyterian and Reformed Publishing Co., 1982), pp. 88-95.

PART 2

Chapter 10. Peter at Pentecost: A New Kind of Preaching

1. J. Behm, '*apophthēngomai*' in *Theological Dictionary of the New Testament*, One volume edition, ed. Gerhard Kittel and Gerhard Friedrich (Grand Rapids: William B. Eerdmans Publishing Co., 1985), p. 75.
2. See chapter 3.
3. Lysias (c.458 - c.380 BC), after one political speech in 405, in accusation of Eratosthenes (one of the 'Thirty Tyrants' in Athens), became a professional speech writer for the law courts. The approximately thirty surviving speeches of Lysias are fluent, simple, and graceful, imbued with both fiery passion and gentle humor. See *Lysias* (Loeb Classical Library, Vol. 244), trans., W. R. M. Lamb, (Cambridge: Harvard University Press, 1979).
4. *enōtisasthe*, aorist imperative from *enotizomai*.
5. Compare it to the language of Hebrews 12:26 f. (a quotation of Hag. 2:6), which is altogether appropriate, as it speaks of judgment as well: 'At that time his voice shook the earth, but now he has promised, 'Once more I will shake not only the earth but also the heavens.' The words 'once more' indicate the removing of what can be shaken – that is, created things – so that what cannot be shaken may remain.'
6. Isa. 2:12-19; 50:3; 63:4; Ezek. 32:7-8; Joel 3:14-15; Hos. 10:8; Nah. 1:6; Mal. 3:2.
7. Kenneth L. Gentry, Jr., *He Shall Have Dominion* (Tyler: Institute for Christian Economics, 1992), pp. 324-28. Herman Ridderbos, *The Speeches of Peter in the Acts of the Apostles* (London: Tyndale Press, 1962), pp. 8 ff. Dennis E. Johnson, *The Message of Acts in the History of Redemption* (Phillipsburg:

Presbyterian and Reformed Publishing Co., 1997), pp. 53-6.

8. Peter begins with Jesus 'the man' for it was in his evident humanity that Peter knew him so well, and others in his audience knew (or knew of) him.

9. The Greek term, *apodedeigmenon*, means 'to point out, approve' in the sense of a *public* demonstration.

10. See chapter 6, pp. 80-3.

11. This was the Father's answer to Jesus' prayer from the cross: 'Father, forgive them, for they do not know what they are doing' (Luke 23:34). Now, through Peter's preaching, they do know what they have done, and they are called to repent and receive God's forgiveness purchased on the cross.

12. Believers who are introduced to expository preaching after a steady diet of orthodox non-expository preaching sometimes say things like, 'The preaching I was used to in the past was true, but it did not come from the Bible.' That sounds paradoxical until you realize that preaching, to be truly orthodox (true), must be biblical in *both* its content and in its method.

13. See, for example, *Expository Preaching for Today,* Andrew W. Blackwood, (New York: Abingdon-Cokesbury, 1953), *Rediscovering Expository Preaching*, John F. MacArthur, Jr., Richard L. Mayhue, and Robert L. Thomas, (Dallas: Word Publishing, 1992), *Christ-Centered Preaching: Redeeming the Expository Sermon*, Bryan Chapell (Grand Rapids: Baker Academic, 1994), and *Biblical Preaching: The Development and Delivery of Expository Messages*, 2nd edition, Haddon W. Robinson (Grand Rapids: Baker Academic, 2001).

14. All preaching is evangelistic in the sense that it announces the good news which is in Christ, and draws out the implications of his redemptive work in one way or another, but not every sermon need be evangelistic in the narrow, 'altar call' sense (see below, ch. 17, p. 288 ff.).

15. Since, according to Paul (2 Tim. 3:16-17), *all* Scripture is God-breathed, then it is *all* profitable for the life of God's people. The preacher thus must endeavor with all his strength to bring as much of it as possible to his people.

16. Jay E. Adams, *Preaching With Purpose* (Grand Rapids: Baker Book House, 1982), p. 17.

17. *Ibid.*, p. 30.

18. Romans 10:14 – True 'hearing' may be more than merely physical, but it surely cannot be anything less.

19. See David Hwang, *From Conservatory to Pulpit*, D.Min. project at Westminster Theological Seminary in California, 1997.

20. That's why, when you lose your place in your notes sometimes during preaching, the congregation does not notice, because what seems to you an interminable silence is to their hearing a very natural pause.

21. Benjamin Franklin, *The Autobiography of Benjamin Franklin* (New York: Vintage Books/Library of America Edition, 1990), p. 104-05.

Chapter 11. Peter's Further Messages to the Jews

1. See chapter 18.
2. Remember that Peter contradicted the opinion of the audience at the beginning of his Pentecost sermon as well: 'These men are not drunk, as you suppose. It's only nine in the morning!' (Acts 2:15).
3. On another occasion in Acts, Paul and Barnabas will have to redirect the attention of the Lystran townspeople, who also thought that they were the source of healing power and were prepared to worship them (Acts 14:11-15).
4. Adams, *Preaching with Purpose* (Grand Rapids: Baker Book House, 1982), pp. 60-1.
5. Bruce, *The Book of the Acts, Revised Edition*, The New International Commentary on the New Testament (Grand Rapids: Wm. B. Eerdmans, 1988), p. 80.
6. This emphasis on the fact that the gospel of Christ is a message from the 'God of our fathers' is a repeated emphasis throughout the sermons of the apostles when addressing a Jewish audience (cf. Acts 13:32; 24:14; 26:6).
7. F. F. Bruce, *The Book of the Acts, Revised Edition*, p. 88.
8. I. Howard Marshall, *The Acts of the Apostles*, Tyndale New Testament Commentaries (Grand Rapids: Wm. B. Eerdmans, 1980), pp. 96, 119.
9. John R. W. Stott, *The Message of Acts* (Downers Grove: InterVarsity Press, 1990), pp. 92-3.
10. Liberal critics have denied that the early church was theologically sophisticated (or even interested in theological matters), and therefore have concluded (arguing in a circle) that Acts reflects a later stage in the development of the church and its theological reflection read back into an earlier period.
11. Stott, pp. 94-5.
12. J. C. Ryle, *Holiness* (London: James Clarke & Co., 1956), pp. 57-8.
13. See chapter 10, p. 127.
14. Johnson, *The Message of Acts* (Phillipsburg: Presbyterian and Reformed Publishing Co., 1997), pp. 63-4.
15. *Ibid.*, p. 65; cf. Bruce, pp. 84-5.
16. Isaac Watts, 'How Sweet and Awesome Is the Place,' *The Trinity Hymnal* (Atlanta & Philadelphia: Great Commission Publications, Revised edition, 1990), #469.
17. The call to repentance was also prominent in the message of John the Baptist in preparing the way for the Messiah (Matt. 3:2; cf. Acts 13:24; 19:4), and of the generations of old covenant prophets, of whom John was the last (cf. Ezek. 14:6; 18:30, 32).
18. The Greek term is *metanoeō*, which means to change one's way of thinking. When one's former way of thinking is perceived as being wrong or hurtful, *metanoeō* carries the sense of 'remorse' or 'regret,' though

there is another word (*metamēlomai*) which captures the emotional side of repentance. Though these two elements (the feeling and the change) frequently come together in true repentance, they must not be confused. It is possible to feel sorry without repenting (e.g., Judas, Matt. 27:3), and sometimes one can make radical changes toward godliness without an antecedent period of grieving over their sin (cf. O. Michael, '*metamēlomai*' in *Theological Dictionary of the New Testament*, One volume edition, ed. Gerhard Kittel and Gerhard Friedrich, [Grand Rapids: William B. Eerdmans Publishing Co., 1985], pp. 589-590; and J. Behm, 'metanoéo and metanoia in the NT,' *Ibid.*, pp. 642-43).

19. Jay E. Adams, *How to Help People Change* (Grand Rapids: Zondervan Publishing Co., 1986). p. 142.

20. C. John Miller, *Repentance and 20th Century Man* (Fort Washington: Christian Literature Crusade, 1975), p. 7. I commend to my readers this brief but very helpful contemporary study of the subject of repentance, notable for its searching insights and pastoral concern.

21. *Ibid.*, p. 17.

22. Peter and John will appear before the Sanhedrin again (Acts 5), and later Stephen (ch. 7), and Paul (ch. 23) will make their defenses.

23. Bruce, *The Book of the Acts, Revised Edition*, p. 92.

24. See chapter 5.

25. Note the play on the word 'salvation' (*sōtēria*). In verse 9 it refers to the physical healing of the crippled man (cf. Luke 6:9; 8:48, 50; 17:19; 18:42; Acts 14:9) and in verse 12 it refers to 'salvation' in the more comprehensive sense.

26. See our earlier discussion of this passage on pp. 23-4.

27. F. F. Bruce comments: 'It is particularly striking that neither on this nor on any subsequent occasion did the authorities take any serious action to disprove the apostles' central affirmation – the resurrection of Jesus. Had it seemed possible to refute them on this point, how eagerly would the opportunity have been seized! Had their refutation on this point been achieved, how quickly and completely the new movement would have collapsed! It is plain that the apostles spoke of a bodily resurrection when they said that Jesus had been raised from the dead; it is equally plain that the authorities understood them in this sense. The body of Jesus had vanished so completely that all the resources at their command could not produce it. The disappearance of his body, to be sure, was far from proving his resurrection, but the production of his body would have effectively disproved it. Now the apostles' claim that Jesus was alive had received public confirmation by the miracle of healing performed in his name. It was, for the Sanhedrin, a disturbing situation' (Bruce, *The Book of the Acts, Revised Edition*, p. 96).

28. Marshall, p. 102; Bruce, *The Book of the Acts, Revised Edition*, p. 96.

29. Again Peter and John are echoing the words of the Master, who said to the Jews, 'You have let go of the commands of God and are holding on to the traditions of men.... You have a fine way of setting aside the commands of God in order to observe your own traditions!' (Mark 7:8-9).

30. Note again that 'preaching' and 'teaching' are often used in a virtually synonymous sense. Preaching is the proclamation, exposition, and application of the Scripture to the hearts and lives of men.

Chapter 12. Stephen Before the Sanhedrin: The 'Aroma of Death'

1. See pp. 276ff.

2. John Calvin frequently described the preaching of the Scriptures as one of the forms of the Word of God. Ronald Wallace summarizes Calvin's view as follows: 'The task of the preacher of the Word is to expound the scripture in the midst of the worshipping Church, preaching in the expectancy that God will do, through his frail human word, what He did through the Word of His prophets of old, that God by His grace will cause the word that goes out of the mouth of man to become also a Word that proceeds from God Himself, with all the power and efficacy of the Word of the Creator and Redeemer. The word preached by man can become "God speaking". "The Word of God is not distinguished from the word of the prophet." [Calvin's comment on Hag. 1:12] "God does not wish to be heard but by the voice of His ministers." [Calvin's comment on Isa. 50:10]' (Ronald S. Wallace, *Calvin's Doctrine of the Word and Sacrament*, [Edinburgh: Oliver and Boyd, 1953], p. 83). Calvin, of course, does not mean to suggest by this that preaching is infallible or revelatory, but uses the analogy of prophetic proclamation to stress the authority and powerful usefulness of faithful biblical preaching.

3. F. F. Bruce quotes L. E. Brown, 'We can hardly doubt that it was Saul who remembered that look, a look which burnt into his soul until he too was turned to accept Jesus as his master and learnt in his own life to experience the presence of the Holy Spirit.' (F. F. Bruce, *The Book of the Acts, Revised Edition*, The New International Commentary on the New Testament, [Grand Rapids: Wm. B. Eerdmans, 1988], p. 128, n. 37).

4. In the tradition of the OT prophets, Stephen brings a covenantal suit against God's people for their unfaithfulness and rebellion.

5. J. M. Stifler, *An Introduction to the Study of the Acts of the Apostles* (New York: Fleming H. Revell, n.d.), pp. 61-7.

6. That is, Stephen's method of bringing his audience to conviction (from the Gk. *elenchō*, 'to convict'). For a detailed discussion of 'elenctics,' see J. H. Bavinck, *An Introduction to the Science of Missions* (Philadelphia: Presbyterian and Reformed Publishing Co., 1960), pp. 221-23.

7. 'By stoning the speaker [Stephen] they [the Sanhedrin] add one more bloody proof to their wickedness, which was so plainly portrayed, while

Stephen, in the spirit of the Master whom he sees, prays for his tormentors. The rejection of Jesus is completed in the person of his first martyr, and now soon we must follow his church elsewhere. The beginning of Jerusalem's end has come' (Stifler, p. 67).

8. Transcribed by the author from a audio tape of the sermon 'The Christ and Our Confession,' preached by Dr. Richard B. Gaffin at Calvary Orthodox Presbyterian Church, Glenside, PA (n.d.).

9. George Whitefield once spoke approvingly of having garbage thrown at him – it was a clear indication that his message was getting through! Better, in his mind, to be opposed than to be ignored.

10. Jay E. Adams, *More Than Redemption* (Phillipsburg: Presbyterian and Reformed Publishing Co., 1979), p. 227. This same term also appears in a variety of other New Testament passages: 1 Timothy 5:20, where Paul reminds Timothy that this convicting is to be done in public at times; Titus 1:13, where Paul calls upon Titus to silence rebellious talkers and deceivers, who were troubling the church, by this kind of effective rebuke; 2:15, where Titus is further reminded that he should encourage (*parakalei*) and rebuke (*elengchei*) 'with all authority.'

11. Cf. Harold O. J. Brown, *Heresies* (Garden City: Doubleday, 1984); Louis Berkhof, *The History of Christian Doctrines* (Grand Rapids: Baker Book House, 1937, reprint 1975); R. J. Rushdoony, *Foundations of Social Order* (Nutley: Presbyterian and Reformed Publishing Co., 1968).

12. Frequently in the writings of the Puritans a citation of a biblical text is given with the first few words only and an etc. The reader was expected to (and did) know and mentally fill in the quotation. Events in biblical history are likewise alluded to in the most sketchy way, but the Bible knowledge of the hearers or readers was such that that was no impediment to their getting the point. Today even seminarians would be hard pressed to catch some of the allusions without a concordance or Bible dictionary. The reason for the difference is the fact that the Puritan movement in England and America was undergirded by a vast growth in both the accessibility of the Bible and its consistent and careful study in private by individual Christians (cf. Christopher Hill, *The English Bible and the Seventeenth-Century Revolution*, [London: Allen Lane/The Penguin Press, 1993], pp. 4-44)

13. See pp. 28 ff.

14. To be sure it is 'assumed' that students will be reading their Bibles extensively, but hundreds of ministerial students can testify to the fact that non-assigned reading (i.e., the Bible) is woefully neglected.

Chapter 13. Peter's Sermon to the Household of Cornelius

1. F. F. Bruce, *The Book of the Acts, Revised Edition*, The New International Commentary on the New Testament (Grand Rapids: Wm. B. Eerdmans, 1988), p. 202.

2. J. M. Stifler, *An Introduction to the Study of the Acts of the Apostles* (New York: Fleming H. Revell, n.d.), p. 81.

3. 'It is further important to observe that Cornelius, though a Gentile, was a worshiper of the God of Israel. Such Gentiles are commonly called "God-fearers"; while this is not a technical term, it is a convenient one to use. Many Gentiles of those days, while not prepared to become full converts to Judaism (the requirement of circumcision being a special stumbling block for men), were attracted by the simple monotheism of Jewish synagogue worship and by the ethical standards of the Jewish way of life. Some of them attended synagogue and became tolerably conversant with the prayers and scripture lessons, which they heard read in the Greek version; some observed with more or less scrupulosity such distinctive Jewish practices as sabbath observance and abstention from certain kinds of food (notably pork). Cornelius's attachment to the Jewish religion appeared particularly in his regular prayer to the God of Israel and acts of charity to the people of Israel. One may say, indeed, that he had every qualification, short of circumcision, which could satisfy Jewish requirements' (Bruce, *The Book of the Acts, Revised Edition*, p. 203)

4. It is important to remember that the Jews were not opposed to Gentiles embracing Judaism. Jesus alludes to the fact that the scribes and Pharisees were 'evangelistic' (Matt. 23:15), and the presence in the New Testament of both Gentile converts ('proselytes') and near-converts ('God-fearers') is evidence that the Jews accommodated heathen converts to a point. The issue was their status within Judaism (and later the church) – were Gentile converts to be received into full fellowship as equals, or would they remain separate from Jews (and later Jewish converts to Christ)? This is the issue with which the apostolic church struggled (cf. Acts 15). Peter's experience at Cornelius's house set the pattern, though that pattern was not always followed, even by Peter himself (cf. Gal. 2:11-21).

5. Jesus' prediction in this passage that Jews and Gentiles would share fully and equally in the fellowship of the Kingdom is fulfilled in Peter's ministry to Cornelius's family, and the later inclusion of all Gentile converts to Christ as equal members of the growing apostolic church (Acts 15:28-29; cf. Eph. 2:11-22).

6. I. Howard Marshall, *The Acts of the Apostles*, Tyndale New Testament Commentaries (Grand Rapids: Wm. B. Eerdmans, 1980), p. 180.

7. 'Therefore it pleased the Lord, at sundry times, and in divers manners, to reveal himself, and to declare that his will unto his church; and afterwards, for the better preserving and propagating of the truth, and for the more sure establishment and comfort of the church against the corruption of the flesh, and the malice of Satan and of the world, to commit the same wholly unto writing: which maketh the Holy Scripture to be most necessary; those former ways of God's revealing his will unto his people being now ceased'

(*The Westminster Confession of Faith*, ch. 1, sect. 1).

8. Stifler, p. 88.

9. John R. W. Stott, *The Message of Acts* (Downers Grove: InterVarsity Press, 1990), pp. 194-95.

10. Though not included in Luke's summary, the implications of the universal lordship of Christ are no doubt similar to those sketched by Paul in Romans 3:29-30, 'Is God the God of Jews only? Is he not the God of Gentiles too? Yes, of Gentiles too, since there is only one God, who will justify the circumcised by faith and the uncircumcised through that same faith.'

11. 'If by birth he was a heathen, by heart and life he was equal to the best Jew' (Stifler, p. 84).

12. *Ibid.*, p. 83.

13. A further confirmation of the authenticity of Luke's record of the apostles' sermons in Acts can be seen by the 'Aramaisms' which have been detected by scholars in Peter's message here, and by the awkward sentence structure in verses 36-38 (Bruce, p. 213; Marshall, p. 190-91).

14. As usual Luke's summary is relatively brief, and it may well be that Peter fleshed out this 'outline' with more details during the delivery of the sermon.

15. The Bible rejects any notion of a 'second chance' for repentance and faith following death. Every man is 'destined to die once, and after that to face judgment' (Heb. 9:27). Though final judgment does not follow immediately upon death, one who dies in his sins (John 8:24) will certainly face the condemnation of God on that day (cf. Robert A. Peterson, *Hell on Trial: The Case for Eternal Punishment*, [Phillipsburg: Presbyterian and Reformed Publishing Co., 1995], pp. 150-52; Stephen Travis, *Christian Hope and the Future*, [Downers Grove: InterVarsity Press, 1980], pp. 130-31).

16. Bruce, *The Book of the Acts, Revised Edition*, p. 223.

17. Marshall, p. 189.

18. Adams, *A Consumer's Guide to Preaching* (Wheaton: Victor Books, 1991), p. 7.

19. Commenting on 1 Corinthians 3:7, Calvin writes, 'Christ puts forth His own power in the ministry which He instituted, in such a way that it is evident that it was not instituted in vain.... For He is not separated from the minister, but rather His power is made known as efficacious in the minister.' (*The First Epistle of Paul the Apostle to the Corinthians*, Calvin's New Testament Commentaries, ed. David W. Torrance and Thomas F. Torrance, tr. John W. Fraser, [Grand Rapids: Wm. B. Eerdmans, 1960], p. 70). At 2 Corinthians 3:6, Calvin further comments, 'Through us [the ministers] Christ enlightens men's minds, renews their hearts and wholly regenerates them.' (*The Second Epistle of Paul the Apostle to the Corinthians and the Epistles to Timothy, Titus and Philemon*, Calvin's New Testament Commentaries, ed. David W. Torrance and Thomas F. Torrance, tr. T. A. Smail, [Grand

Rapids: Wm. B. Eerdmans, 1960], p. 70.)

20. Adams, p. 9.
21. *Ibid.*, p. 12.
22. *Ibid.*, pp. 12-14
23. *Ibid.*, pp. 14-16.
24. *Ibid.*, pp. 23-30.
25. *Ibid.*, p. 25.
26. *Ibid.*, p. 27.
27. *Ibid.*, pp. 17-22.
28. *Ibid.*, p. 19.
29. For more on the important matter of teaching your people to grow in spiritual discernment, see Jay Adams' *A Call for Discernment* (Woodruff, SC: Timeless Texts, 1998).
30. Adams, p. 27.

Chapter 14. Paul at the Synagogue at Pisidian Antioch

1. See pp. 34.
2. Antioch of Pisidia was actually in Phrygia 'over against' (nearby) Pisidia. It was an important city in the Roman province of Galatia, and was probably chosen by Paul for strategic purposes with a view to the evangelization of the whole region (F. F. Bruce, *The Book of the Acts*, New International Commentary on the New Testament, [Grand Rapids: Eerdmans, Revised edition, 1988], p. 251).
3. 'We are indebted to Luke for accounts of two synagogue services – one in Palestine, in the Nazareth synagogue at the beginning of Jesus' public ministry (Luke 4:16-27), and the other, given here, in a synagogue of the dispersion. These two accounts make a valuable contribution to our knowledge of synagogue procedure in the first century AD' (*Ibid.*, p. 252).
4. The preaching in the synagogue, as we shall see, was generally 'expository' (though subject no doubt to many of the interpretive abuses present in the rabbinic tradition), and followed the reading of the Law and the Prophets which was done according to a prearranged cycle which would cover the entire Scriptures over a given period of time. This *systematic* exposure to the *whole* Scripture had many advantages over that which many Christians receive in their churches today, where there is no systematic reading of God's Word as part of worship, and sermons are often 'topical', chosen at the whim of the pastor.
5. See chapter 13 above.
6. William Ramsay, *The Cities of St. Paul: Their Influence on His Life and Thought* (Grand Rapids: Baker Book House, 1960 reprint), p. 311.
7. *Ibid.*
8. Jay E. Adams, *Audience Adaptation in the Sermons and Speeches of Paul* (Nutley: Presbyterian and Reformed Publishing Co., 1976), p. 12.

9. Ramsay, p. 301.

10. 'But, while the Gentiles are associated on a footing of such perfect equality with the Jews in this address, they are regarded entirely on the side of their approach to the Jewish beliefs, and not the faintest reference is made to their own religious conceptions apart from and previous to Judaism. In that respect this sermon stands in marked contrast to the oration to the Athenians and the brief address to the Lystran mob, in which Christian doctrine is set before the auditors as the development of their own natural conceptions of and aspirations towards the Divine power. Here, on the contrary, the God-fearing Gentiles are addressed as standing on the same plane of thought with the Jews.... The topics were so purely Jewish that the appeal to the Gentiles, though clearly marked, was ignored as a mere piece of courtesy or regarded as accidental by the Jews generally (*Ibid.*, p. 303).

11. *Ibid.*, p. 304.

12. 'Paul, as a former Sanhedrist, and Barnabas, as a Levite, and both of them as men of superior Jewish education, might fairly have claimed to sit in the chairs or benches set apart for the elders. But perhaps they had been told what their Lord had said on the subject, and took their seats among the ordinary worshippers.' (F. W. Farrar, *The Life and Work of St. Paul*, [London: Cassell, Petter, Galpin & Co., n.d.], vol. 1, p. 366.)

13. *Ibid.*, p. 366-67.

14. Bruce, *The Book of the Acts, Revised Edition*, p. 252.

15. Farrar, vol. 1, p. 367.

16. Bruce, *The Book of the Acts, Revised Edition*, p. 252, n. 41.

17. Farrar, p. 368. He goes on to say, 'And when turning to the Jewish Lectionary, and bearing in mind its extreme antiquity, we find that these two very lessons are combined as the *Parashah* and *Haphtarah* of the same Sabbath, we see an almost convincing proof that those were the two lessons which had been read on that Sabbath Day in the synagogue of Antioch more than 1,800 years ago' (p. 369). In a footnote he adds, 'They are read on the Sabbath which, from the first word of the chapter in Isaiah, is called the Sabbath *Hazon*. In the present list of Jewish lessons Deut. i.- iii. 22 and Isa. i.1-22, stand forty-fourth in order under the Masoretic title of myrbd. This brilliant conjecture is due to Bengel.' For another opinion on the texts underlying Paul's sermon, see Bruce, p. 254.

18. Adams, p. 15.

19. See p. 79.

20. There is no specific mention of the presence of 'God-fearers,' and if some were present is was a negligible factor.

21. It is true that, on a larger scale, the covenantal rejection of Israel involved Jews in every place (Rom. 9–11), and the course of Paul's ministry in Pisidian Antioch and beyond bears that out (Acts 13:45-48; 28:23-28). But

it does seem that the apostles approach the Jews of Jerusalem in a manner more strongly confrontational than they do elsewhere, because of the Lord's particular judgment upon that generation of Jews in the land (cf. Luke 23:27-31; 21:20-24).

22. The repentance of many Jews on the day of Pentecost was the Father's answer to the prayer of the Savior from the cross, 'Father, forgive them, for they do not know what they are doing' (Luke 23:34). Once they came to see what they had done through Peter's sermon, they repented, and they were forgiven (Acts 2:38).

23. See Bruce's commentary for a start (pp. 253 ff.); also I. Howard Marshall *The Acts of the Apostles*, Tyndale New Testament Commentaries, (Grand Rapids: Wm. B. Eerdmans, 1980), pp. 220 ff.

24. An unusual way to refer to God in speaking to a Jewish audience, but one aptly suited to the Gentiles who may still have thought of many kinds of 'gods' when they heard the term 'God.'

25. Bruce assesses the textual variation as follows: 'The textual evidence is fairly evenly balanced between ἐτροπηοπηῦόῦρεσεν, "he nourished them" ("carried them like a nurse") and ἐτροποφορησεν, "he endured their ways." The same two variants are found in Deuteronomy 1:31 LXX (to which Paul is here alluding). The Hebrew text reads simply *nasa*, "bore."' On balance Bruce prefers the reading 'sustained'/'nourished' (Bruce, p. 253 n. 45).

26. The language of Psalm 2 is also used by the Father at both the baptism of Jesus, which was His messianic 'anointing' at the inauguration of His public ministry (Matt. 3:17), and His 'transfiguration,' which was a glimpse of His future glory as the resurrected and exalted Lord (Matt. 17:5).

27. Peter came to the same conclusion – 'Therefore let all Israel be assured of this: God has made this Jesus, whom you crucified, both Lord and Christ' – by means of a citation of Psalm 110:1 (cf. Acts 2:34-36).

28. 'The raising up of Jesus to be his people's Messiah, rather than his being raised from the dead, seems to be the sense in verse 33 (his being raised from the dead is mentioned in v. 34)' (Bruce, pp. 259-60, n. 79).

29. 'The rabbinical exegetical principle of *gezerah shawah* (in which the sense of two texts is linked to their sharing a common term) is here applied to the Greek text (as in Gal. 3:10, 13)' (*Ibid.*, p. 260, n. 83).

30. *Ibid.*, p. 260.

31. Peter and Paul both make the point that the promises cannot apply to David himself, for he is known to have died, and remained dead and buried, whereas Jesus was raised from the dead (compare 13:36 with 2:29, 34).

32. Earlier apostolic sermons concluded with the offer of forgiveness of sins through faith in Christ (cf. 2:38; 3:19; 5:31; and 10:43).

33. Note well, Paul's preaching is 'the word of the Lord' on a par with the message of the prophets of the old covenant.

34. Even this turn of events was in accordance with the sovereign plan of

God and the predictions of the Scriptures. In declaring his turn to the Gentiles, Paul supports it with a reference to the prophet Isaiah (49:6): 'I have made you a light for the Gentiles, that you may bring salvation to the ends of the earth' (v. 47; cf. Luke 2:29-32).

35. 'Throughout, Paul identified himself with his audience and their common heritage. The words "brethren," "our fathers," etc., are typical indicators of this.

The gradual progression of his argument was achieved this way: In the first third of the sermon, Paul used the third person when referring to the past: "our fathers," "them," "they," etc. (vv. 16-25); in the second third, he changed to the first person and the general present – what God has done for us in our day (vv. 26-37). Finally, in the last third, he adopted the second person, calling his audience to personal decision in the immediate present: "you must understand ..." "you are offered ..." "your sins ..." "you could never be found ..." "take care ..." "fall on you" (vv. 38-41). Each section is introduced by a transition phrase. They are similar: verse 16: "Israelites and God-fearers," verse 26: "brethren, children of Abraham's line and Gentiles of the synagogue," and verse 38: "brethren" ' (Adams, pp. 15-16).

36. Jay E. Adams, *Preaching with Purpose* (Grand Rapids: Baker Book House, 1982), pp. 21-26.

37. For an historic example, one need only think of the decline of a robust, gospel-centered Puritanism in New England in the seventeenth century into a moralistic, Christless Unitarianism at the end of the eighteenth century. In the 1920s, J. Gresham Machen leveled the same charge against the 'liberals' in his church when he charged in his book *Christianity and Liberalism* that 'liberalism' was not a variety of Christianity, but rather a completely different, nonredemptive religion (cf. J. Gresham Machen, *Christianity and Liberalism*, [Grand Rapids: Wm. B. Eerdmans, 1923, reprint 1987]).

38. See chapter 8, pp. 99-104.

Chapter 15. Paul and Barnabas at Lystra: Putting the Brakes on Idolatry

1. I've had some not very fruitful discussions with this kind of pagan across the picket lines during anti-abortion demonstrations over the years.

2. F. F. Bruce, *The Book of the Acts, Revised Edition*, The New International Commentary on the New Testament (Grand Rapids: Wm. B. Eerdmans, 1988), pp. 272-73.

3. C. H. Rieu, *The Acts of the Apostles by St. Luke* (Baltimore: Penguin Books, 1957), p. 144. F. F. Bruce, however, believes there probably was a synagogue in Lystra (cf. Bruce, p. 278).

4. William Ramsay, *Paul the Traveller and the Roman Citizen* (Grand Rapids: Baker Book House, 1949), p. 119.

5. The threefold description of the man's condition in verse 8, 'crippled in his feet, ... lame from birth ... had never walked' serves to emphasize the fact that this man was truly afflicted, and had been known to be such over many years by the people of the small town. As the sequel shows, there was no question in the popular mind that this miracle had not been 'staged'.

6. Ramsay (p. 116) suggests that perhaps the lame man was a 'God-fearer', though there is no indication in the text that this was the case.

7. That Paul, who had been faithfully discipled by Barnabas in the early days, had become the chief preacher by this stage of the missionary journey is evident both because Paul is mentioned before Barnabas most of the time in Acts 13, and by the fact that here Paul is identified with Hermes, the spokesman for the gods.

8. 'It was no time now, in the urgency of the moment, to preach Christ to them, the sole object being to divert them from an idolatrous sacrifice, and to show the futile character of the polytheism of which such sacrifices formed a part. Paul, who was evidently the chief speaker, does this with that inspired tact which can always vary its utterances with the needs of the moment. No one can read the speech without once more perceiving its subtle and inimitable coincidence with his thoughts and expressions.' (F. W. Farrar, *The Life and Work of St. Paul*, [London: Cassell, Petter, Galpin & Co., n.d.], vol. 1, p. 383)

9. Jay E. Adams, *Audience Adaptation in the Sermons and Speeches of Paul* (Nutley: Presbyterian and Reformed Publishing Co., 1976), p. 22.

10. *Ibid.*, pp. 23-24.

11. *Ibid.*, p. 24.

12. The Western text indicates that Paul and Barnabas ministered in Lystra for some time before the arrival of the troublemaking Jews (Bruce, p. 278, n. 43).

13. Though F. F. Bruce's comments (*Ibid.*, p. 278) suggest that these Jews, being strangers in town, might have worked through the Jewish community in Lystra in order to gain an influential hearing with the local Gentile community. If the Jews arrived immediately after the sermon, in the midst of the hubbub that resulted, they might have been able to persuade the Gentiles to turn violently against Paul and Barnabas.

14. When this word is used elsewhere in the New Testament it does not imply that there is a predisposition toward becoming convinced on the part of the one being persuaded (e.g. Acts 12:20), and sometimes the opposite is assumed (e.g., 2 Cor. 5:11).

15. Adams, p. 23

16. Bruce, *The Book of the Acts, Revised Edition*, p. 276.

17. *Ibid.*, p. 277.

18. 'Just as old or bleary-eyed men and those with weak vision, if you thrust before them a most beautiful volume, even if they recognize it to be some

sort of writing, yet can scarcely construe two words, but with the aid of spectacles will begin to read distinctly; so Scripture, gathering up the otherwise confused knowledge of God in our minds, having dispersed our dullness, clearly shows us the true God' (John Calvin, *Institutes of the Christian Religion*, The Library of Christian Classics, ed. John T. McNeill, tr. Ford Lewis Battles, [Philadelphia: Westminster Press, 1960], I, vi, 1, p. 70).

19. See chapter 1, pp. 18 ff.

20. See p. 237.

21. We will point out in the next chapter that there is a 'pre-evangelistic' quality to what Paul says both in his brief message to the Lystrans and the more extended address to the Areopagus in Athens. He is laying out a context of ideas in which the message of the gospel finds its meaning. In Athens his purpose was intellectual, here it was urgently practical. These differences in circumstance have an effect upon his shaping of the message preached.

22. 'Strategy' having to do with your overall plan for the conduct of your pastoral ministry, especially your ministry of preaching. Paul states one of the strategic goals for his ministry in Romans 15:20, 'It has always been my ambition to preach the gospel where Christ was not known, so that I would not be building on someone else's foundation.'

23. 'Tactics' meaning your short-term more immediate plans for accomplishing your strategic goals for ministry. 'But now that there is no more place for me to work in these regions, and since I have been longing for many years to see you, I plan to do so when I go to Spain. I hope to visit you while passing through and to have you assist me on my journey there, after I have enjoyed your company for a while' (Rom. 15:23-24).

24. Luke does not record this as if it were a miraculous restoration of the apostle to life. He appeared to be dead to the satisfaction of the angry crowd, but was not. Nevertheless, it is a testimony to the God-given strength and commitment of the apostle that he was able to get up and walk, and when he did he went back into Lystra!

25. Even Jay Adams, a great champion of Paul's preaching methods, believes the apostle's performance at Lystra demands a 'largely negative judgment'. Of the sermon he writes, 'As a means of winning the Lycaonians from polytheism to Christianity, there is no evidence whatever of any success' (*Audience Adaptation*, p. 24). This is an unusual statement, especially in view of the fact that earlier on the same page Adams acknowledged that 'the missionaries won enough converts to begin a church.'

26. Bruce, *The Book of the Acts, Revised Edition*, p. 280.

27. *Ibid.*, p. 303-04.

Chapter 16. Paul and the Greeks: Facing the 'Cultured Despisers'

1. F. W. Farrar, *The Life and Work of St. Paul* (London: Cassell, Petter, Galpin & Co., n.d.), vol. 1, p. 534.

2. Cf. Allan Bloom, *The Closing of the American Mind* (New York: Simon and Schuster, 1987); Russel Kirk, *Decadence and Renewal in Higher Education* (South Bend: Gateway, 1978); Charles J. Sykes, *ProfScam* (Washington, D.C.: Regenery Gateway, 1988); Ronald H. Nash, *The Closing of the American Heart*; (Waco: Word/Probe, 1990); David F. Wells, *God in the Wasteland: The Reality of Truth in a World of Fading Dreams* (Grand Rapids: Wm. B. Eerdmans, 1994); and Thomas Sowell, *Inside American Education* (New York: Free Press, 1993).

3. *Parōxuneto* (from *paroxunō*): 'to spur' or 'to stir to anger'; passive: 'to be provoked, incensed' (H. Seesemann, 'paroxyno' in *Theological Dictionary of the New Testament*, One volume edition, ed. Gerhard Kittel and Gerhard Friedrich, [Grand Rapids: William B. Eerdmans Publishing Co., 1985], p. 791).

4. Farrar, p. 533

5. 'Reasoned' (διελεγετο, impf. from διαλεγομαι). The verb tense indicates repeated, continual action.

6. 'The Greek word for Paul's activity recalls the "dialogues" of Plato wherein Socrates discusses issues of philosophical importance; it is the same word used by Plutarch for the teaching methods of a peripatetic philosopher. Paul did not simply announce his viewpoint; he discussed it openly and gave it a reasonable defense. He aimed to educate his audience, not to make common religious cause with their sinful ignorance.' (Greg L. Bahnsen, *Always Ready: Directions for Defending the Faith* [Texarkana: Covenant Media Foundation, 1996], p. 246).

7. *Ibid.*, pp. 240-44; cf. also F. F. Bruce, *The Book of the Acts, Revised Edition*, The New International Commentary on the New Testament, [Grand Rapids: Wm. B. Eerdmans, 1988], pp. 330 f.; Dennis E. Johnson, *The Message of Acts* (Phillipsburg: Presyterian and Reformed Publishing Co., 1997), p. 195.

8. 'Both systems, had they followed their logical tendencies, would have annihilated idolatry, though neither could ever have found the true God. But it may safely be assumed that in Paul's day both schools moved with the popular current, and were practically idolaters. They had too little moral earnestness to oppose the worship of the gods, and Paul gives them the credit of being in full sympathy with it.' (J. M. Stifler, *An Introduction to the Study of the Acts of the Apostles*, [New York: Fleming H. Revell, n.d.], p. 166-67)

9. 'At any rate, when he came to address them he makes no allusion to the more popularly known points of contrast between the schools of philosophy, but is entirely occupied with the differences between their views and his own as to the nature and attributes of the Divine. Even to

the philosophers who talked with him in the marketplace the subject-matter of his conversation had been neither pleasure nor virtue, but Jesus and the Resurrection' (Farrar, p. 537).

10. Too much is made, I believe, of the differences between what Paul was doing in Athens and what he and the other apostles did elsewhere in bringing the gospel to the lost. To be sure this was a unique situation, and that uniqueness influenced Paul's approach, but his goal in preaching was the same here as elsewhere. It is noteworthy that Luke describes Paul's preaching in Athens in very similar terms to those used to describe the ministry of Peter and John to the Jews of Jerusalem: 'The priests and the captain of the temple guard and the Sadducees came up to Peter and John while they were speaking to the people. They were greatly disturbed because the apostles were teaching the people and proclaiming in Jesus the resurrection of the dead' (Acts 4:1-2).

11. Some have claimed that Paul used a different method for reaching the Gentiles in Athens from that which he adopted later in Corinth and elsewhere, allegedly because of his 'failure' in Athens (cf. Bahnsen's discussion of this question, pp. 237-40). This reading of the passage fails to recognize the emphasis upon the Person and work of Christ, rather than mere philosophical speculation, which is evident in Paul's ministry in Athens. Though it is the resurrection of Jesus which is emphasized in Luke's summary, one cannot imagine how Paul could speak about that glorious event without also telling his audience how Jesus came to be crucified, and why.

12. *spermologos*. Literally 'seed-picker,' a reference to a bird which picks up scraps to build a nest, but applied figuratively as a term of derision to someone judged to be an eclectic plagiarist, without the imagination or mental discipline for original thought. This is an ironic name to call Paul in view of Luke's later comment about the Athenian intellectuals (v. 21)!

13. Bahnsen, p. 247.

14. 'The Council of the Areopagus was a venerable commission of the ex-magistrates which took its name from the hill where it originally convened. In popular parlance its title was shortened simply to "the Areopagus", and in the first century it had transferred its location to the Stoa Basileios (or "Royal Portico") in the city marketplace – where the Platonic dialogues tell us that Euthyphro went to try his father for impiety and where Socrates had been tried for corrupting the youth with foreign deities. Apparently the Council convened on Mars' hill in Paul's day only for trying cases of homicide. That Paul "stood in the midst of the Areopagus" (v. 22) and "went out from their midst" (v. 33) is much easier understood in terms of his appearance before the Council than his standing on the hill (cf. Acts 4:7)' (*Ibid.*, p. 248).

15. *Ibid.*, p. 248

16. *Ibid.*, p. 249
17. 'Quite likely, in Acts 17 Paul is portrayed by Luke as again appearing before a court without sentencing. Had there been the legal formality of charges against Paul, it is inconceivable that Luke would not have mentioned them or the formal verdict at the end of the trial. Therefore, Paul's appearance before the Areopagus Council is best understood as an informal exploratory hearing for the purpose of determining whether formal charges ought to be formulated and pressed against him. Eventually none were' (*Ibid.*, p. 249).
18. 'Without the proper theological context, the resurrection would simply be a monstrosity or freak of nature, a surd resuscitation of a corpse. Such an interpretation would be the best that the Athenian philosophers could make of the fact. However, given the monism, or determinism, or materialism, or the philosophy of history entertained by the philosophers in Athens, they could intellectually find sufficient grounds, if they wished, for disputing even the fact of the resurrection. It would have been futile for Paul to argue about the facts, then, without challenging the unbeliever's *philosophy of fact*' (*Ibid.*, p. 251).
19. Farrar, p. 533.
20. 'It must first be noted that Paul's manner of addressing his audience was respectful and gentle. The boldness of his apologetic did not become arrogance. Paul 'stood' in the midst of the Council, which would have been the customary attitude of an orator. And he began his address formally, with a polite manner of expression: "You men of Athens." The magna carta of Christian apologetics, 1 Peter 3:15, reminds us that when we offer a reasoned defense of the hope within us, we must do so "with meekness and respect." Ridicule, anger, sarcasm, and name-calling are inappropriate weapons of apologetical defense. A Spirit-filled apologist will evidence the fruits of the Spirit in his approach to others' (Bahnsen, p. 251).
21. Farrar, p. 542, n. 1.
22. J. M. Stifler, *An Introduction to the Study of the Acts of the Apostles*, (New York: Fleming H. Revell, 1892), p. 168.
23. Bahnsen, pp. 254-55.
24. 'In Greek antiquity cases were not altogether rare in which "anonymous" altars "to unknown gods" or "to the god whom it may concern" were erected when people were convinced, for example after experiencing some deliverance, that a deity had been gracious to them, but were not certain of the deity's name' (Adolf Deissman, *Paul: A Study in Social and Religious History* [London: Hodder and Stoughton, 1926], pp. 287-91).
25. N. B. Stonehouse, *Paul Before the Areopagus and Other New Testament Studies* (Grand Rapids: Wm. B. Eerdmans, 1957), p. 4.
26. 'It is not in the least likely that he supposed the altar to have been intended as a recognition of that Jehovah who seemed so mysterious to

the Gentile world. He regarded it as a proof of the confessed inadequacy, the unsatisfied aspirations, of heathendom. He saw in it, or liked to read *into* it, the acknowledgment of some divinity after whom they yearned, but to the knowledge of whom they had been unable to attain; and this was He whom he felt it to be his own mission to make known' (Farrar, p. 532).

27. Bahnsen, p. 255.

28. See chapter 1, pp. 22 f.

29. Bahnsen, p. 257.

30. Cf. chapter 15, n. 18, p. 362 f., above.

31. F. F. Bruce, *The Defense of the Gospel in the New Testament* (Grand Rapids: Wm. B. Eerdmans, 1959), pp. 38, 46-47.

32. Kurt Aland, *et. al.*, eds., *The Greek New Testament*, (New York: American Bible Society, 1966, 1968), pp. 486-87.

33. Bruce, p. 263.

34. Bahnsen, p. 266.

35. Bruce, p. 338, n. 73, 'The verb ψηλαφάω [*psēlaphao*] conveys the idea of 'groping' after God in the darkness or semi-darkness, when the light of his full revelation is not available.' Or, when the revelation of God is being 'suppressed in unrighteousness' (Rom. 1:18).

36. F. W. Farrar dissents from this opinion, claiming that Paul's citations in Acts 17 evidence no more knowledge of the Greek poets than was current in the culture at large (cf. Farrar, pp. 630-37).

37. Bahnsen, p. 261

38. Farrar, p. 547

39. 'Paul wanted the philosophers at Athens to not simply refine their thinking a bit further and add some missing information to it; but rather to abandon their presuppositions and have a complete change of mind, submitting to the clear and authoritative revelation of God. If they would not repent, it would be an indication of their love for ignorance and hatred of genuine knowledge' (Bahnsen, p. 268).

40. Again, Paul uses the Old Testament Scriptures as the basis of his argument without *citing* them directly. Note the parallels between Psalm 96 (and Ps. 98) and verse 31 (cf. Johnson, p. 200, n. 40).

41. Cf. Johnson, p. 195.

42. Cornelius Van Til, *Paul at Athens* (Phillipsburg: L. J. Grotenhuis, n.d.), p. 3.

43. Bruce, p. 362.

44. J. S. Steward, *A Faith to Proclaim* (New York: Charles Scribner's Sons, 1953), p. 117.

45. Stonehouse effectively refutes these claims (*Paul Before the Areopagus*, pp. 39 ff.).

46. I remember years ago hearing a paper delivered at an academic conference by a pastor (who was also a very capable theologian) which critiqued the theological defections from the truth of Scripture of another scholar. At

the end of the paper this pastor declared that these theological problems were at bottom spiritual in character, they constituted unfaithfulness to Christ and thus called for self-humbling and repentance on the part of the theologian in question. That personal plea for the soul of his opponent was so out of place in such an intellectual setting that it left many in the audience speechless.

47. See chapter 6 above.

48. Gary DeMar, *Surviving College Successfully* (Brentwood: Wolgemuth & Hyatt, 1988), pp. 5-7.

49. Van Til, p. 14.

50. D. A. Carson, *The Gagging of God* (Grand Rapids: Zondervan, 1996), pp. 504-05.

Chapter 17. Paul at Miletus: Comfort to the Faithful

1. This kind of appeal not only involves the audience more closely in the sermon, but it calls upon them to believe what is being spoken even as the sermon is being delivered.

2. I think verses 33-35, though very important to Paul's overall message here, are structurally a kind of postscript to the sermon.

3. The landmark volume, *Competent to Counsel*, by Jay E. Adams (Phillipsburg: Presbyterian and Reformed Publishing Co., 1970), who is also, perhaps not surprisingly, one of our more innovative contemporary homileticians, was both a call to, and a primer in, the art of biblical counseling addressed specifically to pastors.

4. While every Christian is responsible and should be able to teach and counsel as part of the general office of the believer, these tasks are given in a special way to the 'pastor-teacher' (or 'elder') as part of his special calling and office. For this task he is equipped and called by God, and is recognized and set apart by the Church to that task through ordination. Jay E. Adams, while having contributed so much to the mobilization of the laity for the work of biblical counseling, nevertheless repeatedly mentions this very important distinction, cf., *Ready to Restore* (Phillipsburg: Presbyterian and Reformed Publishing Co., 1981), pp. 3-4; *Competent to Counsel* (Phillipsburg: Presbyterian and Reformed Publishing Co., 1970), pp. 42 ff.; *More Than Redemption* (Phillipsburg: Presbyterian and Reformed Publishing Co., 1979), pp. 278-80.

5. Jay E. Adams, *Preaching With Purpose* (Phillipsburg: Presbyterian and Reformed Publishing Co., 1982), p. 6.

6. Perhaps we ought to remind ourselves at this point, by way of caution, that any information that derives from actual individual counseling cases must be made sufficiently generic before use in a sermon so as not to violate any of the legitimate confidences which protect the ministry of counseling. If your people begin to identify themselves as 'sermon

illustrations' your effectiveness as a counselor, and perhaps as a preacher, may come to an end.

7. This interest in the 'counseling dimension' of preaching is not new. The English Puritans lay heavy emphasis upon particular application of the passage being preached which takes into account the different conditions of the hearers. William Perkins, for example, in his *The Art of Prophesying*, distinguishes 'seven ways in which application should be made, in keeping with seven different spiritual conditions' (William Perkins, *The Art of Prophesying*, [Edinburgh: Banner of Truth, 1996], pp. 56-63) His concern for specific and pointed application is very much a 'counseling' concern.

8. Adams, *Preaching with Purpose*, pp. 36-38.

9. See Peter Jones, *The Gnostic Empire Strikes Back* (Phillipsburg: Presbyterian and Reformed Publishing Co., 1992) and *Spirit Wars* (Mukilteo, WA: WinePress Publishing, and Escondido, CA: Main Entry Editions, 1997).

10. See chapter 10, p. 137.

11. Some pastors, whose preaching is almost exclusively focused upon evangelism, lose people because they fail to instruct them comprehensively. After a year or so of invitation messages, the converted believer begins to wonder if there is life after the altar call. He may become mired in endless 'rededications' rather than moving on to maturity under the instruction of the whole counsel of God.

Chapter 18. Paul to the Jews in Jerusalem: The Final Confrontation

1. For example, Luke records five times where Christ and his servants appear before the Sanhedrin: Jesus Himself, Peter and John (twice), Stephen, and Paul. In each instance the opposition of the Jews to the cause of Christ is clear. The preaching of the gospel is forbidden, and in two cases (Jesus and Stephen) the death of the accused is ordered. In the last instance (which we will study in this chapter) Paul is able easily to provoke a total breakdown in the meeting of the Sanhedrin, so irrational have the Jewish leaders become.

2. In addition, James Stifler points out, 'The gospel as it was, the gospel as it had shaped itself in the mind and heart of the great apostle, had never been offered by him in Jerusalem' (J. M. Stifler, *An Introduction to the Study of the Acts of the Apostles*, [New York: Fleming H. Revell, n.d.], p. 212).

3. F. F. Bruce, *The Book of the Acts, Revised Edition*, The New International Commentary on the New Testament (Grand Rapids: Wm. B. Eerdmans, 1988), p. 406.

4. It is obvious that, for those who are gifted and called by the Lord to preach, we get better at it the longer we do it. A minister of twenty years' experience is much more capable of preaching under unusual or difficult

circumstances than the pastor who is just getting started. That should be an encouragement for those of you who are new to the preaching ministry – for whom technical sermon preparation is still such an overwhelming, time-consuming task. You will always have to devote significant, quality time to working on your sermons, but your work of preparation does have a very substantial cumulative effect.

5. See my 'Counseling and Church Discipline' in the *Journal of Pastoral Practice*, 6:1 (1982), pp. 21-30; 6:2 (1983), pp. 25-34; 6:3 (1983), pp. 33-41.

6. Take John Calvin as an example, cf. T. H. L. Parker, *Calvin's Preaching* (Louisville: Westminster/John Knox Press, 1992), pp. 57-64.

7. What's more, many of the responsibilities pastors get saddled with (especially in smaller churches) are not even pastoral duties. Get some deacons and delegate to them everything that is not 'prayer and the ministry of Word' (cf. Acts 6:4).

8. Paul apparently had a dual citizenship: in the city of Tarsus and in the empire (cf. I. Howard Marshall, *The Acts of the Apostles*, Tyndale New Testament Commentaries, [Wm. B. Eerdmans, 1980], p. 352). The apostle does not mention his Roman citizenship until later (cf. Acts 22:25).

9. There are several 'apologetical approaches' favored among evangelicals, and many classical texts which have been written within the various 'schools'. There has also been considerable debate among these 'schools' as to which apologetical approach is most consistent with Scripture and most effective in defending the faith to the nonbeliever. You may check the bibliographies of several seminary apologetics textbooks for sources. One recent publication which is comprehensive and nontechnical, written from a Reformed 'presuppositional' apologetical approach, is the book cited several times during our discussion of Acts 17, *Always Ready: Directions for Defending the Faith* (Texarkana: Covenant Media Foundation, 1996), by the late Greg L. Bahnsen, one of the most capable and effective apologists of our day.

10. Bahnsen, pp. 109-10.

11. *Ibid.*, p. 111.

12. When Paul argued to Jews elsewhere that the Person and work of Christ fulfilled the expectations of the Old Testament, he was engaging in a form of apologetics (e.g., Acts 13:27). Likewise when he explained to Gentile pagans that the order and provision they observed in the world surrounding them was the gracious gift of the Creator whom he proclaimed (e.g., 14:17). Thus we see that the line between exposition, defense, and application can be a very fine one.

13. Because of Paul's unique role as an apostle and eyewitness of the risen Lord (1 Cor. 15:8-10), his testimony was qualitatively different from that of later witnesses. Through Luke's report in Acts, Paul is still laying the apostolic 'foundation' of Scripture (3:10-11). His words are the very words

of God the Spirit speaking through him in a unique way. We must distinguish the authority of our 'personal testimonies' to our experience of the saving grace of God from that of an exposition of the Word of God in Scripture in a manner Paul the apostle need not.

14. Stifler, p. 218; cf. J. S. Hawson, *Five Lectures on the Character of St. Paul* (Longman, Greene, Longman, Roberts, & Green, 1864), pp. 26 ff.

15. *Ibid.*, pp. 218-19.

16. The identification 'the Nazarene' (not 'of Nazareth' as the NIV has it) is not mentioned in the account in Acts 9.

17. In Acts 9 the emphasis falls upon the initiative of Christ Himself in calling and commissioning Saul ('the Lord – that is, Jesus,' 9:17). Again the subtle shift of emphasis is made in view of Paul's particular purpose in this message.

18. *Ibid.*, p. 221.

19. The details of the next part of Paul's account of his commissioning are not paralleled by Luke in Acts 9. Luke there tells of Paul's visit to Jerusalem, of his (at first, reluctant) reception by the church, of his ministry among the Jews and their increasingly hostile response which forced him to Caesarea and then Tarsus (vv. 26-30). There is not even a hint of his further encounter with the risen Christ in the Temple.

20. Paul uses only the pronoun, the NIV translators have supplied the noun.

21. The words of the prophet Isaiah, confirmed by Jesus Himself at His 'cleansing' of the Temple confirm the purpose of the Temple as a 'house of prayer.' But interestingly in view of Paul's mission the Temple is to be a house of prayer *for all nations* – for Jew and Gentile alike! Isaiah wrote, '... these I will bring to my holy mountain and give them joy in my house of prayer. Their burnt offerings and sacrifices will be accepted on my altar; for my house will be called a house of prayer for all nations' (56:7).

22. Bruce, p. 419.

23. Stifler, pp. 222-23.

24. *Ibid.*, p. 224.

25. The 'I' (*egō*) is placed in a position of emphasis, and Paul may have intended to contrast his good conscience with the hidden guilt of the Jewish leadership. Cf. Rieu, *The Acts of the Apostles by St. Luke* (Baltimore: Penguin Books, 1957), p. 164. Adams adds, 'It is even remotely possible that by this initial sentence he was 'baiting' them into precipitous action' (Jay E. Adams, *Audience Adaptation in the Sermons and Speeches of Paul*, Studies in Preaching II, [Nutley: Presbyterian and Reformed Publishing Co., 1976], p. 49).

26. F. W. Farrar, *The Life and Work of St. Paul* (London: Cassell, Petter, Galpin & Co., n.d.), vol. 1, p. 539.

27. Cf. Marshall, p. 362-63, and Bruce, p. 425.

28. 'The metaphor of the 'whitewashed wall' suggest a tottering wall whose

precarious condition has been disguised by a generous coat of whitewash: in spite of appearances, a man who behaved as Ananias did was bound to come to grief.' (Bruce, p. 426).

29. *Ibid.*

30. Marshall, p. 363.

31. Bruce, p. 426.

32. Marshall, p. 364.

33. Bruce p. 246; cf. Adams, p. 49.

34. It is ironic that in the course of the vigorous argument that ensued, some of the teachers of the law who were Pharisees admitted what they would never have declared under any other circumstances: 'We find nothing wrong with this man' (v. 9).

35. Adams, p. 49.

36. *Ibid.*

37. See Cornelius Van Til, *Christ and the Jews* (Nutley: Presbyterian and Reformed Publishing Co., 1968), for an enlightening and helpful discussion of the theological and philosophical reasons for the rejection of Christ by the Jews of Jesus' day.

Chapter 19. Paul's Defenses: The Gospel Before Kings

1. B. Rapske, *The Book of Acts and Paul in Roman Custody* (Grand Rapids: Eerdmans, 1994), p. 159, cf. note 35

2. *Ibid.*, pp. 158-59.

3. *Ibid.*, p. 159.

4. *Ibid.*

5. Both Tacitus the Roman and Josephus the Jew agree in their condemnation of Felix' regime. Tacitus expressed his opinion that Felix 'practiced every kind of cruelty and lust, wielding the power of a king with all the instincts of a slave' (*Annals*, 12.54).

6. B. Winter, 'The Importance of the *Captatio Benevolentiae* in the Speeches of Tertullus and Paul in Acts 24:1-21,' *JTS* 42 (1991), pp. 505-31.

7. Rapske, pp. 161-62.

8. 'Related to war, rebellion and civil disturbance, *stasis* was a capital crime and preeminently prisonable as well' (*Ibid.*, p. 160; cf. F. F. Bruce, *The Book of the Acts, Revised Edition*, The New International Commentary on the New Testament, [Grand Rapids: Wm. B. Eerdmans, 1988], p. 439.)

9. Rapske, p. 161.

10. *Ibid.*, p. 162.

11. Bruce, p. 442.

12. Rapske, p. 162.

13. He has served as a deputy in Samaria under his predecessor Cumanus since AD 48, and was chosen to succeed the latter upon his removal from office in AD 52 (cf. *Ibid.*, p. 162, n. 57).

14. 'The emphasis of the comparative *akribesteron* ... is upon the considerable certainty, definiteness, and accuracy of this knowledge' (*Ibid.*, p. 164).

15. *Ibid.*, p. 163.

16. *Ibid.*

17. *Ibid.*

18. *Ibid.*, p. 164.

19. 'Acquitting Paul could raise great political trouble for Felix with the plaintiffs. They were the indigenous spiritual and political powerbrokers of his province. Their co-operation was essential to a relatively smooth Roman overlordship. Moreover, Felix need not have strained himself to think of specific instances of compelling Jewish political pressure and of the disaster that the Jewish leadership, despite Roman legal obstacles, could bring upon the heads of provincial procurators who failed to administer the law with sympathy to the Jewish point of view. His immediate predecessor, the convicted and exiled Ventidius Cumanus, was a case in point. Had Felix been tempted to forget, Tertullus' opening remarks reminded him of the link between responsible administration of law and Jewish gratitude and passivity. Felix's awareness of the Jews' power to do him well or ill as he left office compelled him to do them the favour of leaving Paul incarcerated' (*Ibid.*, p. 165).

20. Peter Jones, *Spirit Wars*, see chapter 7, note 4 above.

21. Bruce, p. 447; cf. I. Howard Marshall, *The Acts of the Apostles*, Tyndale New Testament Commentaries (Grand Rapids: Wm. B. Eerdmans, 1980), p. 381; John R. W. Stott, *The Message of Acts* (Downers Grove: InterVarsity Press, 1990), p. 363.

22. 'Since Drusilla was a Jewess, [Paul] must have rehearsed the facts of the life, death and resurrection of Jesus and deployed his customary arguments that this Jesus of Nazareth was the Christ of Scripture. He will also have presented Jesus not only as a figure of history and the fulfilment of prophecy, but also as the Saviour and Lord in whom Felix as well as Drusilla should put their trust. Paul never proclaimed the good news in a vacuum, however, but always in a context, the personal context of his hearers' (Stott, p. 364).

23. Clarence E. Macartney, *Paul the Man: His Life and Work* (Grand Rapids: Kregel, 1992), pp. 140-43.

24. Bruce, pp. 448-49.

25. Marshall, p. 383; cf. Bruce, p. 449, n. 44.

26. Bruce, p. 449.

27. 'Marcus Julius Agrippa, as he calls himself on his coins (using his name as a Roman citizen), was the son of Herod Agrippa I. He was in Rome when his father died in AD. 44, and the Emperor Claudius was disposed to make him king of the Jews in succession to his father; but because of the younger Agrippa's youth (he was seventeen years old at the time) he was dissuaded

from this plan, and Judaea was once more administered by Roman governors. In AD 50, however, Claudius gave him the kingdom of Chalcis (in Lebanon), in succession to his father's brother Herod, together with the right of appointing the Jewish high priests. In 53 he gave up this kingdom in exchange for a larger one consisting of the former tetrarchies of Philip and Lysanias. This territory was augmented three years later by Nero, who added to it the regions of Tiberias and Tarichaea, west of the lake of Galilee, together with Julias in Peraea and fourteen neighboring villages. In token of gratitude to Nero, Agrippa changed the name of his capital, Caesarea Philippi (modern Banyas), to Neronias' (Bruce, p. 456).

28. The procurator's claim that he had nothing to write concerning Paul's case is hardly accurate. There were plenty of specific charges made against Paul. What Festus (and his predecessor) lacked was any *evidence* that the charges were true.

29. Stott, p. 370.

30. Bruce, p. 461.

31. Marshall, p. 386.

32. Stott, p. 370.

33. R. B. Rackham, *The Acts of the Apostles: An Exposition* (London: Methuen, 4th ed. 1909), p. 457; cf. Stott, p. 370.

34. Stott, p. 379.

35. Jay E. Adams, *Audience Adaptation in the Sermons and Speeches of Paul*, Studies in Preaching II (Nutley, NJ: Presbyterian and Reformed Publishing Co., 1976), p. 59.

36. J. S. Hawson, *Five Lectures on the Character of St. Paul* (London: Longman, Greene, Longman, Roberts, & Green, 1864), p. 32.

37. Paul uses the term 'to declare', to describe his preaching ministry to Festus in verse 25, 'What I am saying is true and reasonable' (NIV). This verb means to speak out loudly and clearly, and is used of philosophers, prophets, singers, and ecstatics. In Acts it is used of those who, under the control of the Spirit filling them, speak out ecstatically (2:4) or prophetically (2:14). (J. Behm, 'apophthéngomai' in *Theological Dictionary of the New Testament*, One volume edition, ed. Gerhard Kittel and Gerhard Friedrich (Grand Rapids, MI: William B. Eerdmans Publishing Co., 1985), p. 75)

38. Stott, p. 378.

39. *Ibid.*, p. 379.

Other books
of interest
in the
Mentor Imprint

_____

™GOD-CENTERED
PREACHER

DEVELOPING A PULPIT MINISTRY APPROVED BY GOD

ROBERT L. REYMOND

The God-Centered Preacher
Developing a Pulpit Ministry Approved by God
Robert L. Reymond

Walk into most Christian churches in the western world today, and the chances of you hearing a biblically based and penetrating relevant message is to be polite, slim. Even churches claiming to be evangelical or reformed all too often tend towards market led, comforting talks on the one hand and impenetrable, jargon-filled theological lectures on the other. How can preachers maintain a sensible balance?

Robert Reymond has trained hundreds of pastors, and has an intimate understanding of the areas where preachers are inclined to fail. He points to 8 qualities that all Pastors should aspire to in their ministries, qualities that are all too often lacking. These include the need for a Scripturally Grounded Pulpit, the need for a Theologically Articulate Pulpit and the need for an Evangelistic Pulpit.

'Among the growing number of books on preaching, this one should take its place at the top echelon and be made a consistent and ready reference for reminding us that truth, passionately believed, fervently lived, and articulately presented governs the preaching task.'

Tom Nettles,
Southern Baptist Theological Seminary, Louisville, Kentucky

'...a very stimulating read. The first chapter alone offers immense encouragement to the preacher, buttressing confidence in the 'mere words' of Scripture to communicate the truth of God with power, and those following issue a much-needed call for robust theology, truly biblical evangelism, and genuine piety in the pulpit.'

William J U Philip,
St George's Tron Church, Glasgow, Scotland

Robert L. Reymond is Professor of Systematic Theology at Knox Theological Seminary, Florida. He is a well-respected author whose books include *Paul – Missionary Theologian* (ISBN 1-85792-497-5) and *Jesus, Divine Messiah* (1-85792-805-2).

ISBN 1-85792-896-2

And the Word Became...A Sermon
A Practical Guide to Biblical Expository Preaching
Derek Newton

There is a steady stream of sermons delivered across the world, week by week. Amidst this flow of speech from the church's pulpits a frightening number of listeners remain essentially unfed and unchanged by what they hear.

Few would be surprised that in churches where the Bible is not taken seriously there will be little grasp of spiritual truth. More worrying, however, is that even in churches that give strong recognition to the inspiration and authority of scripture, the lives of many sermon hearers fail to show real evidence of transformation.

A large proportion can be classified under the following categories
1. Hobby Horse
2. Rocket
3. Heart-on-the-sleeve
4. Skyscraper
5. Grasshopper

What sort of sermons do you deliver?

'A serious and major work on expository preaching. Thorough, detailed, carefully researched material with many in-depth examples. A goldmine of Biblical resource material...'

David Ellis, OMF

'Derek Newton writes with experience of preaching both in the United Kingdom and abroad which makes the book rich. It is thoroughly practical and yet full of deep teaching on the whole theme of preaching within the biblical context.'

Philip H Hacking

'...it offers rich dividends for those who will submit to its suggested discipline of study and preparation.'

Derek Prime

Dr. Derek Newton has been an OMF International missionary for over 20 years. Derek is currently seconded by OMF International to teach at The International Christian College, Glasgow, Scotland.

ISBN 1-85792-767-2

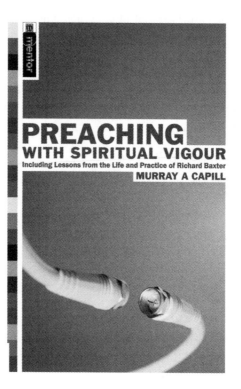

PREACHING
WITH SPIRITUAL VIGOUR
Including Lessons from the Life and Practice of Richard Baxter
MURRAY A CAPILL

Preaching with Spiritual Vigour
including lessons from the
life and practice of Richard Baxter
Murray Capill

Two trends are to be avoided in preaching. On the one hand a subjectivism and entertainment orientation for the crutch of popularity: on the other a dry intellectualism, a zimmer frame encouraging impressions of depth and thoughtfulness. We need guidance and help for our preaching that doesn't send us skittering down the road of the latest fad adapted from the world.

Richard Baxter is regarded as one of the Christian church's models of pastoral practice, many books have been written about his pastoral skills and methods to aid the modern pastor, but Baxter was also an effective preacher. It is one of the reasons why his ministry showed that spark of vitality that changed his surrounding community for the better.

Murray Capill, who himself lectures on preaching at the Reformed Theological College in Australia, set out to discover Baxter's secret. From a thorough study of Baxter's preaching ministry he has constructed a useful framework for us to follow.

This book is not theoretical or historical in orientation, but seeks to inspire and assist pastors to greater vitality in their preaching.

Chapters include -
>Who was Richard Baxter?
>Baxter's rules of preaching
>Spirituality in the preacher
>How pastoral ministry relates to effective preaching
>What should you preach?
>Driving the truth into the listener's heart
>Style and presentation
>Spiritual sermon preparation

Murray Capill was born in New Zealand and currently lectures at the Reformed Theological College in Geelong, Australia in Practical Theology.

ISBN 1-85792-857-1

MY
HEART
FOR THY
CAUSE

BRIAN BORGMAN

'I find Al Martin's preaching to be compelling....
He cuts it straight.'
John MacArthur

Albert N. Martin's Theology of Preaching

My Heart for Thy Cause
Albert N. Martin's Theology of Preaching
Brian Borgman

'I find Al Martin's preaching to be compelling.... He cuts it straight.'
John MacArthur

When asked to take some meetings at a conference for pastors, revered preacher and theologian, Professor John Murray stated *'If Al Martin is to be there I really think he should be asked to take the three evening services you propose for me. He is one of the ablest and moving preachers I have ever heard... I have not heard his equal.'*

How is it that someone stands out in this way? Pastor Martin would be the first to direct our attention to God's grace, yet is there another element that we can learn from and apply in our own lives? Is there such a thing as a 'theology of preaching' that we can adopt?

Brian Borgman has painstakingly researched just this question. The result is a book that will help preacher's everywhere to be used more greatly for God's glory.

'His preaching is powerful, impassioned, exegetically solid, balanced, clear in structure, penetrating in application. I have seen him touch audiences of several nationalities, of all ages and social backgrounds, ranging from well-instructed believers to pagans.'
Edward Donnelly, Reformed Theological College,
Belfast, Northern Ireland

'[Albert Martin's preaching is] very clear, forthright, articulate.... He has a fine mind and a masterful grasp of Reformed theology in its Puritan-pietistic mode.'

J.I. Packer, Regent's College, Vancouver, British Columbia

'Consistency and simplicity in his personal life are among his characteristics - he is in daily life what he is in the pulpit.'
Iain Murray, Banner of Truth, Edinburgh, Scotland

Brian Borgman is the pastor of Grace Community Church in Gardnerville, Nevada.

ISBN 1-85792-716-8

Christian Focus Publications

publishes books for all ages

Our mission statement –

STAYING FAITHFUL

In dependence upon God we seek to help make His infallible Word, the Bible, relevant. Our aim is to ensure that the Lord Jesus Christ is presented as the only hope to obtain forgiveness of sin, live a useful life and look forward to heaven with Him.

REACHING OUT

Christ's last command requires us to reach out to our world with His gospel. We seek to help fulfill that by publishing books that point people towards Jesus and help them develop a Christ-like maturity. We aim to equip all levels of readers for life, work, ministry and mission.

Books in our adult range are published in three imprints.

Christian Focus contains popular works including biographies, commentaries, basic doctrine and Christian living. Our children's books are also published in this imprint.

Mentor focuses on books written at a level suitable for Bible College and seminary students, pastors, and other serious readers. The imprint includes commentaries, doctrinal studies, examination of current issues and church history.

Christian Heritage contains classic writings from the past.

Christian Focus Publications, Ltd
Geanies House, Fearn, Tain,
Ross-shire, IV20 1TW, Scotland, United Kingdom
info@christianfocus.com

For details of our titles visit us on our website
www.christianfocus.com